Farm Buildings

From Planning to Completion

by Richard E. Phillips

Doane-Western, Inc., 8900 Manchester Road, St. Louis, Missouri 63144

Library of Congress Catalog Card Number: 81-67057
ISBN: 0-932250-12-2

Printed in U.S.A.

The Author

Dr. Phillips is a native of New York State and was raised on a dairy farm located near Oswego. He received his B.S. and M.S. degrees from Cornell University in 1958 and 1960, respectively.

From 1960 to 1963, he worked as a test engineer for International Harvester Company. In 1963 he went to the University of Connecticut as an extension specialist in farm structures and environmental control.

He completed graduate work for the Ph.D. in agricultural engineering at Michigan State University in 1970. In 1971, he accepted his present position at the University of Missouri, where he is a professor of agricultural engineering and state extension specialist.

Dr. Phillips has authored over 100 articles and publications in the area of farm structures and environment. His publications have received several awards in national competition among agricultural engineers.

He is a senior member of the American Society of Agricultural Engineers and is currently serving as a member of their national board of directors. He is a registered professional engineer in the state of Missouri.

Contents

Part 3 BUILDING CONSTRUCTION

Part 5 ENVIRONMENTAL CONTROL

Preface

One hundred years ago, the farmer who wanted to add a building to his farmstead had few decisions to make. The construction material was wood; the labor force would be himself and a few neighbors; and he didn't have to worry about providing for equipment access, wiring, or plumbing. Today's farm building is a stark contrast to that of even 50 years ago. It is a highly specialized facility that must be carefully integrated into the farmstead in order to achieve maximum production efficiency. The hundreds of decisions that must be made between initial planning and final occupancy are described in this book. It is not a textbook and contains only a few mathematical expressions and equations. It is designed to provide a general background in farm buildings, which hopefully will assist the prospective owner throughout the construction process.

The initial planning section includes items such as a financial analysis, selecting a plan, and locating the building within an organized farmstead. Sources of professional help, including how to choose and work with a farm building consultant, are detailed in this section. Also included is material that can be used to evaluate plans prepared by yourself, package building companies, or the professional consultant.

The general purpose barn doesn't exist on today's commercial farm. Each building has a specific function to serve and must be built to accommodate the needs of that function. Twelve chapters are devoted to buildings for specific enterprises. Included are chapters on farm shops, crop growing buildings, storages, livestock handling facilities, and each of the major livestock enterprises (beef, dairy, swine, and poultry). There is also a chapter devoted to private and commercial horse facilities.

The actual construction process is detailed in a nine-chapter section. Building it yourself or working with a contractor, including contracts, specifications, and insurance, is discussed. The actual construction process for different types of buildings is described in a logical "from the ground up" order. One complete chapter is devoted to the subject of fire resistant construction.

The selection and use of building materials and fasteners is covered in the fourth section of the book. Chapters are devoted to concrete, masonry, wood, surface coverings, paints, plastics, and the selection of fasteners. Illustrations show product use and what to look for when making purchases.

The final section deals with environmental control and the physical and mechanical systems necessary to achieve it. Insulation, ventilation, and heating systems each receive a separate chapter. There is also a discussion of alternate energy systems for farm buildings, including the current state of the art in solar collection systems and a review of wind power.

Richard E. Phillips
April 30, 1981

Part I

Initial Planning

CHAPTER **1**

Building Economics

You are going to build a new facility. . . . Why? That may sound like a strange question coming from someone who spent a considerable amount of time writing a book telling you how. It is, however, the single most important question you need to answer before starting any construction. It is essential to the success of the project that you have a complete understanding of the effects of a new facility on your farm operation. It will also go a long way toward pleasing your banker when you ask him for money to do the job.

Why Build?

Over the past 20 years or so we have had the opportunity to visit with thousands of farmers like yourself, who were planning new construction projects. Here are some of the more common reasons we have heard.

Increased output. We just can't get by anymore without expanding our operation. This new building will allow us to double our output.

Reduced labor. Now that I am getting older, I can't put in the hours I used to. A new building is going to enable me to maintain farm output with less labor.

Protect investments. Expensive machinery needs protection from the elements in order to keep maintenance costs down and resale value up.

Improve scheduling of production. A controlled environment building will eliminate the need to rely on weather and enable production at all times of the year.

Market flexibility. A new grain bin will keep us from having to take market price at harvest.

Tax advantage. Last year was a good one and we need to invest some money in facilities in order to reduce our tax liability.

Reduce production costs. Our energy costs are rapidly becoming a major element in cost of production. A new, well insulated building can save us hundreds of dollars a year in fuel costs.

Find any new reasons in the above list? If so, remember them. They may come in handy later on. Now let's look at the other side of the coin—why new facilities can cause farm business failures.

Buildings designed to expand farm production generally require additional investment in other areas. Take for example, a dairy farmer expanding from 50 up to 100 milking cows. Unless he already has 100 cows, it will cost $60,000 to $100,000 to get them and, even then, they may not be up to expected quality. If he didn't plan on the investment, or can't make it, he will have to grow into the new 100-cow unit. This means making payments for a 100-cow system with a 50-cow milking herd. It has also meant bankruptcy for many farmers.

One thing leads to another and the other generally costs. A new farrowing house must be utilized fully in order to spread its high cost over a maximum number of pigs. This frequently means weaning at 3 to 4 weeks in order to farrow on a monthly basis. Early weaning means some type of nursery building will be required. Consider carefully the effect of a new building on your total farm enterprise.

Management requirements increase rapidly as farm enterprise size increases. It's three times as hard to manage a 60-cow herd as it is to manage a 30-cow unit. You will have to take a long hard look at your personal desires and capabilities in order to answer this one. More management frequently means less direct involvement with day to day chores and more dependence on hired labor. This is a change that many persons are unwilling or unable to make.

Too much capacity for the farm. You can always buy some production inputs to make up for lack of farm production, but you will usually have to pay a premium for them which may eliminate any increase in profit. In these days of increased concern for the environment, it is also possible to exceed the farm's capability for waste disposal. This can lead to legal action or lawsuits.

Perhaps you can think of other whys or why nots. If so, they will help you rationalize your final decision. Now, let's turn our attention to collecting some of the facts we will need to make your next move successful.

The First Step

We hope you have been participating in some type of organized record-keeping system for your farm business. The numbers which good records provide can point out opportunities for improvement of your present operation. The first step is to compare your operation with averages for your area or state. You can get average numbers on production costs, feed

Figure 1-1. A modern, well-planned facility can add to farm productivity and reduce labor costs—if it is fully utilized.

efficiencies and production rates from your county extension office or through professional farm management organizations, such as Doane. If you are below average in any of the following categories, stop right now and find out why. There is not much sense in expanding your operation with a new building if it is only going to multiply some problem in your present operation.

- Animals per man
- Production per animal
- Feed efficiency
- Yield per acre
- Net income per animal or per acre
- Net income per man

Facilities Costs

Although a new building usually appears as a large one-time expenditure, it will last several years and its costs must be allocated over the expected useful life in order to give a true cost to the farm enterprise. This is done by developing a schedule of annual fixed costs for the proposed structure. These fall into the following five categories:

Depreciation. This is the cost associated with normal wear out of the system. It may be calculated in several different ways for tax purposes; however, the straight line method is usually used for cost estimating. This method determines annual depreciation by dividing initial costs by the anticipated years of useful life. Most farm buildings will have a useful life of 15 to 20 years. This means annual depreciation on a $60,000 building will be in the $3,000 to $4,000 cost range.

One note of caution. If the facility you are planning is for an enterprise where technology is changing rapidly, it may become obsolete before it is fully depreciated. You will have to get out the crystal ball to figure out appropriate depreciation costs for these cases.

Interest. This is the cost of borrowing money to build the system; or, if money is not borrowed, it is the money which could be earned in interest if you were to make some other investment. Use your present interest costs to estimate this one.

Repairs. If you don't have a good idea of building repair costs on your farm, you can figure 1% to 3% of the initial cost as an estimate of annual repairs. This will cover such things as repainting, roof repairs, and normal wear and tear.

Taxes. Real estate and/or personal property taxes will be assessed against your facility. These should be included at a rate equivalent to your best estimate of costs.

Insurance. This is the cost of protecting your investment against catastrophic loss. It will vary with location, building use and type of construction. Your insurance agent can provide an estimate.

An annual cost of owning a 20-sow central farrowing house which costs $50,000 might look like this:

Depreciation	$50,000 / 20 year life	=	$ 2,500
Interest	$50,000 x 12%	=	6,000
Repairs	$50,000 x 2%	=	1,000
Taxes	$50,000 x 1.5%	=	750
Insurance	$50,000 x 1%	=	500
Total annual fixed costs			$10,750

Annual fixed cost as a percentage of initial cost would be 21.5%.

It is interesting to note that annual fixed costs go on whether you use the system or not. For the most part, they are also independent of how much you use the building. If you farrow 160 litters per year in the above building, fixed cost per litter will be $67.18. On the other hand, farrowing only 40 litters per year will cost $268.75 per litter. That's the kind of thing we mentioned earlier that can get people into trouble fast.

How Much Can You Spend?

The only way to answer this one is through development of a budget which will provide an estimate of costs and returns for the proposed building. The more detailed the budget, the better your answer will be.

Partial budgeting is a method of balancing or considering likely gains or losses which will occur from a change in your farm business. It is used when you wish to look at only one part of the farm business. Only those costs and returns which will result from a proposed change are considered. Partial budgeting can also be used to determine the break-even point for an enterprise or how much capital investment you can make in facilities.

Partial budgeting results will only be as good as the figures you use in developing them. Therefore, it is important that you have accurate information on your actual costs to use in the budgeting. Following is an example of a partial budget for a proposed new farrowing house.

Once you have arrived at the money available for fixed cost and management returns, you will be in a position to estimate how much you can afford to spend for the new building. If annual fixed costs average 21.5% of the initial cost and you decide that the entire $9,284 can be used to offset them, you can afford to spend

$$\frac{\$9{,}284}{.215} = \$43{,}181$$

for your new farrowing house and any other needed capital facilities. You may be able to go above this figure if you are investing your own money and are willing to accept a lower rate of return on it.

Collecting Cost Data for Buildings

Once you have arrived at a limiting price for your new building, you are ready to start shopping and comparing. The most important number to you will be the total cost. However, as you shop you will find that the building industry has developed a system of unit pricing just as other industries do. Although there may be some local variations, Table 1-1 will provide you with some of the more commonly used units.

Table 1-1. **Commonly Used Units in Pricing of Agricultural Structures**

Item	Unit
Site preparation	
Earth moving	Cubic yard
Blasting	Cubic yard
Water line installation	Lineal foot
Concrete work	
Forming charge	Cubic yard
Flat work	Square foot
Concrete	Cubic yard
Steel	Pound
Buildings	
Storage buildings	Square foot
Livestock housing	Animal unit capacity
Greenhouses	Square foot
Grain storage	Bushel
Specialty buildings (shops, milking parlors, cold storages)	Complete building
Silos	Ton capacity
Fencing	Lineal foot

The major advantage of unit price comparisons for buildings is that they more nearly reflect the true cost to your farm operation. For example, cost per square foot for a new dairy housing unit is of little interest to you if

Partial Budget Worksheet

Change considered: Build new 20-sow farrowing house to enable addition of 80 sows to feeder pig production system.

I. Projected income to be added

1.	1,280 feeder pigs @ 40 lbs.	$50,176
2.	Salvage 40 sows	6,720
3.	Salvage 2 boars	288
	Total annual income	$57,184

II. Projected additional cost

1.	Purchase 2 boars	$ 500
2.	Replacement Sows-40	5,000
3.	Feed	26,000
4.	Veterinary	2,560
5.	Labor @ $3.50/hr.	6,160
6.	Machinery Costs	1,920
7.	Utilities	2,560
8.	Livestock Materials & Misc.	3,200
		$47,900

III. Estimated money available for fixed cost and management.

Added income	$57,184
Added costs	− 47,900
	$ 9,284

Note: The figures used in the above analysis were adapted from records accumulated in the University of Missouri farm record program.

you happen to be considering two different designs for a 50-cow addition. What you really need to know is how much per cow it is going to cost. Then you can compare buildings to see if any cost differential is merited by some particular features in the designs.

CHAPTER **2**

Selecting a Plan

Sources of Planning Help

Unless you have construction experience or know exactly what you want, you are probably going to need some help in planning that new building. There are three sources of help—builders, cooperative extension, and professional consultants. We suggest you contact people in at least two of the three categories in order to get different viewpoints.

Most builders offer some planning and design assistance as an aid to building sales. If you are not familiar with the farm builders active in your area, check with local lumber dealers and people you know who have built recently to find their names. Many builders also put regular advertisements in farm papers and magazines serving their areas. The amount of help you can expect from a builder will depend on his particular operation. It can vary from a verbal description or rough pencil sketch of his particular building up to preparation of a complete set of detailed construction plans. Development of detailed plans to fit your personal situation is a costly operation for a builder. Because of this, many builders have established a fee schedule for plan development. In some cases the plan fee will be applied against the contract price for the building should you decide to buy from the builder who developed them. Fees for design and plan preparation will range from a few dollars up to 3% to 4% of the construction cost of the building.

Over the past 30 years, the United States Department of Agriculture (USDA) has developed and published more than 400 plans for agricultural buildings and equipment. These plans are distributed through county extension offices in all 50 states. In addition to these plans, Agricultural Engineering departments at most of the state universities develop and distribute plans appropriate to their state through the extension service. The Northeastern and North Central states are also served by the cooperative plan services maintained by their respective state universities. They are the Northeast Regional Agricultural Engineering Service (NRAES) and the

Midwest Plan Service (MWPS). Addresses for NRAES, MWPS, and agricultural engineering departments with plan distribution services can be found in the appendix of this book. Cost for plans distributed through the extension service is minimal, usually just enough to cover costs of reproduction and distribution. Assistance with plan selection and some modification of standard plans is also available through the extension service.

Modern farm buildings are becoming increasingly complex and many farmers do not have the time or inclination to do all the work associated with planning and construction. Because of this, many farmers are employing professional consultants to help with their building programs. These consultants are usually registered professional engineers (P.E.) with specific training in agricultural engineering. They function with regard to agricultural buildings in the same manner that architects function with other types of structures. Their services are contracted for and fees are based on an hourly, daily, or percentage of total cost basis. Things which they can be employed to do include the following.

Site investigation. This can include surveying, test borings to determine foundation needs, and evaluation of potential sites with regard to utilities and waste disposal.

Preliminary planning. This includes development of alternative proposals to meet your stated needs. Normally this also includes sketches of potential floor plans, a description of suggested construction, cost estimates, and integration of plans into your existing facilities.

Construction plans. A complete set of drawings, including needed structural and environmental design, suitable for construction of the facility. Written specifications and construction contract development may also be included.

Construction supervision. The consultant makes visits to the construction project on a specified basis to verify that the building is being constructed according to plan and to approve any needed changes or substitutions.

Names of professional consultants serving your locality can be obtained from your state agricultural engineering department, the state board of professional registration, or from: *American Society of Agricultural Engineers, 2950 Niles Road, St. Joseph, Michigan 49085.*

If you hire a professional consultant, make sure you have a written agreement specifying the work he is to do for you and your payment schedule to him. All reputable consultants will insist on this. One item you should be aware of is that design and ownership of plans customarily remain with the consultant. Your fee purchases the right to use the plans in construction of your facility, but does not give you license to reproduce and distribute or sell copies to others. If this is not an agreeable arrangement to you, be sure to work out some alternative with the consultant and have it included in your written agreement.

Types of Construction Used in Farm Buildings

A building provides a physical barrier which separates two different environments. It must also be functional, economical, efficient and many other things, too, but we will spend time on them later. Right now let's take a look at the general types of construction you will have to choose from when you go shopping.

Conventional (Stud-Frame) Buildings

Unless you happen to live in a log cabin or some radically new type of home, the house you live in is probably of stud frame construction. Almost all homes built in the United States during the past 50 years have used this system.

There are two general systems of stud frame construction; platform and balloon. Platform framing involves building each floor or level one at a time. There are no continuous structural members that extend between floor members. Platform framing is the simpler of the two systems and is the one which we most often see used today.

A balloon framing system uses exterior wall studs which extend

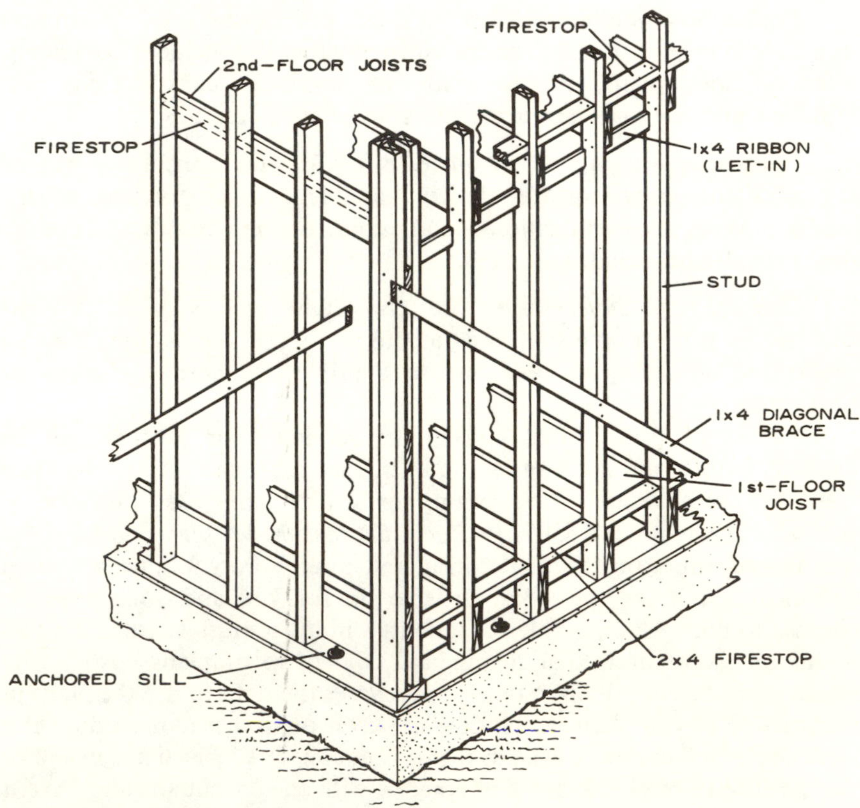

Figure 2-1. Balloon framing wall construction. (USDA)

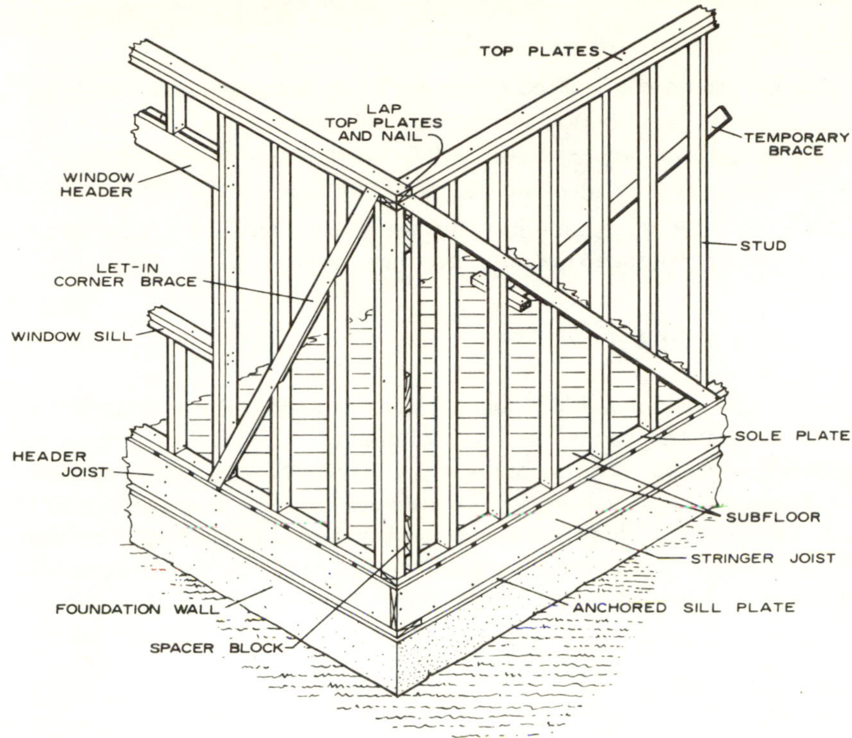

Figure 2-2. Western or "platform" framing system. (USDA)

through two or more levels. Floor joists for upper levels are supported by some type of ribbon board attached to the wall studs instead of resting on top of a plate as they do in platform framing. Balloon framing is much stronger than platform because of the exterior studs which extend through two or more levels. Balloon framing is most commonly used in areas of the country which experience high winds. In farm buildings, it was very popular in the two story poultry buildings constructed in the 1940's and 1950's.

Figures 2-1 and 2-2 illustrate platform and balloon framing. Take a few minutes to study the parts and learn a few of their names. It will help you as we look at some of the other types of framing. You can also use your new knowledge to impress the builders with whom you will be talking.

Advantages of stud frames:

1. Nearly all builders are familiar with this framing system. This means a wider choice for you and you won't have to "pay the tuition" for a builder to learn a new type of construction.
2. Buildings are easily insulated.
3. A wide choice of components such as windows and doors that are designed to fit this type is available.
4. Wiring and plumbing are easily concealed in stud spaces.

Disadvantages:

1. Usually the most expensive type of construction.
2. Conventionally spaced (16 inches and 24 inches on center) units frequently result in highly overdesigned structures.
3. Installation of conventionally used masonry foundations is frequently held up by weather conditions.
4. Extremely wide buildings without interior partitions may require special framing to maintain structural integrity of the walls.

Post and Beam

Post and beam buildings use relatively heavy timbers to carry the normal structural loads on the building. Depending on their orientation—vertical or horizontal—they are referred to as posts or beams. This heavy timber framework is then covered with non-load bearing sheathing or siding. This type of construction was a natural outgrowth of early U.S. construction when heavy timber members were readily available and saw mills were far apart. The oldest buildings of this type used hand

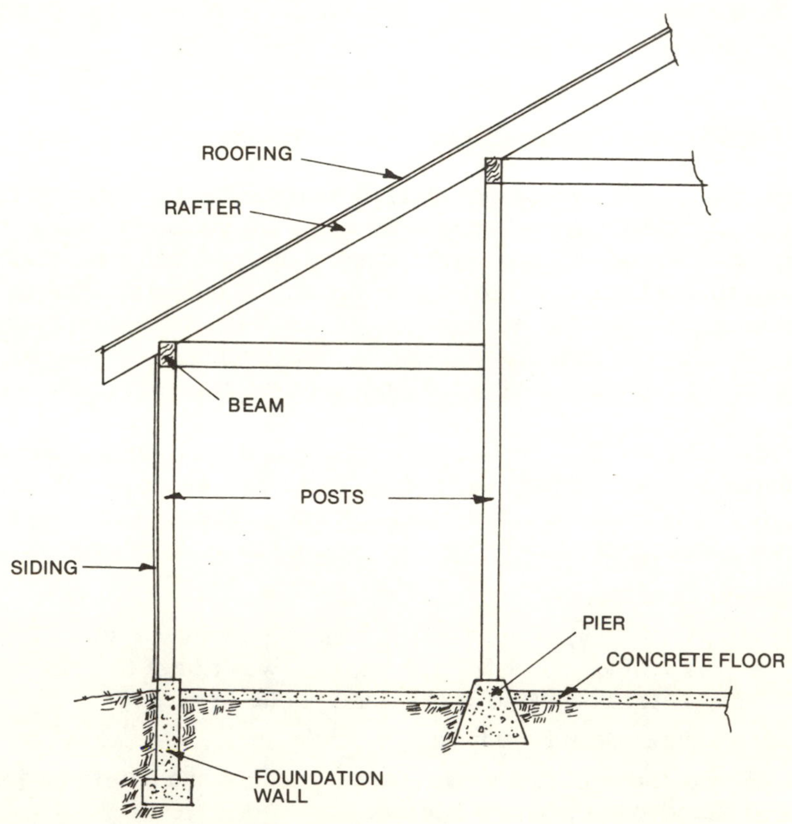

Figure 2-3. Post and beam framing system.

hewn timbers which were frequently fastened together with wooden dowel pins. Later versions used sawn timbers or, in some cases, members which were laminated or built up from two inch planking.

The use of post and beam in farm buildings diminished rapidly in the 1940's and 1950's due to costs, material availability, and the emergence of new construction techniques. Today, about the only place we see post and beam in light construction is where someone is trying to achieve special effects.

Advantages of post and beam:

1. Exterior walls are non-load bearing and window or door openings can be easily accommodated between posts.
2. Exposed posts and beams are architecturally pleasing in many structures.

Disadvantages:

1. Heavy timber members used are frequently costly and in some cases not readily available.
2. Not all builders are familiar with this type of construction and this may restrict choice of contractors.
3. Insulation required for today's energy efficient designs is not easily incorporated.

Pole-Frame Construction

Pole-frame or, as it is more commonly known, pole barn construction is the most popular type of building now in use on farms. Two things are responsible for this popularity. First, the development of reliable methods of preservative treatment has eliminated decay of structural members as a major problem. And second, use of rectangular framing members and trussed rafters has provided a means of enclosing large areas at an economical cost. There are few types of farm buildings which cannot make effective use of pole frame construction.

This type of building is similar to post and beam in that relatively heavy timbers are used to provide structural support. The major difference is that the vertical posts or poles are treated with preservative and placed in the ground where they also serve as a replacement for the building foundation.

In earlier days, pole buildings were considered to be rather crude, cheap construction. Irregular, round poles made it difficult to align a building and interior poles were frequently in the way of equipment. As a result, pole construction was frequently limited to use for uninsulated cattle barns or storage buildings. Today, most pole buildings use sawn timbers for poles and roof trusses to eliminate interior supports. They can be easily insulated and are used regularly for almost every conceivable purpose on farms and in other industries.

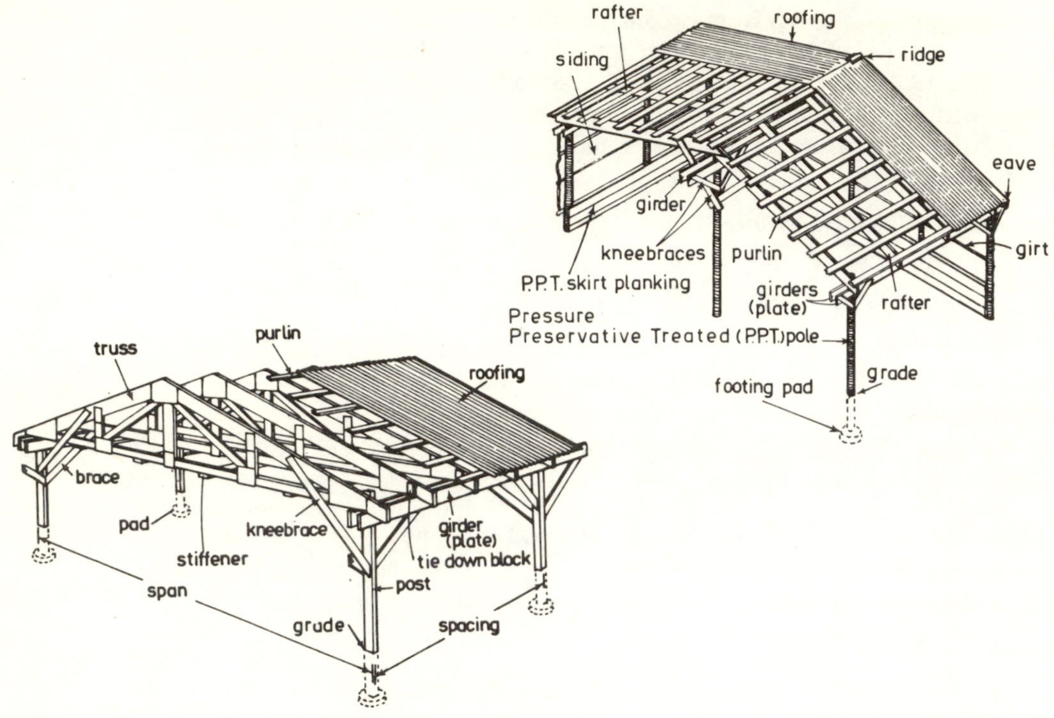

Figure 2-4. Two types of pole frame buildings. The clear span unit with trussed rafters is most common today. (NRAES)

Advantages of pole frame:

1. It is a low cost space enclosure.
2. No foundation is necessary.
3. Easy erection with semi-skilled labor is possible.
4. The building is adaptable to either unfinished interior or complete environmental control.
5. Wide selection of trusses, sidewall heights, and pole spacing make this type construction adaptable to a variety of uses.
6. Buildings are adaptable to a variety of sites with a minimum of site preparation.
7. Sides can be left off to improve accessibility and reduce costs, if necessary.
8. The building is easily lengthened at a later date by adding sections.

Disadvantages:

1. Clear span width is generally limited to a maximum of 50 to 60 feet. Wider units are possible, but cost increases rapidly.
2. Buildings are usually limited to single story.

3. Subsurface problems such as rock or ledge may increase construction costs.

Steel Frame Construction

Steel frame or "metal buildings," initially developed to meet needs of light manufacturing, have become a popular alternative for many agricultural uses. They offer a clear span construction with widths which can range up to 100 feet and can have unlimited length.

The main load carrying structure is the metal frame. The frames may be an open webb truss-like design or a specially formed solid member. The space between members is spanned with either wooden or metal purlins which support the metal roofing and siding.

Frames can be supported on a conventional concrete foundation wall or by specially designed reinforced concrete piers. Manufacturers who supply buildings will also provide plans for the foundation or pier support. These plans must be closely adhered to since there is a considerable amount of outward thrust at the point where the frame is attached.

Metal frame buildings are adaptable to nearly as many uses as the pole frame type structure. They usually will cost slightly more for the conventionally used widths; but are very competitive when the desired clear span width exceeds 50 feet.

Advantages of metal frame:

1. A wide variety of widths and wall heights is available.
2. They are quickly erected once frame supports are in place.

Figure 2-5. Metal frame construction.

3. There is greater salvage potential in the event the building is no longer used.
4. They may have a slightly better insurance rate.

Disadvantages:

1. Foundation supports must be precisely located.
2. Skills in metal working for erection which may not be locally available are required.
3. A crane or other heavy equipment may be required for erection.

Concrete and Masonry Construction

"If you want it to last, make it out of concrete." The durability, cleanability, and decay resistance of concrete and masonry have led to their use or partial use in construction of nearly every farm building. Unfortunately, both concrete and masonry are excellent conductors of heat and cannot be easily insulated. For this reason, their use in construction of

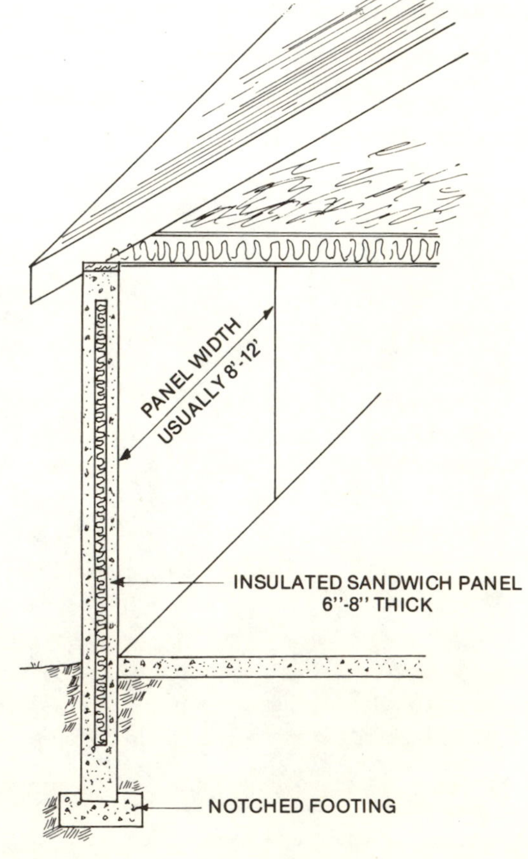

Figure 2-6. Tilt-up concrete sandwich panel construction. Panels are formed and poured on a flat surface and then lifted or tilted up into place. This durable and economical type of construction has not been widely accepted in farm construction.

exterior walls of farm buildings has lessened and will probably continue to decline in the years ahead. However, two relatively new construction techniques may slow this decline. They are concrete sandwich panel construction and surface bonding of blocks.

A concrete sandwich panel is a 6 to 8 inch thick wall panel which contains a center of 2 inch thick foam plastic insulation which is encased or "sandwiched" between two layers of reinforced concrete. The panels are usually poured on a flat surface and then tilted up to form wall sections after the concrete has cured. The resulting wall combines the durability of concrete with a moderately well insulated section adaptable to many farm buildings.

Surface bonding of concrete blocks was developed by USDA researchers as a means of reducing costs and improving strength of block wall construction. Concrete blocks are laid up without mortar and the exterior surfaces are plastered on both sides with a glass fiber reinforced mixture which bonds them together. Cores in the blocks can be filled with certain insulating materials to provide some resistance to heat flow.

In spite of these new developments, concrete and masonry will probably continue to be used only where their special properties are specifically needed.

Advantages of concrete and masonry construction:

1. It is an extremely durable construction.
2. A high degree of fire resistance is achieved.

Disadvantages:

1. Higher cost than other systems.
2. Weather can be a limiting factor on when construction is done.
3. It is not easily adapted to future remodeling.

New Construction Systems

Research in farm buildings by various universities and private industry continues to produce new building types and concepts which may be applicable to your particular situation. Because they are new, it is frequently difficult to determine how they will stand the test of time. If you are not experienced in construction, you should seek professional advice in the evaluation of new concepts. A few of these which have been successfully used are contained in the following list.

Air inflated structures. These are temporary or seasonal use facilities, usually constructed of plastic or rubber coated fabric inflated by a continuously operating blower. Access to the structure is through some type of air lock or is limited by the blower's ability to keep the structure inflated.

Semi Air Inflation. This is a technique, researched extensively by Rutgers University, used in plastic covered greenhouses. A rigid frame is used to form the basic structure and it is covered with two layers of plastic

Figure 2-7. This relatively new form of construction is referred to as a monolithic dome. An air-inflated form is covered with layers of reinforced concrete and insulation to provide a one-piece structure suitable for a multitude of uses. (Monolithic Structures, Inc.)

film, sealed together around all edges. A small blower is used to inflate and maintain pressure between the two layers of plastic. This system reduces considerably the amount of labor required to recover the greenhouse when the plastic film deteriorates.

Prefabricated Panels. Over the years there have been many attempts to bring assembly line techniques to the construction industry. Most of these have taken the form of some type of prefabricated wall or roof panel system which can be factory assembled, transported to the building site, and set into place. Many of these systems use excellent materials and have the potential of making a good building. They have not been widely accepted in farm buildings because of cost and the fact that their standardized pattern does not always adapt to the particular needs of the individual farmer.

Zoning and Codes

There once was a time when a farmer could build anything he wanted anywhere he wanted, provided it was on his own property and he could afford it. In some parts of the country this is still true. However, many of us must now conform to state and/or local governmental regulation when we locate and build a new facility. These regulations fall into two general categories—zoning and building codes.

Zoning laws are developed and implemented by local governments (usually town or county) to bring some degree of order to land use within the governed area. Zoning requirements frequently set aside or "zone" areas for agricultural, light industrial, residential, heavy industrial, or open space usage. They may also determine "set backs" or clearances between structures and property lines for each of the different land use categories. Zoning laws can prohibit construction of a large swine complex in the middle of a residential subdivision. They may also prohibit a manufacturing plant adjacent to your farm.

Zoning laws are usually enforced by local governments through a building permit, inspection, and occupancy permit system. You should be able to find out the specific requirements for your area (if any) through the county clerk's office. In order to secure any needed building permit, you will probably need some type of plot plan showing building location with regard to your property line. There will also have to be some definition of use so that it can be determined if it is in compliance with zoning requirements. When the building is complete, an inspection will be made to see if it is in compliance and if so, a certificate of occupancy will be issued. Without a certificate of occupancy, you cannot legally use your new facility and may be subject to penalty if you do so.

Building codes specify construction standards aimed at ensuring the health and welfare of building occupants. Model building codes are developed and maintained by organizations interested in the construction industry. These model codes are then implemented or promulgated by local or state governments. The government which implements a particular code usually makes some changes or additions to accommodate local situations. The three most commonly used model codes in the United States are the Uniform Building Code (UBC), Building Officials and Code Administrators Code (BOCA), and the Standard Building Code (SBC). Although there are some exceptions, UBC is normally found in use in the western United States, the SBC in the Southeast, and the BOCA Code in central and northeastern areas.

Traditionally, building codes have largely ignored agricultural buildings. Because of this, many conflicts have arisen in code regulated areas when specifications developed for commercial or residential buildings have been randomly applied to farm buildings. This situation is changing slowly; however, it will be many years before the major codes contain fully defined sections on agricultural buildings.

Building codes are also enforced through a permit-inspection system. Zoning and building code regulations are usually operated through the same agency. Code regulated buildings will require more frequent inspection than facilities covered only by zoning. A typical inspection schedule would include visits when the foundation is in place, the roof is on and utilities are roughed in, and on completion. Depending on the local regulation, there may be a fee for each inspection or it may be covered in the building permit fee. If there are construction errors or items of noncompliance, these will have to be corrected before building can proceed. Information on code and inspection requirements can also be obtained through county clerk offices.

Most problems between building officials and farmers erecting new facilities are the result of misunderstanding or missed communications.

Those of you living in areas covered by zoning and/or codes can avoid unnecessary delays by adhering to the following items.

1. Find out in advance what will be required under the laws that govern your particular site.
2. Provide officials with as complete a set of plans as possible when applying for your building permit. This will give officials an opportunity to resolve any questions about construction before the building is underway.
3. Call for any required inspections in advance.

All planning and zoning ordinances, as well as building codes, contain provisions for variance. If your planned structure does not comply with regulations, you may be able to obtain a variance which will enable you to complete the project. Zoning variances are usually acted on by a planning and zoning board in response to a written request. They may also require a public hearing and notification of adjacent property owners before ruling on the request. Code variances often require that you obtain a certification from a registered professional engineer or architect that the particular design is in conformance with accepted practice.

Quality Level

Everyone who purchases anything wants top quality at minimum cost. Unfortunately this is not always possible; nor is it necessarily desirable. The low priced economy model may get you to the same point with considerably less overhead.

We briefly discussed economics in Chapter 1 and by now you should have a pretty good idea of how much you can afford to spend. Determining quality is going to be a much harder job. Anyone can walk through a completed building and decide for himself if it meets his quality expectations. In fact, this is probably a good way to start. Visit several recently constructed buildings in your area to see for yourself how they are put together and if they are performing up to the owner's expectations. This will also give you a chance to do some preliminary evaluation of builders who are working in your area.

It is almost impossible to fully determine quality level from looking at plans. Unfortunately, in many cases it is the only alternative available. The sections that follow cover items which we feel are important in a quality building.

Meeting Functional Requirements

This item is easiest of all to evaluate. Will the building do what you want it to? Is there adequate capacity for the number of animals or other things you want to put in it? Make a list of the things you have to do and the access necessary to accomplish them. Then use the list as a check off for the features contained on the plan.

A sample listing for a 100-cow, free stall barn follows.

1. Free stalls for 100 cows.
2. Silage feed bunk (24 inches of feed space per animal).
3. Drive thru feed alley for silage (12 feet wide to accommodate hired man who has trouble with 8 foot wide wagon).
4. Waterer (located away from silage bunk so cows with full mouths don't drop silage in it).
5. Natural light during daytime hours.
6. Ten foot clearance under roof to accommodate self unloading wagon.
7. Room for hay feeder in case we have to feed hay.
8. End doors 12 feet wide and 10 feet high.
9. Natural ventilation system.
10. Provisions for split herd operation.

Structural Requirements

Four types of loads act on farm buildings—dead, live, snow, and wind. Dead loads are made up of the weights of the individual components of the building. Snow and wind loads are location and climate dependent. Live loads are those imposed by usage or occupancy of the building.

Although dead loads are not normally a major part of building design, they are considered in the overall process of plan development. Light frame buildings used on farms will have dead load requirements which fall into one of three categories.

Low: roof load = 3.5 lbs/sq ft
ceiling = 0 lbs/sq ft

Low dead load structures would include such buildings as pole-frame units using trussed rafters with purlins and metal roofing. No insulation or ceiling is included. Examples would be machine sheds, cold livestock housing, hay storages, etc.

Medium: roof = 3.5 lbs/sq ft
ceiling = 5.0 lbs/sq ft

Similar in construction to the low category except that a ceiling and insulation have been added. Examples include warm livestock housing, milking parlors, and farm shops.

High: roof = 7.5 lbs/sq ft
ceiling = 8.0 lbs/sq ft

These dead loads are typically used with residential design or in buildings having a solid roof deck, asphalt shingles, insulation, and a sheet rock ceiling.

Snow and ice loads are obviously dependent on weather. Because of this, there is always a certain amount of probability, or risk, associated with assignment of a specific design load to accommodate snow.

Farm buildings are usually designed to withstand the maximum snow load expected once every 25 years. Weather bureau records are available which provide these data. A map of the United States showing these values is presented in Figure 2-8. Data for maximum ground level snow load are adjusted downward to account for the fact that sloping roofs seldom have as high a snow pack as the ground. Traditionally this adjustment factor has been 0.6. However, as we write this, there is some indication that there will be an increase in this value in the near future. Design engineers are expected to increase snow load values as needed to meet any unusual conditions, such as high drifting areas or with roof designs which may tend to retain snow.

Remember that snow load assignment is based on probability. Because of this, there is always some element of failure risk. If you

Figure 2-8. Twenty-five year snow-load map. Values shown are the maximum snowpack in lbs per square foot on the ground expected once in 25 years. (ASAE)

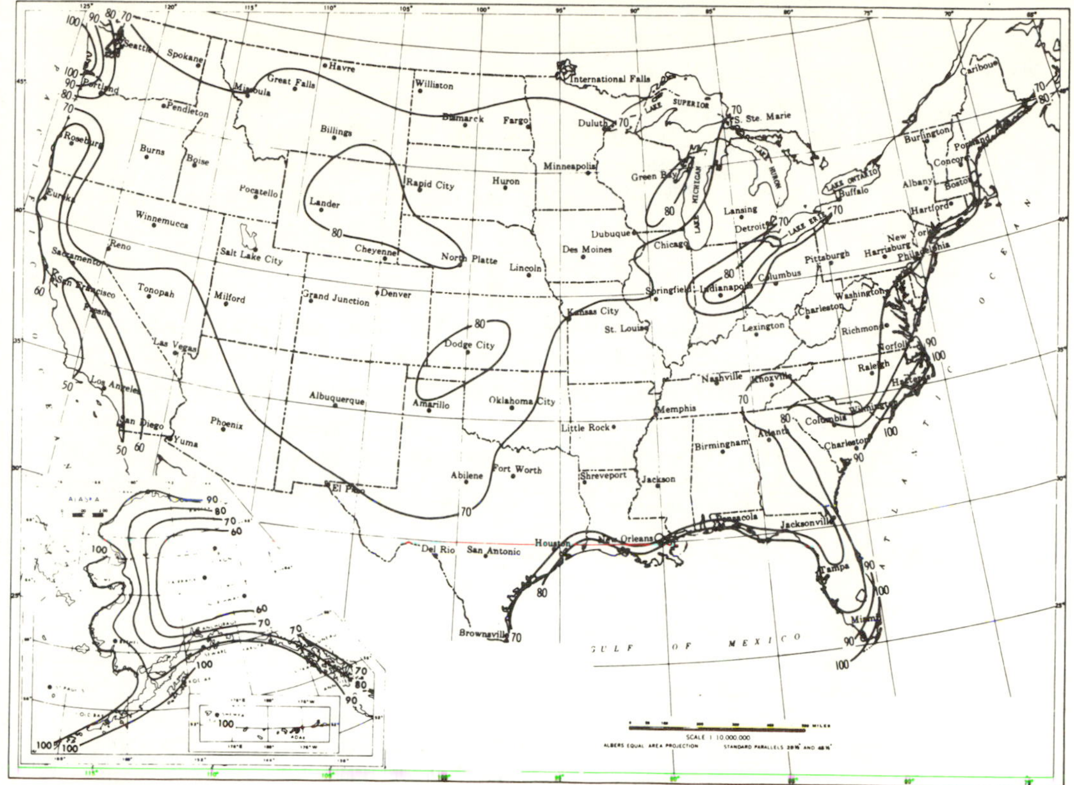

Figure 2-9. Maximum wind velocity expected once in 25 years (miles per hour). (ASAE)

specify the loading expected once in 25 years, there is no guarantee that a once in 100 year storm won't occur next winter, or even for the next two winters in a row. Probability is an accepted design practice which provides a reasonable building at an economical price. It is also what keeps insurance companies in business.

Farm buildings should be designed to withstand all expected wind loads except for tornado. Again, it is accepted practice to use a probability of occurrence factor. A design wind speed of 80 mph will take care of the once in 25 year expectations for all but some coastal areas of the United States. Figure 2-9 depicts the design loads.

The actual load which wind exerts on a surface which is perpendicular to it can be calculated using the following equation:

$Q = .00256\,V^2$ where:
Q = pressure in lbs/sq ft
V = wind speed in mph

Using this equation, you can determine that a wind speed of 80 mph can exert a force of 16.4 pounds per square foot on a surface perpendicular to it. Obviously, not all surfaces are perpendicular to the wind at all times, if ever. Because of this, wind may exert forces in unusual directions. Forces

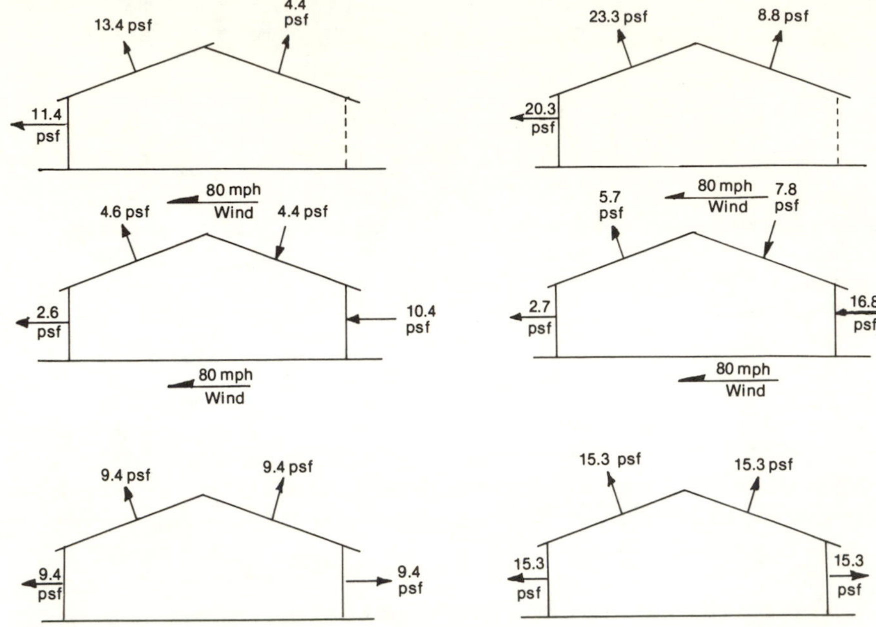

Figure 2-10. Loads on parts of buildings caused by 80 mph wind. Buildings on left side of illustration are located on rolling ground with some tree protection. Buildings on right are on flat, open land. Loads are in lbs per square foot of area.

due to an 80 mph wind on different types of buildings are shown in Figure 2-10. It is not uncommon for a wind load to actually overcome the dead load of a building and lift the roof off.

Live loads are those loads which are imposed on a building by its usage. In most cases these will be floor loads. Structures used for storage of grain, silage, or hay also have to be able to withstand side pressures as part of their expected live loads. The following tables present live load design values used in several types of farm structures.

Table 2-1. **Live Loads To Be Used in Floor Design**

Building Use	**Design Live Load (Lbs/Sq Ft)**
Cattle	
Milking parlors	70
Loose housing	80
Milk rooms	50*
Poultry	40
Sheep	30
Swine-solid floors	40
Horses	100
Greenhouses	50
Shops	70

**Special provisions for support of bulk tanks must also be considered.*

Table 2-2. **Required Design Line Loads for Slatted Floor Areas**

Livestock	Design Live Load	
	Lbs/Ft of Slat	Lbs/Sq Ft Slatted Floor Area
Dairy and beef cattle	250	100
Dairy and beef calves to 400 lbs	150	50
Sheep	120	50
Swine		
To 50 lbs	50	35
To 200 lbs	100	50
To 400 lbs	150	65
To 500 lbs	170	70

Lateral loads, or side pressures developed in storages will depend on depth of product, physical dimensions of storage, and type of construction. Some basic data you may find useful in preliminary planning can be found in the table below.

Table 2-3. **Density and Marketing Unit Weights for Farm Products**

Product	Density (Lbs/Cubic Foot)	Marketing Unit	Weight of Market Unit-(Lbs)
Fescue seed	11 to 24	Bushel	14 to 30
Clover seed	48	Bushel	60
Corn-shelled	44.8	Bushel	56
Corn-ear	28	Bushel	70
Oats	25.6	Bushel	32
Soybeans	48	Bushel	60
Wheat	48	Bushel	60
Baled hay	6 to 10	Ton	—
Corn silage	40 to 50	Ton	—

Judging Labor Efficiency

A farm building's reason for being is to modify the environment surrounding those things it contains. It is hoped it will accomplish this without bringing higher labor requirements to the farm operation.

How does someone judge labor efficiency of a particular design? One way is to attempt to visualize materials flow through the structure. Agriculture is materials handling. We move animals, feed, machines, food products, and manure. Whenever there is a designer imposed bottle neck to smooth movement of material, we have a reduction in labor efficiency.

Let's illustrate this with a closer examination of two different free stall dairy systems shown in Figures 2-11 and 2-12. The system in Figure 2-11 provides the following advantages from the materials flow standpoint:

1. Feed storage is close to point of use. In fact, it could be self-fed, if necessary.
2. Cow traffic is minimized by short, single purpose alleys in free stall barn.

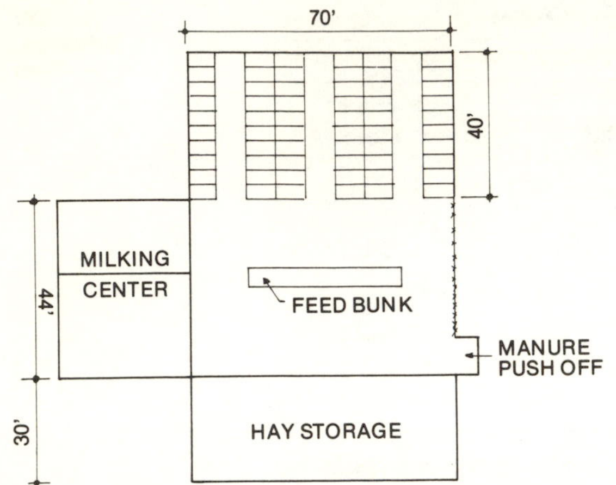

Figure 2-11. Open type free-stall system.

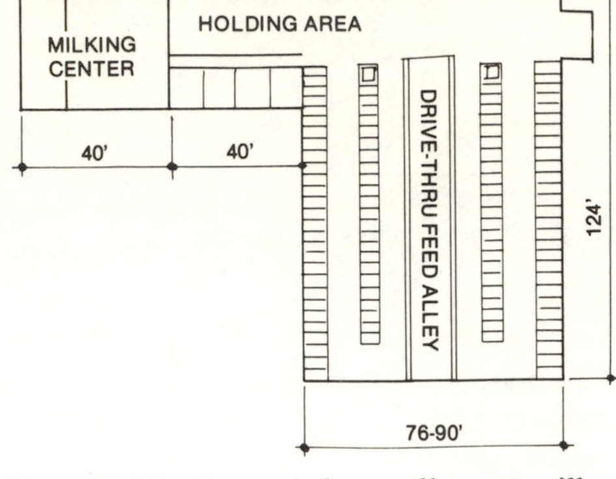

Figure 2-12. Covered free-stall system illustrating straight-line design and multiple-use alleys.

3. Manure push off simplifies loading of solid manure.

Contrast this system with Figure 2-12 which shows the following.

1. Movement of animals and manure is straight line.
2. Manure handling could be done with a flushing system, which would minimize labor still further.
3. Multiple use paving (feed alley and free stall alley) reduces overall size of the system.
4. Herd can be easily divided into groups to facilitate handling or feeding according to production schedule.
5. There are no blind alleys to restrict movement of animals or machines.
6. Door aligns with feed bunk to permit access when feeder breaks down or power is off.

Granted, the second system will require a higher initial investment and is not a design which can grow by bits and pieces as money becomes available. This should be a concern, but you should be even more aware that a design which adds extra man hours to your operation will cost you something every day you own it. Remember this as you look at each plan and ask yourself how each material you have to handle will move through it and what types of problems are likely to occur.

Expansion Potential

"This is as big as we are ever going to get." "I am too old to handle a larger operation and there is no one to take it over after I am gone." At least 80% of the people who are getting ready to build will use these arguments or a similar one to deny any need for future expansion. Almost 90% of the time, they are wrong. A classic example is the two bachelor brothers we visited in 1962. Changes in health requirements were forcing them to upgrade their dairy operation from manufacturing to grade A. At the same time, they were planning to expand "for the last time" from 30 cows up to 50 cows. When we last visited them in 1970 they were milking 140 animals and planning another expansion. Their ages in 1970 were 78 and 80!

Too many times we box ourselves in and prevent easy expansion by selecting the wrong building. Whenever you look at plans, go through some mental planning to see how it could be expanded. If you are dealing with a professional consultant, have him outline expansion potential on the plans he develops for you. It will be well worth any extra money it costs. Even if you don't do the expanding, the potential will add to the salability of your farm.

Figures 2-13 and 2-14 illustrate expansion potential for some different types of farm structures. Issues that need to be raised as you consider expansion potential include the following:

Mechanical feed handling equipment. Often drive units used on this equipment can handle additional footage, provided it is in a straight line or has a minimum of turns. If you are going to use different rations in various parts of the building, this may not work out well.

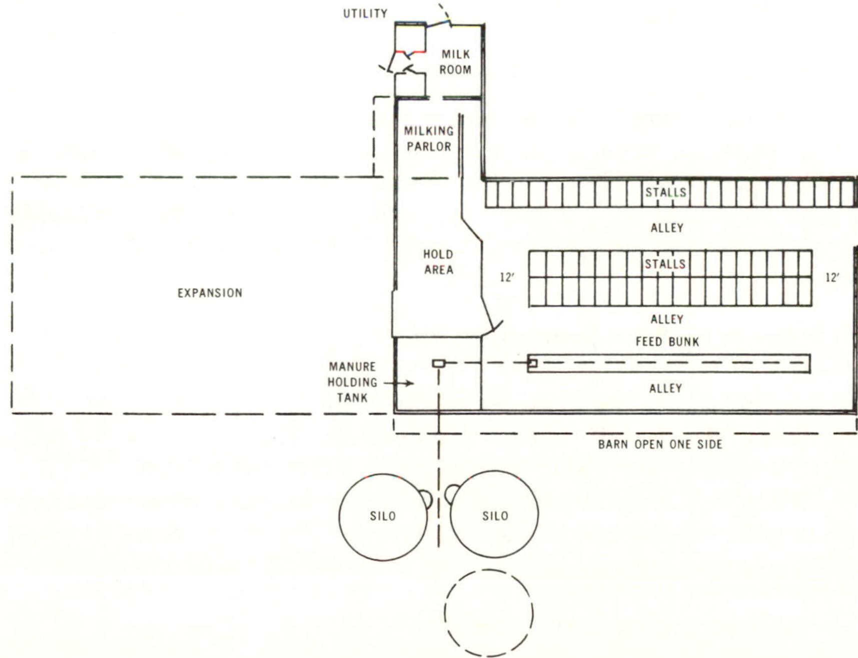

Figure 2-13. A 60-cow free-stall system that can easily be expanded to 120 cows by adding a free-stall barn and additional feed bunk. (Granite City Steel)

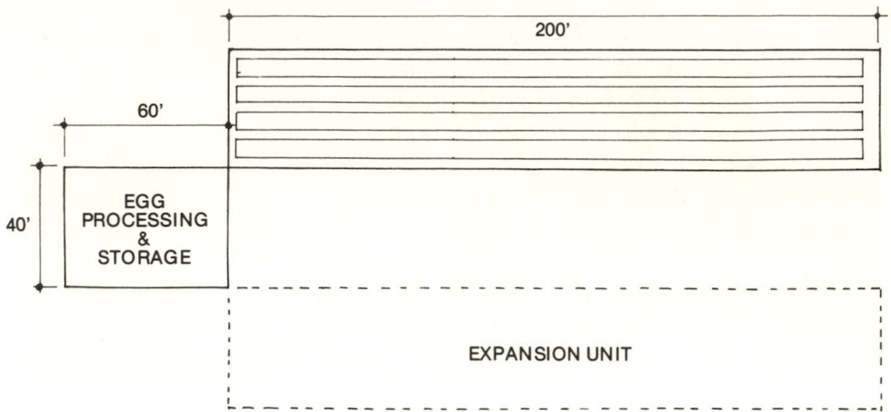

Figure 2-14. One possible method of allowing for expansion of a caged layer poultry operation.

Grouping of animals. As units increase in size, there may be merit in grouping according to age or production level. If animals have to be moved to a central location, such as a milking parlor or a handling facility on a regular basis, merely adding to the length of the building may create traffic problems.

Site development. Farmers who live in the flat lands of the Midwest seldom have to worry about cut and fill problems associated with preparing for building construction. Others are not so fortunate and should pay particular attention to just where that expanded building is going to fit on their farmstead. It is not unusual for poor placement to result in earth moving costs which will become a major obstacle.

Interior flexibility. Many times expansion will lead to a change in use for the particular building. If there is any one thing that causes planners and engineers headaches when they develop plans for change in use, it is interior supporting walls or posts. You will maintain maximum flexibility for future expansion or possible change of use by selecting a clear span type structure.

Matching With Present Facilities

Appearance is important, especially if you plan on selling out in the near future. However, if your existing buildings are more than a few years old, you probably won't want to try to match either style or type.

When we talk about matching with present facilities, we are most concerned with obtaining operational compatibility. We want a structure which will fit in well with present management and not create additional problems.

Is Energy Use Appropriate?

There was a time when building operational cost was considered to be an insignificant item in the cost of maintaining a desirable environment.

Figure 2-15. A variety of building types is the logical result of expansion over a number of years. It may not always be aesthetically pleasing, but the real goal should be a functional, efficient farm operation.

Rapid and substantial increases in energy costs during the last half of the 1970's changed this. Energy costs are now second only to the feed bill in size, particularly for those buildings which are used for rearing of young animals or birds. A study of energy costs in 1980 indicated that Missouri feeder pig producers were spending approximately $1.00 per pig weaned for energy to provide supplemental heat.

The building you select should have a heating system which uses fuel compatible with that which your regular supplier can provide. If you are using LP-gas as a primary fuel source, you probably shouldn't make a switch to fuel oil on a new building unless you have some assurance of a future supply.

Whether or not you wish to incorporate an alternate heat source, such as solar, will depend on economics at the time. As we write this book in 1980-81, many of the highly promoted alternate systems are only marginally cost effective, if at all. We discuss construction, as well as pros and cons, of these in a later chapter.

The single most cost effective item in reducing energy bills is insulation. If your new facility will require any supplemental heat at all, you can afford to spend extra dollars to insure that you have the maximum amount of insulation needed for your building. Insulation will be specified on the plans and should be in terms of R value—not inches of thickness. If you have any question on adequacy of the amount, ask the person who provided the plans for an operational cost estimate. He should have made one when he arrived at the amount of insulation he specified.

Efficient Use of Materials

Did you ever go to the lumber yard and try to buy a 3 by 6 foot sheet of plywood? If you did, the guy behind the counter probably thought you had been spending too much time out in the hot sun.

Building materials come in standardized sizes. Matching building dimensions as nearly as possible to these standards will reduce both labor and material waste. The standard unit or module for overall building size is 2 feet, starting with an even number. For best use of materials, a 4 foot module will be even better. Let's illustrate our point. Suppose you have a choice between three buildings which are 26, 27, and 28 feet wide. All three are going to use exterior plywood siding. Which will make the best use of materials?

Plywood comes in sheets that are 4 feet wide. This means you will have to buy the same number of sheets (7) to cover the end of all three building sizes. For the 26 foot building, the seventh sheet will have to be cut in half. You will be able to use the other half sheet on the opposite end of the building, but you do have to pay for the labor of cutting. When you put siding on the 27 foot wide building, the seventh sheet will also have to be cut, only this time you will be left with a 1 foot wide strip, which probably will go to the scrap lumber pile. The 28 foot width, which is a multiple of the 4 foot module, makes full use of the plywood siding and results in more building for the same materials and labor costs.

Does it always work out that way? Of course not—there may be other requirements, such as specialized equipment needs, which will dictate the exact dimensions of your building, but the module approach will work out to your advantage often enough to at least consider it when choosing a size.

Just about everything you or your contractor will buy for that new building is made in standardized sizes built around some unit module. If you are familiar with these and make use of this knowledge you will get more building for your money and avoid having to pay the premium for special order items. Don't be like the man who insisted on an 11 foot high sidewall and had to trim a foot off all the studs and the siding material. Table 2-4 gives some of the more common sizes and modules for building materials.

***Table 2-4.* Standard Size Ranges and Module Increments for Building Materials**

Material	Range of Standard Sizes		Increment Module	Available at Extra Cost
	Width	Length		
Lumber	2 in. to 12 in.	8 ft to 20 ft	Width-2 in. Length-2 ft	14 in. width 22 ft to 24 ft length
Plywood	4 ft	8 ft		9 ft to 11 ft length
Panelling	4 ft	7 ft to 8 ft		
Metal roofing	24 in. to 48 in.	8 ft to 24 ft	Width-6 in. Length-2 ft	custom lengths
Roof trusses		20 ft to 50 ft	2 ft	50 ft +
Window units	24 in. to 72 in.	24 in. to 72 in.	2 in.	custom sizes
Prehung doors	24 in. to 36 in.	80 in. to 84 in.	2 in.	custom sizes
Rigid insulation	4 ft	8 ft to 16 ft	Length-2 ft	
Wood trim		8 ft to 16 ft	2 ft	
Concrete block	4 in., 6 in., 8 in., 12 in.	16 in.		

Building Packages

An increasing number of farm buildings constructed today are selected from the wide variety of "pre-engineered" structures available from lumber yards or commercial manufacturers. These buildings are commonly referred to as "package buildings" and have been designed to reduce costs through standardization.

Package buildings are available in a variety of sizes and shapes. They contain features which reflect both the needs of their intended use and the choice of their designers. Their purchase can be compared to that of a tractor or automobile—there are high price models, economy units, and usually a variety of optional accessories which add to the cost.

The decision to purchase a package building may mean compromising on some of the features you would like to have. Remember, the manufacturer makes some of his profit through standardization and changes add to his costs. On the positive side, a standard plan probably means there are units just like the one you are interested in already constructed and in operation. This gives you an opportunity to visit a facility and see for yourself how it is functioning.

There are generally three options available in the selection of a packaged unit. They are materials only, materials and labor, and more recently, the prefabricated building module. We will look at each of these possibilities in the following paragraphs. Don't forget though, the successful building package must fulfill all the same criteria we were discussing earlier in this chapter.

Materials-only packages are generally assembled by a local lumber dealer or sometimes by a farm building company that also offers a complete building service. Their packages normally include all the parts necessary for completion of the building with the exception of the concrete. The supplier will also provide a set of plans showing how the materials go together. Some packages will contain preassembled components such as doors, windows, and roof trusses.

The materials only package usually offers the most flexibility for the buyer, particularly if it is being assembled by a local supplier. The dealer should be able to offer a wide variety of materials and any necessary changes in size to accommodate your needs.

Another variation in the materials-only package is to ask several building supply dealers to bid on materials required to complete a building which you supply plans for. This approach will usually get you the advantage of some volume discount prices. It will also provide a chance to lock in a price for materials ahead of actual construction and make overall cost estimation more accurate. This helps keep your banker happy.

Whenever you get prices on materials packages, be sure to insist on a complete listing of what is to be supplied. If you are not sure the list is complete enough, ask for help. Too many times we have seen materials packages that did not include items such as siding, doors, or finish trim. You can get some idea of the pieces that are needed from later sections of this book. If you are planning to have a local builder help assemble your package, ask him to go over the list of materials to see if there are any missing items you will need.

The materials-plus-labor package is the most common unit in the farm building industry today. The company supplying it will generally offer one or two basic buildings with a series of options designed to make it fit your needs. These will include such things as size, wall height, window and door sizes and locations, insulation, interior finish, and possibly equipment. The supplier usually prefers that the owner do the basic site preparation work, including removal of top soil, grading, and installation of water and electric supply lines. This can usually be arranged through local contractors more economically than if the builder who is usually at some distance from the site has to do it. As soon as the site is prepared, the construction crew moves in and erects the building.

Materials and labor packages are available in metal frame, pole frame, and conventionally constructed buildings. There is no general rule as to which type will be most economical for your particular situation. In fact, it is not unusual to find more price variation between similar types of construction offered by different companies than between different types of construction.

The materials plus labor package provides the least amount of owner involvement in the actual building process. Once the contract is signed, responsibility for completion of the unit is in the hands of the supplier. Before you sign, however, make sure the contract, plans, and specifications adequately describe the building you want and the performance you expect from the supplier. It is a good idea to include a completion date for the facility and a procedure for handling any unexpected changes that may be required in the basic design.

The prefabricated module is the newest concept in farm building packages. These units are assembled in factories much like a mobile home and delivered to the farm on a trailer. Because of transportation restrictions, their size is more limited, much as it is with mobile homes. Generally, they will not be more than 28 feet wide and 60 to 70 feet long. Units more than 14 feet wide are shipped in halves and assembled at the site.

The size restriction limits the types of buildings adaptable to this type construction. At the present time, available buildings include swine farrowing and nursery units, calf housing, milking parlors, and a variety of small portable buildings.

As you might expect, manufacturers of these units are not interested in or able to do much in the way of site preparation work. They should, however, be expected to provide detailed plans and instructions for this work. If you deal directly with the manufacturer, you will have to make arrangements for site preparation. If there is a local dealer you are working with, he may be in a position to provide these services for you.

This type of building package offers the least amount of flexibility in planning. The size restriction imposed by transportation limits both the capacity and any variation of floor plan arrangement. The assembly line nature of their construction cannot provide both economy and customized features.

These buildings do offer the advantage of rapid installation at the site and they do have the potential of relatively easy relocation should you desire to move your farm operation or sell the building. Many manufacturers now offer them on a lease basis, which may provide some financial advantage to your particular farm operation.

CHAPTER **3**

Locating the Building

Proper placement of your new structure can be as important to its success as selecting it in the first place. In most cases, proper location is a lot harder decision, too! The average livestock farmer spends up to 75% of his working hours in and around his farm buildings. When it comes to adding a new building, we are often in a position of being so close to the forest we can't see the trees.

This chapter is designed to present many of the factors which influence building location. These have been separated into environmental, utilities, safety, and general farmstead arrangement. At the end of the chapter, we have included a section on how you can develop your own farmstead plan.

Environmental Factors

A building protects its interior from the effects of the outside climate or environment. How well it does this can depend on the kind of job we do in placing it. Items we need to be concerned with include sun, wind, snow, and drainage.

Solar

Extensive research over the years has provided both graphical and mathematical expressions as to just where the sun is located at any particular instant on any day of the year. By using this information in selecting a building site we can maximize solar effects in winter and minimize them in summer. This technique is part of a process known as passive solar design.

Let's show how this works by using an example. Consider the open front livestock housing building shown in Figure 3-1. The general recommendation for locating this building is to orient the long dimension or

Figure 3-1. Proper orientation with regard to sun and wind is as important to the performance of this building as is the selection of quality materials and good construction.

ridge line of the roof East-West; leaving the open front facing the South. This provides the following advantages:

1. Facing the smaller end wall to the West minimizes exposure to the late afternoon summer sun.
2. The relatively longer south wall is open to direct radiation from the winter sun which is low in the sky. At the same time, a roof overhang can be used to keep out the summer sun, which is high in the sky.

Solar penetration and shading effects can be calculated for different parts of the country during various months of the year. Figure 3-2 will enable you to determine the approximate latitude of your location

***Table 3-1.* Horizontal and Vertical Factors Used in Calculating Solar Penetration and Wall Shading on a South Facing Wall at Solar Noon**

Season	Latitude							
	30° N		35° N		40° N		45° N	
	Vert.	Horiz.	Vert.	Horiz.	Vert.	Horiz.	Vert.	Horiz.
Spring	1.7	.6	1.4	.7	1.2	.9	1.0	1.0
Summer	8.8	.1	4.9	.2	3.4	.3	2.5	.4
Fall	1.7	.6	1.4	.7	1.2	.9	1.0	1.0
Winter	.7	1.4	.6	1.6	.5	2.0	.4	2.5

Note: Above table values were calculated for the first day of each season; i.e., winter values are for December 21.

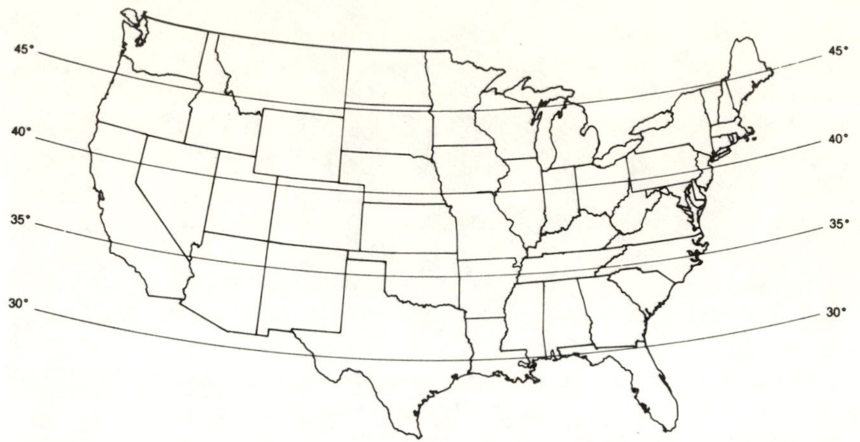

Figure 3-2. The latitude of your farm determines how much solar penetration you will get with a particular building and how much overhang is needed to provide summer shading. (American Plywood Association)

in the United States. Table 3-1 gives multiplier factors for different latitudes and different times of the year. If we know how much overhang we have on the south side of our building and the height of the eave above the ground, we can calculate the sunlight penetration at noon for different seasons of the year. The horizontal penetration of sun behind the overhang will be equal to the eave height times the horizontal factor from Table 3-1. For example, the eave height of a building at 40 degrees North latitude is 12 feet. On December 21, the horizontal factor is 2 and the noon time solar penetration will be 12 × 2 = 24 feet behind the eave line.

We can use a similar procedure to determine how effectively a roof

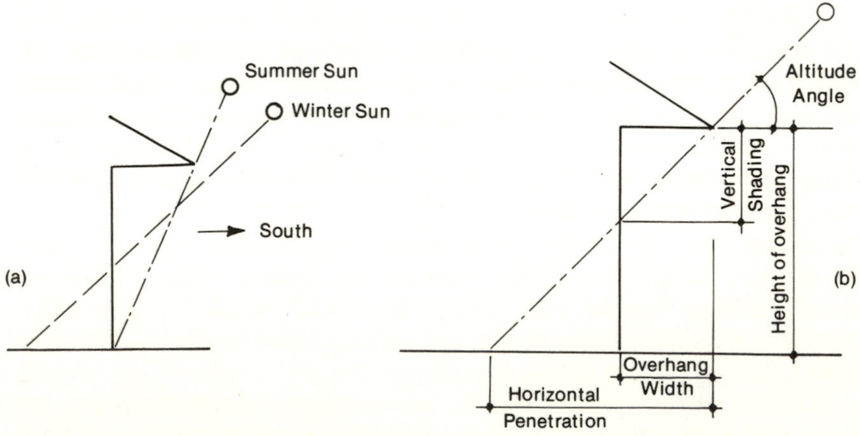

Figure 3-3. (a) Solar effects on a building change throughout the year because of changes in sun altitude. (b) Both vertical shading and horizontal penetration can be calculated using solar angles and building measurements.

overhang shields the front of a building from the summer sun. This is done by using the vertical factor from Table 3-1. If the building we used above has a 2 foot roof overhang, calculate the vertical shading on the south wall at noon on June 21. Table 3-1 yields a multiplier factor of 3.4. Multiplying this by the 2 foot overhang gives 6.8 feet of vertical shading. This means that over half the wall will be shaded by a 2 foot overhang. We can do a little mathematical manipulation and find out how much overhang is needed to fully shade the south wall at noon. This is done by dividing wall height by the vertical factor in Table 3-1. Our 12 foot wall would require a 12 ÷ 3.4 = 3.5 foot overhang to fully shade it on June 21.

You will find that an overhang large enough to provide complete south wall protection in June will restrict winter sunlight penetration. It will also add significantly to the cost of roof construction. A better solution is to compromise and accept some summer sun in return for lower cost and better winter sun. At 40 degrees latitude, a good compromise for most farm buildings is a 2 to 2.5 foot south overhang.

Suppose your site won't allow an exact East-West ridge orientation. What is next best? My preference has always been to orient the long side toward the Southeast if unable to get a true South location. Turning toward the Southeast rather than the Southwest will do two things for you. First, it faces the long side of the building toward the sun a little earlier in the day. This helps speed up warming during a cold winter day. It also results in a little earlier shading from the hot afternoon sun in summer. Second, it faces the building slightly away from west and northwest winds in winter months.

Most of our discussion so far has concerned open front buildings. The same principles apply to closed, insulated buildings. The main difference is that closed buildings are not as sensitive to deviation from the East-West ridge orientation as open front units.

Current energy costs have caused engineers and farmers to focus even more attention on passive solar design techniques than in the past. A major problem with all solar systems is that of storing energy for nighttime and cloudy day use. The so-called active solar systems generally use some type of insulated container holding rock or water to absorb energy during periods of sunshine and give it up at night. We will look at some of these systems in a later chapter.

Several years ago, a Frenchman named Felix Trombe patented a system for providing solar energy storage in passive systems. Known generally as the Trombe wall, this system involves placing a massive structure in a location where it will intercept solar energy directly and then release it directly to the building at night.

Trombe design features can be incorporated in farm structures by placing high mass (concrete or masonry) building components where they will intercept the sun's energy. The most common elements are concrete floors and walls. To provide maximum benefits, place some type of waterproof insulation between the storage unit and the ground. A 2 inch thickness of expanded polystyrene is sufficient for this purpose.

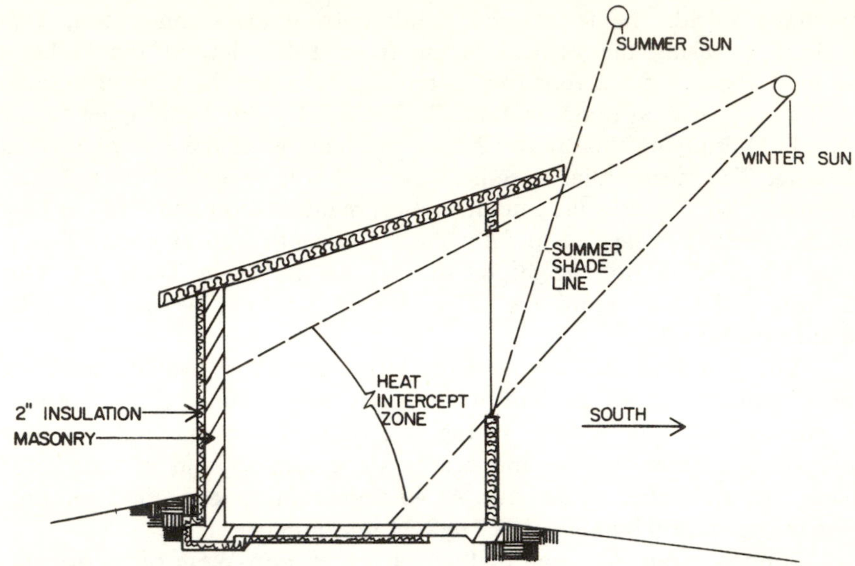

Figure 3-4. Proper design and orientation will allow a building to act as a natural or "passive" solar collector and storage unit. Often this can be done with little or no additional construction cost. (University of Missouri)

Predicting exactly how much energy a particular design will store is impossible. The specific heat of concrete is 0.2 Btu per pound per degree Fahrenheit. Concrete has a density of 150 pounds per cubic foot or 50 pounds for every square foot of 4 inch thick floor. This means that if you raise floor temperatures 15 degrees during the day, it will release $15 \times 50 \times 0.2 = 150$ Btu of heat energy as it cools during night hours. At this rate, a 500 square foot floor area would store energy equivalent to 1 gallon of LP-gas.

Figure 3-4 shows how passive solar collection and storage might be incorporated into a simple shed type structure.

Wind

Wind helps the performance of natural ventilation systems and provides cooling summer breezes. It also helps make snow drifts, causes wind chill factors, and carries undesirable odors from one location to another.

In most areas of the United States the prevailing winter winds blow from the North and Northwest. During summer they switch to a southerly direction. This means that open or partially open front buildings should be oriented with their open sides toward the South. It is fortunate indeed that the southerly orientation also works out best from the standpoint of passive solar design.

There are exceptions to every design rule and prevailing winds are no exception. If you happen to live in an area where prevailing winds are not "normal," you will have to make adjustments in your building orientation.

In the case of completely closed buildings, wind orientation is more a matter of deciding what undesirable effects the building will have on wind patterns around it. A large, tall building located on the northwest corner of the farmstead may do a good job of breaking the winter wind. It may also add considerably to your snow removal problems by providing a calm place where drifts can accumulate.

If at all possible, buildings should not be placed where they will interfere with desirable summer breezes, either. Most domestic animals, including man, will suffer as much from summer heat as from the winter cold. Natural air movement in the form of breezes is an important factor in helping maintain some degree of comfort during hot weather.

Some areas of the United States and specific localities in almost all parts of the country can benefit from specific wind control devices. The two devices most commonly used are shelterbelts and windbreaks. Studies in high wind areas such as North Dakota have shown that wind control devices can reduce heating costs by 20% to 30%, control snow drifting, reduce erosion, and improve animal performance.

A shelterbelt consists of one or more rows of trees located on the windward side of the farmstead. Figure 3-5 shows a cross section of a typical shelterbelt. In general, you can expect significant reduction in wind for a distance of about 20 times the maximum tree height on the downwind side. For example, 20 foot high trees would give about 400 feet of protected area.

In areas where snow is a problem, a multiple row shelterbelt is recommended. This will provide space for snow to accumulate within the planted area. Observations have shown that snow will accumulate for a distance of about 180 feet downwind of the first row of the shelterbelt. This means that if you have a 120 foot wide shelterbelt, you should

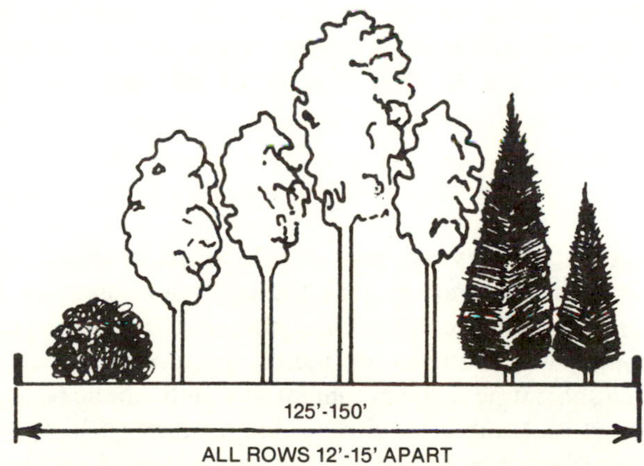

Figure 3-5. A tree windbreak or shelterbelt on the north and west sides of the farmstead will help minimize wind and snow problems. This cross section shows how evergreen and deciduous trees can be combined into a shelterbelt. (North Dakota)

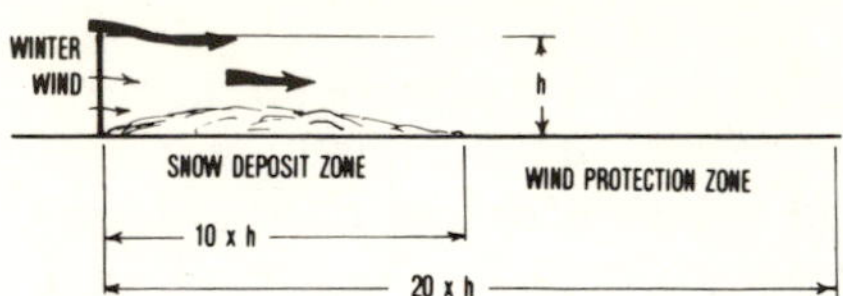

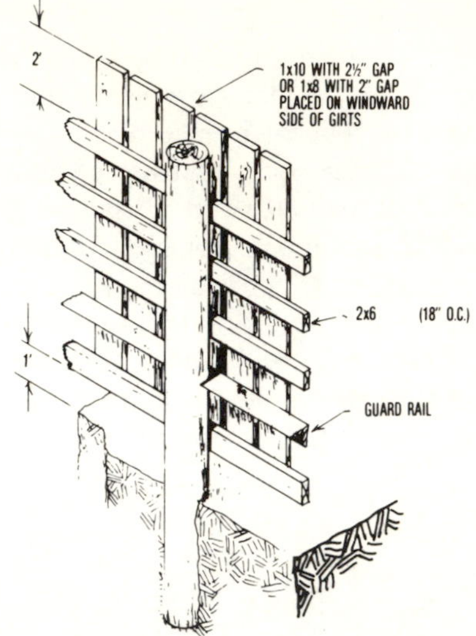

Figure 3-6. Construction details and expected performance for a manmade windbreak fence. (Purdue University)

allow about 70 feet between the inner row of trees and the nearest building for snow accumulation.

Shelterbelts should extend about 150 feet beyond the area they are intended to protect. This will minimize the swirling effect of the wind as it goes around the end of the plantings.

Unfortunately, it will take 5 to 10 years to establish an effective shelterbelt if you are starting with new plantings. If you can't wait or if you need protection on a more localized basis such as next to a feed bunk, consider a mechanical windbreak. One of the most effective devices is a board fence (Figure 3-6) about 10 feet high with openings between the boards. University research has shown that a ratio of 80% solid to 20% open area will provide good wind protection and also minimize snow problems.

If you are involved in construction of a mechanical windbreak, make sure it is well anchored. A strong gusty wind can exert nearly 1-½ tons of force on a 20 foot section of 10 foot high windbreak fencing.

Snow

If you live in the western part of Michigan or New York where heavy snowfall is the rule rather than the exception, placement of your new building should be done with some planning for winter access. For most of us though, winter snows are merely an inconvenience which can be dealt with in a short time with equipment available on the farm.

Our main snow trouble is with problem areas such as the feedlot that drifts 6 feet deep every time we get more than 4 inches of snow. By knowing the "lay of the land" and how snow tends to accumulate, we can avoid some of these. However, not everyone is good at making these predictions and even those who are sometimes make mistakes. I

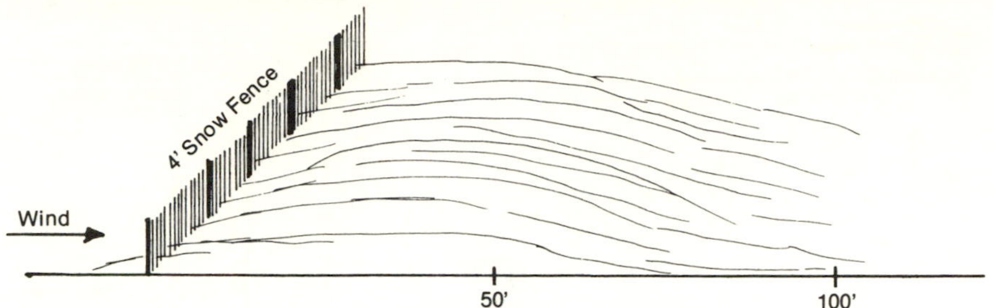

Figure 3-7. Normal drift and protected area pattern for standard 4-foot high slatted snow fence.

remember several years ago recommending that a farmer face his open front free stall barn toward the East to avoid an unusual wind pattern in the valley where he was located. During the first winter, he experienced two unusual snow storms, each of which left a 4 foot deep drift right down the middle of his new barn. Fortunately (at least for me), this has not happened since.

This type of problem is most easily handled with some type of wind control system or snow fencing. We discussed shelterbelts and mechanical wind breaks previously. Snowfence functions in a similar way, although it normally has a higher ratio of open to solid area than does a windbreak. Standard snowfence is 4 feet high and is about 40% open. It is effective in providing snow protection up to about 80 feet downwind. Figure 3-7 shows the expected drift and protection zone for snow fence.

Slope

The perfect location for a new building is absolutely flat over the area covered by the structure and has a 2% to 4% slope away in all directions. In nearly 25 years of working with farm buildings, we have yet to see the perfect site.

Drainage may well be the single most important consideration in final selection of the building site. Keeping water out of and away from the building means the building will perform at its best and you will have easy year-around access to it. If you have a ground surface slope of at least 2% (2 feet of fall per 100 feet) you can almost always correct any other drainage problems.

Slopes greater than 4% on an individual building site may add significantly to the cost of construction. Take, for example, a 40 × 250 foot poultry house proposed for a site having a 6% slope. Six percent means a 15 foot difference in elevation over the 250 foot length of the building. If we fill an area 50 feet wide and 260 feet long to provide a level spot for construction, it will take more than 3,600 cubic yards of fill. And, we would probably have to wait a year for the fill to settle before starting construction.

We are not trying to discourage earth moving as a means of securing a satisfactory building site. It is a necessary factor in at least 80%

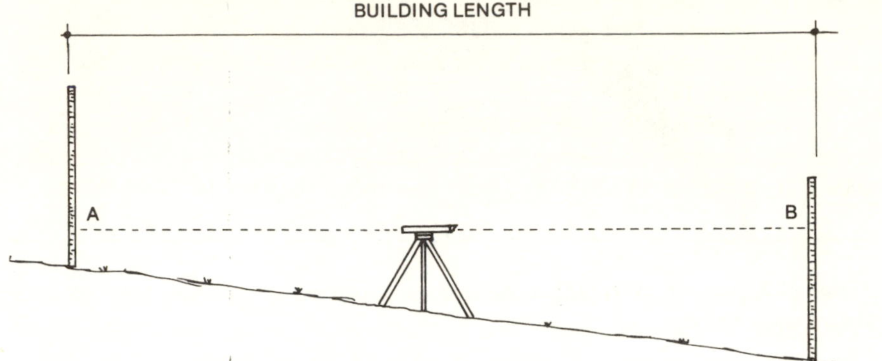

Figure 3-8. You can estimate earth-moving requirements using a simple farm level. See example in text for how it's done.

of all farm buildings. We are trying to alert you to the fact that it can add materially to the cost of a building. You can calculate how much earth moving will have to be done on a particular site using a simple level. Set up your level at the approximate center of your proposed building site. Referring to Figure 3-8, take rod readings at locations A and B, which are at the ends of the proposed building. Subtract reading A from B to get the total difference in height between them. Multiply this number by the total floor area of the building in square feet and divide by 54. This will give you the number of cubic yards of soil that need to be moved to level your site. Add 10% to 15% to account for extra required around the edges of the building. You can get a good estimate of current earth moving or fill costs in your area from local contractors or by calling the county ASCS (Agricultural Stabilization and Conservation Service) office.

Another important drainage consideration is the control of runoff from outside livestock production areas. Most states now have pollution control laws which prohibit the release of this contaminated runoff from the property on which it is produced. You should become familiar with these requirements and how they can best be met before making a final selection of a building site.

Utilities

Almost every new structure will have to be provided with one or more utilities. These include services for water, electricity, and sewage disposal.

Water

This essential element can be provided by a commercial utility or a private well or pond. The important thing is to make sure it is available in the amount and quality that you need to satisfy the demands of the facility you are planning. If you have to drill a well or build a pond to accommodate your needs, make sure this expense is planned in advance and doesn't come as a big shock when you are about ready to occupy your new facility.

If you need help with water system planning, the Midwest Plan Service (address in appendix) has an excellent reference book entitled PRIVATE WATER SYSTEMS, which you may want to order from them.

Electricity

The manner and type of electric service to the building will likely be determined by the company that serves you. Plan on contacting them at an early stage in your planning process. They probably have a farm service adviser who can help you plan all the electrical needs for your facility. They should also be in a position to give you an estimate of operating costs, too! If you have special needs, such as 3 phase power or unusually high demands, be sure to find out in advance if your utility will be able to accommodate them and if there will be any priority assigned to your usage.

Sewage

Increasing numbers of farm buildings are incorporating bathroom facilities, which require the installation of some type of sewage disposal system. These systems must, in many cases, meet requirements of local health authorities. If the building itself is associated with milk production, sewage disposal facilities will also have to meet the requirements of the market in which the milk is sold.

The major concern at the time of site selection is to be sure there is adequate area for the type of sewage system you are planning to install. In fact, it's not a bad idea to leave room enough for two systems in the event that the first one has to be replaced at some future date. Ideally the sewage disposal area should be located down slope from the building in order to allow for gravity movement of sewage. If it just cannot be done, there are automatic pumps available which can pump sewage to uphill disposal sites. This will add to both cost and maintenance chores throughout the life of the system.

You will find a discussion of the three commonly used individual sewage disposal systems in a later section on plumbing.

Safety: Fire and Security

Fires in farm buildings cost American agriculture millions of dollars every year. This loss could be reduced substantially through better site selection and improved construction techniques.

Building location may help prevent fire spread to or from adjacent buildings. Two things are responsible for fire spread; radiation and direct contact with burning particles. Radiation is the direct transfer of heat energy from a burning fire. A building located too close to a fire can become hot enough to actually burst into flame because of radiant heat transfer. Burning particles are carried from one structure to another by wind and natural updrafts surrounding a fire.

Recommended minimum separation between farm buildings is 50 feet. Shops or fuel storage areas should be at least 100 feet from any other buildings. Consider using greater separation whenever buildings are in alignment with prevailing winds.

Information on selecting materials and construction methods to improve the fire resistance of a particular building can be found in a later chapter of this book.

The rapidly rising rural crime rate is making building security an important factor on many farms. Probably the best way to secure a building is to place it where it can be easily observed by someone who is nearly always available. Unfortunately, this is an option which is not available to many farmers. This has led to development of a considerable number of electronic devices, including closed circuit television, which can be selected to "watch over" your investment. It is not within the scope of this book to discuss these systems; however, you should be aware that for a few hundred dollars, you can provide an increased measure of protection for your investment. It may even pay off in terms of some reduction in insurance premium.

One effective security device you can plan and install is outdoor night lighting. Outdoor lights will discourage unwanted night activity and also reduces the risk of accidents when you have to be out at night. In selecting lighting fixtures for outdoor use, you will have a choice of incandescent, fluorescent, mercury vapor, and metal halide. Incandescent will be the least expensive initially, but will cost more in the long run because of bulb replacement cost and a relatively low light output. (Light output is measured in lumens and you can compare energy use efficiencies for different lights by comparing the number of lumens they produce per watt of power input.) Fluorescent lights are efficient light producers but their efficiency drops off rapidly at low temperatures and they are not generally recommended for outdoor farm lighting. For the past 25 years, the mercury vapor lamp has been the standard for outdoor lighting on the farm. It combines yard light output with long bulb life and makes an ideal outdoor unit.

More recently we have seen the development of metal halide and other exotic lamps which have a much higher light output per watt than do mercury vapor lamps. Although these units cost more initially, operational cost will be substantially lower and this should be your primary concern in selecting a lighting system. As the lighting industry seeks to improve energy efficiency, we will probably see even better light sources in the future. Check with your electric supplier for any new developments before making a final decision.

Table 3-2 below will tell you how much illumination is necessary for various areas around your farmstead. Your electric supplier can help you size and locate light sources which will provide these levels.

Table 3-2. **Recommended Levels of Illumination**

Area	Footcandles
Driveway entrance	1.0
Sidewalks	1.0
Garage and fuel storage area	3.0
Outdoor auto parking area	1.0
Office or house entrance	3.0
Silo control areas	3.0
Bulk tank loading area	3.0
Barn lots	1.0
Feed bunks	1.0 to 3.0
Feed processing area	3.0
Livestock loading	3.0
Building perimeters	0.2

Farmstead Arrangements

We have looked at lots of pieces—now comes the hard part—putting it all together into an organized farmstead plan. It has been said that good farmstead arrangement is an art, not a science. To be sure, there are many basic principles which can help steer us in the right direction, but the person who can do it best is the one who has had the most experience to go with his book learning. Now that we have told you it's a tough job to do, let's look at some of the techniques you can use to help.

The Midwest Plan Service, in its FARMSTEAD PLANNING HANDBOOK, has developed what it refers to as the zone concept of farmstead layout. The zones consist of a series of concentric circles spaced about 100 feet apart. The innermost circle or zone 1 is the family living area. This includes the house, lawn, recreational area, and guest parking. This zone needs special attention with regard to protection from noise, dust, and odor.

Zone 2 is the machinery area and contains the machinery storage and farm shop. It is a relatively quiet, dust, and odor free area which can be located next to the family living zone. It may also include fuel and chemical storage, provided they are at the outer limits of the zone and at least 200 feet from the house.

Zone 3 is reserved for grain storage, feed handling, and some livestock. Although grain drying and feed processing are noisy and dusty, they do require relatively large amounts of electric power and good access. Livestock enterprises located in this zone should be those that require frequent attention. These include the milking center, farrowing house, calf housing, poultry brooding, and housing for any pet or hobby animals.

Zone 4 contains major livestock facilities such as finishing buildings, drylots, and milking herd housing. This large zone will provide space for waste management and, it is hoped, for future expansion of the enter-

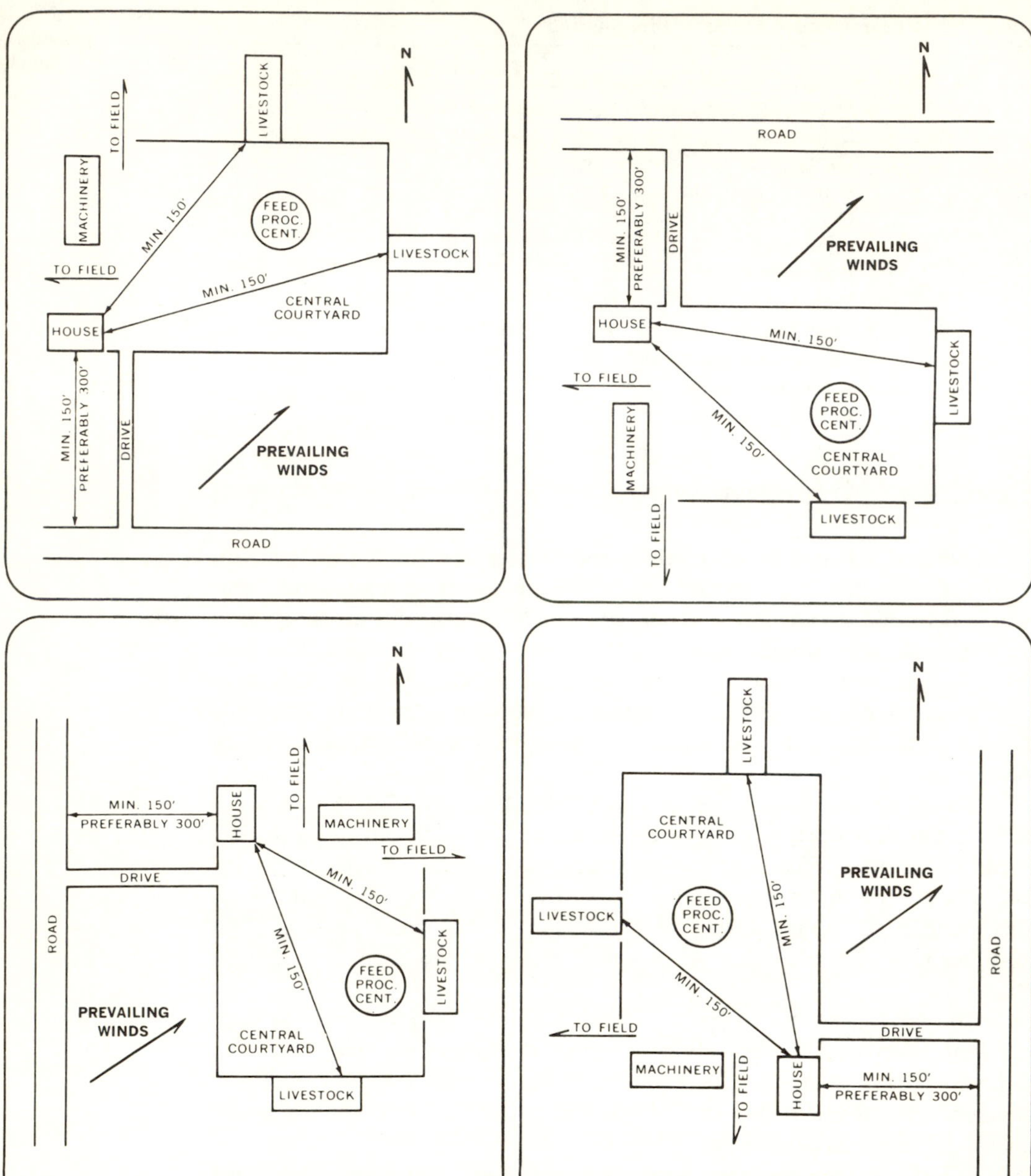

Figure 3-9. Four farmstead layouts that place buildings in proper relationship to wind and highways. (Granite City Steel)

prise without interference from facilities in other zones.

One reason we have found the zone concept useful in planning is that it can be applied to just about any arrangement of highway access to the farmstead. Look at the four layouts in Figure 3-9 and see if they satisfy most of the desired characteristics we have discussed.

Planning Your Farmstead

So much for the theory, what we really wanted to do all along was come up with a plan for your farmstead so you will know where to put that new building. Here is a step by step procedure we think will help you do just that.

1. Go down to the ASCS office and get a copy of the aerial photo for your farm. You are going to be looking at the farmstead from the top down (engineers call it a plan view) and the aerial photo will help you get a feel for working from this angle. Looks different, doesn't it?
2. Use a cross section paper with 10 by 10 divisions per inch to make an actual map of your existing farmstead site. Let each inch equal 40 feet and locate all existing buildings, driveways, trees, wells, fences, or anything else that is a working part of your present farmstead. Leave out anything you are planning to tear down or remove in the near future.
3. See if you can identify the zones we explained in the last section. Do you see any principles of good planning that have been violated so far? If you do, you may be able to work around them in future planning.
4. Using the proper scale, sketch in the location of all the things you would like to have in your farmstead 10 years from now. Try to locate each item where it will add to both convenience and workability of the farmstead. (It may speed this process up if you take another sheet of paper and cut out pieces scaled to represent different items you want. These pieces can then be moved around to different locations on your original sketch.)
5. Use dotted lines to sketch in those features that will be needed 20 years from now. This is going to be a wild guess at best, but we would like to make sure there is plenty of room for expansion around the buildings you located in Step 4.
6. Examine your plan for potential problems. One way to do this is to visualize the way materials will be moved through the farmstead. Imagine how machinery, feed, animals, and manure will be handled. If you see any bottlenecks, go back to Step 4.
7. Take a tape measure and some stakes or surveyors' flags and actually locate the buildings you drew in your plan. Sometimes the layout looks different on the ground than it did on paper. (Remember how much difference there was between the aerial photo and the way you see things from ground level?) If you see any bottlenecks, go back to Step 4.
8. Now that you have completed a workable plan for your farmstead, use it as a guide for organized future development. It may have taken you several hours or even days to go through these steps, but think of how much easier it was to make changes with an eraser than it would be with a bulldozer.

Part II

Special Buildings

CHAPTER **4**

Machinery Storage

There is probably no area of agriculture that has changed more rapidly in the past 20 years than machinery. Farm machines have increased rapidly in size, complexity, and cost. Along with this has come a greater awareness of the consequence of not having a particular machine ready to go when it is needed. Machinery storage buildings have become an integral part of the management system required to keep today's complex machines going.

Machinery requires only protection from precipitation, wind blown dust, and sunlight. It has no need for controlled temperature or positive ventilation. Because of this, we can make effective use of relatively low cost pole frame or metal frame buildings with no insulation or floor.

The best way to determine how much machinery storage you need is to plan it out on paper. Use graph paper with 10 × 10 to the inch lines to scale out the machinery you plan to accommodate in your storage. Use a scale of 1 inch equals 10 feet. It's best to use actual known dimensions of the equipment you have, but if you don't have this information, you can find some typical dimensions in Table 4-1. Cut out your scaled implements and arrange them into a storage system you are comfortable with.

There are three basic systems for storing machinery. You can use a 20 to 24 foot wide open fronted building and back all the machinery into storage through the open side. A 30 to 40 foot wide building with open front to the south and doors on the back can be loaded or unloaded by backing into either side. The third system is to use a 50 foot or wider closed building with a drive through center alley, storing machinery on both sides. The wider closed building provides more security and an overall better appearance, even though its use of floor space is not as efficient as the others.

A major consideration in selecting a machinery storage building will be the size and location of access doors. Most farms in the Midwest have need for at least one door that is 24 feet wide and 14 to 16 feet high. Make

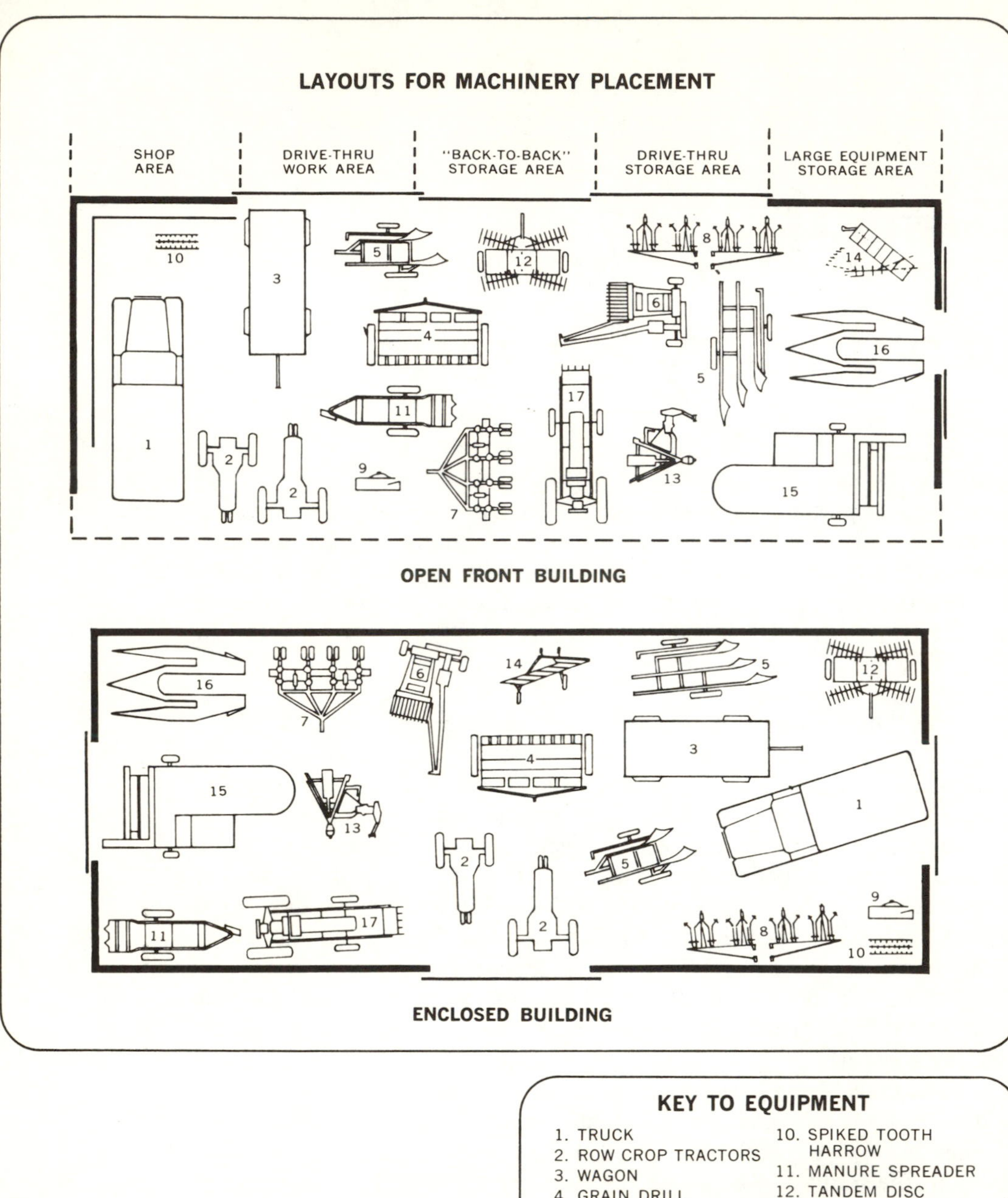

KEY TO EQUIPMENT

1. TRUCK
2. ROW CROP TRACTORS
3. WAGON
4. GRAIN DRILL
5. PLOWS—2 & 3 BOTTOM
6. FORAGE HARVESTER
7. CORN PLANTERS 2 & 4 ROW
8. CORN CULTIVATORS 2 & 4 ROW
9. BLADE GRADER
10. SPIKED TOOTH HARROW
11. MANURE SPREADER
12. TANDEM DISC
13. MOWER
14. SIDE DELIVERY RAKE
15. ONE MAN COMBINE
16. MOUNTED CORN PICKER
17. TRACTOR WITH MOUNTED MANURE SCOOP

Figure 4-1. Two different possible layouts for machine storage. (Granite City Steel)

sure any building you select can accommodate this size door or you may find yourself parking an expensive piece of equipment outside.

The choice between pole frame and metal frame buildings should be made on personal preference or, better yet, price. They perform equally well as machinery storages. Some people prefer metal frames because of their supposed fire resistance. Unfortunately, when a machinery storage burns it is almost always the contents which start on fire and burn first. A metal frame building exposed to the intense heat of a machinery fire will last no longer, and may even fail sooner than the pole frame units.

Table 4-1. **Storage Area Requirements for Typical 1980 Farm Equipment**

Item	Width	X (Feet)	Length
60 hp tractor	8		12
100 hp tractor	9		14
100 hp tractor with dual tires	13		15
4WD tractor	14		18
20 ft S.P. combine	30		20
Stacker	12		23
Forage harvester	11		15
Batch dryer	8		14
Rotary cutter	7		12
Large round baler	8		13
Feed wagon 150 bu	7		14
5 Bottom plow	8		19
4 Row corn head-combine	10		13
18 ft Disk	19		15
Forage wagon	8		20
Twine tie square baler	9		17
Grinder-mixer	8		15
Beet harvester	15		16
140 bu manure spreader	7		17
Mowing machine	7		7
Side delivery rake	10		8
8 Row corn planter	25		12

Note: The above dimensions are adequate for general planning but may not exactly fit the particular equipment you have.

CHAPTER 5

Farm Shops

The farm shop is an essential part of today's machinery based agriculture. Not only does it provide an organized setting for maintenance and repair, but also fabrication capabilities to allow the farmer to construct or change equipment to fit his particular needs.

Size

No matter how large you build it, your shop will be too small! The ideal size would be a building large enough to accommodate your largest piece of machinery with plenty of work space on all sides. Unfortunately, you probably won't be able to justify tieing up that much investment and will have to compromise on size. Probably the minimum size you should consider would be a 30 by 40 foot building. This will provide a clear work area about the size of a double garage, with room around the edges for workbenches, parts storage, and fixed equipment. A 30 by 50 foot or 40 by 60 foot unit would be even more desirable if it can fit into your budget.

Construction

Since the shop will be a year-round use building, it should be constructed so that insulation and a heating system can be incorporated in it. It will also require a concrete floor, which should be 4 to 5 inches thick and reinforced under the main work area.

Next to the farm home, the shop is the most probable location for a farm fire. This means selection of materials which are fire resistant is a must. It also means you should plan more than one way to exit the shop in case of fire. If the shop is to be attached to or part of the machinery storage building, consider building a 60 minute fire rated wall between them.

No matter what type construction you use, make sure it is clear span in order to provide maximum freedom of space usage inside. Since wall space is the desired location for many storages, keep window area at a minimum. Preferred window locations are on the wall opposite the main entry door, where they provide cross ventilation in summer.

Ventilation

The welding area and the paint area (if there is one) should be provided with separate exhaust fans to remove smoke and fumes as they are produced. A 1200 to 1500 cfm fan should be adequate for most farm shops. Summer ventilation is best handled by opening doors and windows and using portable fans to blow air around in the shop. If you want to install a more complete summer ventilation system, it should be capable of changing the complete volume of air in the shop every 5 to 10 minutes.

Access

As we mentioned earlier, it would be nice if you could get your largest piece of equipment into the shop, but this may not be possible. The large door to the shop work area should be a minimum of 18 feet wide with a 24 foot width preferred for larger shops. A 14 foot height will accommodate tractors with cabs and most other farm equipment. Overhead type doors are more convenient to use and generally fit tighter to keep out winter wind. They are, however, considerably more costly to install, require more head room than horizontal sliding units, and may interfere with interior lights.

Electric Service

The shop should have its own electric service distribution panel and a remote disconnect to be used in case of fire. Minimum size should be 100 amps with 150 to 200 amps preferred for larger shops.

Plan for one light outlet for every 100 square feet of floor area and concentrate them over work areas. If you plan to keep minimum winter temperatures in the 50 to 60 degree or higher range, fluorescent lights will provide greater electrical efficiency. Use mercury vapor lamps to illuminate outside work areas adjacent to the shop.

Plan on one convenience outlet for every 5 feet of workbench, plus separate outlets for each piece of permanently located equipment. Convenience outlets should be located every 10 feet on walls away from the workbench area. Place outlets 4 feet above the floor and use 3-wire grounded type outlets. Don't forget to locate weatherproof convenience outlets next to the outdoor work area.

Floor Plans

Among the illustrations shown in this chapter are three possible shop floor plans. The plan you choose should fit your needs and it might not look anything like one of these. There are some accepted practices in developing shop plans that you should consider in planning your facility.

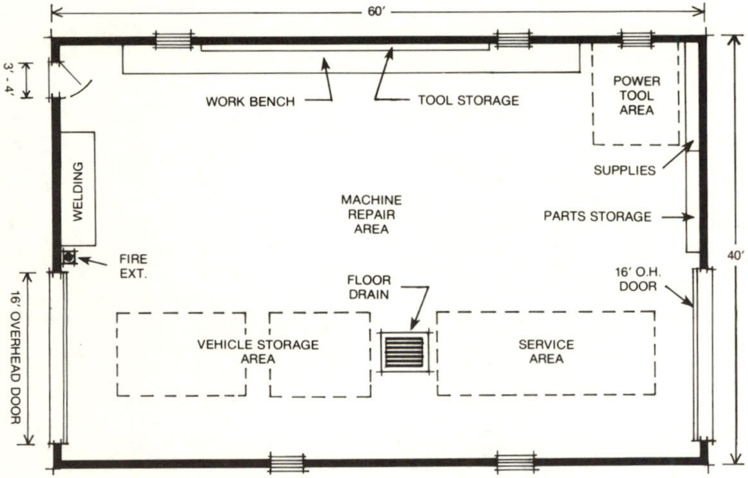

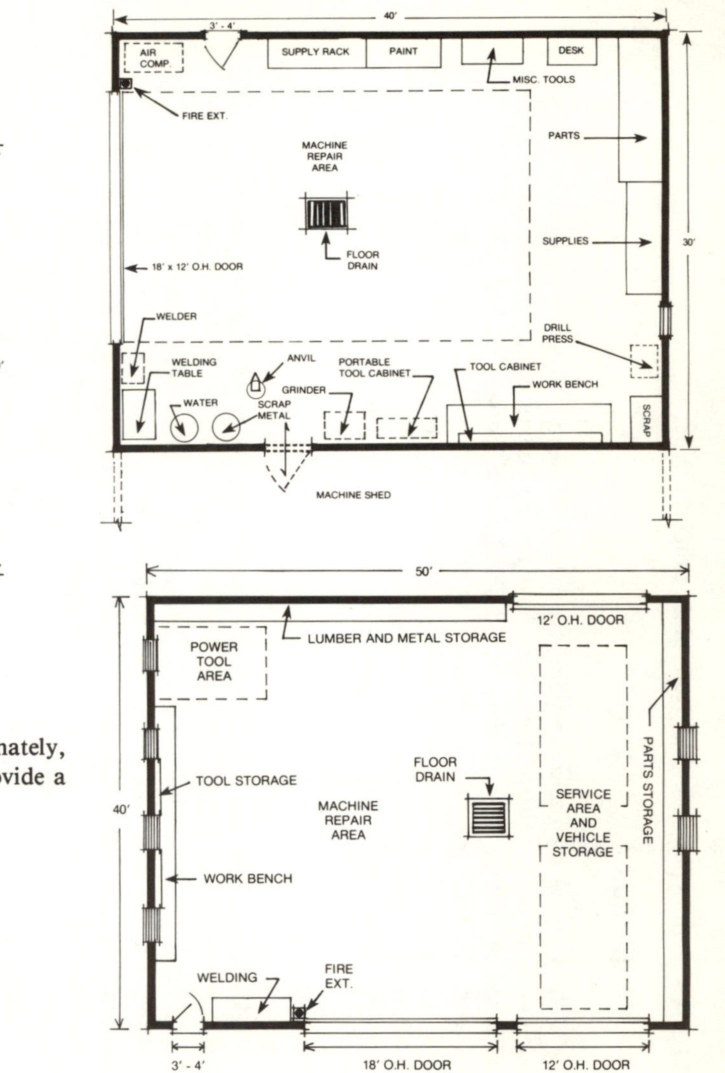

Figure 5-1. The bigger, the better, when it comes to the farm shop. Unfortunately, cost will probably limit the size on your farm. These three layouts can provide a starting point for your planning. (North Dakota)

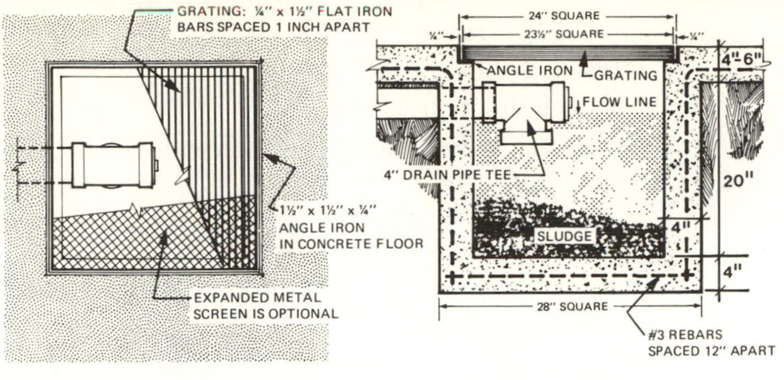

Figure 5-2. Here is a floor drain that will take the mud and dirt you wash off equipment in the shop without having to be cleaned out every day. In order to make it work the way it's supposed to, be sure to slope the floor toward it from all directions. Another good drain choice is to use a gutter that extends all the way across the service area. Use the same cross section shown above to plan a gutter type drain. (North Dakota State University)

Table 5-1. **Average Floor Space Requirements for Shop Storage and Equipment**

Item	Width x Length
Storage	
Horizontal lumber or metal	1.5 ft x 16 ft
Vertical lumber or metal	1.5 ft x 4 ft
Small parts bins	2 ft x 4 ft
Garden & fence tools	2 ft x 4 ft
Paint cabinet	2 ft x 3 ft
Metal working equipment	
Electric welder	1.5 ft x 2 ft
Oxy-acetylene welder	2 ft x 3 ft
Welding table	2 ft x 3 ft
Grinder	2 ft x 2 ft
Work bench	2.5 ft x 8 ft
Power hack saw	1.5 ft x 3 ft
Drill press	1.5 ft x 2 ft
Anvil	1.5 ft x 2 ft
Tool Cabinet	1.5 ft x 3 ft
Wood working equipment	
Bench	2.5 ft x 8 ft
Table or radial arm saw	3 ft x 3 ft
Jointer	1.5 ft x 3 ft
Band saw	1.5 ft x 2 ft
Lathe	1.5 ft x 5 ft
Miscellaneous	
Air compressor	1.5 ft x 3 ft
File cabinet	1.5 ft x 2.5 ft
Desk	2.5 ft x 5 ft
Fire extinguisher	1 ft x 1 ft
Hoist-floor type	5 ft x 10 ft

- Locate welder and air compressor near the large access door where they can be easily used for outside maintenance and repairs.
- Locate fire extinguisher near an exit door.
- Locate lumber and paint storage away from the welding and metal working areas.
- Install a large floor drain with a sludge accumulation trap near the center of the work area. (See Figure 5-2.) Floor pitch to the drain should be a minimum of 1/8 inch per foot, with 1/4 inch per foot preferred.
- Install a telephone or intercom unit for convenience and safety.
- Place a file cabinet and desk to keep service records and those all important service manuals.

Table 5-2. **Recommended List of Tools and Equipment for the Farm Shop**

Item	Size
Stationary tools	
Arc welder	225 Amp
Welding table	
Drill press	15 in. w/½ in. Chuck
Grinder	8 in.
Power hack saw	6 in. x 10 in.
Vises	
Machinist	6 in.
Blacksmith	6 in.
Anvil	
Air compressor	5 SCFM
Bench grinder	6 in. w/1 in. Stones
Portable Power Tools	
Right angle grinder	6 in.
Electric drills	1/2 in., 3/8 in., 1/4 in.
Electric hand saw	7 in.
A frame	12 ft
Hoist	1000 lbs
High pressure washer	
Battery charger	
Hydraulic jack	5 Ton
Jack stand	2 Ton
Complete tool sets	
Mechanic	
Plumbing	
Carpentry	
Optional items	
5 KW portable generator	
Impact wrench	
Hydraulic press	10 Ton
Shop vacuum	
Radial arm saw	10 in.

CHAPTER **6**

Swine Confinement Buildings

The past 15 years have seen a major shift in swine production away from pasture and toward partial or complete confinement systems. There is every indication that this trend will continue as farmers seek to produce a continuous supply of pork with minimum labor.

One major problem brought about by confinement systems is the increased demand for scheduling management. These buildings represent substantial investments and in order to pay off, they must be utilized at full capacity a maximum amount of time. This is complicated by the fact that individual buildings are no longer complete in themselves. They must function as a part of a complete system and be sized to fit in with other units. The most important thing you can do before deciding on a new swine building is to carefully analyze your production system to be sure that the change you want to make will fit into your farm operation.

Farrowing Buildings

The most complex and most expensive of the swine confinement buildings is the farrowing house. The successful unit has to be an environmentally controlled building capable of satisfying the different needs of adult and newborn pigs in an efficient and sanitary manner.

Size

Farrowing house size is typically expressed in terms of sow capacity. Sows are normally handled in groups and farrowing house size is generally determined by sow group size, the total number of sows to be farrowed per year, and the frequency of farrowing or turn around time for the farrowing house. For example, a producer with a 60-sow herd would nor-

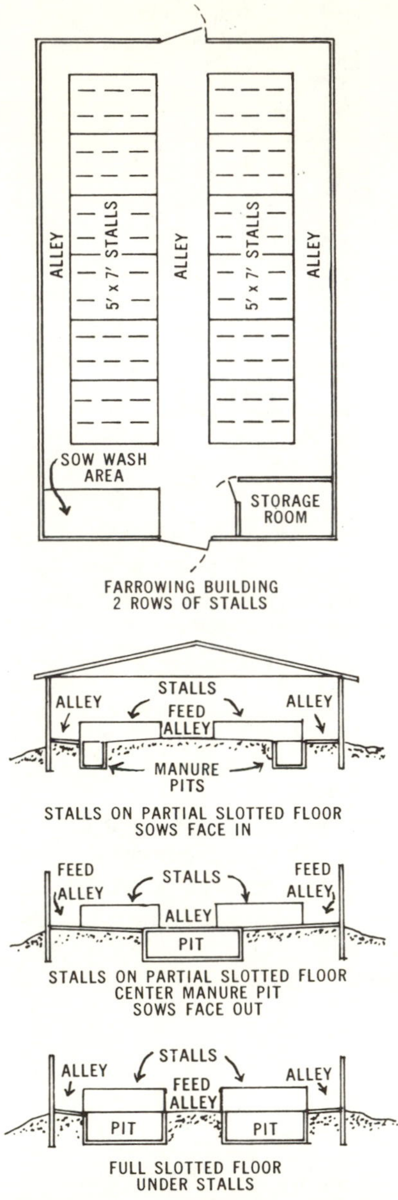

Figure 6-1. The traditional central farrowing house has two rows of stalls and can have several waste-handling options as shown. (Granite City Steel)

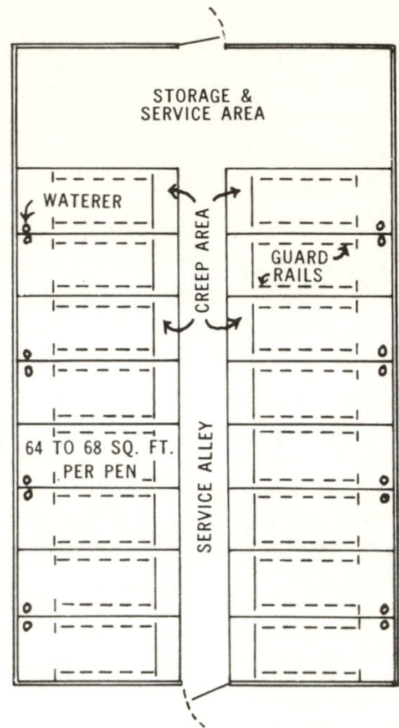

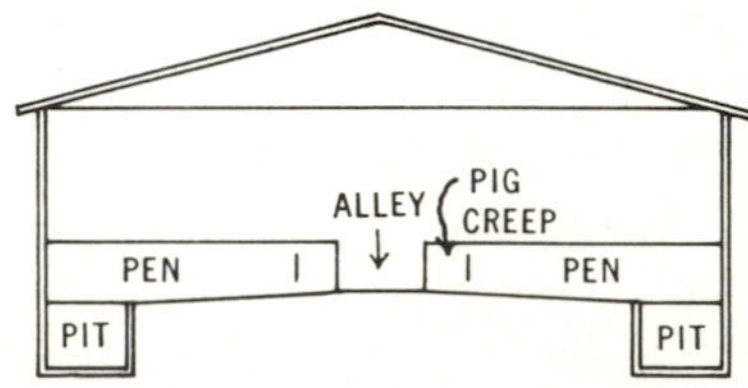

Figure 6-2. Pen type farrowing is becoming less popular due to high building costs. Farmers cannot afford to allocate extra floor space that is not really necessary for successful farrowing. Likewise, the indicated farrow-to-finish option is not economically feasible on most farms. (Granite City Steel)

mally expect to farrow 120 litters per year. If farrowing was done on an every other month basis, the farrowing house would need to be 120 ÷ 6 = 20 sows in size. If this same farmer was to farrow on a quarterly basis, he would require a 30-sow unit.

It is easy to see from the above example that frequency of use has a major effect on size of building required. As buildings increase in cost, there has been a definite trend toward more continuous usage in an attempt to minimize the capital costs per unit of animal. The same 60-sow herd could be farrowed in a 10 sow farrowing house if pigs were weaned at 3 weeks and farrowing was scheduled on a monthly basis. This practice is being adopted successfully on some farms, but it is not as easy as it appears. Unfortunately, mother nature does not always cooperate with precise scheduling of animal reproductive cycles.

For a number of years, the typical farrowing house has been a 24 to 26 foot wide single story building with two rows of farrowing crates or pens facing a center alley. Building length is determined by

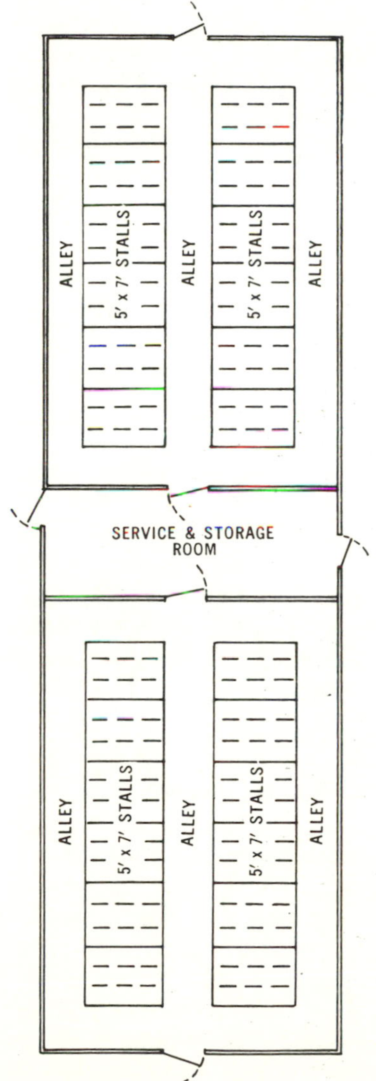

Figure 6-3. One variation of the room concept popular on larger farms is to use the two ends of the building as separate rooms. Disease control becomes an important management factor in buildings that are never completely empty. (Granite City Steel)

required capacity, ranging from about 50 feet for a 16-sow unit up to 85 to 90 feet for a 30-sow building. The exact dimensions will be determined by the type of equipment and internal arrangements selected by the individual producer.

A desirable feature from the animal health standpoint is to operate the farrowing house on an all in-all out basis. This allows an opportunity for complete cleaning and disinfection between usages. As herd sizes increase, farrowing facilities increase, and the all in-all out concept becomes more difficult to accommodate. One way around this problem is to use the farrowing room concept. This involves the use of larger buildings with a series of individual farrowing rooms, each containing equipment for 8 to 10 sows. The individual rooms can be isolated and operated on an all in-all out basis. This type of unit has several advantages for the medium to large swine producer. It can reduce the possibility of disease spread, providing the operator is careful in his travels between rooms. It reduces some of the scheduling problems in that it is easier to coordinate breeding of smaller groups of animals. And, the larger size of the overall building will reduce per unit construction costs and also reduce total heating costs during winter months.

Construction

Most farrowing houses utilize conventional stud frame construction with clear span trussed rafters and concrete foundations. Traditional 2 by 4 stud walls are used for interior partitions with 2 by 6 studs being preferred for outside walls in northern parts of the country where higher insulation levels are used.

Poured concrete floors, 4 inches thick, provide an easily cleaned surface. Reinforcing is not necessary unless the unit is constructed over an area of fill which has not been properly compacted or settled.

Since supplemental heat will be required in winter, insulation is a necessary part of farrowing house construction. Insulating to the same level that you would for a home will not add much to initial cost and will reduce energy costs considerably. For Missouri conditions, we currently recommend that farrowing house ceilings be insulated to an R value of 24 to 30 and sidewalls to R = 13 to 19. It is extremely important that insulation be protected from high moisture conditions inside the building by using a vapor barrier. A 4 mil polyethylene film is suggested.

In most designs, interior walls are not subjected to continual animal contact. This means they can be covered with some of the less expensive construction materials or paneling. We have even seen exterior grade sheetrock used successfully in farrowing houses, provided it is well sealed with 2 or more coats of a good enamel paint. If you select sheetrock or other material which is brittle, the lower 3 to 4 feet of wall should be covered with a stronger material to provide some mechanical protection.

Washing down and sanitizing are important parts of farrowing house management. Materials selected and construction techniques used on the interior should withstand washing and not retain or channel water into other parts of the building.

Ventilation

Animal density in the farrowing house is relatively low compared to other swine housing units. This results in relatively low ventilation rates, particularly in winter. A winter minimum rate of 20 cfm (cubic feet per minute) per sow and litter is the current standard recommendation.

A blended air pressure type ventilation system will provide good distribution and control over the low amounts of air required during winter months. For the remainder of the year, conventional exhaust fans and adjustable slot inlets are satisfactory.

Heating

Supplemental heat will be required in the farrowing house during all seasons of the year. Sows are most comfortable at temperatures in the 50 degree to 60 degree F range. Baby pigs require 90 degrees to 95 degrees F during the first few days of their life. These two widely differing requirements have led to the development of two level or zoned heating systems for farrowing houses. Typically, an electric or gas fired space heater is used to maintain room temperature in the 50 degree to 60 degree F range preferred by sows. Heat lamps, infra red heaters, floor heat, or hovers are then used to maintain higher temperatures in areas accessible to the baby pigs.

Heat lamps and other radiant heaters transfer heat energy by the process of radiation. Radiation is a straight line heat transfer process between the heater and the object being heated. Radiant heat heats objects it strikes without heating the air it passes through. We get our heat from the sun by the radiant heat transfer process. That is why you can feel warm when you are out in the sun; even on a zero degree day.

The major problem with radiant heat is that it is either on or off. With a few exceptions, there is no in between setting which will accommodate lower heat needs in spring, summer, and fall. This is usually not a problem in winter since the extra heat output can usually be used to maintain desired room temperature. For this reason, radiant heaters will usually be somewhat more costly to operate on a year-round basis than will other types of baby pig heaters. If you select radiant heaters, look for units that have some type of input controls and compare the initial cost carefully with potential long run savings.

Hovers use a mechanical barrier to contain high temperatures desired by baby pigs in the areas they can get to. Heat in the hovered area is usually supplied by a light bulb or occasionally by a hot water radiator. Hovers offer the potential of being the most economical type of creep heat for the farrowing house. Their main disadvantages are that they restrict direct observation of baby pigs in the farrowing unit and they do represent additional things that must be cleaned between usages.

Most producers agree that the most satisfactory creep heating system for the central farrowing building is floor heat. This system uses either electric heating mats or hot water pipes that are imbedded in the concrete floor under the creep area. They are controlled with thermostats to provide a 90 degree to 95 degree F surface temperature for the baby pigs to lie on.

Insulation is required to make the best use of energy in floor heating. A 2 inch thickness of expanded polystyrene foam (R = 8) or equivalent expanded polyurethane is required under the concrete floor in areas to be heated. This amount of insulation will reduce operating costs by approximately 25%.

Figure 6-5 shows the major components of a hot water system. All of these systems will have these items:

1. A thermostatically controlled boiler to provide a source of hot water. Most systems operate at 140 degrees F.
2. An expansion tank to take care of expansion and contraction of water as it heats and cools.
3. Pipes imbedded in the floor to transfer heat.
4. A thermostatically controlled circulating pump to circulate hot water through the floor. This thermostat should be equipped with a remote sending bulb which can be located in the floor to insure that floor temperature is controlled.

Pipes passing through sections of the floor which are not to be heated or through other parts of the building should be covered with a 1 inch thickness of pipe insulation. This will reduce heat loss by 80% and can save well over $1.00 per day in an average 20-sow farrowing house.

The total amount of heat the system must supply will depend on length of pipe, shape of the surrounding concrete, and temperature difference between the floor and the room. Table 6-1 presents recommended design values. Use these along with total feet of pipe for your planned system to determine the size boiler you need.

The most commonly used "boiler" is either a residential or commercial, domestic water heater. Electric, gas, or oil may be used. Table 6-2 gives expected heat output for different sized units.

Table 6-1. **Heat Needed by Hot Water Pipe Located in Floors of Swine Buildings**

Pipe Configuration	Btu/h per Foot**
Imbedded in 5 in. x 5 in. concrete slat	55
Imbedded in 5 in. x 12 in. concrete slat	90
Pipes 12 in. on center in 4 in. thick floor	35*
Pipes 18 in. on center in 4 in. thick floor	50*
Pipe with 1 in. insulation cover in slab or in 60° air	10

**These values assume insulation under slab.*

***Values given are in Btu per hour (Btu/h) per foot of pipe length.*

Table 6-2. **Heat Which Can be Supplied by Domestic or Commercial Hot Water Heaters Expressed as Btu/h**

	Type & Size	**Btu/h**
Electric	2,500 W	8,100
	4,000 W	12,900
	4,500 W	14,600
	6,000 W	19,500
	9,000 W	29,200
Oil or Gas	30,000 Btu/h input	21,000
	40,000 Btu/h input	28,100

Copper, black iron, and plastic are the types of pipe most often used in floor heat systems. Plastic pipes should be selected for their ability to withstand 140° F water temperatures without deformation. Hot water systems operate under very low pressures and do not require high pressure pipe. Pipes in slabs should be placed directly on the insulation at the bottom edge of the concrete slab. Location as far as possible from the surface of the slab improves temperature distribution. Pipes in slats should be located near the center of the slat. Allow for expansion and contraction when using heated slats. A heated slat should have 1/16 inch per foot of length available for expansion.

Pipe size and length must be designed to keep friction losses at a

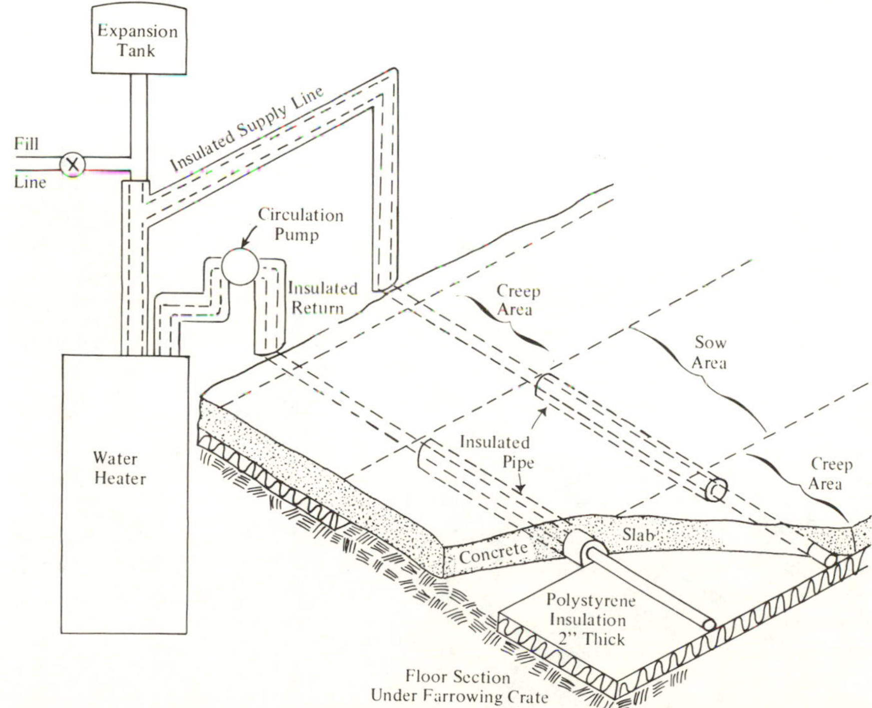

Figure 6-4. Typical components used in a hot water floor heating system for farrowing crates. Note that pipes are insulated except where heat is required. This practice can save considerably on the energy bill. (University of Missouri)

Table 6-3. **Friction Loss in Feet of Head per 100 Feet of Pipe**

Flow Rate	Friction Loss		
Gal./Min	Plastic Pipe	Copper Pipe	Iron Pipe
½ Inch pipe			
1	.49	.55	.91
1.5	1.03	1.16	1.92
2	1.76	1.97	3.28
¾ Inch pipe			
2.0	.45	.52	.84
2.5	.68	.78	1.26
3.0	.95	1.10	1.77
3.5	1.26	1.46	2.35
4.0	1.61	1.87	3.01
1 Inch pipe			
3.0	.30	.32	.55
4.0	.50	.54	.93
5.0	.75	.82	1.48
6.0	1.06	1.14	1.97
8.0	1.80	1.96	3.36

minimum. Most circulating pumps will not handle much over 5 feet of friction head loss. Table 6-3 presents friction head for different flow rates in pipe sizes usually selected for hot water floor systems.

Electric floor heating systems use resistance type heating wires which are imbedded directly in the concrete. Several manufacturers offer these units already pre-packaged in a nylon or plastic mesh which insures cor-

Figure 6-5. An alternative to hot water is the electric heat pad being installed here prior to pouring the concrete floor. The insulation under the mats keeps heat from escaping into the ground.

rect spacing and prevents the wires from becoming crossed and causing hot spots or burn outs. Select units which match the size of spaces you wish to heat and which provide a heat density of 30 watts per square foot. Make sure units you purchase are Underwriters Laboratory (UL) listed and install them in accordance with manufacturers' instructions. Pay particular attention to requirements for grounding of the electrical units.

Some manufacturers produce an electrically heated pad which can be placed on the surface of the floor in the pig creep area. These are designed to be used in existing buildings or over completely slatted floors.

Air Conditioning

Many farrowing houses contain air conditioning systems to reduce the effects of high summer temperatures on sow performance. Research has shown that if a supply of cool air is blown on the snout area of the sow, it is as effective in reducing stress as complete room air conditioning, and less expensive.

General recommendation is to provide 1,200 Btu per hour of cooling capacity per sow. This should be installed so that clean outside air is drawn over the cooling coils and discharged just above the sows' snouts through an overhead duct and drop tube system. The distribution system should supply about 40 cfm of cooled air per sow. Ducts and drop tubes are sized to keep air velocities in the 700 to 1,000 foot per minute range.

Waste Handling

Manure volume from the farrowing house is relatively low compared to other areas of the production system. Because of this, you should strive to install a handling method which is compatible with the system you plan to use, or are using in other housing units.

Most frequently used manure handling system is the partially slatted floor located over a collection pit or gutter. The collection pit is periodically drained to a lagoon or pumped out with a liquid manure handling system. Gutters are usually flushed or scraped on a daily basis to keep odors at a minimum.

When planning your waste system, consider installing a narrow slat covered gutter at the front of the farrowing crate to handle spilled feed and water.

Farrowing houses equipped with farrowing pens may have either a partially slotted floor system or use bedding and solid handling of manure. If your decision is to use solid handling, make sure the room arrangement and building size will accommodate any mechanization you plan to use.

Special Areas

Depending on your particular operation, there are several items you should consider incorporating in your farrowing building. They are a sow wash, feed storage, medication storage, and an office or employee rest area.

The spread of internal parasites and disease between sows and baby pigs can be greatly reduced if only clean sows are admitted to the farrowing area. A wash rack or pen, complete with floor drain, makes sow washing a relatively easy chore. The rack should be designed to restrain the sow and should be located conveniently to the main entrance of the unit. Use concrete curbing to control wash water and provide a small water heater to preheat wash water during winter months.

Feed storage does not require much room in the farrowing house. A 6 by 8 foot space will usually be adequate to store several days' needs, or if an outside bin is used, to store feed cart and related items. The feed storage should be walled off from the farrowing area to keep dust problems to a minimum.

Most medication for swine is done in the farrowing house. At the very least, provide space for a refrigerator to keep medications in and a sink to wash up syringes and other veterinary tools. You may also want to add space for a record keeping system.

The farrowing house is the most labor intensive operation on the swine farm. For some reason or other, sows always seem to farrow late at night or very early in the morning. The farm with the highest average pigs per litter is the one where someone spends a considerable amount of time in the farrowing house. A small rest area will make the farrowing house a more enjoyable place to work for you or the person who has to be there. This area should be directly accessible from the outside and provide space for a change of clothes and perhaps a shower if your management system dictates.

Electrical Service

The farrowing house may or may not be a high electric use area, depending on the type of supplemental heat used. If electricity is used, the building should probably have its own service entrance. For other heat sources, a sub panel fed by the main distribution panel will be adequate for most buildings.

Nursery Buildings

The nursery unit provides the transition between the farrowing building and the finishing house. It must provide an environment similar to the creep area in the farrowing house. The building itself will cost nearly as much as the farrowing house when compared on a cost per square foot basis.

The traditional nursery unit is designed to receive pigs at weaning time or about 6 weeks of age, and hold them until they are large enough to go directly to the finishing house at about 12 weeks of age. Early weaning (3 to 4 weeks) of pigs has placed greater demands on the environmental control system of the nursery. Pigs weaned at this age need to be housed

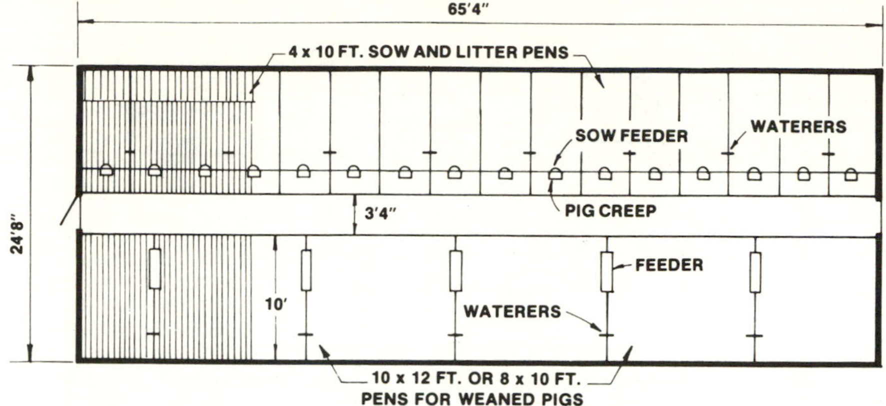

Figure 6-6. One way to put more pigs through the farrowing house is to move both sow and litter to a nursery unit prior to weaning. (Purdue University)

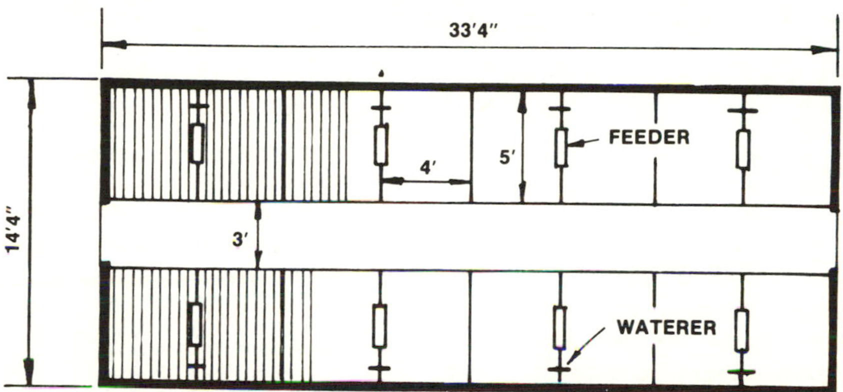

Figure 6-7. Slotted floors work well in nursery buildings. This unit is set up to provide pens for individual litters. Individual litter grouping works well with early weaning. (Purdue University)

where temperatures are maintained at 80° to 85° F and do not need as much space as the larger pigs in a conventional nursery. This has led to development of so called "hot nursery" units and grower buildings on some farms. The hot nurseries provide the higher temperature needed until pigs reach a size where they can be sold as feeder pigs or transferred to a growing unit which is similar to the more conventional nursery.

The cost per animal unit of nursery buildings can be substantially reduced by the use of double decked cages. These metal framed units allow for the stacking of two layers of pigs within the same floor space that one layer used to occupy. This increases equipment cost, but reduces building cost per pig. In many cases, the same waste handling system can be used for both layers or decks. Placing more pigs in the same volume of space also reduces the need for supplemental heat and tends to improve operation of the ventilation system. The double deck system does require more labor and a higher degree of management skill.

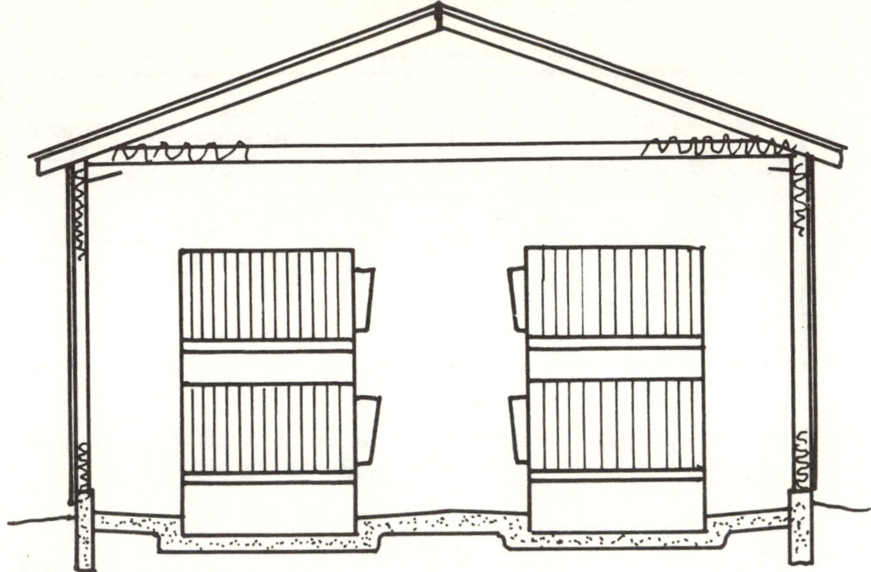

Figure 6-8. Cages double building capacity and reduce supplemental heat costs. There is some added labor associated with pig handling.

Size

The "all in-all out" management scheme is desirable for disease control in nurseries also. This means that nursery size should be carefully matched to farrowing house output. A nursery pig to 40 pounds will require about 3 square feet of floor space. From 40 to 100 pounds, space should be increased to 4 square feet per animal. The building should be divided into pens, each of which will hold about 25 pigs. Research has shown that larger groups will not grow as well and lead to greater variation in pig size.

Nursery units have been successfully combined with farrowing houses to provide some economy in construction of a larger building. This has been done by using individual rooms within the larger building for nurseries or by dividing the building in half and using one end for a

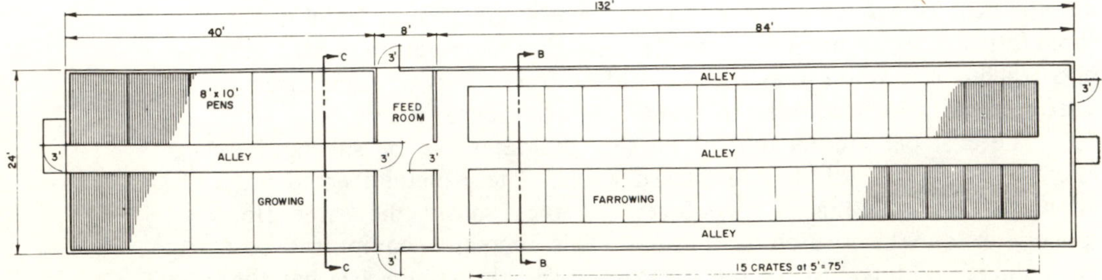

Figure 6-9. Combination farrowing-nursery buildings such as this are becoming more popular as swine producers switch to early weaning programs in order to minimize farrowing house cost per litter. The combination building simplifies moving pigs at weaning time and concentrates high labor operations into one structure. (USDA 6247)

nursery and the other for farrowing. These arrangements provide some added disease risk. They do, however, simplify moving of pigs from the farrowing area to the nursery.

A 24 to 26 foot clear span building is normally used for nurseries, with wider units chosen for buildings containing individual rooms or in combination with farrowing buildings. Length is determined by the particular pen arrangement and the capacity needed.

Construction

Most nursery building floor plans place pigs in contact with exterior walls. This means that some type of durable construction must be used for at least the lower half of the wall section. Many designs use conventional poured concrete foundations and extend the foundation walls to a height of 3 to 4 feet above the floor level. Conventional stud frame construction completes the wall, with trusses used for the roof section. This satisfies the requirements for durability; however, it leaves a large section of uninsulated wall area, which adds to pig discomfort and winter heat loads.

Some builders have attempted to reduce the cold wall problem by banking soil up against the walls of the building. This is only marginally effective since soil is only a fair insulating material and it cannot be piled over the full height of the concrete. A better, but more costly, solution is to place a 2 inch layer of polystyrene over the exterior concrete portion of the wall and extend it to a depth of 2 feet below ground. The polystyrene can be placed inside the concrete forms before pouring and the concrete will adhere well to it. Exterior, above ground surfaces of the polystyrene can be protected from mechanical damage by plastering with a cement mortar mix or by covering with an asbestos-cement board cover.

A newer, but not well accepted, method of wall construction which provides both insulation and durability is the concrete sandwich panel. These panels are 6 to 8 inches thick and are made up of outer layers of reinforced concrete and a center core of foam plastic insulation. They are usually formed and poured on a flat surface and tilted into place. The University of Nebraska has been active in the development of this type construction for swine buildings and has working drawings available.

Pole frame and metal frame buildings are also adaptable to nursery building use. They too must have extra care taken to make sure the lower wall is durable enough to withstand animal contact. This has been successfully done by covering the lower part of the wall with a high strength material such as plywood, and then facing it with sheet metal or one of the newer glass fiber reinforced plastic sheets. When doing this, try to plan so that joints between the cover sheets occur behind pen or partition walls.

Poured concrete, 4 inches thick, makes a satisfactory floor and needs no reinforcing unless poor subgrade preparation has been done. Solid floors in pen areas should be sloped ½ to ¾ inch per foot toward the manure collection system. Flatter slopes will not permit hoof action to move manure.

Pen partitions can be constructed of poured concrete, surface bonded concrete blocks, or welded steel paneling. The concrete and masonry units have proven to be the more durable units. If flushing gutters are used, pen dividers over the gutter area should be constructed of welded metal. This promotes "socializing" between adjacent pens and encourages dunging in the gutter area.

Ventilation

A positive ventilation system must be installed in the nursery area. Exhaust fans with adjustable slot inlets will do a satisfactory job if properly installed and operated. The minimum ventilation rate for winter should be approximately 1 cfm per 20 pounds of body weight. Total installed fan capacity to accommodate summer heat should be 9 to 10 cfm per 20 pounds of body weight. Additional information on ventilation system design can be found in Chapter 29.

Heating

The greatest need for supplemental heat in a well constructed insulated nursery is to offset losses caused by the ventilation system during cold months. This can be accomplished with space heaters or, in buildings without totally slatted floors, floor heat. Floor heat is installed in the area of the pens that is farthest from the waste disposal system. This also promotes good dunging habits since pigs do not normally dung in the area where they lie down. Floor heat systems are designed and installed in the same manner as they are for farrowing buildings. Surface temperatures can be operated at lower levels as pigs increase in size.

It is possible to incorporate solar collection and storage systems into swine nursery buildings. These systems appear to be most feasible economically when used to provide some preheating of ventilation air. More details on their construction and use are in Chapter 37.

Special systems for summer cooling are not usually incorporated into nursery buildings. Pigs of this size have a relatively high ratio of surface area to body weight and are able to withstand heat much better than larger hogs. If you feel a need for some type of cooling, the misting system described in the finishing unit section is suggested.

Waste Handling

The larger the animal, the bigger the waste volume and the greater the planning that must be done. A 100 pound nursery pig produces about 3 quarts of waste material per day.

The nursery waste handling system should also fit into the overall waste management system for the farm in order to minimize investment in equipment and simplify the management program. The two alternatives generally chosen for nursery wastes include handling as a liquid manure and flushing to a lagoon.

Liquid manure systems for nurseries normally incorporate a collection and storage area within the building directly under either a partially or fully slatted floor. Physical dimensions of the holding pit will depend on the number of animals housed and the desired interval between clean outs. Outside access ports are provided at intervals along the building to permit agitation and pump out of the storage pit.

Advantages of liquid manure systems include the following:

- Storage can be sized to permit disposal at times when it fits field schedules and when crops can make optimum use of nutrients.
- Odors are at a low level except during pump out.

Manure stored in pits under slatted floors undergoes some decomposition. During this process, toxic gases are produced and may be released into the building above. This is a particular problem during times when manure is being agitated and pumped. It is recommended that some type of positive ventilation system be installed for pit ventilation whenever this type of manure handling system is used.

Gutter flushing systems offer an attractive alternative to slatted floors and storage pits for swine wastes. They utilize a solid floor which is sloped to a shallow gutter at one edge of the pen area. Manure that is not deposited directly in the gutter is soon worked into it by action of the animal hooves on the sloped floor. Periodically, a large charge of water is dumped into the upper end of the gutter, flushing waste materials to a lagoon system.

Advantages of flushing include:

- Very low odor in the housing unit.
- Completely automated, trouble free system.
- More economical construction.
- No toxic gases produced within the building.
- Flush water can be recycled from the lagoon.

The major objection to the flushing system has been the anaerobic lagoon system. This method of swine waste processing and disposal has not been well accepted in all areas of the country. No waste handling system is management free and lagoons are no exception. They do cause occasional odor problems and must be pumped down on a periodic basis to insure that they will continue to function in a satisfactory manner. Although pump down can be done with a liquid manure handling system, irrigation equipment which can handle larger volumes in shorter time periods has proven to be more satisfactory. *Caution: Successful gutter flush systems require careful design, good construction, and a matching of flush tank volume to gutter needs. Make sure you and/or your builder understand gutter slopes and any channel requirements that may be in the plan you select before the concrete work is done.*

Another handling system which has been satisfactorily used in farrowing and nursery buildings is the "gravity drain" system. This system utilizes a slatted floor section, usually about 2 feet wide over a Y shaped gutter. Manure is allowed to accumulate in the gutter for 3 days, at which time a plug is pulled allowing it to drain by gravity to a lagoon. The system offers advantages similar to the flush system in that few odors are produced. It also eliminates the need for recirculating pumps and flush tanks. The cost of the floor slats and the form work involved in the "Y" gutter will probably offset any equipment cost savings when compared to the gutter flush. This system does offer the potential of being used as part of a liquid manure system if a manure storage tank were used instead of a lagoon.

Special Areas

A small utility room should be a part of every nursery unit. This room can be used to contain the electrical service entrance, hot water heater for the floor heating system, a refrigerator for storing medications, and equipment needed to meter any needed medications into the water system. The utility room should also contain a pan of disinfectant and be located so that it can serve as a visitor entry point to the nursery, if needed. An 8 by 8 foot or 8 by 10 foot area will be sufficient in most cases.

Feed handling in the nursery can be done manually by periodically filling feeders or through an outside storage bin with an automated filling system. Manual handling will require a feed alley wide enough to get through with a feed cart and feeders which are located immediately adjacent to the alley for easy filling. It will also require a storage area for the cart and perhaps for feed. Dust and problems caused by it will be minimized if this storage area is not combined with the utility room.

Finishing Buildings

Finishing takes pigs from the nursery at about 100 pounds to a market weight of 220 to 230 pounds. At this stage of a pig's life, he is able to withstand a wide variation in climatic extremes and many older finishing systems took advantage of this by providing only minimal protection from the elements. Even today, some new systems utilize large outside paved areas located on the south side of low cost shed-roofed, open fronted shelters in an attempt to minimize capital investment.

Finishing hogs grow fastest and have the best feed conversion ratios when they are in an environment where temperatures are 55° to 60° F. This temperature range can be maintained fairly easily during fall, winter, and spring in a completely covered, insulated finishing building. During summer months, the completely covered units help relieve heat stress by shading the animals from the hot sun.

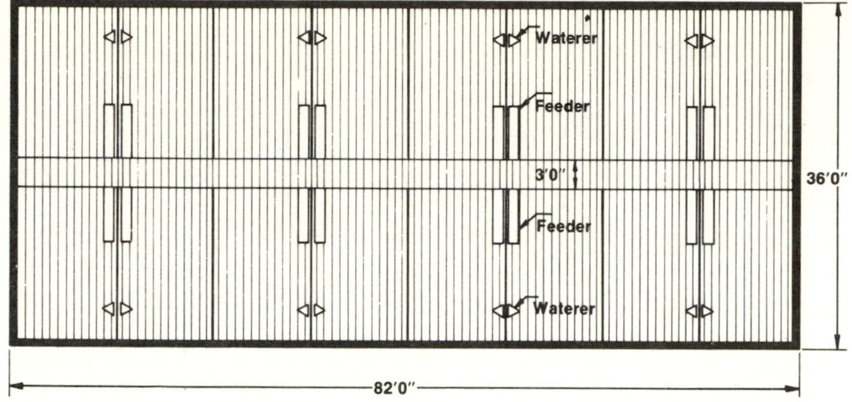

Figure 6-10. Finishing building with completely slotted floor and under-floor manure storage. This type is the most costly type to construct. (Purdue University)

Size

Overall size of the finishing unit will depend on factors such as the number of pigs available for finishing, either from your nursery or a feeder pig supplier, the amount of feed available, and possibly the waste management system. A pig will require about 6 square feet of pen space until he reaches 150 pounds, and then about 8 square feet until he goes to market. If the facility uses an outside paved area in conjunction with an open fronted shelter, provide 6 square feet inside and 6 square feet of outside area per pig.

Pigs need to be grouped into pens of not more than 25 to 30 animals to minimize problems of social stress. A pen width of 8 to 10 feet is usually chosen. This results in pen lengths of 24 to 28 feet. Buildings with a single row of pens are usually 28 to 32 feet wide. Buildings with two rows of

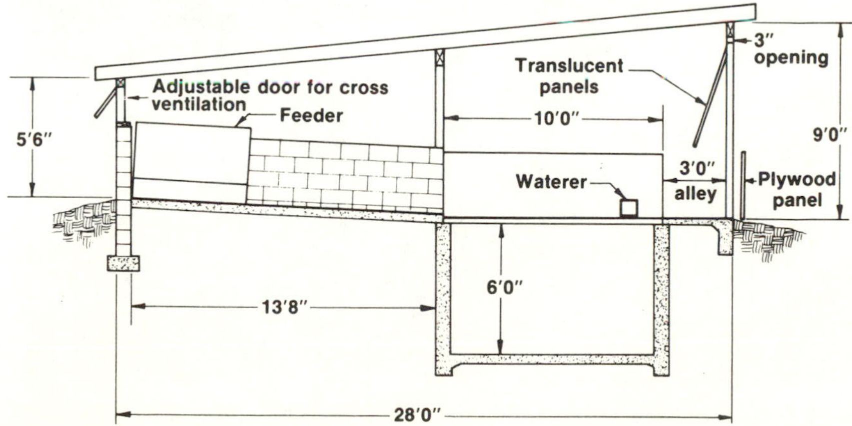

Figure 6-11. Modified open-front shed roofed building developed in Nebraska. (Purdue University)

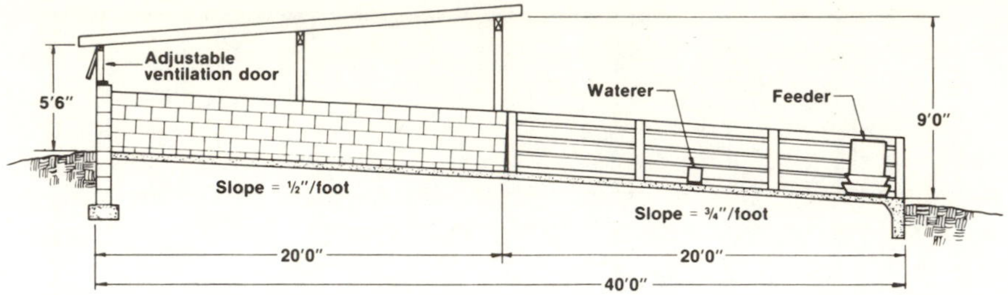

Figure 6-12. Shed roofed building with outside paved yard areas. Waste management and runoff control can be a problem with this system. (Purdue University)

pens are 36 to 40 feet wide and frequently have a middle alley which is offset from the center of the building. This provides two sizes of pens to accommodate pigs' needs as they grow. One hundred pound pigs entering the system are placed in the smaller pens on one side of the alley and then moved directly across the alley when they are large enough to need more room.

Construction

There are few things as destructive as a pen of finishing hogs. A fellow engineer once remarked to us that he felt a pen of finishing hogs could probably destroy a blacksmith's anvil if you left it in the pen for more than a day.

Figure 6-13. This modified open-front building has the floor sloped toward the back and wastes are removed to an anaerobic lagoon by a gutter flushing system. Note that all parts of the building that are exposed to the hogs are of masonry or steel construction.

Any part of the finishing building accessible to the animals should be durable enough to withstand them. Poured concrete and masonry units have withstood the test of time for many producers. Another alternative is to use oak planking as a lining in the pen areas. Post frame and conventional frame buildings are the usual choices for finishing buildings. A wide range of interior arrangements and roof designs have been successfully used. A ceiling is not necessary, so long as adequate insulation is provided at the roof.

Concrete is the preferred floor material, with a 4 inch thickness used for most buildings. Systems using partially or fully slatted floors have used concrete, metal, and synthetic slat materials with equal performance. Wood slats are a poor choice since they will require considerable maintenance after 2 to 3 years of continuous usage.

Pen partitions of poured concrete or concrete block are most durable. When using concrete block in finishing pen partitions, cores should be filled and vertical reinforcing bars installed every 2 to 3 feet.

Finishing hogs provide enough excess body heat to maintain desired building temperatures during winter months, provided insulation is used in the building. Minimum insulation levels for the central Midwest are R = 9 to 12 for sidewalls and R = 12 to 16 for ceiling or roof areas.

Ventilation

Both natural and mechanical ventilation systems have been satisfactorily used in finishing buildings. Natural systems require more management during winter months when outside weather conditions change rapidly. However, in summer their use will save considerably in both initial equipment cost and operating cost. Some producers have selected the best of both, using automatic fan ventilation during winter and opening up sidewall areas to provide natural ventilation in the warmer seasons.

Summer Cooling

Hogs do not sweat when they are hot. This means that body heat must be lost by evaporation from the lungs or by convection from the skin surface. Panting during hot weather is the hog's way to increase the amount of evaporative cooling from the lung area. As animals increase in size, the surface area available to lose heat through, decreases in proportion to their weight. We must compensate for this and find ways for finishing animals to lose body heat if we are going to maintain maximum productivity during summer months.

The most effective way to do this is through the use of a spray or mist cooling system. Spray cooling covers the hog's skin with a layer of moisture which will evaporate and cool the animal. It takes about 1,200 Btu to evaporate a pint of water and a high proportion of this heat will come from the animal's body.

It takes a very small amount of water to provide spray cooling—about .09 gallon of water per hour per pig is sufficient. Systems are designed to spray for 2 minutes every hour. This provides 58 minutes of evaporation or cooling time.

For a pen of 25 pigs, select a single spray nozzle with a rated capacity of about 1.15 gallons per minute at your minimum water pressure. This should be a nozzle which puts out a cone shaped pattern of droplets. Pattern spread should cover an 8 foot width at floor level when the nozzle is mounted out of reach of the hogs. Locate the spray nozzles over the manure accumulation area of the pen. For systems with covered sleeping areas and outside paved feed areas, locate the nozzles under the front overhang on the sleeping area roof and aim them slightly outward toward the paving.

The low volume used in spray cooling can lead to nozzle problems. An in-line filter with disposable cartridge will eliminate problems of plugging with foreign material. If your water is corrosive or is extremely hard, you may have to select a special nozzle material to take care of the problem.

The system is turned on and off with a solenoid valve. The valve is controlled with both a timer and a thermostat. The timer should be a 60 minute timer and set to turn on for 2 minutes out of every 60. Locate a cooling type thermostat (closes on temperature rise) between the timer and the solenoid. Set the thermostat at 75° to 80° F.

When installing the spray cooling system, pitch all water lines to a low point and locate a drain valve there. This will allow you to drain down the system for frost protection during the winter months.

Waste Handling

In terms of volume, waste is the largest single product produced in the finishing unit. A number of systems have been developed to handle swine waste. Most of these handle it as a liquid. Among the more successful units are liquid storage pits located under slatted floors and gutter flush systems with lagoon disposal. Both of these were discussed under nursery facilities. Other handling systems which have been used with varying degrees of success are the oxidation ditch and direct depositing of manure into a lagoon.

The oxidation ditch is a manure treatment system which uses mechanical means to mix oxygen with manure so that it can be broken down by aerobic organisms. Aerobic (with oxygen) break down is desirable because it is relatively odor free and produces an end product which can be easily disposed of. The ditch is usually constructed under the floor of the finishing building and covered with a slatted floor. It is circular in design, similar to a race track, so that waste can be circulated around in it. A paddle wheel or other type mechanical device is used to agitate the manure and stir in the air required for the aerobic organism. Oxidation ditches have not gained wide acceptance in the swine industry because of their cost and the fact that some additional system is required to handle the output from it.

Direct deposit of manure into lagoons reached its peak in popularity during the mid 1970's. This system involved construction of the finishing building directly over a waste disposal lagoon. A slatted floor allowed manure to enter the lagoon directly. Periodic pump down of the lagoon was all that was required to keep the system functioning. The development of gutter flushing systems led to a dramatic decrease in the use of these systems. Gutter flush buildings with their solid floors reduced construction costs and provided considerably more flexibility in farmstead arrangement.

Housing the Breeding Herd

Looking at the entire area of swine housing, it becomes obvious that little attention has been paid to the development of systems for housing of the breeding herd. The main reasons for this have been that breeding animals are able to tolerate a wide range of environmental conditions, existing facilities can be used to house them, and it is a lot easier to spend money on facilities which have a more immediate return.

As swine farms become larger, problems with efficiency and handling and management have led to greater interest in confinement of breeding animals. Some of the advantages of confinement include the following:

- Opportunity for closer observation of breeding animals.
- Reduced labor in handling animals.
- Less land required for housing.
- Improvement in control of parasites.

When compared to the more traditional pasture system for housing, these advantages must be weighed against the following possible disadvantages:

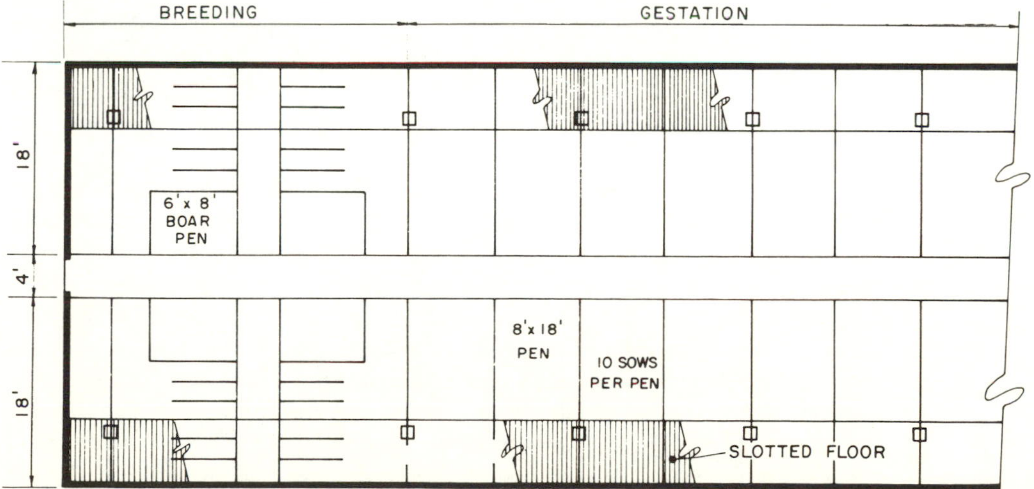

Figure 6-14. Completely enclosed breeding and gestation building with partially slotted floor. A gutter-flush system with open gutter could be adapted to this unit. (Purdue University)

- Larger capital investment.
- Poorer reproductive efficiency in both sows and gilts.
- Increase in feet and leg problems.

A wide variety of possible housing systems has been used for breeding animals and there has been very little research aimed at defining the ideal system. Later in this section, we show some floor plans that have been successfully used. One of these may fit your needs, or perhaps a combination of features from all of them can be used on your farm.

Size

Sows are best handled in groups of evenly sized animals to minimize fighting and other social problems. Most systems provide for groups of 10 to 16 sows. Feeding may be incorporated into the group housing area, or groups can be rotated to a common feed area. Boar pens should be designed to hold 1 to 2 animals and located convenient to where breeding is to be done. Some producers locate boar pens between sow pens to stimulate more regularity in estrus.

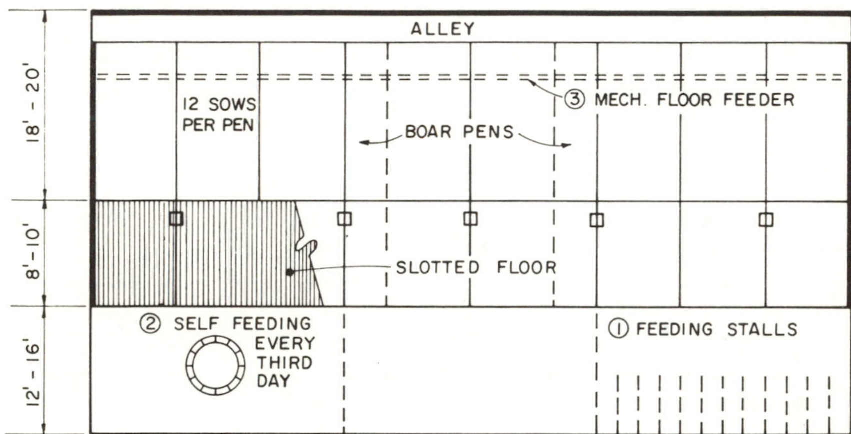

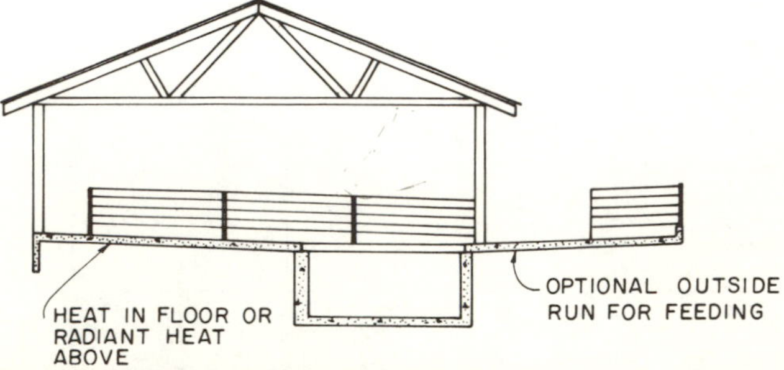

Figure 6-15. Breeding-gestation system with outside paved area. Two options for feeding are illustrated. (Purdue University)

Table 6-4. **Recommended Floor Space per Animal for Breeding Herd Housing**

Animal	Square Feet per Animal	
	Solid Floor	**Partial or Total Slats**
Boars	70	50
Gilts	15	15
Sows	18	18
Gestating gilts	17	14
Gestating sows	18	15

Construction

Almost any type of building can be used for housing the breeding herd. Depending on the particular design, special attention may have to be given to protecting a portion of the wall from the animals.

Insulation should be incorporated into the building both for keeping in heat in winter and for reducing summer heat gain. Recommended levels are the same as for finishing buildings.

Ventilation

Most breeding herd units can be satisfactorily ventilated using natural ventilation techniques. These are discussed in more detail in Chapter 29.

Cooling

Reproductive efficiency of the breeding herd can be seriously affected by exposure to high temperatures. In boars, this decrease can persist for several weeks after exposure to high temperatures. For this reason, some type of cooling is suggested for these buildings. In most cases, the spray cooling system described for finishing buildings will be satisfactory.

Waste Handling

Sows and boars which are limit fed will produce about 1.5 gallons of waste per animal per day. This is approximately equal to the output of a mature market hog. Waste systems used in other swine units are also satisfactory for breeding units. The system you select should be chosen to fit in with your overall waste management program, not just because it happens to look good in the breeding building.

Special Areas

Following is a listing of special purpose areas which can be incorporated into your breeding herd housing unit to improve its usefulness to you.

- Breeding Pens-separate areas where boars and sows are brought for breeding purposes. Some producers omit floor paving and fill these pens with sand to improve animal footing.

- Artificial insemination facilities. These include an area for semen collection and processing and an area for breeding of females.
- Treatment Area-working chute and holding device where individuals or groups can be restrained for medical treatment, pregnancy testing, or routine vaccinations. If space is available, an isolation pen adjacent to these facilities is a desirable addition.

Swine Housing Data

A. Suggested interior temperatures-winter

Farrowing buildings	60°-70°F
Farrowing creep areas	90°-95°F
Nurseries	70°-75°F
Finishing buildings	55°-60°F
Breeding animal buildings	55°-60°F

B. Manure production per day

	Gallons
Sow & litter	4.0
Pigs 40 lbs	.3
100 lbs	.75
150 lbs	1.1
210 lbs	1.6
Breeding animals	1.5

C. Floor space in buildings

Breeding animals	15-20 sq ft
Nursery pigs	
to 40 lbs	3 sq ft
to 100 lbs	4 sq ft
Finishing animals	
100 to 150 lbs	6 sq ft
150 to 220 lbs	8 sq ft

D. Slot widths in slotted floor systems

Baby pigs 3/8 in. or 3/4 in.-1 in.*
Nursery pigs 1/2 in.-1 in.
Finishing pigs 3/4 in.-1 in.
Breeding animals 1 in.-1 1/4 in.

*Avoid slot widths between 3/8 in. and 3/4 in. because young pigs tend to get legs caught.

E. Feeder and water space

Self feeders: 1 space for every 4 pigs
Waterers: 1 space for 20 to 25 pigs

CHAPTER 7

Beef

Beef cattle production has been long considered to be a relatively low margin type of farming operation. This fact, plus the ability of the beef animal to do well under a wide variety of climatic conditions, has resulted in most animals being raised with very minimal housing facilities.

The systems used in cattle production can be grouped into four general types.

- Pasture systems
- Open lots
- Barn and lot
- Complete confinement

The pasture system is used almost exclusively throughout the United States for cow-calf operations. Cows remain out of doors on pasture year-round and breeding is synchronized to avoid calving during severe winter months. Pasture areas are frequently planned so that cows can be confined near the farmstead during calving season. In some cases, a simple pole type building is constructed to provide a sheltered area for calving or sick animals. Figure 7-1 shows a floor plan of construction for a unit of this type. Plan on providing capacity for 4% to 6% of your cow herd.

Cattle on pasture generally have lower rates of gain and poorer feed conversion than cattle in confined feeding areas. For this reason, few cattle are maintained on pasture past weaning age.

Finishing Systems

Open Lots

This is the least cost system in use for finishing cattle and is extensively used in all the major cattle feeding areas of the United States. It utilizes

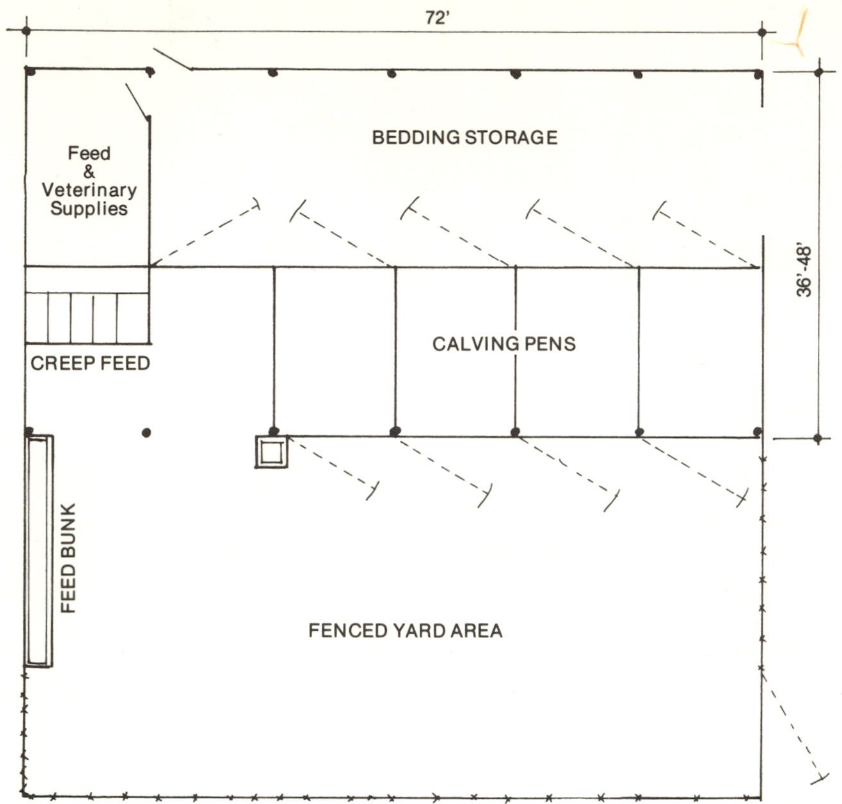

Figure 7-1. A simply arranged pole frame type structure can provide an excellent calving facility for the cow-calf beef operation.

unpaved lots with a fence line bunk feeding system. The ideal location for this system is on a south slope with reasonably good drainage. Desirable extra cost features for the open lot system include windbreaks, paving adjacent to feed bunks, shades, and mounds for soil that is less than well drained.

Windbreaks improve the comfort level for cattle during winter months and can reduce the amount of snow that must be removed from lots. Design and placement was discussed in Chapter 3.

Paving a strip 10 to 12 feet wide along the feed bunk eliminates pocketing and mud in this high traffic area. This will not only improve cattle traffic to and from the bunk, but also will reduce maintenance chores for the operator. Paving should be of 4 inch thick concrete and placed as shown in figure 7-2. The slope on the surface will keep manure and dirt worked away from the bunk. A step next to the bunk keeps animals from backing up to the bunk and also helps reduce fighting among animals at the bunk.

A shaded area improves cattle comfort during hot weather. In some instances shades can be located with the feed bunk to keep precipitation out of the feed. In order to provide shade for the complete herd, allow 20 to

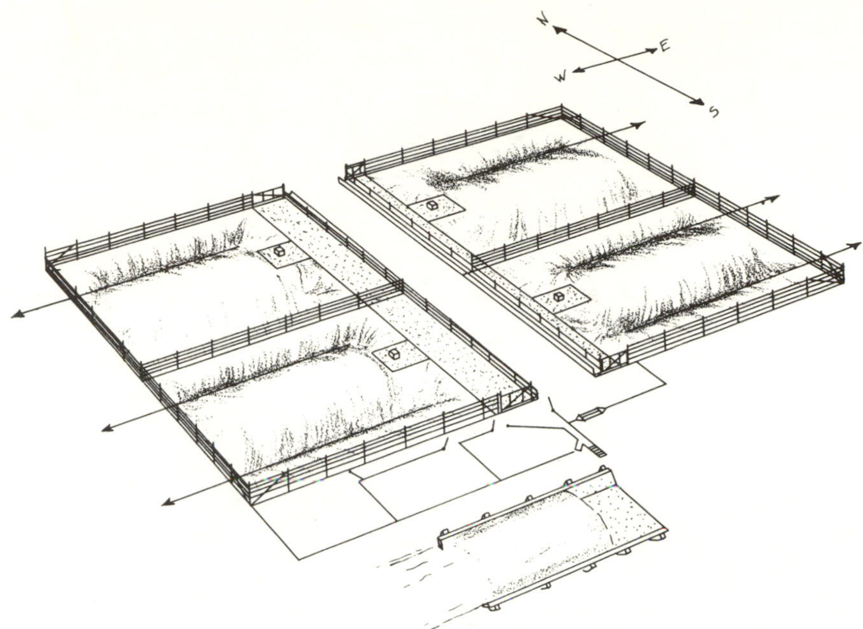

Figure 7-2. An open-type finishing lot showing installation of mounds and orientation with regard to prevailing winds normally found in the Midwest. (University of Missouri)

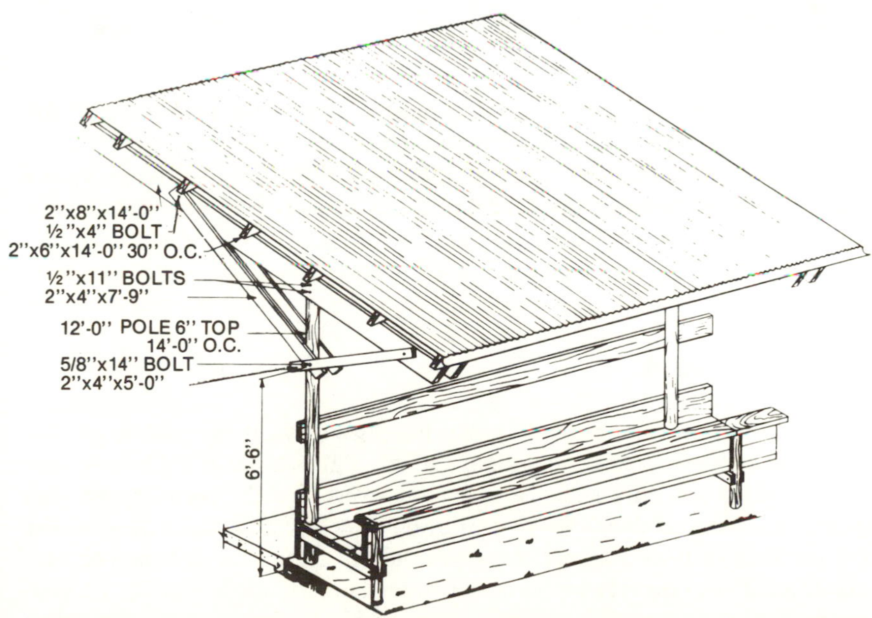

Figure 7-3. A simple structure such as this can keep water out of the feed bunk and provide shade for animals in an open type system. (University of Minnesota)

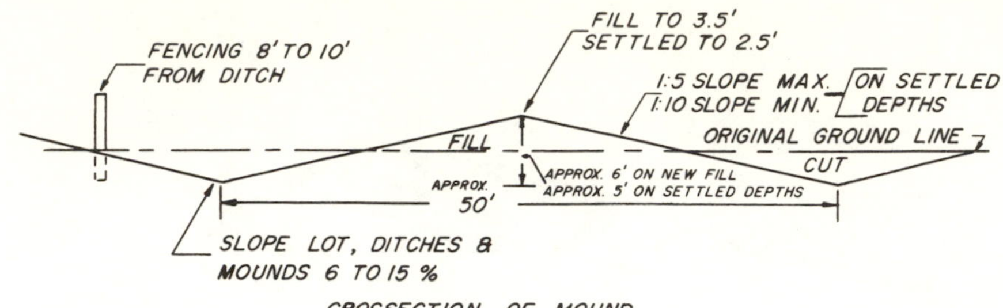

Figure 7-4. Proper mound construction is essential for good control of both mud and runoff. (University of Missouri)

Figure 7-5. A well-designed and well-built mound in use.

25 square feet per animal. Shades should be located 8 to 10 feet above ground level to allow cooling breezes to pass under them.

Mounds are artificially created hills which are designed to provide a mud free resting area in the feed lot. They are generally designed to be 6 feet high with a 6 foot wide top and side slopes of 5:1. Mounds should slope lengthwise a minimum of 6%. Construction details are shown in Figure 7-4.

Barn and Lot

These systems are basically open lot systems with the addition of an open fronted barn to provide animal shelter. Barns are usually simple pole frame structures with a ridge oriented east-west and the entire south wall open. Some type of drop down ventilating panels should be located in the north wall to provide summer cross ventilation. Barns are designed to provide 20 to 25 square feet of floor space per animal. Barns should be constructed with an open ridge to promote natural ventilation and a minimum amount of insulation (R = 2 to 5) located under the metal roofing will help control condensation and provide greater summer comfort. Research has

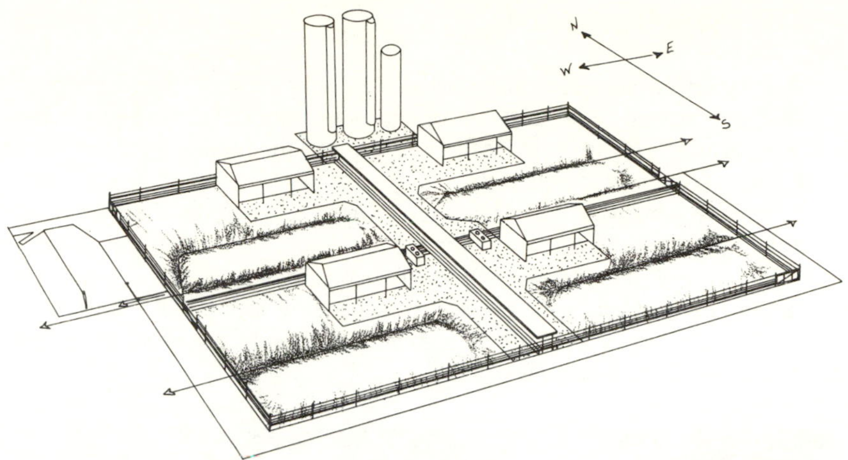

Figure 7-6. This barn and lot layout is planned for use with mechanical feeding. Mounds have been incorporated into this system to control mud and pollution. (University of Missouri)

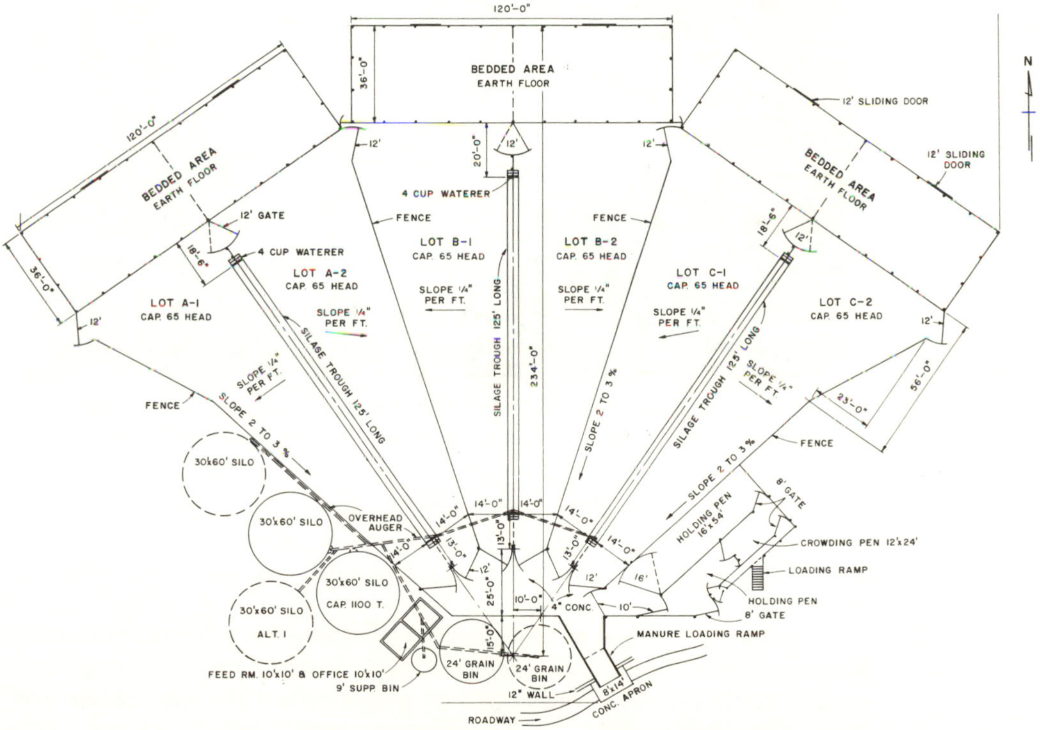

Figure 7-7. The so-called "pie shaped" system layout enables handling of large numbers of animals from a centralized feed-processing and animal-handling facility. (USDA 6210)

shown that barns will pay for themselves by providing better animal performance, especially in the central and eastern Corn Belt where wet windy conditions are common.

Complete Confinement

A completely covered and enclosed feedlot system will eliminate problems such as drifting snow, mud, and excessive runoff from the beef production operation. It also requires less space and the handling of both feed and manure can be easily mechanized.

Complete confinement systems most often use pole frame type buildings 40 to 60 feet wide. Sidewalls are 10 to 14 feet high to promote better air movement and provide accessibility for equipment. The preferred ridge orientation is east-west, with the south side being left open. Minimal insulation is provided in the roof to control condensation and summer heat gain. No side-wall insulation is used.

Figure 7-8. Completely covered and enclosed units such as this reduce total space required per animal and also eliminate the problem of feedlot runoff control.

New buildings usually incorporate a floor surface which will allow for some type of automated manure handling. Most commonly used are slatted or partially slatted floors over a liquid manure storage pit and flushing system.

Buildings are sized to provide 18 to 20 square feet of space per animal and are usually divided into pens holding from 40 to 100 head. Pen size is usually determined on the basis of anticipated animal receiving or shipping schedules.

Special Areas

All beef cattle operations will need to plan for several support facilities when designing and locating their systems. These include isolation pens for sick animals, conditioning lots, working facilities, and possibly an office area.

Isolation or hospital pens can be located next to the working corral. Pens should be under roof and in a comfortable area to minimize stress. Provide space for up to 5% of the system capacity. Isolation is an important part of disease control and this area should be located so that contact with healthy animals is minimized.

Conditioning lots are used to help arriving cattle make the transition to the finishing operation and to relieve the stress of handling and shipping. These lots should be located near the corral to allow for ease in treatment of animals. Provide 100 square feet of space per animal in lots sized to take one truck load. Allow for 2 feet of bunk space per animal.

Corral and handling facilities for livestock are covered in more detail in Chapter 11. For feedlots with fewer than 1,000 head, provide one holding pen for every 250 head capacity. For 1,000 to 5,000 head lots, provide four pens plus one for each 600 to 700 animals above 1,000. Holding pens are sized to hold about one truck load of animals to 10 square feet per head capacity.

Beef System Data

A. Space requirements

Housing System	*Sq Ft Per Animal*
Open lot	150 to 800
Barn and lot	20 to 25 in barn
Complete confinement	30 For bedded floor
	18 to 20 slotted or flushed
Calving pen	100
Mounds	25
Sick pens	40 to 50

B. Feed and water

Bunk Space	*Inches Per Animal*
All animals fed at once	
600 to 1,000 lb animals	24 in.
Mature cows	28 in.
Feed in bunk at all times	4 in. - 6 in.
Water: 1 space per 40 animals	

C. Manure Production: daily

1 cubic foot per 1,000 lbs of animal

CHAPTER 8

Dairy

The farmer who is about to embark on planning and construction of dairy facilities is facing one of the most difficult tasks in the farm building field. Not only does he have to sort through a wide variety of choices and new technology, but he also must contend with a set of regulations unequaled in any other area of production agriculture. It would be impossible for us to cover all the types of dairy facilities currently in use in the U.S. within the confines of this book. Because of this, we will limit our discussion primarily to the type of system which appears to best fit the majority of family operated dairies in the northern half of the U.S.—the free stall loose housing system. In doing so, we will be omitting discussion of traditional stable or stall barns and of the extremely large dairy systems located in several of the southern states.

Facilities for dairy housing fall into four general categories. They are housing for the milking herd, milking centers, calf housing, and housing for the replacement herd.

Housing the Milking Herd

Loose housing has long been recognized as the most efficient means of handling dairy cattle. It allows animals to be grouped and moved from one location to another, thus simplifying both the handling of materials and the mechanization of the milking operation. However, it was not until the development of the free stall in the early 1960's that loose housing came of age as the system for dairying in the U.S. The free stall reduced the high bedding requirements of earlier housing, improved cow cleanliness, and allowed engineers to increase housing densities and to more closely integrate components into efficient housing systems.

There is a wide variety of free stall housing systems in use today, all of which have some advantages and disadvantages. Those that work well will satisfy the following requirements.

- Provide a clean, dry and comfortable resting place for the milking animal.
- Adequate shelter from weather extremes accessible to all animals.
- Provide for the orderly and efficient movement of materials, including feed, manure, animals and equipment.

Free stall housing systems have been classified into four general areas or types, depending on the degree of protection or confinement afforded the animal. These are as follows.

Open. The open system uses buildings to cover only the free stalls. Feeding areas and connecting trafficways are open. The free stall barns may be pole frame buildings with one side open in the more severe climates or

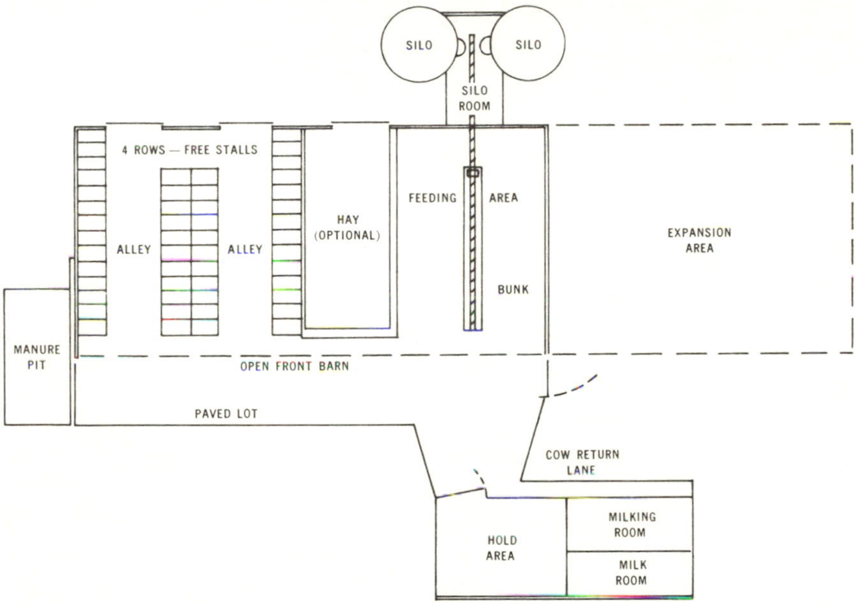

Figure 8-1. The open type free-stall system requires the least amount of building space, but runoff control and increased labor may offset the initial cost advantage. (Granite City Steel)

may be only a simple roof with no sides in milder areas. The earliest free stall systems evolved from bedded pack housing and were almost always of the open type. There is a common belief that the open system with its minimal building structure is the most economical type free stall system. However, new designs in other types have provided compactness and labor efficiency that tend to offset some of the supposed cost advantages of the open system.

The major disadvantage of the open system is the exposure of large outside areas to precipitation. In winter this means snow and ice to contend with, along with the usual manure handling problems. During the rest of

Figure 8-2. Open systems that cover only the free stalls are popular in warmer, relatively snow-free areas of the country. This unit is sometimes referred to as a "Utah type free stall."

the year, mixing of rainfall runoff with manure poses a potential pollution problem.

Partially Open Systems. This was the first step away from the traditional open system. Free stalls and feeding areas were located in a building and an outside paved area was provided for animal exercise. These units utilize relatively low cost pole frame and metal frame buildings with no insulation. Ridge lines are oriented east-west and the south is generally open to the outside paved area.

Partially open systems considerably reduce the total area involved in the housing system and they provide a sheltered access to feed in all kinds of weather. They do not, however, eliminate the problems of snow handling and runoff control from the outside yard area.

Covered Cold Systems. The first of these systems appeared in the mid 1960's and their development and refinement has progressed steadily ever since. Well over half of the new systems built today fall into this category.

The complete housing and feeding unit, along with any planned exercise area is covered with a low cost uninsulated pole frame or metal frame building. Depending on the system layout, the south side of the building may be left entirely open or only partially open. A continuous ridge opening works in combination with openings in both major walls to provide natural ventilation. There is little attempt to modify interior temperatures beyond what is provided by the ventilation system.

These designs eliminate lot runoff as a concern and provide a year-round housing and management system which has been most satisfactory.

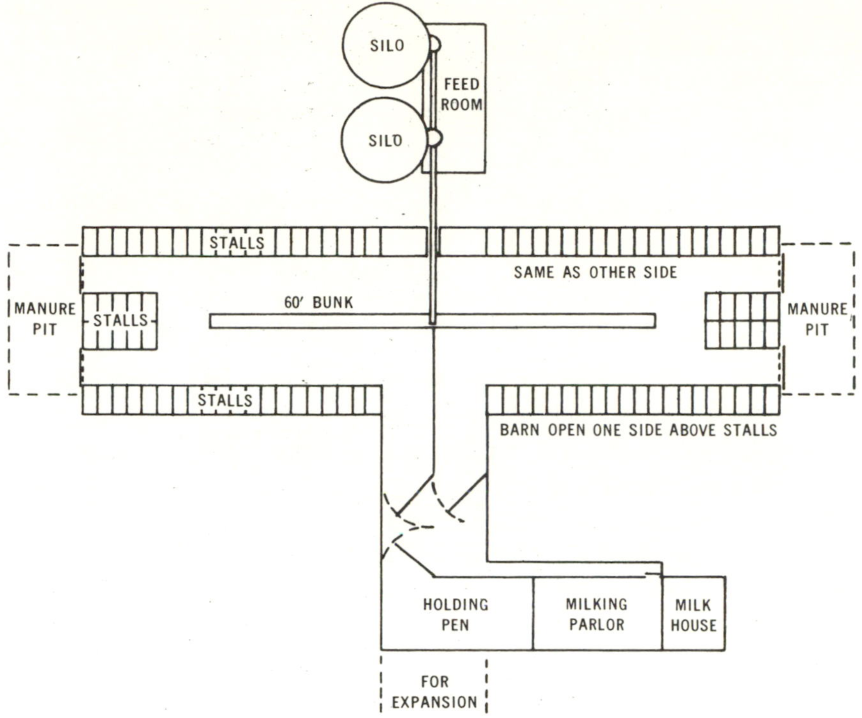

Figure 8-3. The covered cold system gets more cows in less area and greatly simplifies movement of materials. Some newer designs using 80 to 100-foot wide buildings with four to six rows of free stalls are even more efficient space users than this older type layout. (Granite City Steel)

Enclosed Warm Systems. These are similar to the covered cold systems in basic layout. The major difference is that these units are housed in a completely closed, insulated and mechanically ventilated building. They are the most costly of all the free stall systems to construct and operate. Their main advantage appears to be the higher degree of comfort that they provide to the persons who work within them. This effect is apparently wasted on the cows since all the research indicates there is no particular advantage in production efficiency for animals housed in these systems.

Moisture control in the warm enclosed system poses some interesting problems for the designer. The major heat source in these buildings is the cow herd. If the building is laid out in such a manner that animals move from one area to another in a group, the shifting heat source can lead to excessive condensation and even fog within the building. For example, suppose the feed bunk is in the opposite end of the building from the free stalls and that feeding is done on a twice a day basis. On a cold winter night cows lying in the free stall area have warmed up their end of the barn and at the same time added moisture from respiration and evaporation of wastes. In the morning the feeder comes on and the entire herd moves to the other end of the barn, taking their heat source with them. Temperature in the free stall area can drop to the point where condensation and fog will occur. Well designed warm systems will attempt to avoid this problem by integrating feeding and resting areas and by promoting management schemes which will not cause rapid shifts in animal occupancy.

Size

Free stall barns can be built with from 2 to 6 rows of stalls and from 1 to 6 or more alleys. Successful systems have used buildings as narrow as 22 feet and as wide as 100 feet. This book contains layouts of several systems which will give you some idea of the variety of possibilities. As you study these floor plans, keep in mind the following good design practices.

- Match stall size to the animals to eliminate wasted space and to control manure deposition.
- Eliminate dead end alleys which cause problems with movement of both machines and animals.
- Provide some means of separating animals into groups of 50 to 75. This will enable feeding according to production level and also make it easier to handle cows at milking time.
- Alleys should have the following minimum widths:

Location	*Minimum Width*
Between adjacent rows of free stalls	8 ft
Between row of free stalls and a feed bunk	10 ft
Drive through feed alley	
Separate from cows	12 ft
Accessible to cows	15 ft

- Main alleys should run lengthwise with the building and be of constant width. This simplifies both removal of manure and installation of bedding in stalls.

***Table 8-1.* Recommended Free Stall Sizes for the Milking Herd**

Average Cow Weight Lbs	Stall Size W x L
1,000	3 ft 6 in. x 6 ft 10 in.
1,200	3 ft 9 in. x 7 ft 0 in.
1,400	4 ft 0 in. x 7 ft 0 in.
1,600	4 ft 0 in. x 7 ft 6 in.

Construction

As noted above, most of the cold free stall housing utilizes pole frame or metal frame construction. A sidewall height of 8 to 10 feet is adequate for good performance of natural ventilation systems. A clear span building is desirable from the standpoint of flexibility in making any future changes; however, some of the systems require buildings that are too wide for

Figure 8-4. Alleys must be wide enough to accommodate animals on a daily basis. If they are also wide enough to allow for equipment movement, labor involved in routine maintenance will be reduced.

economical clear span construction. Buildings which use deep roof purlins should be avoided if at all possible. Natural ventilation systems function best with a smooth flow of air entering the building at the eave line, flowing up along the under side of the roof, and exiting at the continuous ridge vent. Deep roof purlins interfere with this flow and may cause winter condensation problems.

Stud-frame buildings with conventional foundations and interior linings and ceilings are used for warm free stall systems. These buildings are fully insulated and must also be provided with a mechanical ventilation system.

Insulation is recommended for roof areas of partially open and covered cold buildings to reduce summer heat gain. A rigid type of insulation board having R value in the range of 2 to 5 is adequate for this purpose.

Natural lighting during daylight hours can be improved by installation of translucent panels of fiberglass reinforced plastic in the roof. An area equal to 5% to 8% of the floor area will be adequate.

Concrete floors, placed over a well compacted fill, should be 4 inches thick. Floors are generally flat unless a manure flushing system is planned. Slope for flushing will depend on the size of the facility, and the type of flush system planned. You should make this decision before starting construction.

Waste Handling

Manure represents the largest single volume of material to be handled on the dairy farm. The system you choose should satisfy the following requirements.

- Prevent pollution of public waters.
- Help reduce odors and fly breeding.
- Maintain cow cleanliness.
- Operate efficiently in terms of labor and management requirements.
- Protect the public health.
- Save a maximum amount of fertilizer nutrients.

Regulatory requirements prohibit the accumulation of manure in areas to which cows have access. This means cleaning of the free stall system floors and alleys on a fairly regular basis. During fly season, not more than a four-day accumulation of manure is allowed unless an approved fly control program is in effect.

Manure may be disposed of as a solid or semi-solid on a daily basis, as a liquid by using a storage tank, pump and spreader, or through a properly designed lagoon.

Solid disposal systems are generally least cost in terms of initial investment required. They work best in open type systems that have a large amount of paved area. They are also highly adaptable to farms which have scattered facilities. The main disadvantage of solid handling systems is their regular demand for labor. Manure has to be moved at all seasons of the year, which may not be compatible with climatic conditions and probably will be inconvenient during the growing season when fields are in crops.

Liquid handling systems are attractive to many dairymen because of the flexibility they offer to the manure management program. In most cases, storage tanks can be combined with either slatted floors or some type of automated scraping, which reduces the daily collection chore for the labor force. Manure can be spread at times when labor is available and a higher percentage of nutrients is preserved than with other handling systems.

Many states require that liquid manure systems provide a minimum of 60 to 90 days storage. Storages are generally designed on the basis of about 2 cubic feet of capacity per cow per day. These storages must be water tight to prevent either entry of outside water or escape of manure to ground water. Most are constructed of reinforced concrete or of steel. The cost of storage combined with the cost of pumping and spreading equipment makes the liquid manure handling system the most expensive of the possible options. The other disadvantage of liquid manure is the odor associated with agitation and spreading. Farms located close to developed areas and using liquid manure systems have to carefully select days when manure is handled and must incorporate manure into the soil as it is spread or immediately thereafter.

The anaerobic lagoon can be effectively used to receive and treat dairy wastes in many areas of the country. It fits in well with almost any type of system for removal of manure from the housing area, including flushing. Sizing and planning of a lagoon will depend on your particular climate and health requirements and should be done by someone experienced in your area.

Stall Construction

The first free stalls were constructed of wood and performed very satisfactorily. Manufactured stalls are generally made of steel frames. Durability and design are the important factors in stall construction, not the material chosen by a particular builder or manufacturer. Stalls must be rugged enough to withstand the day after day pushing and shoving of 1,400 to 1,600 pound dairy cows, as well as an occasional hit from a misguided piece of equipment.

Stalls must be designed to provide a comfortable place for the cow to lie. If they do not do this, cows won't use them; it's as simple as that. We listed overall sizes for different sized cows in Table 8-1. Now, let's look at some of the other factors.

Partitions between stalls must be high enough to keep the cow from turning around in the stall and solid enough to keep her from sticking her head through into the next stall. This means a height of 40 to 48 inches above the curb at the rear of the stall. The bottom rail or board of the partition should be 12 to 15 inches above the top of the curb. This allows some foot and leg movement under the partition, but is open enough to prevent injury to pin bones and legs. In order to maintain these dimensions

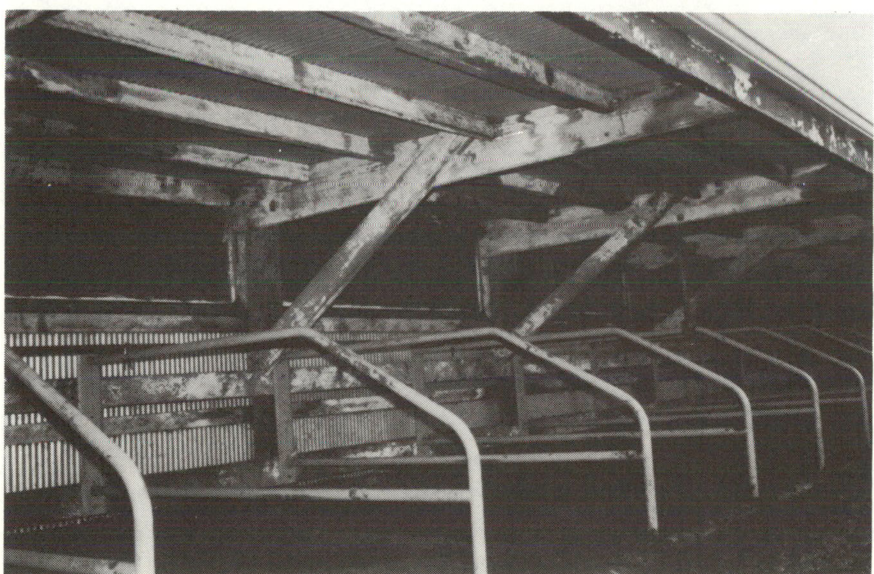

Figure 8-5. These stall dividers look rugged enough but are not likely to stand up to several years of pushing and shoving from 1,500 to 1,800-lb cows. Also, the wide spacing between bars will allow cows to stick their heads into the next stall and turn around.

Figure 8-6. This head piece forces the cow to step back when she gets up, causing manure to be deposited in the alley. Devices such as this should not be installed until cows are accustomed to using the stalls.

Figure 8-7. The free-stall system should include a well-built feed bunk that provides 2 feet of feed space for each cow to insure maximum feed intake. The step adjacent to the bunk reduces fighting and keeps manure from being deposited in the bunk.

during usage, it is important that stall bases be constructed of material that packs well and resists pocketing. Well compacted clay or stone dust works well. It should be leveled about 3 inches below the top of the curb and topped with bedding. Another alternative is to use concrete stall floors with rubber mats for cows to lie on. These will reduce maintenance, but add considerably to initial costs.

Restraining devices such as pipes or cables across the top of stalls at the withers or brisket boards in the bottom of the stall are sometimes suggested to make sure the cow backs out of the stall as soon as she stands up. If stall size is properly matched to cow size, these devices are of questionable value. They do detract from the comfort of the stall and should probably not be used until cows are well adjusted to using the free stalls.

The Milking Center

The milking center, including milk room, parlor, utility room, and holding area, represents the most complex arrangement of building and equipment in use on the farm today. This complexity is reflected in the fact that milking centers are also the most costly of our farm buildings.

Traditionally, milking centers have been of concrete masonry construction. Masonry provided a material which would take the abuse of cow traffic, withstand high moisture conditions usually found in the center, and satisfy the milk inspector's demand for a cleanable interior surface. Unfortunately, masonry is not easily insulated and rapidly increasing energy costs have produced milking center heating costs approaching $1,000 per year in many northern states. Because of this, we now feel that an effort must be made to move toward types of construction which can be more easily insulated. In most cases, this will mean conventional stud frame construction. This can be done without major problems, provided we exercise care in selecting construction techniques which will avoid the traditional problems with moisture and cleanability. We will place extra emphasis on these as we proceed.

Size

The milking center is a production system made up of specialized equipment and a building to house it. Size of the structure will be completely dependent on the type of milking parlor selected, and to a lesser extent on the particular brand of equipment that is selected for that parlor.

The most popular types of parlors for milking herds of up to 150 cows are the herringbone and the side opening. The herringbone provides for group handling of cows, places cows closer together in the parlor, and requires less equipment. The side opening system permits individual cows to proceed at their own pace in the parlor, allows more individual attention, and is more compatible with automatic cow wash and preparation

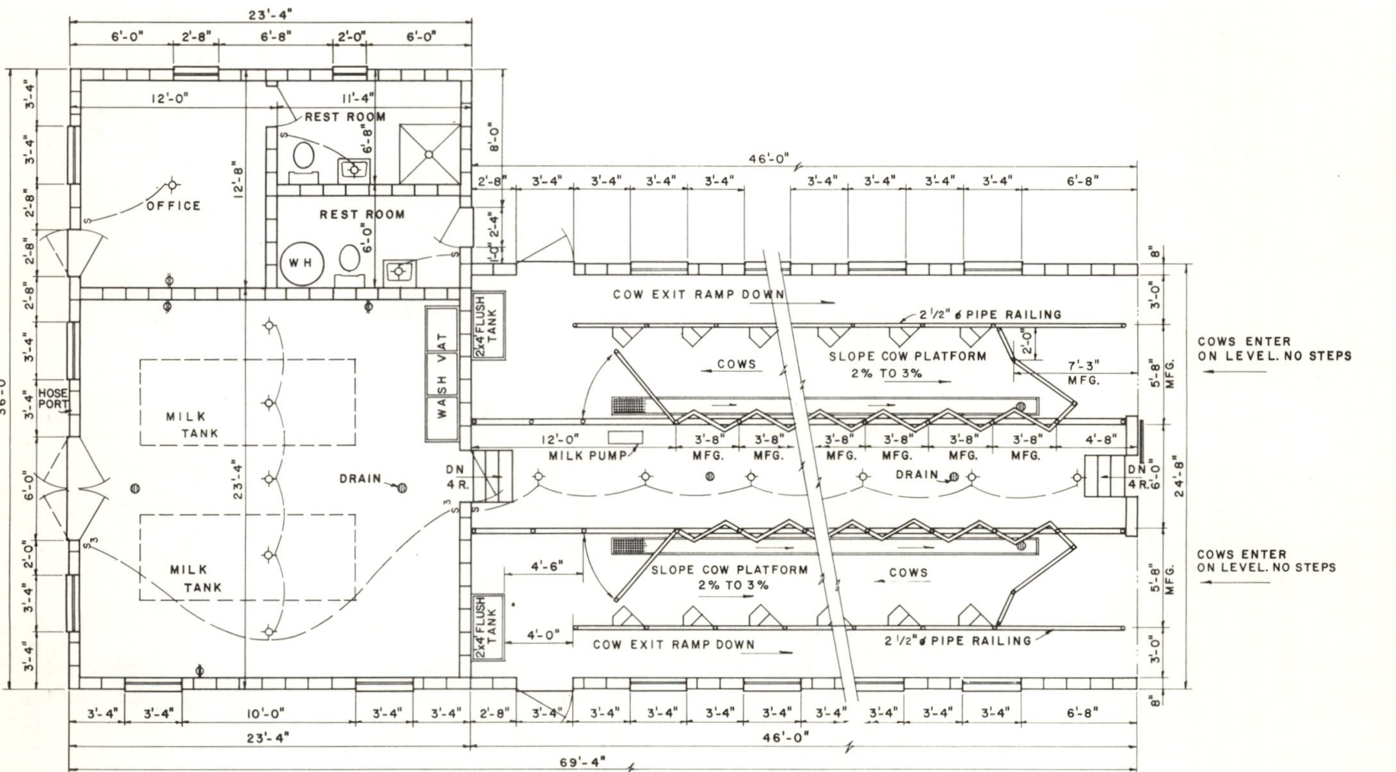

Figure 8-8. Plan view showing the basic components of a milking center featuring a herringbone parlor. Working drawings for milking parlor construction are provided by most of the equipment manufacturers. Since there are some differences in equipment requirements, you should decide on the type of equipment you will be installing and then secure plans for a parlor to fit it from the manufacturer. Although this plan shows masonry construction, well-insulated frame construction is preferred today. (USDA 6203)

equipment. Table 8-2 presents some representative numbers of cows per hour and per man hour for different parlor sizes.

Table 8-2. **Average Capacities of Milking Parlors Without Automatic Prep Stalls or Machine Detachers**

Parlor Size	Cows/Hr	Cows/Man Hr
Herringbone		
Double 3	34	29
Double 4	41	39
Double 6	58	30
Double 8	71	35
Double 10	92	44
Side Opening		
Double 2	41	41
Double 3	51	47

A double 4 herringbone parlor will require a room in the milking center that is approximately 19 by 24 feet. A larger area will be required if cow returns or other traffic ways are incorporated into the parlor room. The milk room size will be determined by the physical size of the bulk tank and requirements for work space around it. A minimum clearance of 36 inches between the working sides of the tank and walls or other equipment is usually required. Also required is 24 inches minimum clearance at the rear of the tank and on the side opposite the drain valve.

Bulkhead tanks can be successfully used to reduce the size of the milk room. The major portion of these tanks is located outside the milking center building, with only the end containing the access port and the drain valve extending into the milk room. Even with a bulkhead tank, milk rooms should probably be a minimum of 14 by 16 feet.

The utility area must be large enough to house water heating equipment and, depending on design, the vacuum pump and/or bulk tank compressor. It should also include lavatory and toilet facilities as required.

The holding area is sized to provide 12 to 15 square feet per cow immediately adjacent to the milking parlor. Total capacity should match the herd grouping size in the housing system.

Construction

Conventional concrete foundations with stud-frame or insulated prefabricated wall panels are preferred for energy efficient milking centers. Interior wall and ceiling surfaces in the milk room and parlor must be covered with an easily washed impervious material. Recommended for this is fiber glass reinforced plastic sheeting. This is available in a variety of sizes and can even be purchased already bonded to a plywood backing board. Joints in the lining material should be sealed with caulking or pre-formed closure strips to keep moisture from entering the wall cavity. A suggested method of handling the floor to wall joint is shown in Figure 8-9.

Floors in the milking center must be constructed of concrete or other impervious material with a non-slip finish.

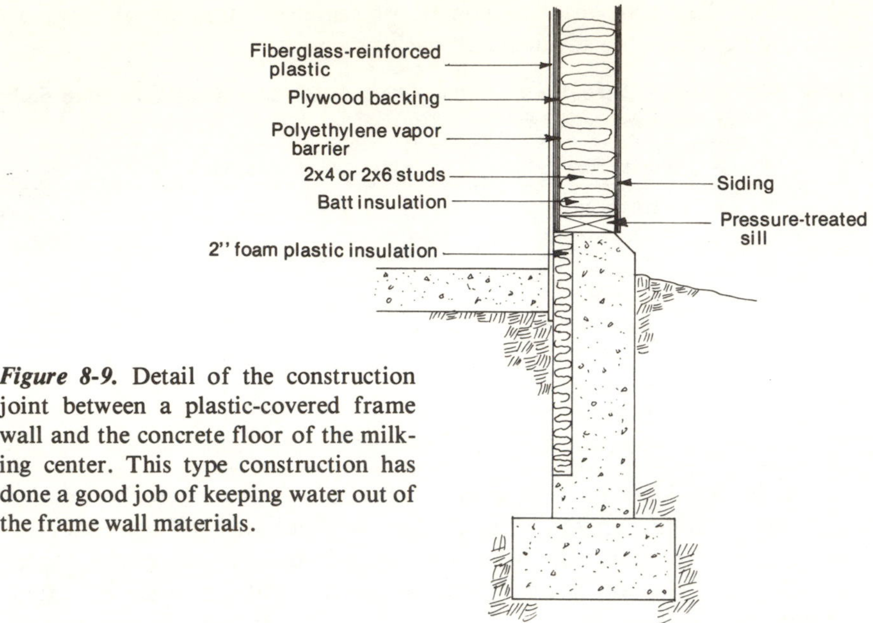

Figure 8-9. Detail of the construction joint between a plastic-covered frame wall and the concrete floor of the milking center. This type construction has done a good job of keeping water out of the frame wall materials.

The most desirable non-slip surface is provided by using aluminum oxide grit in the surface of all traffic areas. One hundred pounds of aluminum oxide will treat 400 square feet of concrete surface.

A second choice is to use a rough broom finish on floors in all traffic areas. An even coarser or rougher finish may be used where floors are cleaned by flushing. This can be provided by using expanded metal with 3/8 inch to 5/8 inch holes. Commonly called a jitterbug, this is an excellent device for surfacing traffic areas throughout the free stall system also.

Milking center floors are subject to acid conditions which can cause rapid surface erosion. About the only way to combat this is by using high quality concrete. Use at least six sacks of cement per cubic yard of concrete, and not more than 6 gallons of water per sack of cement. The use of air entraining cement is recommended. It provides a higher resistance to acid action than does ordinary cement.

Floors and other concrete work in the milking center will require a considerable amount of form work to accommodate required drainage and equipment. Persons who are not skilled in form work and concrete placement and finishing should be carefully supervised if allowed to work on a milking center.

Windows are a source of heat loss, increase maintenance work, and add to construction costs. They should be kept to a minimum in the milking center. At one time, window area equivalent to 10% of the floor area was required in the milk room and suggested in the parlor. Most areas are relaxing this requirement now that we are becoming more energy conscious.

A special foundation or reinforced floor area will be required to support the bulk milk tank. One way to do this is to thicken the floor to about 8 inches in the bulk tank area and use two layers of 6 by 6 inch by 10 gauge reinforcing mesh in the floor. Bulkhead tanks require foundations which extend below the frost line to prevent heaving during freeze-thaw cycles.

All exterior walls of the milking center should be insulated to a R value of 13 and ceilings to R = 24. A polyethylene plastic vapor barrier must be used to prevent moisture from inside the structure from reaching the insulation.

Ventilation

A mechanical ventilation system is required to control moisture, minimize odors, and maintain a degree of summer comfort in the milking center. Regulations require that ventilation air for the milk room come from outside, and not from any other part of the milking center or animal housing area. Because of this, a pressurized fan ventilation system is generally recommended for the milk room. With this type system, a pressure fan forces air directly into the milk room. Recommended fan location is near the ceiling on an outside wall, away from the animal housing or feed handling areas. The fan should be equipped with a filter to screen out dust and a shutter which closes when it is not in operation.

Milk room fans are sized to provide 12 air changes per hour in the room and controlled with a thermostat-timer unit. An outlet for ventilation air must be provided for the milk room. This is usually located in the wall between the milk room and the parlor. The outlet must be screened and covered with gravity type anti-backdraft shutters. Size the opening to provide 1 square foot of area for every 500 cfm of fan capacity.

Parlor ventilation is designed to provide moisture control year-round and operator comfort during warm weather. An exhaust fan system is usually used. A fan which can provide one complete air change every 1-½ minutes is adequate for summer heat control. Moisture control can be provided by running the summer fan periodically using a timer or by installing a second fan with a lower volume rating. A fan that provides one air change every 10 to 12 minutes is adequate to control moisture. Screened air inlets must be provided in order to achieve optimum performance of the parlor ventilation system.

Heating

Milking centers require supplemental heating systems to provide freeze protection during winter months and for operator comfort. A wide variety of heating units has been used satisfactorily in milking centers. Electric heating units are most often selected. Electric space heaters with individual thermostats can be located in each room of the milking center and set to maintain room temperatures of 45° to 50° F. Additional radiant type heaters are located in the operator area of the parlor to provide comfort during the milking operation. Radiant heaters are preferred in the

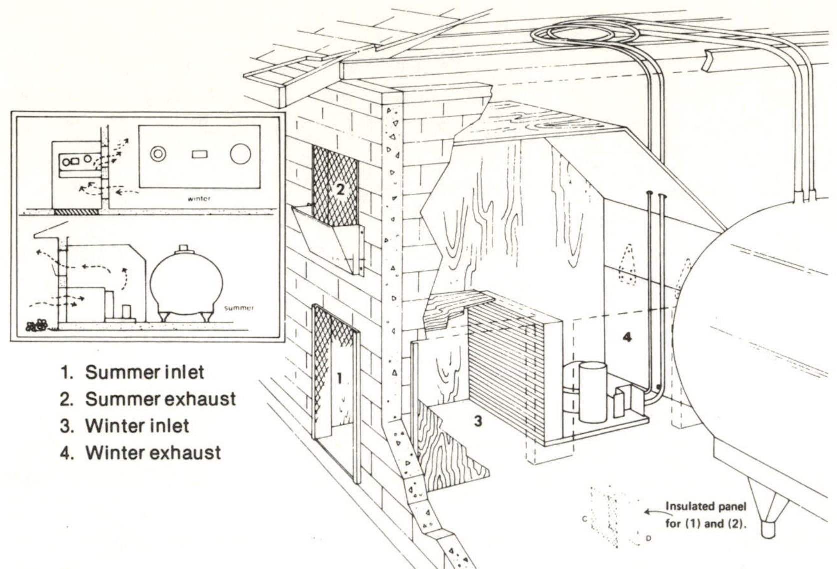

Figure 8-10. Location of the bulk milk tank compressor so that it can provide milking center heating during winter months will greatly reduce energy bills associated with its operation. Each pound of milk that is cooled releases nearly 100 Btu. (University of Missouri)

parlor because they have the capability of heating people directly without heating surrounding air. The frequent opening and closing of doors in the parlor during milking makes heating of air almost an impossible task.

The refrigeration unit used to cool milk can also be used to help warm the milking center during cold weather. Cooling one pound of milk from 100° to 37° F will produce nearly 100 Btu of heat energy at the compressor. For every 1,000 pounds of milk cooled, the compressor releases an amount of heat about equal to 1 gallon of LP-gas or 21 KWHR of electricity. A number of different systems can be used to direct heat energy from the compressor to the milk center in winter and to the outside during summer. Two different systems are shown in the accompanying figures. Care must be taken when designing systems of this type to make sure air flow over the condenser coils is not restricted. Any restriction will reduce cooling efficiency and may shorten compressor or motor life.

Hot Water Supply

Two hot water heaters are recommended for milking centers. One is used to provide 100° to 110° water used in the parlor to wash udders. The other provides 160° water for cleaning of pipe lines and equipment. Locating the two heaters in series so that 100 degree water from the low temperature heater supplies the high temperature unit will increase the recovery rate for the high temperature heater, allowing use of a smaller heater which will save energy.

For a quick estimate of recovery rates in gallons per hour of water

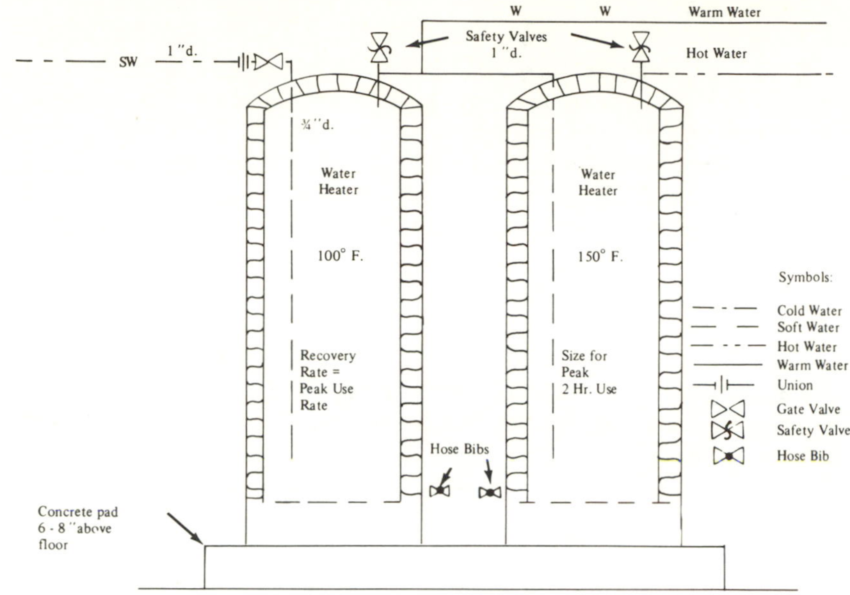

Figure 8-11. Schematic diagram of the two-tank water heating system recommended for the milking center. (University of Missouri)

raised 100° above inlet temperature, divide the watts of the heating element by 500 or the rating of the heater in Btu per hour by 1,200.

Examples:

1. A 53,000 Btu per hour input gas hot water heater would have a recovery rate of

$$\frac{53{,}000}{1{,}200} = 44.2 \text{ gallons per hour}$$

2. A 6,000 watt electric heater would have a recovery rate of

$$\frac{6{,}000}{500} = 12 \text{ gallons per hour}$$

If the water is heated only 50° instead of 100°, the recovery rates would be doubled. This is what happens with the high temperature heater placed in series with the low temperature unit.

Heat from the milk cooling process can also be used to provide warm water for the milking center. Commercially available heat recovery units can be installed to capture nearly all of the compressor heat. These units are capable of producing one gallon of 140 degree water for every gallon of milk cooled. A small heater can then be used to boost cleaning water temperature up to the required levels. Hot water recovery units will produce more hot water than is needed for cleaning purposes in most herds. At least one farmer we know of is using the excess hot water in unit heaters to keep milking center temperatures above freezing.

Drainage

Four inch diameter lines should be used in the milking center drain system. Waste does not contain any large particles and the 4 inch line will promote scouring.

A 4 inch line has a capacity of 150 to 300 gallons per minute, depending on the slope and the amount of head provided in loading the line. A 6 inch line has two times this capacity and an 8 inch line, four times the capacity.

Drain lines require a minimum slope of 2% (¼ inch per foot). Problems with plugging will occur in lines that have less slope. It is interesting that some persons think you should increase pipe size when you anticipate trouble with plugging; just the opposite is often true. Smaller pipes promote higher velocity which helps prevent solids from settling in the line and plugging it.

Cast iron, copper, polyvinylchloride (PVC) plastic, transite, or other permanent types of piping are suggested for drain lines within the milking center. Bituminous fiber pipe should not be used since acid compounds used in cleaning parlor equipment tend to soften it, leading to collapse.

Vents for drain lines are needed to release odors and prevent siphoning of traps. Vents should extend above the roof line of the milking center.

Floor drains in the milking center must be trapped. Deep box water seal drains are most satisfactory for this purpose. They have a high flow rate and will collect sediment particles which might tend to plug drain lines.

All drains should be located in corners or against walls to aid in hose wash down of the floors. The top surface of the drain should be located ½ inch below the floor surface. Wash vat and hand washing facilities should be plumbed directly to the drainage system and not allowed to drop directly onto milk room floors where cleaning compounds will erode the concrete.

Milking center floors that continuously remain wet provide a good place for bacteria and mold to grow. They also contribute to more rapid deterioration of both the building and its equipment. The best way to prevent this problem is to install adequate slopes on parlor and milk room floors. A minimum slope of 2% is suggested for all floor areas.

Most milk rooms can be adequately drained with a single drain. Slope the floor uniformly from the outside wall to the wall between the parlor and milk room. Locate the drain next to the wall and at the mid point of the partition wall. Place a slight slope from the two corners at the low side of the floor toward the drain. Two different systems for sloping parlor floors are shown in Figure 8-12.

Waste Handling

If a toilet is installed in the milking center, a separate waste disposal system will be required to handle sewage from it. The only exception is where aerobic lagoons are used for milk center waste disposal. In these

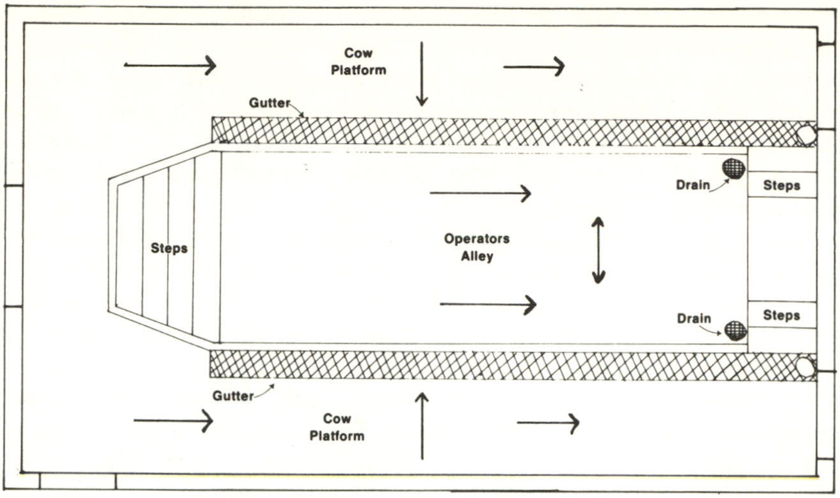

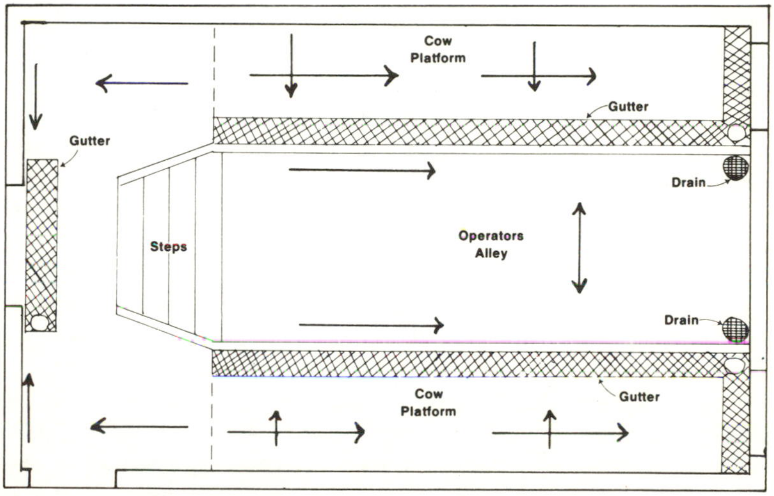

Figure 8-12. Two floor-slope systems that have proven satisfactory for milking parlor floors. (University of Missouri)

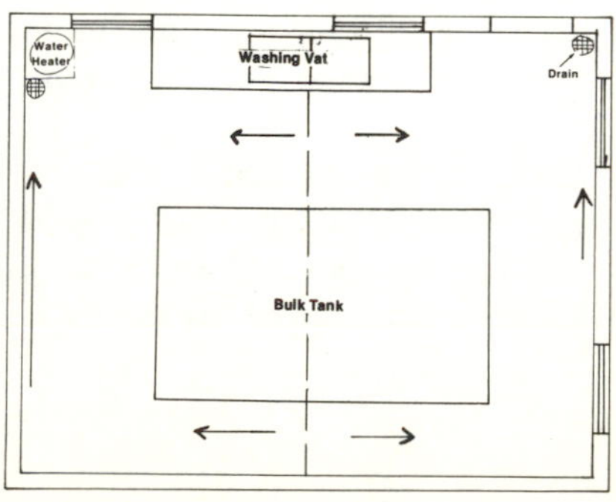

Figure 8-13. Details of the two-way milk room floor-slope system. This method of water control simplifies both the forming and pouring of concrete, as well as provides an easier surface to wash down. (University of Missouri)

cases, regulatory officials may permit a single disposal system for all milking center wastes.

Milking center wastes contain a variety of materials, most of which are difficult to handle in conventional disposal systems. Among these are milk solids, cleaning solutions, and dilute animal wastes. Alternatives for disposal include land application, adding to the liquid manure tank, lagoons, and settling tanks.

Land application involves setting aside an area which can be used as a soil-plant filter for applying parlor wastes. Depending on the location and slope, application can be made by flooding or with a sprinkler irrigation unit. Size of area required will depend on soil type, vegetative cover, and the anticipated volume of waste.

Adding waste to the liquid manure tank is one of the simpler solutions, provided it can be done easily. Frequently, elevation differences between parlor pit floors are not sufficient to allow gravity flow to the manure tank. It is possible to use a collection pump and an automatic controlled sewage ejection pump in these cases; however, sand and acid found in wastes do not make for long periods of trouble free operation.

Lagoons offer the most trouble free solution to the waste problem for farms that do not have a liquid manure handling system. Both aerobic and anaerobic lagoons have been used satisfactorily. Anaerobic lagoons require less surface area and are generally less expensive to construct. However, they may produce odor at certain times of the year and cannot be used for treatment of raw sewage from the toilet. Also, they are not acceptable by regulatory officials in all parts of the country. Lagoon design requires special engineering assistance which can usually be obtained through the county extension office or from local SCS officials.

Settling tanks collect wastes, allow solids to settle out, and distribute water to a disposal field similar to those used with septic systems. At one time, settling tanks were generally recommended as the system for handling of milking center wastes. Experience has shown, however, that they are the least desirable of the alternatives. Tanks require frequent attention to prevent plugging with solids and the milk particles which get into the disposal field tend to seal up the soil and prevent absorption. Settling tanks should be sized to provide at least 20 gallons capacity per cow milked and should have a length to width ratio greater than 3:2 to permit maximum settling action. The most desirable type settling system uses two tanks placed in series.

Wastes which collect in the holding area are best handled by the same system which handles waste from the free stall area. If flushing is used, waste water from the parlor and milk room can be collected and used to flush the holding area. This provides the added advantage of getting rid of all the wastes (except the toilet) together.

Special Areas

A hospital area to confine sick animals or hold animals for breeding or other purposes is a desirable addition to the milking center. If located adjacent to the parlor, animals needing attention can easily be diverted to the hospital as they leave the parlor. The hospital area should contain a box stall, four to six treatment stalls, and a maternity pen for every 75 to 100 cows in the milking herd. There should also be a loading chute provided for arriving and departing cattle.

Electrical Service

The milking center will usually have enough electrical demand to merit its own service entrance panel. A minimum of 100 ampere capacity will be required, with higher capacity needed in cases where electric heat and several large motors are required.

Cows are extremely sensitive to electrical currents. For this reason it is very important that all conductive materials used in the milking center be

***Table 8-3.* Illumination Levels for Milking Centers**

Area	Light Level Foot Candles	How Obtained
Milk room-general	20	Install uniformly spaced fluorescent lights with capacity of 1.5 watts per square foot of floor space.
Wash vat	100	One fixture over vat with 2-40 watt tubes.
Bulk tank	100	Mount 150 watt reflector flood lamp to shine into tank.
Milk parlor-general	20	Two continuous rows of 2-40 watt tube fixtures over parlor pit area.
Utility room	20	Single fluorescent fixture with 2-40 watt tubes.
Toilet	15 to 20	Same as utility.
Hospital area	20	Install fluorescent tubes at rate of 1.7 watts per square foot. Concentrate over treatment area.
Holding area	3 to 7	1 incandescent* fixture near entrance to parlor —150 to 200 watts.
Milk loading area	20	1 incandescent fixture* —300 watts.

**Incandescent fixtures required because of difficulty in starting fluorescent lights at low temperatures.*

bonded together and properly grounded. This includes stalls, plumbing lines, equipment, floor grates, and even reinforcing used in concrete work. Stray voltages which are so low that they cannot be detected by a human will cause a cow to stop milk let down, not eat in the parlor, or not even enter the parlor.

Milking center lighting must be good enough to permit close observation of cows and of all cleaning and sanitizing operations which are carried out. Most milk marketing areas have specific lighting requirements which must be followed in order to secure approval for milking center usage. Fluorescent fixtures equipped with cool-white, rapid start lamps provide the most practical and energy efficient lighting system for milking centers. Recommended levels of illumination and how to obtain them are contained in Table 8-3.

In addition to lights, there are a number of special purpose electrical outlets required in the milking center. Your power company can help with planning to accommodate these needs.

Calf Housing

The successful rearing of replacement animals is an essential part of dairying and the most critical part of the operation is calf raising. Dairymen estimate that 85% to 90% of the replacement animals that die do so within the first 60 to 90 days of life. Good housing and management during this period can materially reduce these losses. Calves can be satisfactorily housed either in individual shelters called "hutches" or in environmentally controlled central housing units.

Calf hutches are designed to hold individual calves up to an age of about 3 months. They consist of a shed type building about 4 feet square,

Figure 8-14. The individual calf hutch provides a low-investment, extremely satisfactory method of rearing replacement dairy calves. (University of Missouri)

with an outside pen area also about 4 feet square. A burlap sack or canvas cover is usually provided to close the entry to the shed during extremely cold weather. The success of a calf hutch depends on keeping the calf dry at all times and liberal amounts of bedding must be used during winter months. Calves should be placed in hutches soon after birth, before they become accustomed to some other environment. Hutches should be thoroughly cleaned and moved to clean ground as soon as a calf is removed from it.

Specific advantages include:

1. Calves adapt quickly to a natural environment.
2. Disease buildup is minimized by cleaning and relocating between calves.
3. Initial investment is low.

Disadvantages:

1. Space requirements are higher than for central housing.
2. More labor is required.
3. Separate facilities are needed for feed storage and preparation.

Central housing units eliminate the disadvantages of hutches and provide for maximum convenience and labor savings—at a price. These systems are high in initial cost and do require a higher degree of management skill to make them function properly. They are probably best suited to herds of more than 100 cows or for persons involved exclusively in replacement animal rearing.

Size

Individual calf stalls approximately 2 by 4 feet are most often used in central calf housing. These stalls are elevated 8 to 12 inches above the floor and have a partially slatted floor at the rear to allow for escape of manure and urine. Another alternative is the use of individual pens 3 by 4 feet in

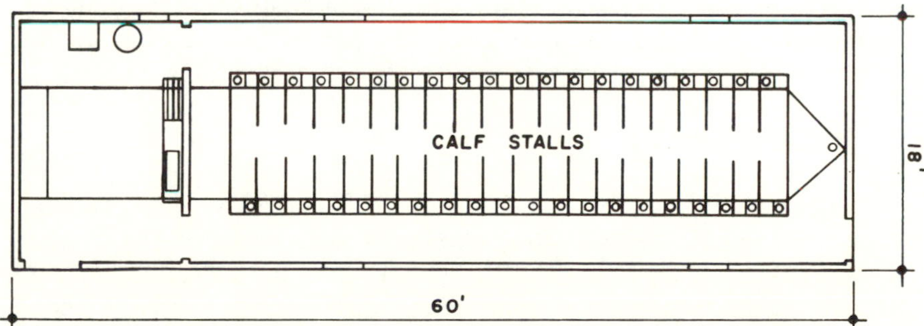

Figure 8-15. This building is designed to handle large numbers of calves with minimum of labor. Manure is removed from the unit by a flushing gutter beneath the grating that forms the floor of the stalls. Plans for the unit are available through the extension service. (University of Missouri)

size. These can be elevated with expanded metal flooring or located on the floor with bedding provided. Overall building size will depend on the number of stalls or pens needed and the floor plan arrangement selected. A unit with two rows of stalls located over a flushing gutter will fit very nicely into an 18 foot wide building. In some cases, calf nursery units have been combined with housing for larger animals in a single building.

Construction. Post frame or conventional stud frame buildings with interior linings and flat ceilings are most adaptable to calf nursery facilities. An 8 foot ceiling is satisfactory unless special equipment access is needed.

Supplemental heat will be needed during cold months and this requires use of insulation in both sidewalls and ceilings. R values of 13 and 24, respectively, are suggested.

Interior surfaces need to be easily cleaned, but need not be as physically strong as milking centers because direct animal contact will be minimal.

A 4 inch thick concrete floor without reinforcement is adequate.

Ventilation

A minimum continuous ventilation rate of 10 cfm per 100 pounds of animal weight should be provided in the winter. A pressurized fan-tube type of system provides the best way to introduce and control this relatively low volume of air. Summer ventilation can be provided by a natural ventilation system using openable insulated wall panels or by an exhaust fan system delivering 75 to 100 cfm per 100 pounds of animal weight.

Heating

Supplemental heat capable of maintaining a minimum temperature of 45^0-50^0 during the coldest expected weather should be installed in the nursery. The size of the heater will depend on building size and insulation levels. Size should be determined on the basis of no animals being present in order to be able to take care of times when few animals are in the building. If a fan tube ventilation system is used, heat can be introduced at the fan and the ventilation system will distribute it through the building.

Waste Handling

The calf nursery produces a relatively small amount of waste. This can be easily handled as a solid, followed by a hose down of floor areas. Another possibility is to use a flushing gutter under the stall area. Flushing eliminates nearly all the labor from the manure handling operation and is an excellent alternative, provided a lagoon is available for waste disposal.

Systems using solid handling should have some type of shallow gutters or positive floor drainage constructed to accommodate liquids from wastes and washdown.

Buildings using individual bedded pens will be restricted to solid handling of wastes. These units should be planned so that there can be equipment access to handle the larger amounts of waste associated with bedding material.

Special Areas

A separate room should be included for feed storage, feed mixing, and cleaning of equipment. It should be large enough to also accommodate a hot water heater and a refrigerator for storage of medicines and vaccines. An area 10 by 12 feet should be considered as a minimum for this purpose.

Housing the Replacement Herd

When calves are consuming at least 2 pounds per day of dry calf starter, they can be moved from the nursery unit or hutches into group housing facilities. These facilities can be "cold" barns, providing only shelter from rain, snow, and winter winds.

Size

Provide space for at least three and preferably four groups of animals between the time they leave the nursery and the time they enter the milking herd. Add one extra group if dry cows are to be housed in this unit. Plan units for groups of 20 or fewer animals. Space requirements per animal will vary from about 30 square feet at 3 months of age, up to about 50 square feet for a dry cow. Specific building size will depend on floor plan layout and whether or not feeding area is included as part of the barn.

Construction

Clear span post frame or steel frame buildings are generally used for housing growing animals. Minimum insulation under the roof is desired for summer heat control. Buildings can be fully or partially open to the south, depending on the severity of winter weather expected.

If a bedded pack manure system is used, the bottom 4 to 5 feet of wall should be lined with treated planking to retain the manure. Bedded pack buildings should also have sidewalls of 10 to 12 feet minimum to allow animal room as manure builds up.

Free stalls can be successfully used for growing animals. They must be carefully managed so that animals are matched to stall size as they grow. Suggested stall dimensions are as follows:

Age of Animal (Months)	*Free Stall Size (W x L)*
2 to 7	2 ft 6 in. x 4 ft 6 in.
7 to 12	2 ft 9 in. x 5 ft 0 in.
12 to 18	3 ft 2 in. x 6 ft 0 in.
18 to 24	3 ft 6 in. x 6 ft 9 in.

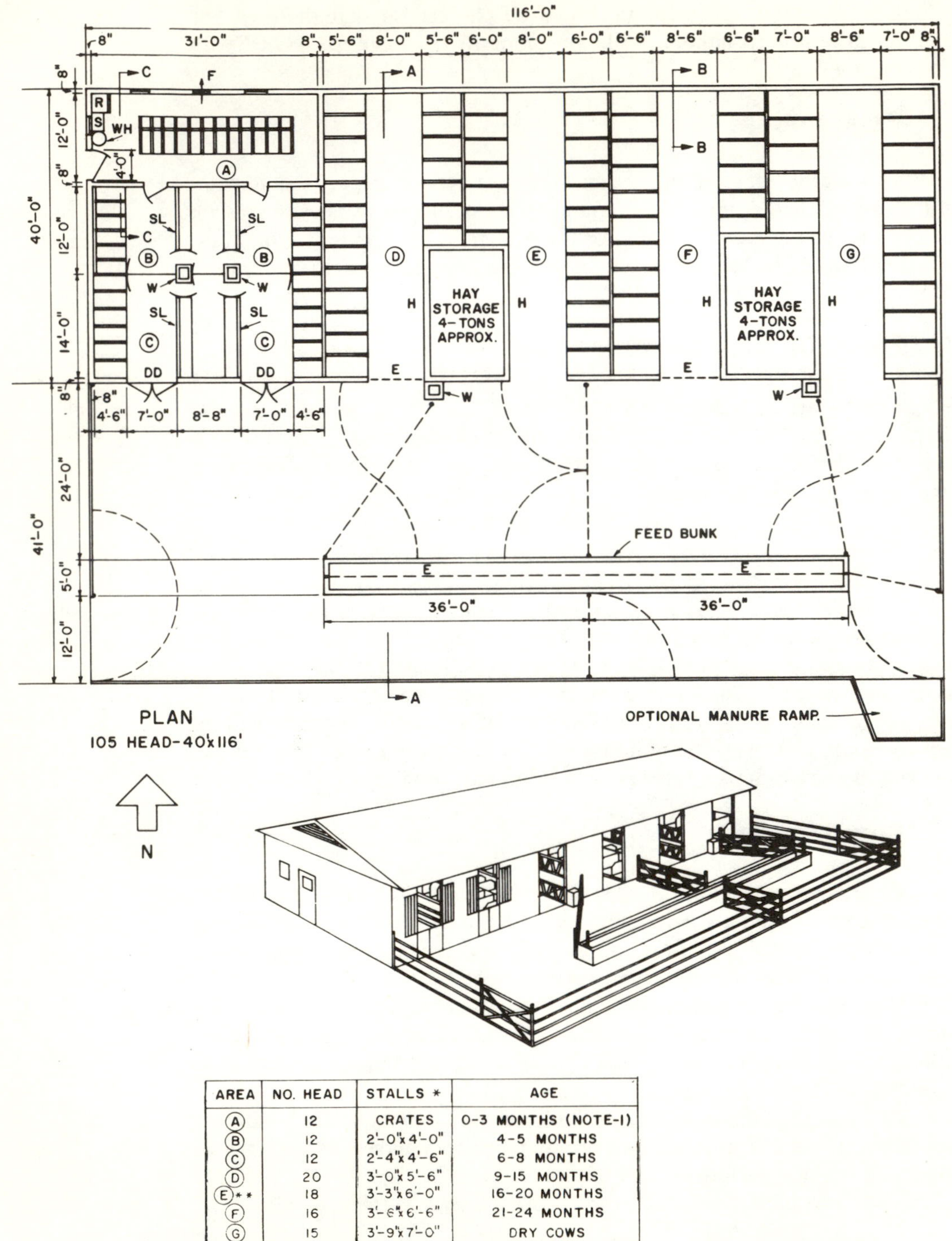

AREA	NO. HEAD	STALLS *	AGE
(A)	12	CRATES	0-3 MONTHS (NOTE-1)
(B)	12	2'-0"x 4'-0"	4-5 MONTHS
(C)	12	2'-4"x 4'-6"	6-8 MONTHS
(D)	20	3'-0"x 5'-6"	9-15 MONTHS
(E)**	18	3'-3"x 6'-0"	16-20 MONTHS
(F)	16	3'-6"x 6'-6"	21-24 MONTHS
(G)	15	3'-9"x 7'-0"	DRY COWS

Figure 8-16. This combination unit contains a nursery area for newborn calves and graduated size free stalls to house animals all the way to maturity. (USDA 6234)

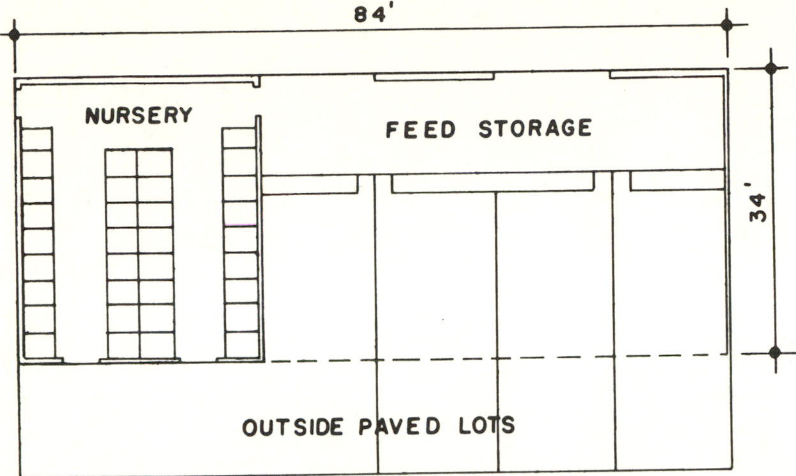

Figure 8-17. This building combines a calf nursery with bedded pack areas for larger animals. The bedded pack offers a lower labor requirement but does take more bedding than the free-stall setup. (University of Missouri)

Ventilation

Natural ventilation systems are satisfactory for buildings used for growing animals. Provide a continuous ridge vent, a continuous 6 inch wide opening under the eave on the north wall, and a partially or fully open south wall. During summer, open up an additional 2 feet at the top of the north wall, using drop down hinged panels.

CHAPTER 9

Poultry

A good poultry house is one which provides optimum environmental conditions for the particular management system at the lowest possible cost. About 30 years ago, a revolution started in the poultry industry. It went from back yard flock operations using manual labor to complete automation and factory-like systems. Housing was a part of this revolution up to a point. A highly cost conscious and competitive industry tended to cut corners when it came to construction, leaving us with a large number of facilities which are not capable of maintaining desired environment and which are proving costly to operate at today's energy costs.

The poultry building being constructed today will have to be more energy efficient than its typical predecessor. The days of 3¢ per gallon LP-gas are gone and it is not unusual to see brooding costs well in excess of 10¢ per bird in buildings considered adequate less than 10 years ago.

There are a wide variety of facilities in use on poultry farms today. Many of these have evolved because of a particular market or climatic conditions existing in the locality. We will attempt to separate buildings into three categories (brooding, growing and egg producing) and outline the fundamental needs of each.

Brooding Facilities

Baby birds have no ability to regulate their body temperatures for the first several days of their lives. This means they must be placed in an environment which is very close to their desired body temperature. Typical brooding schedules call for a 95° F temperature for the first 5 to 7 days, followed by a 5° F per week decrease, down to 55° to 60° F. Although radiant heat systems which heat birds and not the air in the building have been used successfully for brooding, the more common practice is to either heat the entire building to the desired temperature or to provide zone heating.

Positive ventilation must be provided during brooding to control

Figure 9-1. Zone heating is provided by hover type brooders in this turkey brooding building. Ventilation air is being provided through the perforated plastic tube suspended below the ridge of the building.

moisture and supply fresh air for birds to breathe. A minimum rate of 1/8 cfm per pound of body weight is considered adequate during periods when supplemental heaters are in use.

Size

Over the years, poultry houses have gradually increased in width to accommodate both construction techniques and the capabilities of mechanical equipment they house. If we were to survey all the brooding units constructed in the past 10 years, we would find that the preferred width today is about 40 feet. Length will depend on factors such as number of birds to be brooded, capabilities of mechanical feed handling equipment, limitations of the site, and the amount of money available. Very few buildings less than 100 feet long are constructed on commercial poultry farms.

Birds will usually remain in the brooder facility for a minimum of 6 to 7 weeks. In the case of broilers, birds will usually remain in the facility until they are marketed at 9 weeks. Replacement laying chickens may remain in the brooder unit until they are moved directly to the laying house at 20 to 22 weeks. Total floor space required will be based on the needs of the birds at the time they are removed from the unit.

Cages can be used to brood and rear replacement birds for laying flocks. Cages allow a much greater housing density and a somewhat lower risk of disease. They also eliminate the need for litter, permitting a greater variety of choices in manure handling systems. Whether or not they reduce

Table 9-1. **Space Requirements for Poultry Brooding Facilities**

Bird	Required Square Feet per Bird
Chicken	
0 to 4 weeks of age	.5
0 to 9 weeks of age	.9
0 to 20 weeks of age	1.25
Ducks	.5 -1.0
Turkeys	
0 to 7 weeks-hens	1.1
0 to 7 weeks-toms	1.5

labor requirements is a debatable issue. Cages have not adapted well to production of meat birds because of problems with bruising and deformities.

Construction

Poultry brooding units should be constructed using either conventional stud frame or pole frame buildings. Steel frame buildings which are in general usage in the poultry industry are not well adapted to brooding because of the difficulty of installing adequate insulation. Wall height is determined by the size of equipment necessary to clean the building. An 8 foot height is usually selected as a minimum.

Flat ceilings will improve operation of the mechanical ventilation system and make the building easier to insulate. Ceilings can be covered with almost any material which can be easily washed down. Many builders use corrugated metal roofing which can be nailed directly to the lower chords of trusses spaced up to 4 feet on center. Others use exterior sheet rock or plywood fastened to furring strips secured to the trusses. Sidewalls should be protected from birds and mechanical equipment for a distance of at least 2 feet above floor level. Sheet metal or plywood can be used for this purpose.

The building should be fully insulated to keep energy usage at a minimum. For the central Midwest, this means $R = 24$ to 30 for the ceiling and $R = 13$ to 19 in the sidewall. Areas located farther north may be able to justify higher insulation levels, particularly if year-round usage is planned. Provide a polyethylene vapor barrier to protect both wall and ceiling insulation. Exposed concrete around the perimeter of the building requires a 2 inch thickness of expanded polystyrene insulation extending 24 inches below grade to minimize heat loss from this area. Without this perimeter insulation, heat loss from this area will be greater than from the entire frame portion of the wall.

A 4 inch thick layer of concrete provides a satisfactory floor for those buildings where a solid floor is needed. Reinforcing is not necessary unless excessive settling of subgrade is expected.

Ventilation

Exhaust type ventilation systems are most commonly used in conjunction with slot type inlets. Fans providing the minimum ventilation rate should run continuously. A thermostatic control set at 35° to 40° can be used to shut them off in case of a heating system failure. Additional fans sized to provide required winter and summer rates are thermostatically controlled to increase ventilation as needed to maintain desired interior temperatures. Thermostats on these fans should be closely calibrated with heating thermostats to prevent operation of more than minimum ventilation during periods when supplemental heat is on.

Another satisfactory ventilation system is the recirculating fan tube unit. These must also be designed to introduce the required minimum of fresh air and operated to prevent conflict with the heating system.

Heating

The required 95° temperature can be provided as a room temperature with a central heating unit or as zone temperature with individual or central heaters. Most popular is the so called "pancake" hover type unit which is fired with LP-gas. These are suspended from the ceiling and each unit will accommodate about 300 birds. Birds are confined to the heated area for the first 1 to 2 weeks by a temporary fence around the hover.

Hot water boilers can be used either with hovers or as whole room heat sources for the brooder unit. Black iron pipes are suspended along exterior walls to serve as radiators. Conventional finned tubing is not used because it plugs with dust in the poultry environment. Wood or metal hovers can be hinged off the walls above the pipe radiators to provide a heated zone at the floor along one or more walls of the room.

Hot air heaters can also be used to provide room heat in brooder units. If hot air heaters are selected, they must not be of the non-recirculating type. They must be single pass units, bringing in clean outside air, warming it and discharging into the room.

Boilers and other central heating units should be located in a building separate from the brooder unit to minimize the potential for fire. If this is not possible, they should be housed in a separate room with a 1 hour fire rating and be provided with a source of outside air for combustion.

Many producers are reducing energy costs considerably by using a technique known as partial room brooding. Day old or even week old birds do not need all the space designed into a brooding unit. If they are confined to a part of the space (usually one-fourth to one-third of the total) the smaller area can be heated to brooding temperature much more economically. This is often done by using a floor to ceiling sheet of plastic to wall off a portion of the room to be used as a brooding area. As birds reach the point where they need more space and lower temperatures, the temporary wall is removed, giving them access to the entire brooder unit.

Waste Handling

Manure from brooding units is normally handled as a solid since it is relatively low in moisture content. The exception would be cage brooding units where manure is collected without litter in gutters below cages. This manure can be handled either as a solid or a liquid.

Buildings should be provided with access doors large enough to accommodate manure loading equipment. Cleanout is also helped by suspending all equipment from ceilings in such a manner that it can be winched up out of the way at cleaning time.

Special Areas

A small utility room is a desirable addition to the brooding unit. This room should be located so that it serves as an entryway to the bird housing area. Make it large enough to contain a sink with drain board for posting birds, a disinfectant foot bath, equipment for adding medication to water, and some storage area for repair parts.

Electrical Service

Electricity is required for lighting, ventilation, feed handling equipment, and possibly heating in the brooding unit. Except for units with electric heat, total demand is not high and can probably be handled with a distribution panel fed from the main service entrance.

Poultry require a relatively low light intensity. This can usually be provided by 25 watt incandescent bulbs located on 10 foot centers.

Growing Buildings

The growing and/or finishing building for poultry is usually associated with turkey production. Turkeys have a relatively longer life cycle to market and a rapidly changing space demand. Grower buildings meet the changing need for space with lower cost construction. They can also provide the desired environment for larger birds. As construction and energy costs continue to rise, we may see the growing building become a practical system for other poultry operations also.

Size

The 40 foot width is the generally accepted standard for both growing and finishing buildings, as it is for brooding. Length is determined by the square footage required to accommodate birds from the brooding unit.

A wall height of eight feet is generally adequate to provide clearance for manure handling equipment.

It is desirable to locate growing buildings adjacent to brooding units if at all possible. This facilitates driving of birds from one unit to the other, reducing labor considerably.

Table 9-2. **Space Requirements for Growing Turkeys**

Age	Space in Sq Ft per Bird Hens	Toms
7 to 13 weeks		
Light breeds	1.75	3
Heavy breeds	2.25	4
13 weeks to market		
Light breeds	3	5
Heavy breeds	4	6

Construction

Metal frame and pole frame buildings are most suitable for growing units. For year-round use in northern climates, both roof and wall areas should be insulated. An R value of 9 to 12 in both ceiling and sidewall will contain enough body heat from the birds to promote efficient gains. Buildings designed for summer only usage need only light insulation in roof areas to reduce radiant heat load.

Sidewall height of 8 feet is adequate for equipment access. Paved floors are not generally used in growing units.

Ventilation

Both mechanical and natural ventilation systems are used successfully in growing buildings. Natural ventilation systems either omit sidewall covering altogether in warm climates or leave a 3 to 4 foot continuous

Figure 9-2. These ducks are being grown out in a relatively low-cost metal frame building with natural ventilation during summer months. The perforated plastic tubes are used for ventilation in fall, winter, and spring when sidewall curtains are closed.

opening covered by an adjustable curtain. Natural ventilation systems frequently provide large circulating fans inside the building to help relieve heat stress by blowing air over birds during extremely hot weather.

Mechanical ventilation systems use exhaust fans and slot inlets to provide a maximum of about 1 cfm per pound of bird weight. Evaporative cooling systems may also be incorporated into mechanical ventilation systems. Evaporative coolers either pull or push ventilating air through porous pads which are continuously wet with water. Evaporation can cool ventilation several degrees, particularly in the southwestern parts of the U.S. where humidities are relatively low. They are much less effective in locations where high humidities often accompany hot weather.

Birds depend on evaporation of moisture from their lungs to remove much of their body heat. High relative humidities caused by evaporative coolers have a negative effect on this process. For this reason, most research has shown that evaporative coolers are helpful in relieving extreme heat stress, but do not improve bird performance under conditions of extreme temperatures.

Waste Handling

Waste from grower buildings is handled as a solid. It is common practice to use floor buildup as a storage area with disposal being done on an as needed or as land is available for spreading basis. This type of storage requires careful attention to management. Waterers must be well maintained to prevent leakage and wet or caked spots which develop must be broken up. Many producers use a rototiller as a regular part of their manure management program.

Egg Production Buildings

While eggs produced by breeding flocks still use floor management systems, nearly all of the edible eggs today are produced by birds housed in cages. Cages provide several advantages to the egg producer. Among these are the following:

- Higher bird density allowing greater numbers of birds in a given building.
- Lower building insulation requirements.
- Complete mechanization of feed, water, and egg collection is possible.
- Litter is not required, reducing both operating cost and amount of waste to be handled.
- Improved egg quality.

A number of cage systems have been developed and used over the past 20 years. In early days, the colony type cage was popular among many

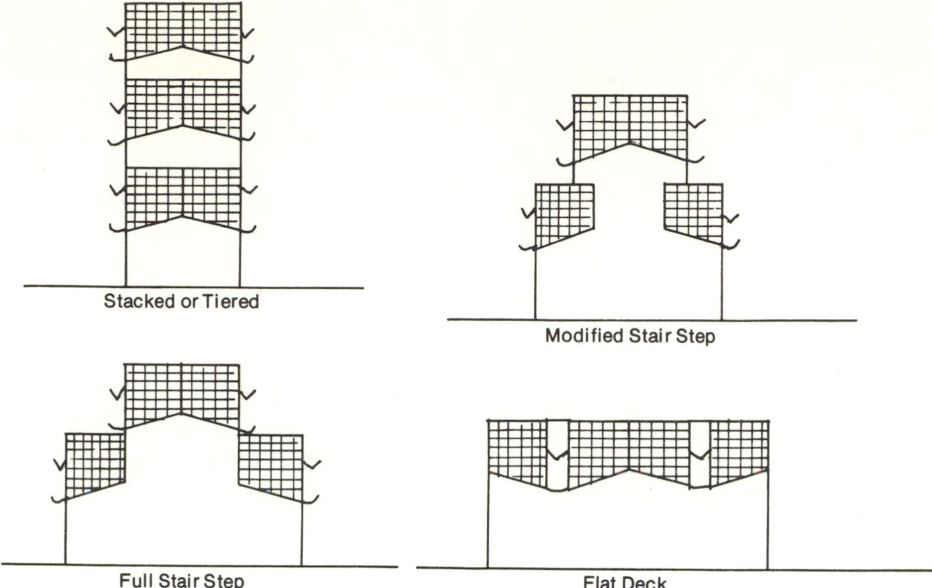

Figure 9-3. Cross-sectional views of different cage types. From top to bottom they are: tiered, stair step, modified stair step, and flat deck.

producers. This was a relatively large cage that held 8 to 10 or even more birds. Later developments showed that smaller cages with fewer birds resulted in higher production. Today, most cages will have about 1.5 square feet of floor space and hold 3 to 4 birds, depending on breed and the particular management system used. Cage systems are generally classified on the basis of how they are arranged in the building. Most common are tiered, flat deck, stair step, and modified stair step arrangements.

Size

Building width will be dependent upon the particular type of cage arrangement selected and to some extent, on who makes the cages. For this reason, it is important to settle on a supplier for the equipment and a particular model early in the planning process for the cage laying building.

Length will depend on the desired size of the operation or possibly limitations of the building site. The most economical length will be that which fully utilizes the drive units associated with feed, egg and manure handling. Building lengths of 400+ feet are not uncommon in the industry. A wall height of 8 feet will accommodate most cage systems.

Construction

Both type of building and degree of enclosure vary widely, depending on climate. Buildings in southern areas frequently are pole supported roof structures with only a minimal amount of insulation to cut down on summer heat. They may or may not have roll down sidewall curtains to help prevent freezing and bird stress during cold periods. In northern states, buildings are usually pole frame or conventional stud frame construction with sidewall and ceiling insulation and mechanical ventilation. For the northeast and midwestern states, insulation levels of R = 9 to 12 are suggested for sidewalls and R = 12 to 16 for ceilings. Lower amounts can be used with the high density 3 and 4 tier cage systems.

Flat ceilings and tight construction are desirable for mechanically ventilated units, but not needed with natural ventilation. Interior surfaces should be cleanable, but need not be particularly strong since they are not exposed directly to birds. A protective rail or covering for the lower portion of the walls will reduce the mechanical damage from feed or egg collection carts, if used.

Roof systems need special attention if cages are suspended from the ceiling. The weight of cages and birds will frequently require at least a doubling of the normal roof design capability. This means using specially designed trusses and often changes in sidewall support to provide adequate structural capability.

Floors in cage buildings are usually constructed of poured concrete with manure collection gutters being cast into the floor area beneath the cages. Collection gutters need to be sized to accommodate the type of removal system being installed in them.

Ventilation

Exhaust fans with adjustable slot inlets have proven to be the most effective type of mechanical ventilation system for cage laying houses. Natural ventilation can be used during summer months or year-round in warmer climates. Tiered cages tend to restrict air flow through buildings and may cause problems for naturally ventilated systems, particularly on hot, still summer days.

Waste Handling

Manure from cage systems is a solid, semi solid or liquid, depending on the species of bird, time of year, and feeding program. It can be moved from the collection areas with mechanical scrapers or gutter flush systems. One thousand birds will produce about 1.25 cubic feet of manure per day. After removal from the building, waste can either be stored in a liquid manure tank or removed directly to fields for disposal. If manure storage tanks are used, they should be emptied completely whenever spreading is done. Poultry manure contains relatively high amounts of calcium, as well as a certain number of broken egg shells. If the tank is not emptied completely, the calcium and egg shells tend to build up as a solid in the bottom of the tank. Removal of this buildup is extremely difficult.

One unique manure system, developed in the state of Maine, utilized a two story building design with manure collection and storage in the lower level. Referred to as a "deep pit" system, the lower story is constructed

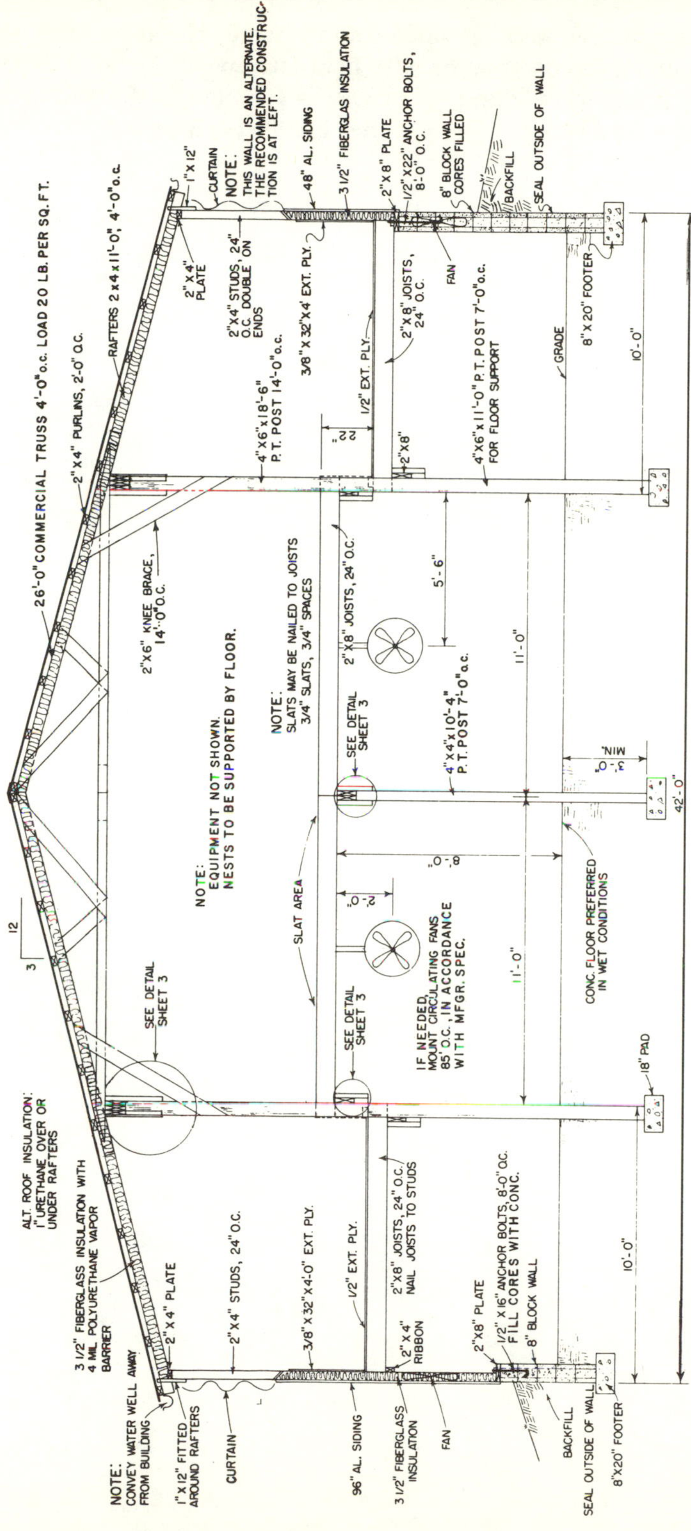

Figure 9-4. Section view of a building with a deep pit manure-handling system and a slotted floor for either broiler or egg production. (USDA 6235)

much the same as a walkout basement in a home. The upper level is conventional stud-frame construction with light framing at the normal floor level to support walk ways between the cage rows. Manure is allowed to collect in the pit area for a year or more and then handled as a solid.

CHAPTER 10

Horses

Horses represent one of the more rapidly increasing segments of the American livestock industry. Unlike most livestock production, however, most of this growth is not taking place on commercial farms. It is occurring in suburbs and in rural areas surrounding our cities. Because of this, and the fact that horses usually represent a recreational enterprise, the design and construction of facilities will vary from the normal agricultural building. Areas which require extra attention and advance planning include the following:

Budget allocation. In most cases horses do not produce income which can offset facilities cost. Careful budget analysis is necessary to set a limit on how much you can afford to spend.

Manure storage and disposal. People who live in suburban settings are usually not accustomed to either the sight of, or odor from, livestock manure. Make sure you will be able to handle this problem satisfactorily before you start.

Building style and appearance should complement surrounding buildings. This may not result in the least cost design.

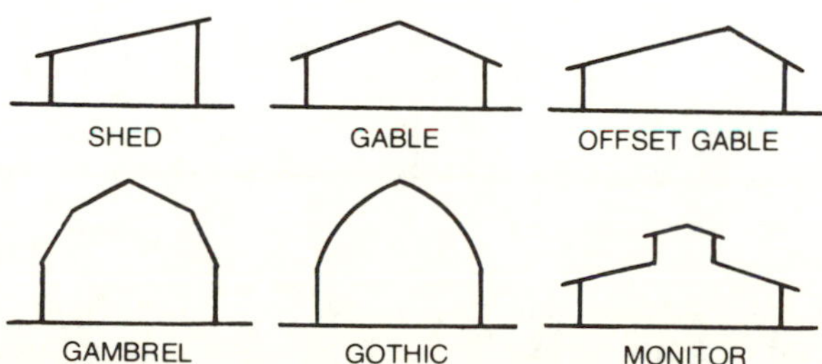

Figure 10-1. Horse barns can be constructed in several different ways to obtain an appearance that fits in well with surrounding structures. Several of the possible shapes are depicted above. (Granite City Steel)

Investigate building codes, zoning ordinances, and any possible covenants or deed restrictions which may affect keeping of horses.

This chapter is divided into two general areas. The first deals with building requirements of the horse and ways to meet these for a small number of animals appropriate to one or two families. The second outlines space requirements and building types for commercial horse enterprises.

Small Private Facilities

The horse is a remarkable animal. Give him a little protection from the extremely cold winter winds and some summer shade and he will do very nicely without ever going into a building at all. In fact, most horse buildings are built primarily to provide some degree of comfort for the horse owner and a place to store feed and tack. The main exception to this is the show horse which must be kept inside in order to maintain the appearance and hair coat desired in the show ring.

Size

Overall size of your building will depend on three things: the number of horses, how much feed and hay storage you need, and whether or not you want to include a tack room. Suggested stall sizes for individual animals can be found in Table 10-1. The very least width of a building would be that required to contain a single stall or row of stalls. This would probably be 10 to 12 feet. A single row of stalls plus a service alley would require an 18 to 20 foot wide building. A tack room suitable for 2 to 3 horses can be located in an 8 by 10 foot room. Hay, grain and bedding stor-

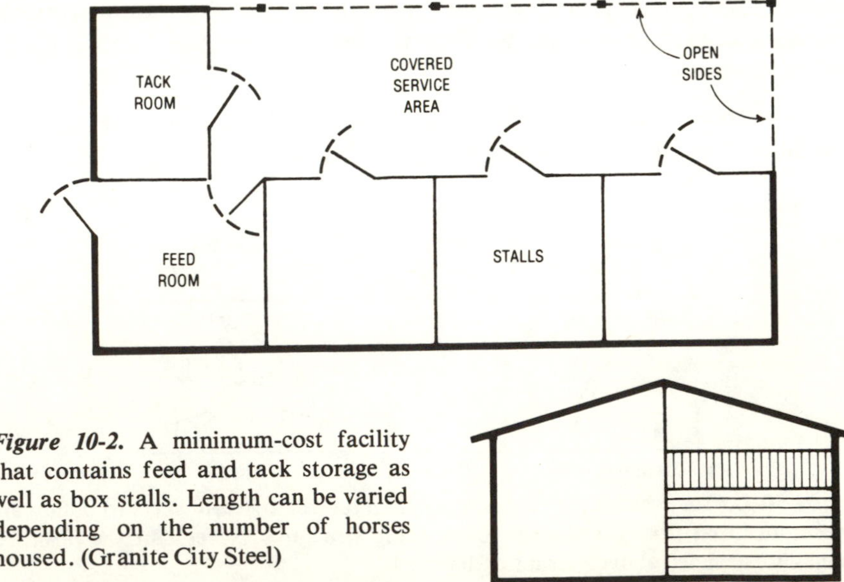

Figure 10-2. A minimum-cost facility that contains feed and tack storage as well as box stalls. Length can be varied depending on the number of horses housed. (Granite City Steel)

age requirements will depend on how often you plan to purchase them. A 1,000 pound riding horse will require 5 to 7 pounds of grain and about 10 pounds of hay per day. Baled hay will weigh about 10 pounds per cubic foot.

Table 10-1. **Suggested Box Stall Sizes for Individual Animals**

Animal	Stall Size (Feet)
Mature horse	
Small— 900 lbs	10x10
1,100 lbs	10x12
1,400 lbs	12x12
Foal up to 2 yrs old	10x10
Stallion	14x14
Pony	9x9

Construction

There is a wide variety of buildings which can be adapted to housing for a few horses. The most popular and economical to construct is the pole frame building. It is, however, not easily adapted to all styles of building. Building styles to which pole frame is adaptable include shed, gable, and offset gable or salt box designs. The classic styles such as gambrel, gothic, and monitor are more adapted to conventional stud frame construction with masonry foundations.

Wall height should provide an interior clearance of 8 to 9 feet if horses are not to be mounted inside. A horse and rider will require a minimum of 12 feet clearance.

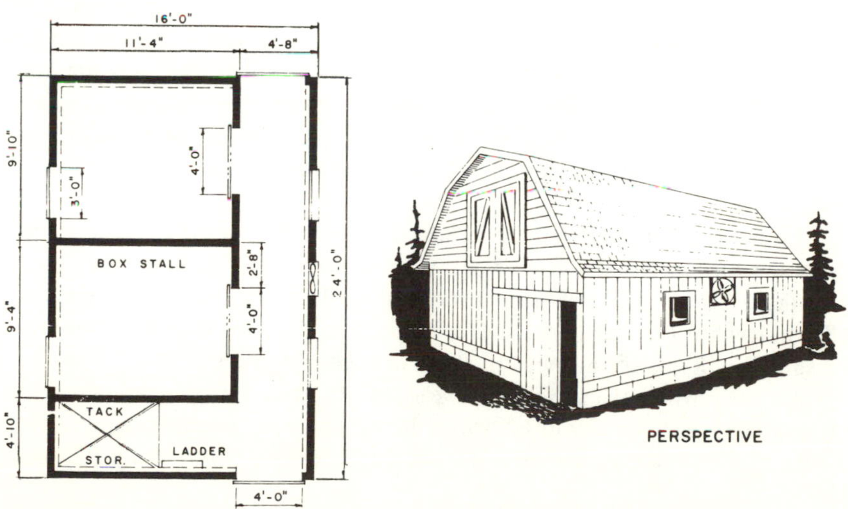

Figure 10-3. An attractive gambrel roofed barn to house two horses with overhead room for storing hay. This type building fits in well in most suburban areas. (USDA 6262)

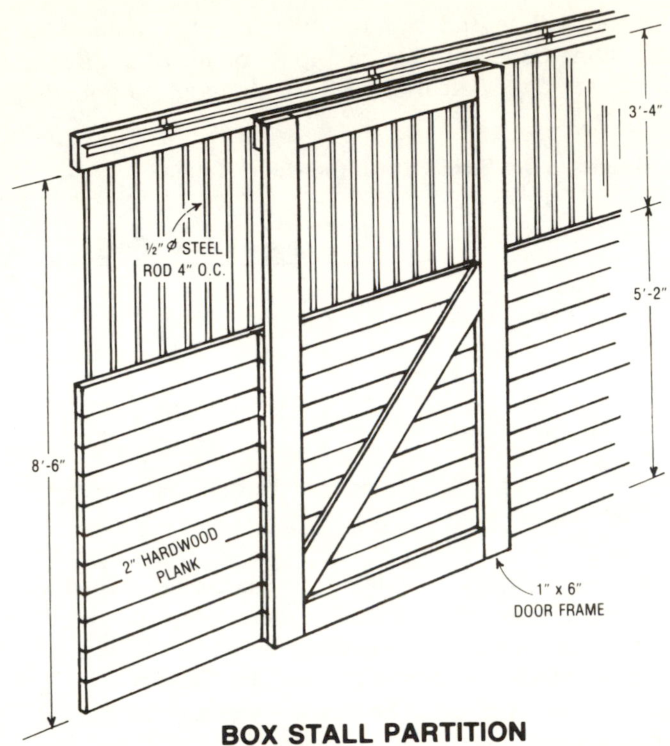

Figure 10-4. Partitions and interior linings need to be sturdily constructed to withstand occasional kicking. You should also avoid sharp corners and rough edges, which can cause injuries. (Granite City Steel)

Insulation is not required unless there is a need to keep inside temperatures above freezing in winter. If metal roofing is used, a layer of rigid insulation immediately under the roofing will reduce summer heat load in the building and help prevent condensation from forming during winter.

Walls of the building which form part of the stall area should be covered with 2 inch thick solid planking to a height of 6 feet above the floor. The bottom plank which contacts the ground should be pressure treated with a wood preservative.

Stall partitions and fronts should also be constructed of solid 2 inch thick planking with metal grille work at the top, if desired. There are several manufacturers of stall partition brackets, grille work, door hangers, and other hardware for horse stalls. If you plan to do your own construction, these items will greatly simplify the stall fabrication process.

Floors in the barn should be made up of a 4 to 6 inch layer of packed clay placed over a well-drained gravel base. The only exception is the feed storage and tack areas, where a 4 inch thick concrete floor may be desirable.

Ventilation

Natural ventilation is used in all but heated horse barns. A continuous opening 2-4 inches wide under the eaves, combined with a continuous ridge ventilator, will provide adequate winter ventilation. If the roof has less than 2 feet of overhang, consider placing a baffle or closable door over the eave opening on the side facing prevailing winter winds. This will aid in keeping out blowing snow during winter storms. For summer, provide an openable panel or window in each stall with an equivalent opening on the opposite side of the barn. The bottom of the panel or window should be a minimum of 6 feet above the floor. Windows in stall areas should be covered with a protective grille.

A mechanical ventilation system and supplemental heat must be provided in warm housing. Either pressure or exhaust type systems can be used. A minimum rate of 25 cfm per 1,000 pounds of animal weight is required during periods when supplemental heat is used. A total fan capacity of 100 cfm per 1,000 pounds of weight will be adequate for normal fall, winter and spring seasons. Natural ventilation is used in warm barns during summer months.

Waste Handling

Horse manure and waste bedding is handled as a solid. The most desirable situation is to provide for immediate disposal as stalls are cleaned. For periods of bad weather, provide 10 to 12 square feet of fenced storage per animal and dispose of manure as soon as possible. During summer months, manure storage must be limited to 4 to 5 days or it will develop into a fly breeding area.

Electrical

Needs of the small barn are minimal and can usually be provided by a single circuit from the main service panel. Provide lights for general illumination of stalls, alleys, tack room and storage areas. Incandescent fixtures are preferred since they will perform under all temperature extremes. Select recessed fixtures or fixtures with metal guards to minimize the possibility of breakage by animals.

Locate a 100 watt light over the center of each stall and at 12 to 15 foot intervals along the alley. Provide at least one light in the tack room and in the feed storage area. If you do not have adequate yard lighting, consider installing an outside light on the horse barn to help light the approach area. Install one or two convenience outlets along the alleyway to provide power for grooming equipment.

Commercial Horse Facilities

Many individuals who own horses have no place of their own to keep them. Others, who enjoy riding and working with horses, have no desire to own an animal of their own. A large number of commercial stables cater to the needs and desires of these people all over the United States.

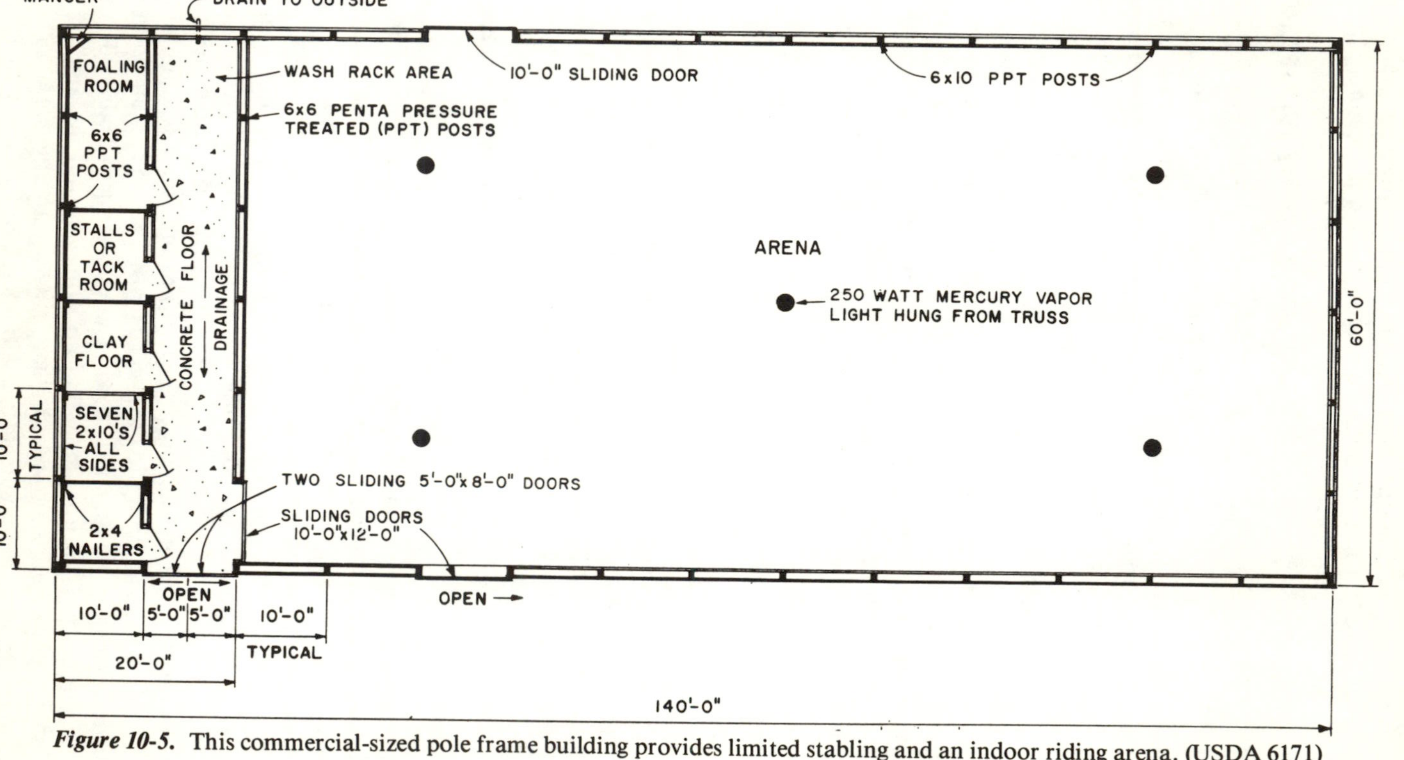

Figure 10-5. This commercial-sized pole frame building provides limited stabling and an indoor riding arena. (USDA 6171)

In many respects, a commercial housing unit is just a large version of an individual stable. They must, however, satisfy a different set of requirements. Floor plans must be developed to accommodate larger equipment needed to handle larger volumes of feed and manure. Also, many governing bodies and almost all insurance companies classify these units as commercial and public occupancy buildings. This means they must conform to an entirely different set of design and construction standards. We do not propose to get into the design detail required to satisfy your local government or your insurance agent. You will have to take those issues up with them; hopefully before you start construction. We will be presenting some basic data and arrangements which have proven helpful to individuals who have previously constructed facilities of this type.

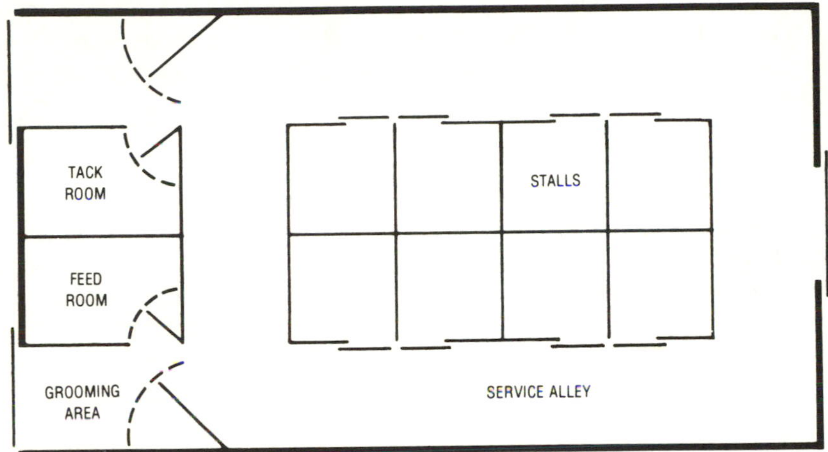

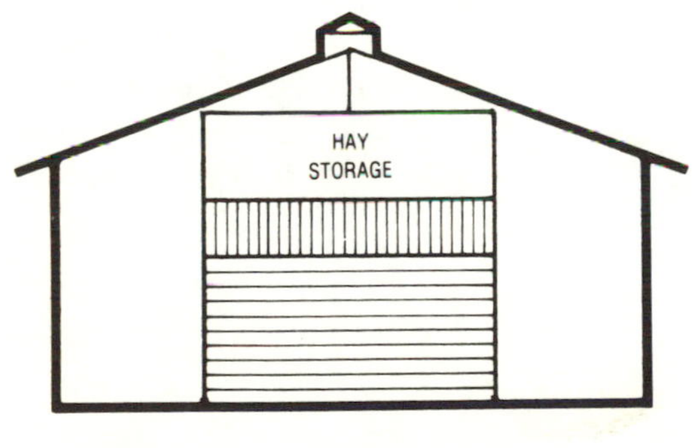

Figure 10-6. A layout of this type can be used for a commercial boarding stable. If the walls are made high enough, the perimeter alley can be used as an indoor riding or exercise area. Some stable operators prefer not to store hay in the same barn with horses because of the fire danger. (Granite City Steel)

Size

Overall building size will depend on the number of animals to be housed and/or its other uses. Stall requirements for individual horses will be the same as those in Table 10-2.

Alleys in larger barns should be at least 10 feet wide to allow access by manure removal equipment.

At least one room for storage of concentrate feed should be provided. A separate building is desirable for storage of hay and bedding material.

Table 10-2. **Sizes for Tie Stalls for Horses***

Animal	Stall Size (Feet)
Mature horse	
Medium—1,100 lbs	5x9
Large —1,400 lbs	5x12
Foal to 2 yrs old	4-½x9
Pony	3x6

**Listed size includes manger area.*

This will reduce the possibility of fire and should save on insurance rates.

Provide a centrally located tack room large enough to accommodate all of the equipment you plan to own. An alternative would be to construct several small tack rooms at different locations in the barn. These can be as small as 4 by 6 feet and can be rented to persons boarding horses with you. Each of the smaller units should be lockable to provide a measure of security.

Construction

Construction is essentially the same as for smaller units, with the exception of changes needed to meet building codes or insurance requirements. Most buildings are either metal frame or post frame construction and are operated as cold buildings. Structures used as riding arenas should have a minimum wall height of 16 feet.

Special Areas

At least one building in the commercial horse complex should contain a small insulated and heated area to house bathroom and office facilities. A 20 by 20 foot area will be adequate to accommodate a 10 by 12 foot office, two bathrooms and a small utility area. This area should be located so that anyone in the office will be able to view both arriving customers and activities in the stable area.

CHAPTER 11

Livestock Handling Facilities

Every livestock farm needs some type of handling facilities to help with sorting, treating, and loading or unloading of animals. Unfortunately, these facilities don't usually get very high priority on the needs list and many farmers are unaware of the benefits of a good set of facilities. Well designed and well constructed facilities save time, reduce injuries to both animals and handlers, and make the job of working animals a routine chore.

General Construction

Components of handling facilities must be capable of taking a considerable amount of abuse. This means using heavy duty construction techniques and durable materials. Posts used to support fences should be set a minimum of 3 feet into the ground and back filled with well tamped earth, or better yet, concrete. Space posts a maximum of 6 feet apart. Planking between posts should be either full inch thick rough sawn material or nominal 2 inch dressed lumber. All lumber should be pressure treated to resist rot. If you use a welded pipe assembly, minimum size should be 1-½ inch pipe. Hinges, latches, and other accessories need to be selected on the basis of sturdiness and durability, not necessarily cost.

Working facilities need to be located on a well drained site, particularly if they will be used on a year-round basis. Concrete paving is not necessary; however, it will eliminate any mud problems and make it easier to handle animals that have been used to concrete floors. A 4 inch thickness is sufficient. Slope any paving at least ¼ inch per foot to prevent accumulation of water.

Swine Facilities

Many swine farms will need two sets of working facilities: one for assembling and sorting of market hogs, and the other for handling of the breeding herd.

Market hog handling facilities require the following components.

- Holding area capable of holding at least one pen of hogs from the finishing floor or building.
- Crowd area to direct hogs into chutes for sorting and loading.
- Holding pen for animals to be shipped. This pen should hold at least one truck load of market animals.
- Holding pen for hogs to be returned to the finishing building.
- Loading chute to accommodate truck or trailer used to move animals to market.

Breeding herd facilities are designed primarily for directing and restraining animals for pregnancy checks and treatment. Components include:

- Collection area to hold 1 group of sows. This pen should have some type of funnel arrangement at one end to direct animals into the chute.
- Working chute. A 12 to 16 foot long chute with a head gate at the end and a blocking gate about 4 feet behind the head gate. The working chute should be 18 to 20 inches wide and have solid sides 36 inches high. Provide a gate between the head gate and blocking gate to allow for access to the sow for pregnancy testing.
- Holding pens for culls and for animals to be returned to the breeding herd.
- Loading chute. If it is not convenient to move animals to the market-hog load-out area or in the case of feeder pig operations, a loading chute is a desirable addition to breeding herd facilities.

There are dozens of different arrangements possible for components of swine handling systems, none of which will be best for all farms. Several layouts which we have found effective are illustrated in Figures 11-1 through 11-5. The best way to evaluate these is to take a pencil and trace

Table 11-1. **General Specifications for Swine Handling Facilities**

Item	Market Hogs	Breeding Animals
Fence height minimum	32 in.	36 in.
Chute width	16 in.	20 in.
Crowd area per animal	6 sq ft	8 sq ft
Holding pen area per animal	6 sq ft	8 sq ft
Loading chute side wall ht	36 in.	42 in.
Loading chute width	16 in. to 18 in.	20 in. to 24 in.

N
SICK PEN
CHUTE
MARKET
HOGS
CUT
GATES
TAILENDERS
FEEDER
HOLDING
PEN
SERVICE
ALLEY

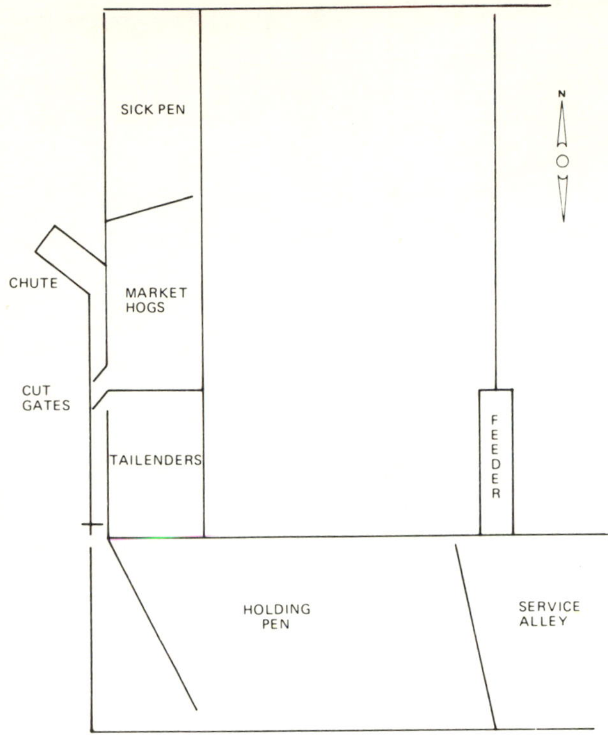

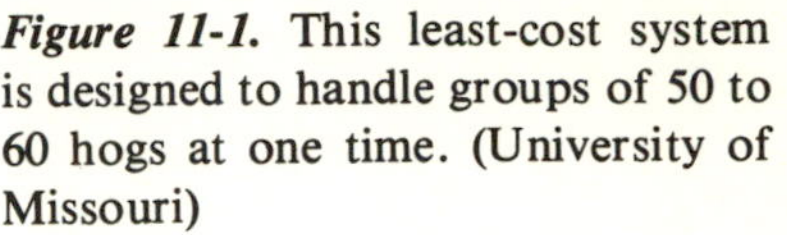

Figure 11-1. This least-cost system is designed to handle groups of 50 to 60 hogs at one time. (University of Missouri)

N
FEEDER
FEEDER
REMOVABLE GATE
MARKET HOGS
TAILENDERS
12'
SERVICE
ALLEY
HOLDING PEN
CUT GATE
TRAFFIC
APPROACH
MAN
GATE
CALLER'S
GATE
CHUTE
ALLEY - 16" WIDE
CHUTE - 20" WIDE
HALF-CIRCLE CROWD
8' RADIUS (10' - 12' PREFERRED)

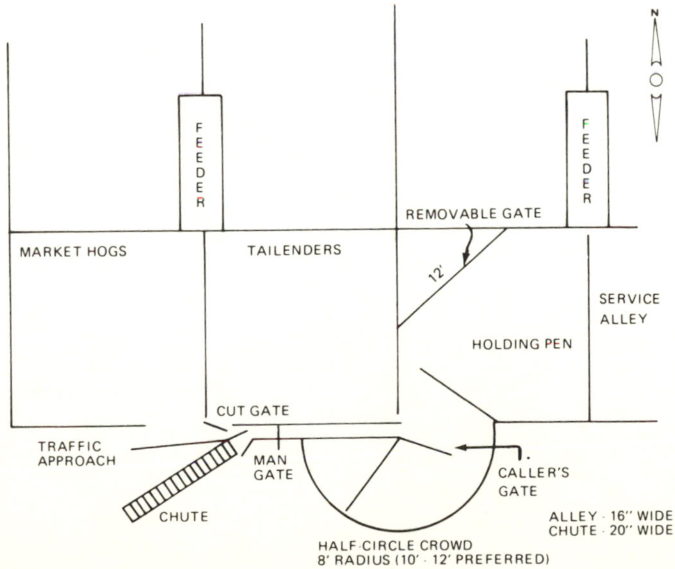

Figure 11-2. This layout features a half-circle crowd with a capacity of about 30 market hogs. It also makes use of the finishing floor service alley as a holding pen. (University of Missouri)

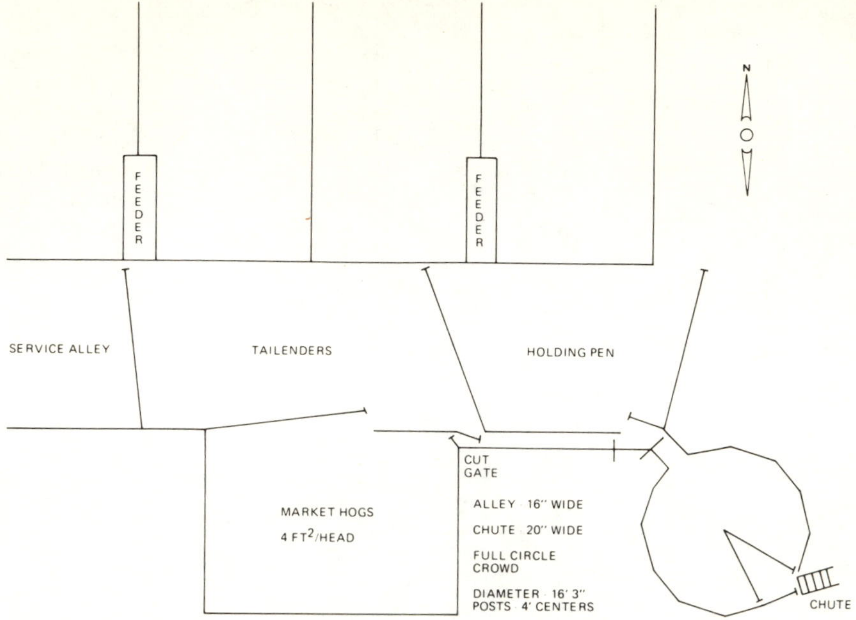

Figure 11-3. Sixty-hog capacity with full-circle crowd is completely separate from the finishing floor system. (University of Missouri)

Figure 11-4. This system provides space for a scale in addition to sorting pens and a circle crowd. (University of Missouri)

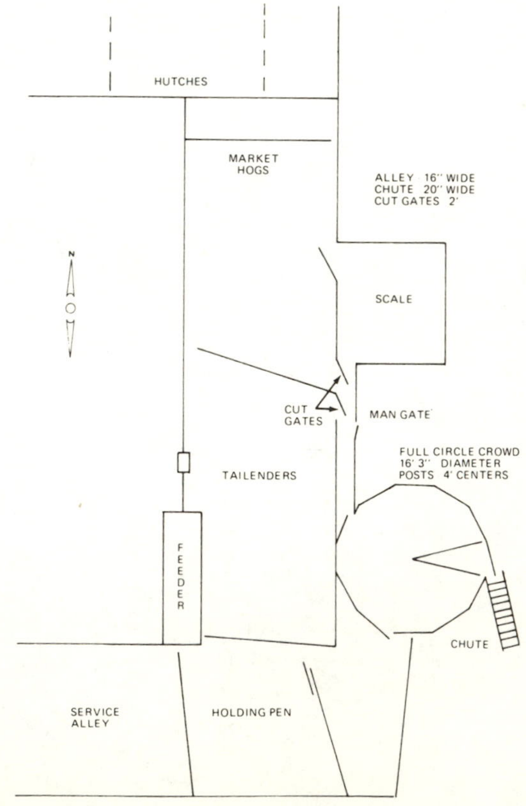

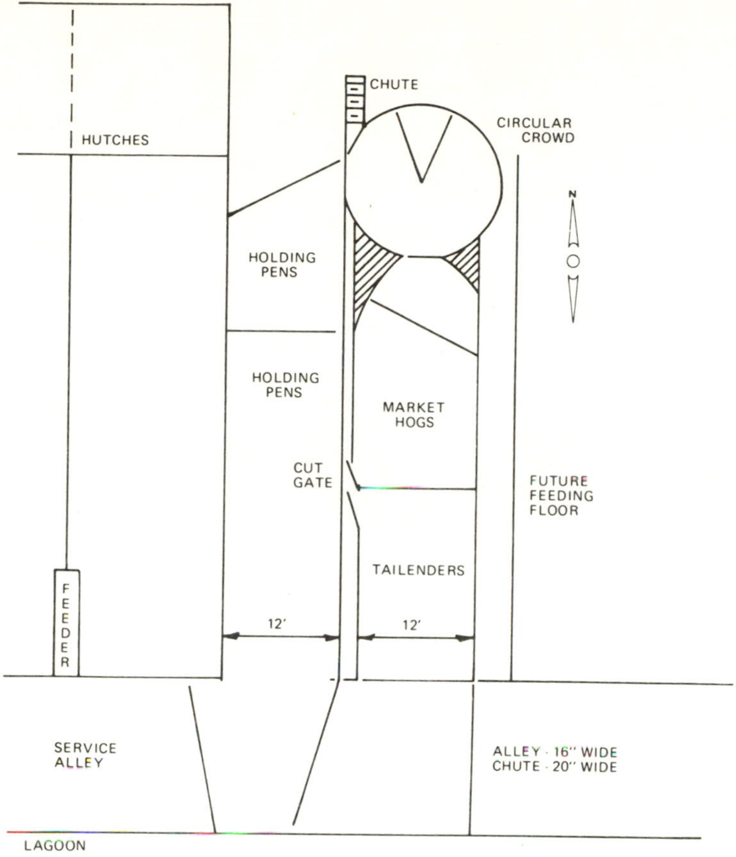

Figure 11-5. This design will accommodate groups of up to 120 market hogs at a time and provides for a three-way sort. (University of Missouri)

animal movement through the facility. Compare this with the way you presently work to see if the layout presents any bottlenecks. If it does, go on to the next system or try to rearrange components into a workable unit for your farm.

Beef Facilities

The basic part of every cattle handling facility is the working chute. Minimum length for a working chute is about 20 feet. The basic chute is equipped with a head gate and some type of crowding arrangement to force cattle into the chute. Larger herds will also need holding and sorting pens, a cutting gate, and a permanent loading chute.

The working chute should be 24 inches wide (28 to 32 inches if it will be used for larger cows). A 4 inch concrete floor in the chute area will eliminate mud problems. The lower half of the chute walls need to be solid construction to prevent animals from sticking legs through the sides.

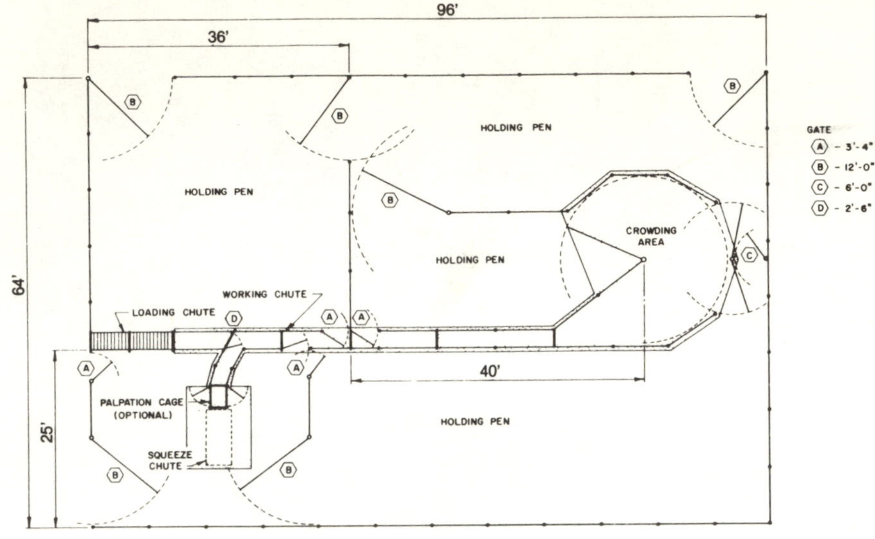

PLAN VIEW

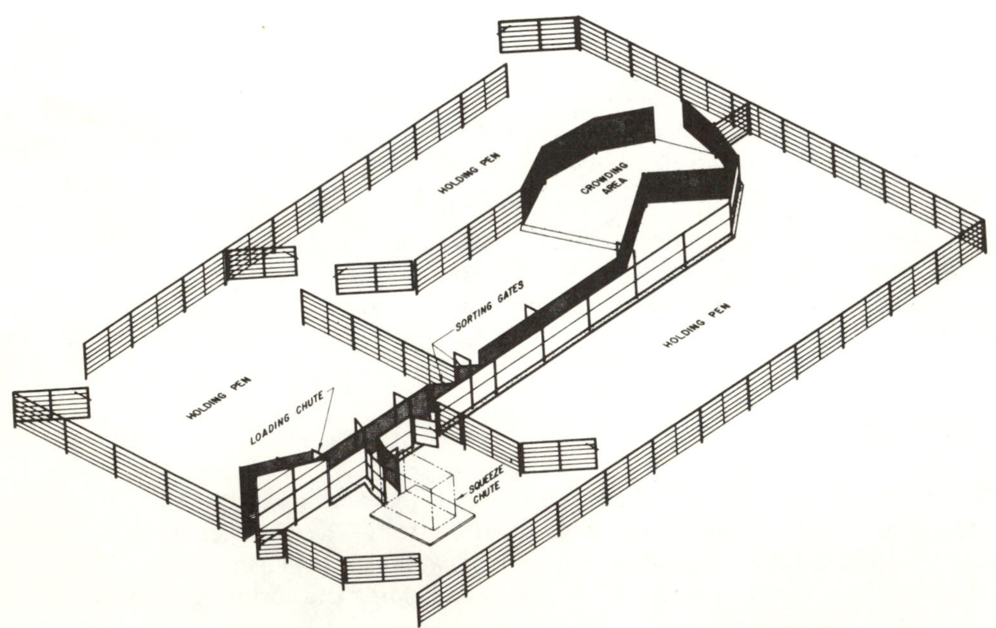

Figure 11-6. Corral and working facility. (USDA 6230)

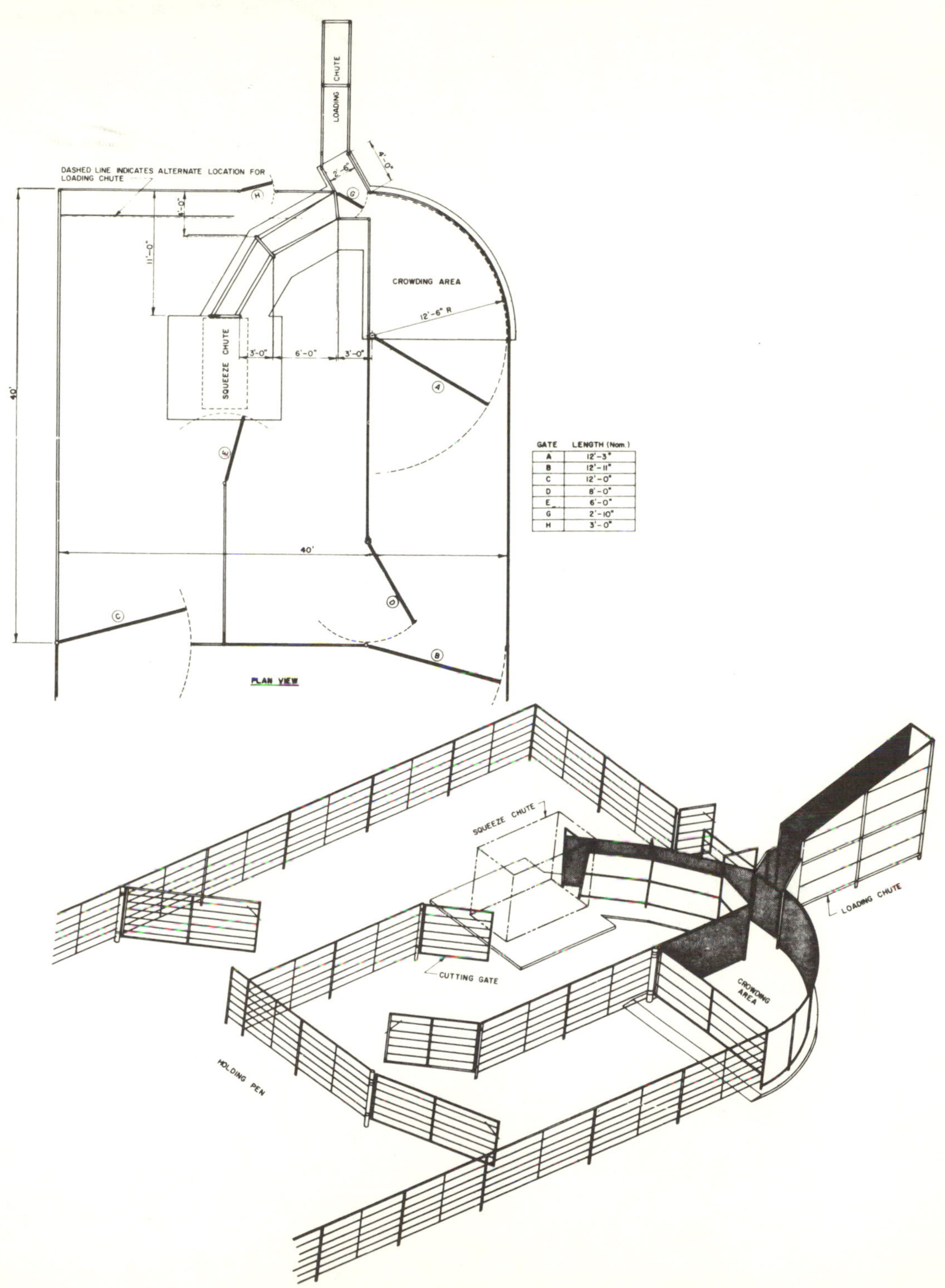

GATE	LENGTH (Nom.)
A	12'-3"
B	12'-11"
C	12'-0"
D	8'-0"
E	6'-0"
G	2'-10"
H	3'-0"

Figure 11-7. Corral with quarter-circle crowd. (USDA 6230)

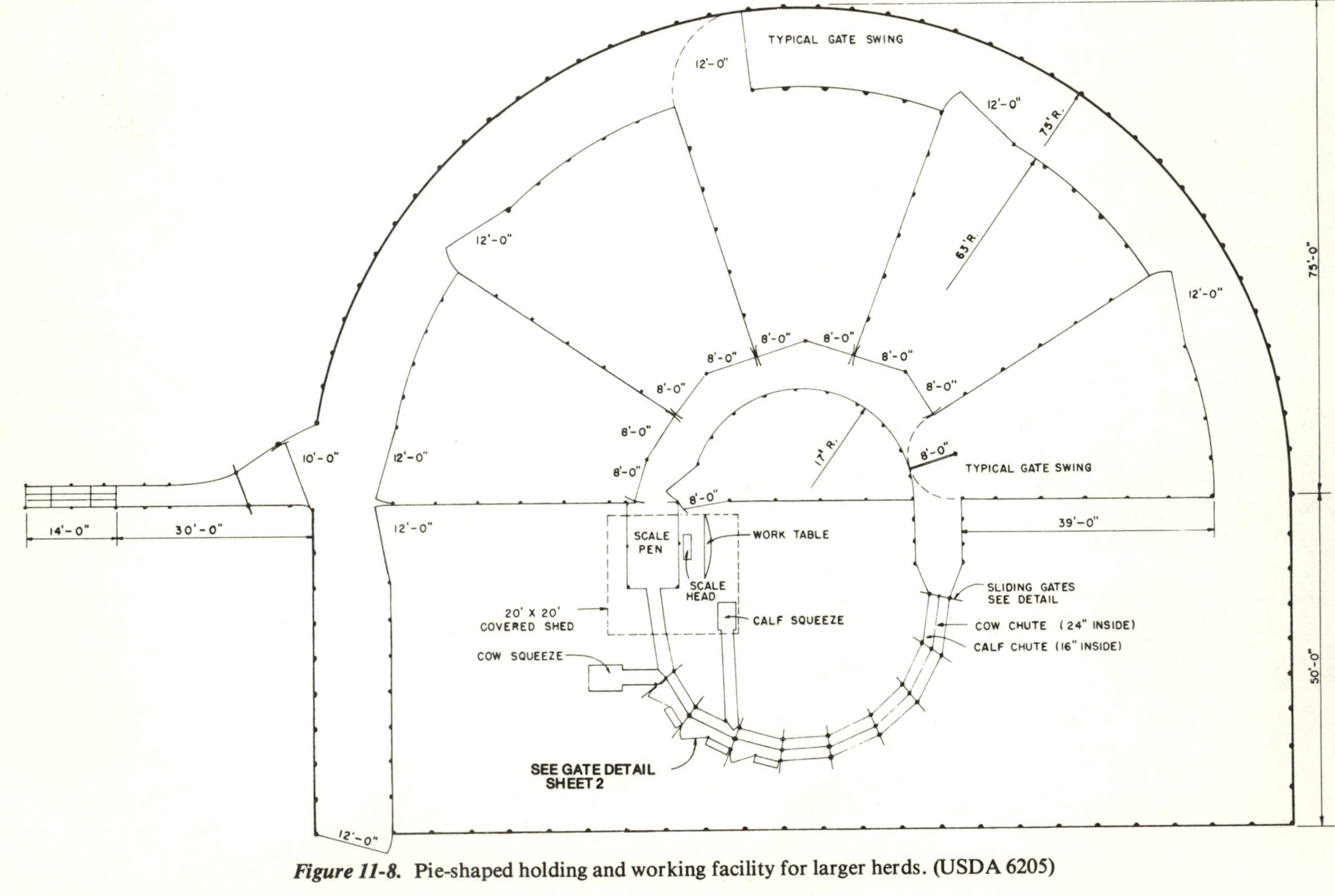

Figure 11-8. Pie-shaped holding and working facility for larger herds. (USDA 6205)

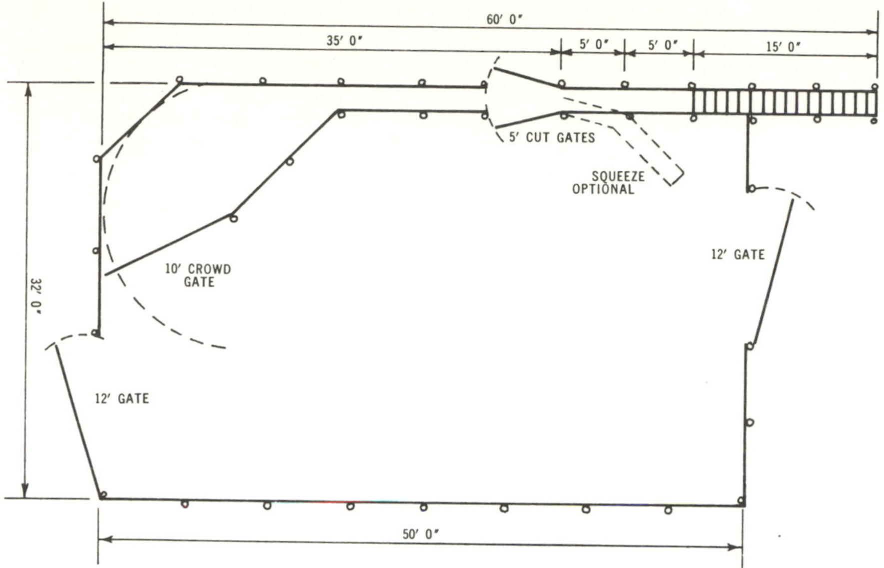

Figure 11-9. Handling unit for the smaller herd (50 to 100-feeder steer capacity). (Granite City Steel)

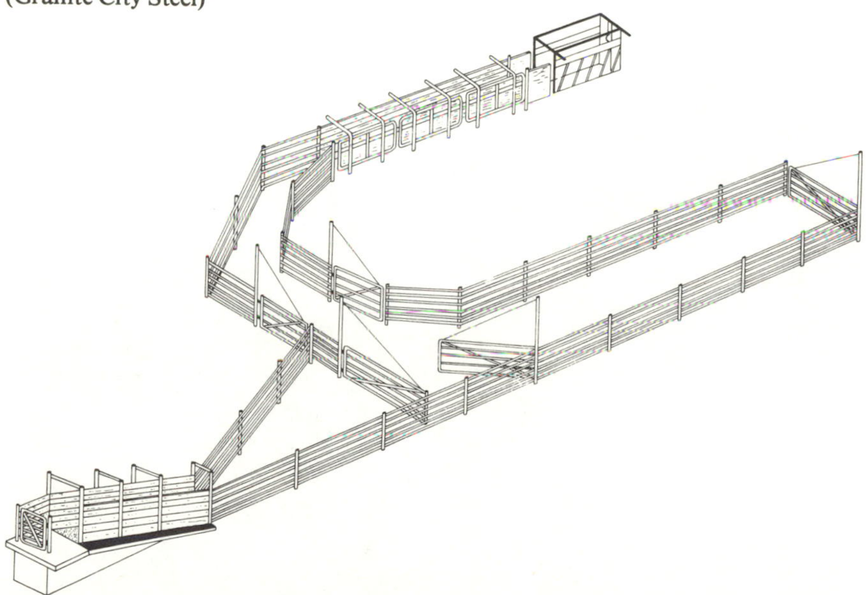

Figure 11-10. "Y" shaped unit originally developed in Oregon. (USDA 6204)

Headgates can be either purchased or farm constructed using wood or steel. Locate a hinged gate next to the headgate to permit greater access to the animal and for releasing the animal. A blocking gate placed 8 to 10 feet behind the headgate will provide a working area for pregnancy testing and examinations. Locate man pass gates 16 to 18 inches wide adjacent to head and tail working areas. Elevated walk ways along one or both sides of the working chute will help in moving animals through the unit and in some treatment procedures.

Safety is a primary consideration when designing cattle handling facilities. Make sure your facilities are built so that there is a substantial fence between you and the animal whenever he is not completely restrained. If this is not possible, make sure there are at least two escape routes from any area occupied by both people and animals.

Examples of different working facilities for cattle are shown in Figures 11-6 through 11-10.

Table 11-2. **General Specifications for Cattle Handling Facilities**

Item	Size
Chute width—calves & steers	24 in.
cows & bulls	28 in. to 32 in.
Chute height—working	6 ft
loading	6 ft 6 in.
Corral fence height	5 ft 6 in. to 6 ft 0 in.
Holding pen area per animal	
Cows	20 sq ft
Steers & calves	16 sq ft
Loading chute width	30 in.
Loading chute rise	3.5 in. per ft of length

Figure 11-11. Sturdy construction pays off both in terms of easier use and in long life with a minimum of repairs.

CHAPTER **12**

Hay Storage Buildings

Storage of hay is largely a matter of protecting it from precipitation. Buildings to do this need not be able to contain any particular environment and several types of construction are adaptable. The only constraints on hay storage design are that the building be able to hold the required amount and be accessible to the equipment used to move bales or other packages in and out.

Pole frame and metal frame buildings with one or more open sides are the most popular types for hay storages. Since the roof area represents the major cost of these buildings, sidewalls are frequently high (16 to 22 feet) in order to obtain maximum capacity at minimum costs. Floors do not need to be paved, but should be higher than surrounding ground level and sloped slightly to allow for positive drainage of water away from the stored crop. A 4 inch layer of gravel over the floor will help reduce hay spoilage at the bottom of the stored area.

Buildings which are open on one or more sides are particularly vulnerable to wind damage. Special attention to wind bracing and tie down of both rafters and poles or metal frames is required.

Traditionally, clear span construction has not been widely used in hay barn construction because of its slightly higher cost and the fact that it reduces total storage volume somewhat. It does provide more freedom of movement for handling equipment and allows greater flexibility in planning if the structure is ever remodeled for another use.

Baled hay typically has a density of 8 to 10 pounds per cubic foot. This means you will need approximately 250 cubic feet of storage space per ton of hay. Table 12-1 presents storage capacities per foot of building length for several typically sized hay buildings. Baled straw has a density about half that of hay. If you are planning on storage for straw, reduce the values in table 12-1 by 50%.

Table 12-1. **Baled Hay Storage Capacity in Tons per Foot of Length for Several Sizes of Buildings**

Building Width Feet	Side Wall Height (Feet) 12	14	16	18	20	22
24	1.1	1.3	1.5	1.7	1.9	2.1
28	1.3	1.5	1.7	2.0	2.2	2.4
30	1.4	1.6	1.9	2.1	2.4	2.6
36	1.7	2.0	2.3	2.5	2.8	3.1
40	1.9	2.2	2.5	2.8	3.2	3.5
48	2.3	2.6	3.1	3.4	3.8	4.2
60	2.8	3.3	3.9	4.3	4.8	5.2

Sidewall Pressures

Rectangular bales which are stacked in the storage building exert little or no pressure on sidewalls. This is not the case for bales which are randomly dumped off an elevator into the storage building. This type of handling requires a building which is designed to withstand high outward pressures on the sidewall. This is usually accomplished by using extra posts, cross ties, or a combination of both.

Large Round Bales

The large round baler was developed in the early 1970's as a combination storage and handling system for hay used in beef cattle operations. Since that time, the convenience of handling hay in these relatively large packages (800 to 1,500 pounds each) has led to their use in nearly all parts of the United States on both dairy and beef farms.

Initial results with grass hay in the drier areas of the Midwest led many people to believe that these bales could be left in the field until needed with only minor losses. Research has now proven that this is not true and that losses can be very high in wetter areas of the country and when using large round balers to package legume and legume-grass mixtures. Research in Missouri showed storage losses can be in the 40% to 50% range in some instances. Because of these results, covered storage of large round bales is becoming a generally accepted practice on many farms.

Storage of large bales imposes two constraints on building design—size and sidewall pressure. Most bales are approximately 5 feet long and 5 feet in diameter. Storage buildings need to be sized to accommodate a specific number of bales plus some maneuvering room. For example, bales stacked three high will require a sidewall height of 15 feet for the bales, plus an additional 1 to 2 feet for maneuvering, for a total of 16 to 17 feet. A 20 foot sidewall will still only accommodate bales stacked three high and will be more costly to construct than the minimum required wall height. The same type of calculations should be used to determine optimum width and

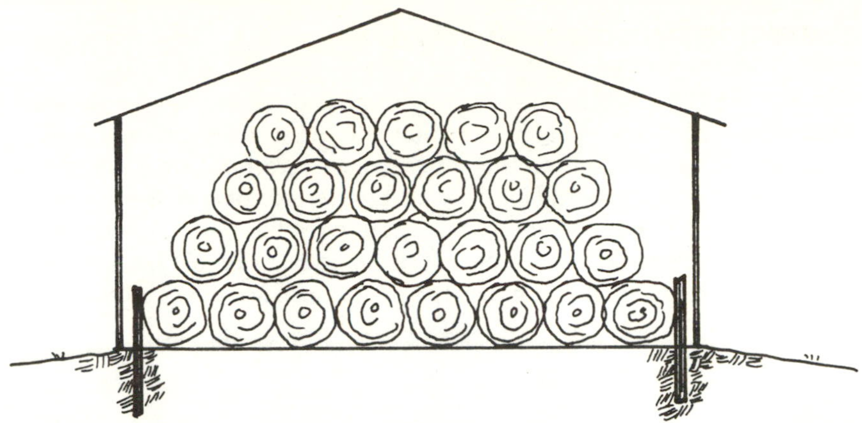

Figure 12-1. The best way to protect a conventional hay storage building from the sidewall pressures imposed by large round bales is to install retainer posts at each end of every row of bales. Retainer posts should be at least 5 inches in top diameter and be set 3 feet in the ground.

length of storage buildings.

Sidewall pressures can be very high unless bales are stacked on their ends. Numerous buildings throughout the U.S. have failed because of sidewall pressures from large round bales. Research is now underway to determine how great these pressures are so that future building designs can accommodate them. In the meantime, stacking bales on end or using retaining posts (shown in Figure 12-1) at the ends of each row of bales are the best ways to protect your building.

Figure 12-2. Combining storage with a feeding system can substantially reduce labor at feeding time.

Combining Feeding with Storage

Labor involved in removing hay from storage and feeding can be reduced considerably by incorporating hay feeding into the storage building. This is usually done by either constructing a permanent feed bunk area along one of the long sides of the barn (south or east preferred) or by using portable feeders across the width of the barn. These portable units are advanced toward the stored hay as it is fed out. If hay is to be available for feed on a continuous basis, plan on 4 to 6 inches of bunk feed space per animal. For once a day feeding, allow one feed space per animal.

CHAPTER **13**

Silage Storage

Most silage can be stored with equal success in either vertical tower type silos or horizontal storages. The major differences between the two are initial cost and the amount of management required to operate successfully.

General requirements which both types must satisfy include the following:

- Construction materials which are restistant to acid action of the silage.
- Walls which are essentially air tight to prevent spoilage of silage.
- An unloading face area sized to permit unloading at a rapid enough rate to minimize spoilage.
- Walls which can withstand maximum expected pressures from stored material.

Some of the advantages and disadvantages of the two types of silos are listed below.

Upright or tower silos

1. Less management required to produce and keep quality silage.
2. More adaptable to mechanized feeding systems.
3. Less space required for construction.
4. More costly than horizontal silos.
5. Relatively slow filling rate may limit harvesting speed.
6. Somewhat lower storage losses; particularly when ensiling haylage and high moisture grain.

Horizontal Silos

1. Less costly and less technical construction. They can be farm built

without having to bring in a specially trained erection crew.

2. Easily filled with dump trucks or rapidly unloading wagons.
3. Silage can be self-fed if the owner is willing to put up with required management.
4. Relatively large, well drained site, preferably sloping to the South or Southeast is required.
5. Surface must be sealed with an air tight cover, usually black plastic, which usually lasts only for one season.
6. Silage must be levelled and packed as the silo is filled. This may mean an extra employee and tractor at a normally busy time.

Vertical Silos

Upright or vertical silos are normally purchased as a package, which includes materials and labor. The package may or may not include the foundation. Since erection crews are highly specialized and often travel over a wide area, many manufacturers prefer to have foundations installed by the farmer or a local contractor prior to arrival of the crew. The selling dealer will provide plans for the required foundation.

Proper location of the upright silo is an important factor in how well it fits into your overall feeding program. Items which we feel are important include the following:

1. Good drainage both on the surface and below the surface. Surface drainage eliminates mud problems when filling and unloading the silo.
2. Proximity to roads over which silage will be transported.
3. Clearance around the silo. Make sure there is plenty of room for tractors and wagons or trucks to be able to get to the silo filling area without an excessive amount of turning and backing. Filling the upright silo will be the major bottleneck in the harvesting system and anything that can be done to reduce time spent in this area will speed up the entire operation.
4. Location with regard to the feeding system. Economical use of mechanical feeders will require that the silo be located reasonably close to the feed bunk—usually within 75 to 100 feet. If a self unloading wagon is used to distribute feed, the silo can be located farther away from the feeding area and an all weather road or travel lane will be an important factor.
5. Locate with expansion in mind. Silos are constructed one at a time, but very few farms end up with only a single silo unit. Plan ahead and make sure your site has room for at least two silos and possibly a concentrate storage and mixing area.
6. Environmental considerations, such as wind and shading, should

also be factors in final selection of a location. Wind tends to swirl around tower silos, carrying snow with it. Location away from the open side of open fronted buildings will help reduce drifting problems inside the building. Winter sun is relatively low in the sky. This means tall objects such as silos will cast extra large shadows during winter months. If these shadows fall across open feedlots, they will slow the melting of snow and ice. The idéal silo location from the standpoint of shadows is on the north side of any open lot area within shadow distance.

There are five general types of construction materials used in building of tower silos, all of which have proven satisfactory over time. The choice between them should be based on your evaluation of performance on your particular farm and the type of service available from the selling dealer.

Glass lined steel. These are generally acknowledged to be the most expensive type of upright silo. They do offer the advantage of air tight construction which reduces the management required with lower moisture silage and high moisture grain storage. Most units are equipped with a bottom unloader which will permit removal of ensiled material at the same time you are adding new material to the top of the silo. The economic feasibility of this type silo will be greatly improved if you are in a situation where the silo can be filled more than once a year.

Fiber glass reinforced plastic. These silos are also sealed units and offer the same reduced management advantages as the steel silos. They are also considerably lighter in weight, which may provide a break in shipping costs, depending on your particular location. Interior surfaces of both the glass lined steel and the plastic units are highly resistant to acid action of the silage.

Poured concrete. A process known as slip forming is used to construct these steel reinforced units. Form rings are set on top of the concrete foundation and a section of silo 5 to 10 feet high is poured and allowed to set. The next day, the form rings are "slipped" upward and another section is poured. This process continues until the entire wall section is complete. Reinforcing steel is placed inside the concrete to enable the walls to withstand pressure of the silage. These units are relatively air tight, but are not "sealed silos." Some type of cover should be placed over the surface of the silage to reduce spoilage during periods when there is no feed being removed. Poured concrete is relatively resistant to silage acid; however, interior coatings are frequently used to prolong silo life. These will usually consist of either an epoxy coating which is installed before the silo is first filled, or a linseed oil coating which must be renewed every 2 to 3 years.

Concrete stave. There are probably more concrete stave silos in the United States than there are all other types together. Concrete staves produced under controlled factory conditions provide a durable and relatively economical form of construction for upright silos. Individual staves vary in size and shape among manufacturers, but are generally about 3 inches thick, 10 inches wide and 30 inches high. They are stacked vertically in rows and held in place by steel reinforcing hoops placed around the outside of the silo. Hoop size and placement will depend on size of the silo and usually change from close spacing at the bottom to wider spacing near the top where pressures are less. The interior surface of the stave silo is plastered with a cement base plaster to seal joints in the staves and provide an air tight wall. The plaster is frequently protected from acidic action of silage with either epoxy or linseed oil coating. Exterior of the silo may or may not be painted, depending on the appearance desired.

Wood. Wood stave silos use pressure treated, beveled boards, usually 2 to 2-½ inches thick to form exterior walls. The boards are held together by steel reinforcing hoops located around the outside. Wood has good resistance to acid action of the silage and these units have given good service over many years. They do require periodic adjustment of tension in the reinforcing hoops to accommodate dimensional changes in wood as moisture content varies.

With the exception of the completely sealed units, upright silos should be sized so that a minimum of 3 inches of silage is removed from the surface each day during the feeding season. This keeps surface spoilage and losses at a minimum. This minimum amount to be removed can be calculated using an average silage density of approximately 50 pounds per cubic foot and the following formula.

$$\text{Minimum lbs fed per day} = 9.82 \times (\text{silo diameter in ft})^2$$

***Table 13-1.* Minimum Daily Amounts Which Must Be Uniformly Removed From Upright Silos to Prevent Surface Spoilage**

Silo Diameter (Feet)	Lbs Silage
12	1,400
14	1,900
16	2,500
18	3,200
20	3,900
22	4,700
24	5,600
30	8,800
40	15,700

***Table 13.2.* Silo Capacity in Tons of Corn Silage at 70% Moisture Content**

Silo Height (Feet)	Silo Diameter (Feet) 12	16	20	22	24	30	40
30	80	143	223	270	321	—	—
40	110	196	307	371	442	690	—
50	—	252	394	477	570	886	—
60	—	—	483	585	697	1087	1935
70	—	—	574	694	827	1290	2285
80	—	—	659	798	950	1484	2637

Height of the upright silo will be determined by the annual needs for storage capacity. If the required height exceeds the diameter by a factor of 4, more than one silo should be erected. Because of pressure produced by stored silage, higher silos will contain more silage per cubic foot than shorter silos. For a given diameter, doubling the height will increase storage capacity by about 3 times. Total capacity in tons of corn silage for several sizes of upright silos can be found in Table 13-2.

Horizontal Silos

Horizontal silage storages are referred to as either bunkers or trenches, depending upon whether they are located above or below ground level. If a suitable location is available, the below ground trench will result in more economical construction and easier filling.

The same site location factors that were important in locating upright silos should also be considered in placement of the horizontal silo. Horizontal silos also have additional requirements for drainage of water which accumulates in the silo itself. Floor surface should slope uniformly toward the open end at ¼ inch per foot. If self feeding is used, floor slope needs to be increased to a minimum of ½ inch per foot. The open or unloading end should face South or East to minimize ice and snow accumulation in the work area.

Horizontal silos are constructed with concrete floors 4 to 6 inches thick. Walls may be either concrete or pressure treated wood. Special care must be taken in constructing walls so that they can withstand lateral pressures exerted both by silage and the tractor used to pack silage. Walls which are tilted outward at the top permit better packing of silage next to the wall and this results in less spoilage. An outward tilt of 4 feet per 6 feet of wall height is usually recommended. Construction details for different types of walls are illustrated in Figures 13-1—13-3.

Sizing of the horizontal silo is even more critical than for the upright silo. Silage is generally at a lower density, permitting rapid penetration of air, and unloading techniques do not remove uniform layers. For these reasons, face area is based on an average daily removal of 4 to 6 inches instead of the 3 inches suggested for upright silos. An average silage density of 40 pounds per cubic foot and face area equivalent to a level full silo is used in making these calculations. Maximum face area to keep down spoilage can be calculated using the following formula.

$$\text{Face area in square feet} = \text{daily feed required in lbs} \div 16$$

The determination of height and width dimensions to achieve the required face area will depend on the type of construction and the particular site. In general, the higher the sidewalls, the smaller the surface area and the lower the spoilage losses will be. However, wall pressures increase greatly with depth and above ground bunkers seldom have sidewalls of more than 8 to 10 feet. Trenches have the advantage of earth support to offset sidewall pressures. As a result, wall heights of 15 to 20 feet have been used

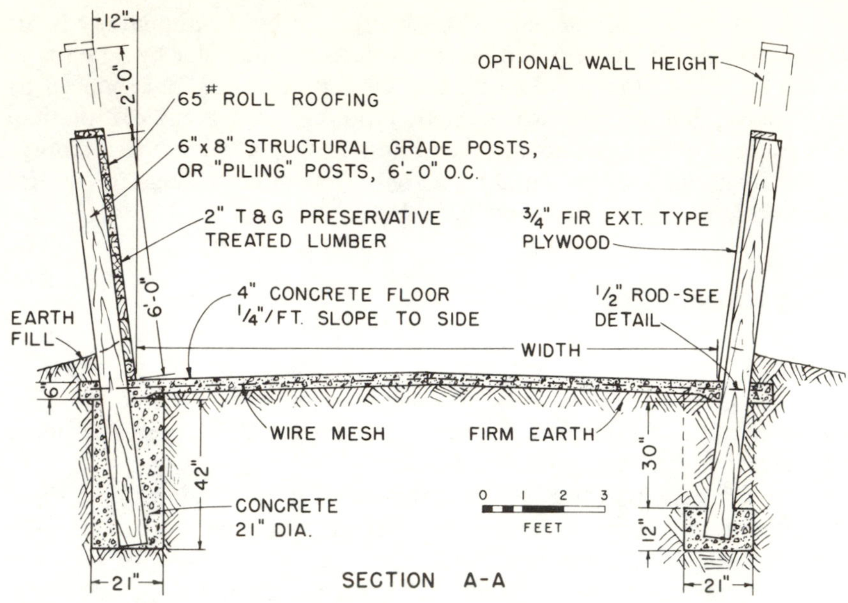

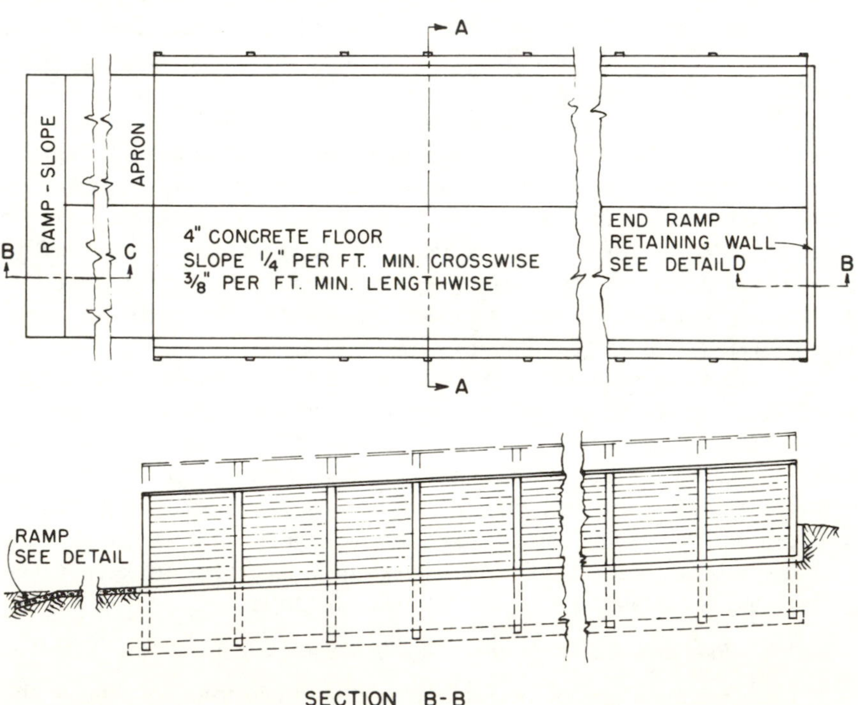

Figure 13-1. Pressure-treated posts and either planking or exterior plywood can be used to build sidewalls for bunker type silos. Plans are available from your extension office. (University of Georgia)

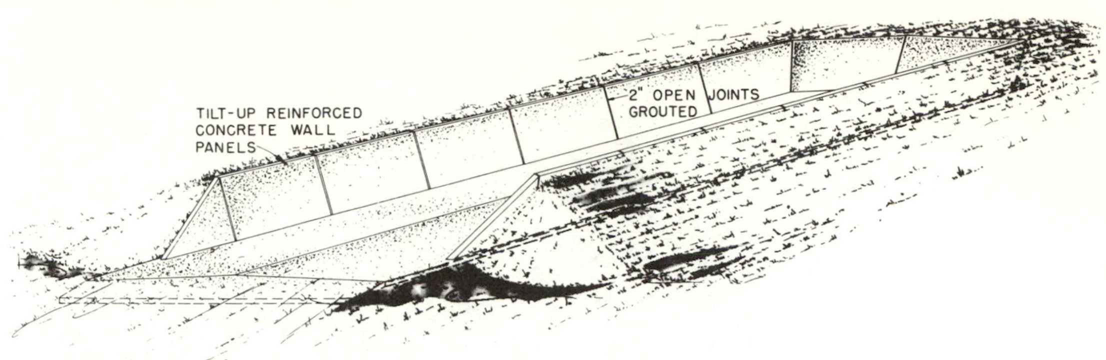

Figure 13-2. This below-ground trench is lined with tilt-up concrete panels which are poured in 2x4 forms placed on the silo floor and then tipped up into place. (University of Georgia)

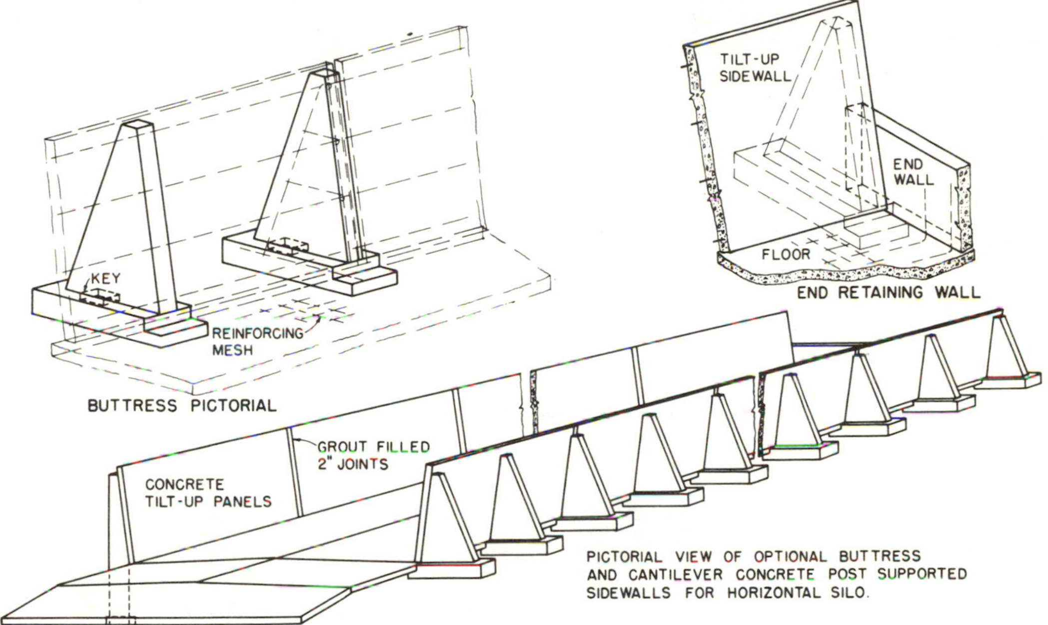

Figure 13-3. Tilt-up construction can also be used for bunker silos; however, some type of supporting buttress will be required to support the panels. (University of Georgia)

successfully.

Minimum width will be determined by space needed for unloading of the silo. If the silo is less than 50 feet long, a 15 foot width will provide adequate room to maneuver a tractor and loader. Silos more than 50 feet in length should be wide enough to permit turning around with the tractor loader and perhaps room to back the feed wagon close to the working face of the silage. Self feeding will require a silo wide enough to provide 4 to 6 inches of feed space per animal. Wall height of units used for self feeding should be limited to a maximum of 6 feet to reduce the possibility of animal injury from cave-ins of the silage face.

In theory, self feeding of silage from horizontal silos represents the

Figure 13-4. Self feeding is the ultimate in labor efficiency, but it requires special attention to management, which many farmers are unwilling to give. Before you try it, better check with someone who is doing or has done it.

ultimate in efficiency. No mechanical equipment is required and the animal does all the work. However, it has been our experience that very few people are able to make self feeding work satisfactorily. Those who are successful spend time every day keeping the feeder adjusted, manure removed, and the silage face worked down evenly. If you don't have any experience with self feeding, we suggest you visit with a few people who are using it before making a decision to incorporate it into your farm operation.

Required length of the horizontal silo is determined by total storage needs. Use an average silage density of 40 pounds per cubic foot and a level

Table 13-3. **Minimum Amount of Silage to Be Removed (Lbs per Day) to Prevent Spoilage**

	Wall Height (Feet)					
Average Silo Width (Feet)	**6**	**8**	**10**	**12**	**15**	**20**
15	1440	1920	2400	2880	3600	4800
20	1920	2560	3200	3840	4800	6400
25	2400	3200	4000	4800	6000	8000
30	2880	3840	4800	5760	7200	9600
35	3600	4480	5600	6720	8400	11200
40	3840	5120	6400	7680	9600	12800

Table 13-4. **Capacity of Horizontal Silos in Tons of Silage per Foot of Length (40 Lbs/Cubic Foot)**

	Wall Height (Feet)					
Average Silo Width (Feet)	**6**	**8**	**10**	**12**	**15**	**20**
15	1.8	2.4	3.0	3.6	4.5	6.0
20	2.4	3.2	4.0	4.8	6.0	8.0
25	3.0	4.0	5.0	6.0	7.5	10.0
30	3.6	4.8	6.0	7.2	9.0	12.0
35	4.2	5.6	7.0	8.4	10.5	14.0
40	4.8	6.4	8.0	9.6	12.0	16.0

full volume to make your calculations. If the length comes out too long for the site you are planning to use, it may be possible to construct two or more storage units side by side.

Figure 13-5. Two horizontal silo units side by side shorten the length of site required and also permit filling with different materials or filling one while feeding from the other.

CHAPTER **14**

Grain Storage

Storage is only one of the components of a successful grain handling system. Unfortunately, many farmers start out to purchase storage without taking time to analyze how it will fit into the entire system. One of the more complete references on grain handling systems is "Planning Grain-Feed Handling," available from the Midwest Plan Service at Ames, Iowa. We would recommend that you obtain and study this publication before making any major investments in your grain handling system.

Horizontal or Vertical

Horizontal or "flat" storage is that which is located in a relatively shallow bin constructed within or as a part of a conventional building. Vertical storages are cylindrical units usually constructed of metal and having a greater depth than diameter. The choice between the two general types will depend on the particular system which you feel will work best on your farm.

Considerations when selecting horizontal storage:

1. It may be possible to adapt existing buildings to storages.
2. Buildings may be able to serve some other function (i.e., machinery storage) when not being used for grain storage.
3. Storage is easier to construct with available farm labor force.
4. System is not easily adapted to drying systems or long time storage unless complex duct work is installed.
5. Loading and unloading is not easily automated.

Considerations when selecting vertical storage:

1. Cylindrical design makes most efficient use of construction materials.

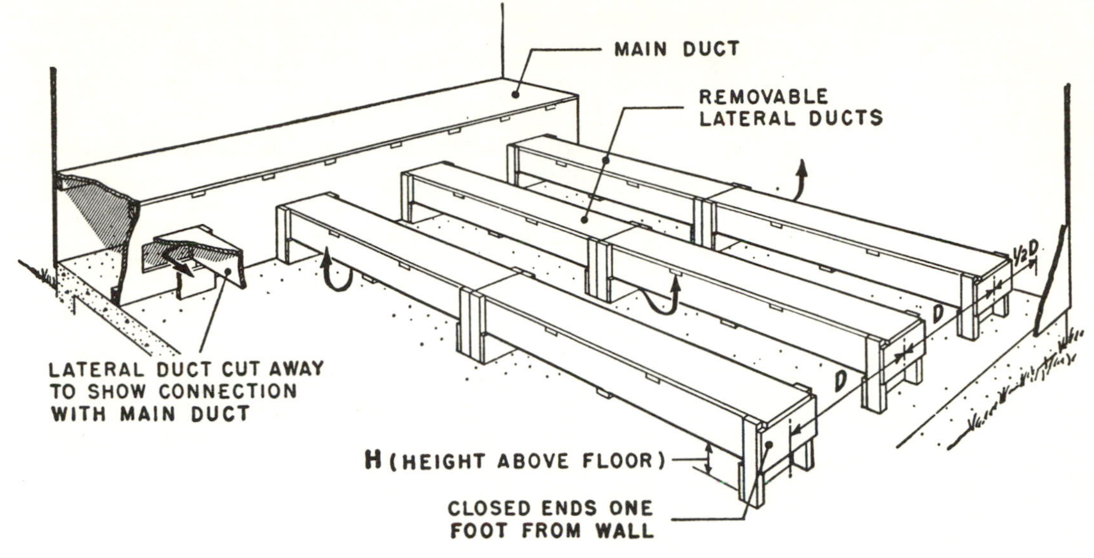

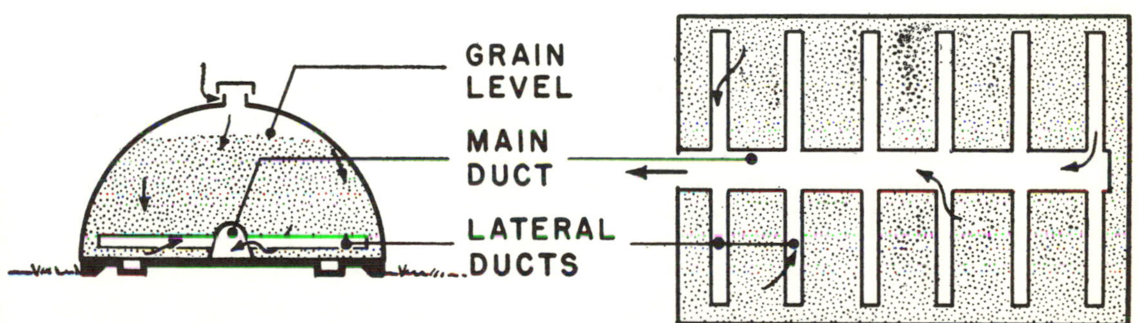

Figure 14-1. An example of the horizontal ductwork which is a necessary part of flat storages that incorporate drying or aeration. (USDA)

2. Less area is required for a given amount of storage.
3. Mechanical handling systems are easily adapted to these storages and automatic control is both practical and available.

Volume

Total storage volume needed will depend on your anticipated yield and disposal system. It requires 1.25 cubic feet of storage space to hold 1 bushel of grain. The capacity of a rectangular storage in bushels is:

$$\text{Capacity} = \frac{\text{Length (ft)} \times \text{width (ft)} \times \text{depth (ft)}}{1.25}$$

For a cylindrical bin, the capacity is:

$$\text{Capacity} = \frac{[\text{Bin diameter (ft)}]^2 \times 3.14 \times \text{height (ft)}}{5}$$

When figuring the height or depth, be sure to deduct for drying floors and the fact that bins are seldom filled completely to the top.

Table 14-1. **Capacity of Circular Bins in Bushels of Dry Grain**

Bin Diameter (Feet)	Grain Depth in Feet 5	10	15	20	25	30
10	314	628	942	1,256	1,570	1,884
12	453	905	1,358	1,810	2,261	2,714
14	616	1,232	1,848	2,464	3,078	3,694
16	804	1,608	2,412	3,216	4,021	4,825
18	1,018	2,036	3,054	4,072	5,089	6,107
20	1,256	2,513	3,769	5,026	6,283	7,539
24	1,809	3,619	5,428	7,238	9,047	10,857

Location and Arrangement

Grain handling and storage facilities should be located in zone 3 of the farmstead. This represents a compromise which is designed to get noise and dust away from the residential area and minimize the length of electrical distribution runs.

Arrangement of individual storage units within the handling facility will depend largely on the physical size and capacity of the connecting

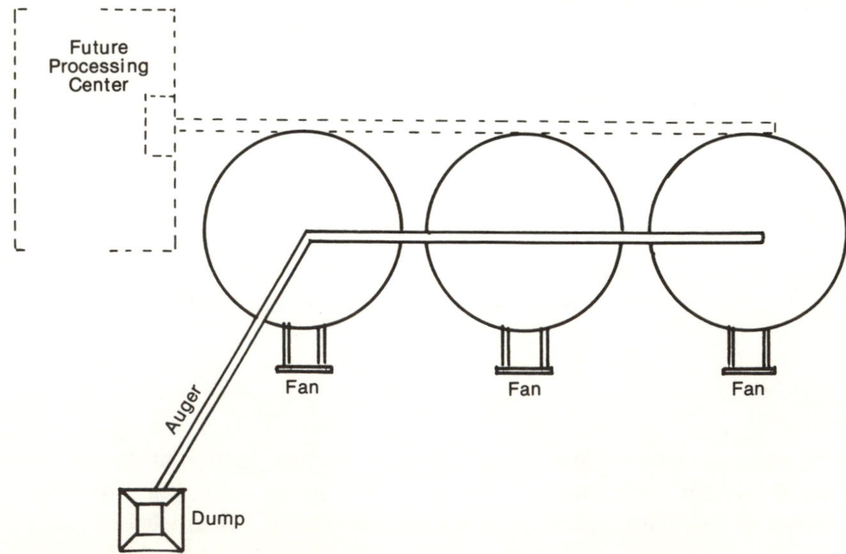

Figure 14-2. A low-cost, straight-line arrangement that can easily be expanded as the operation grows. Bins can be filled with an inclined auger or the optional leg.

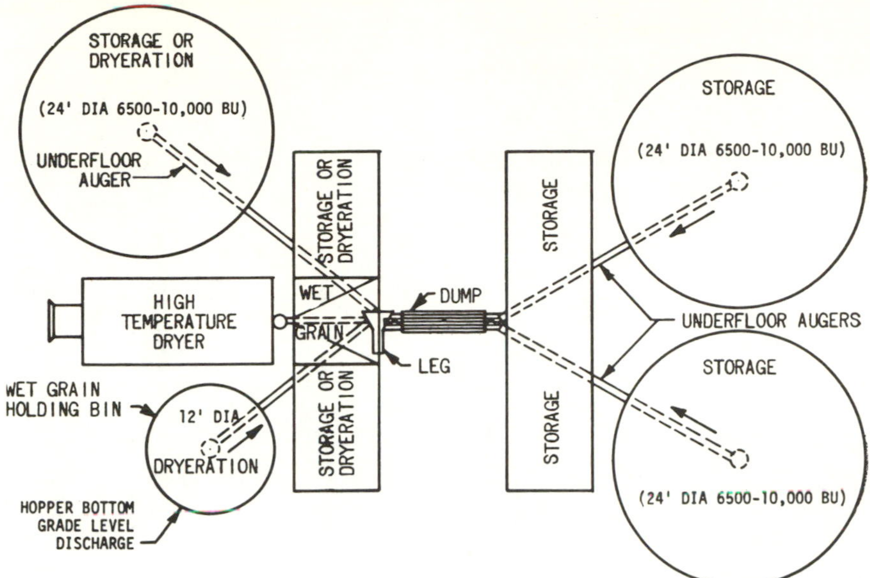

Figure 14-3. A 20,000 to 30,000-bushel storage unit incorporating high-speed drying with dryeration. The centrally located dump area could easily be covered with a building to house feed-processing equipment. (Purdue University)

equipment which moves the grain. A number of possible layouts are illustrated in Figures 14-2 through 14-4.

Two general concepts govern the design and layout of a large majority of on farm handling systems. They are closed loop handling and centralization. Closed loop handling is a design feature which allows grain at any point in the system to be returned to the starting point. This feature is particularly attractive on farms where some type of processing plant is used to grind and/or blend grains into livestock feed. It is less of an advantage on cash grain farms where grain is frequently loaded directly into storage and from storage directly on a truck for shipping.

Centralization places the starting point for each of the storage closed loops at one central location. This usually results in a system with a minimum amount of equipment duplication and can make installation of permanent equipment an economical alternative. The central point frequently provides a convenient location for processing facilities.

Table 14-2. **Average Machine Capacity and Recommended Capacity of Wet Grain Handling Equipment***

Machine Size	Harvest Rate (Bu/Hour)	Wet Grain Handling System Capacities (Bu/Hour)	(Bu/Year)
2 row	150	700	20,000
4 row	300	1,400	60,000
6 row	400	1,800	100,000
8 row	500	2,200	130,000

**Values are based on corn and the number of harvest days available 9 years out of 10.*

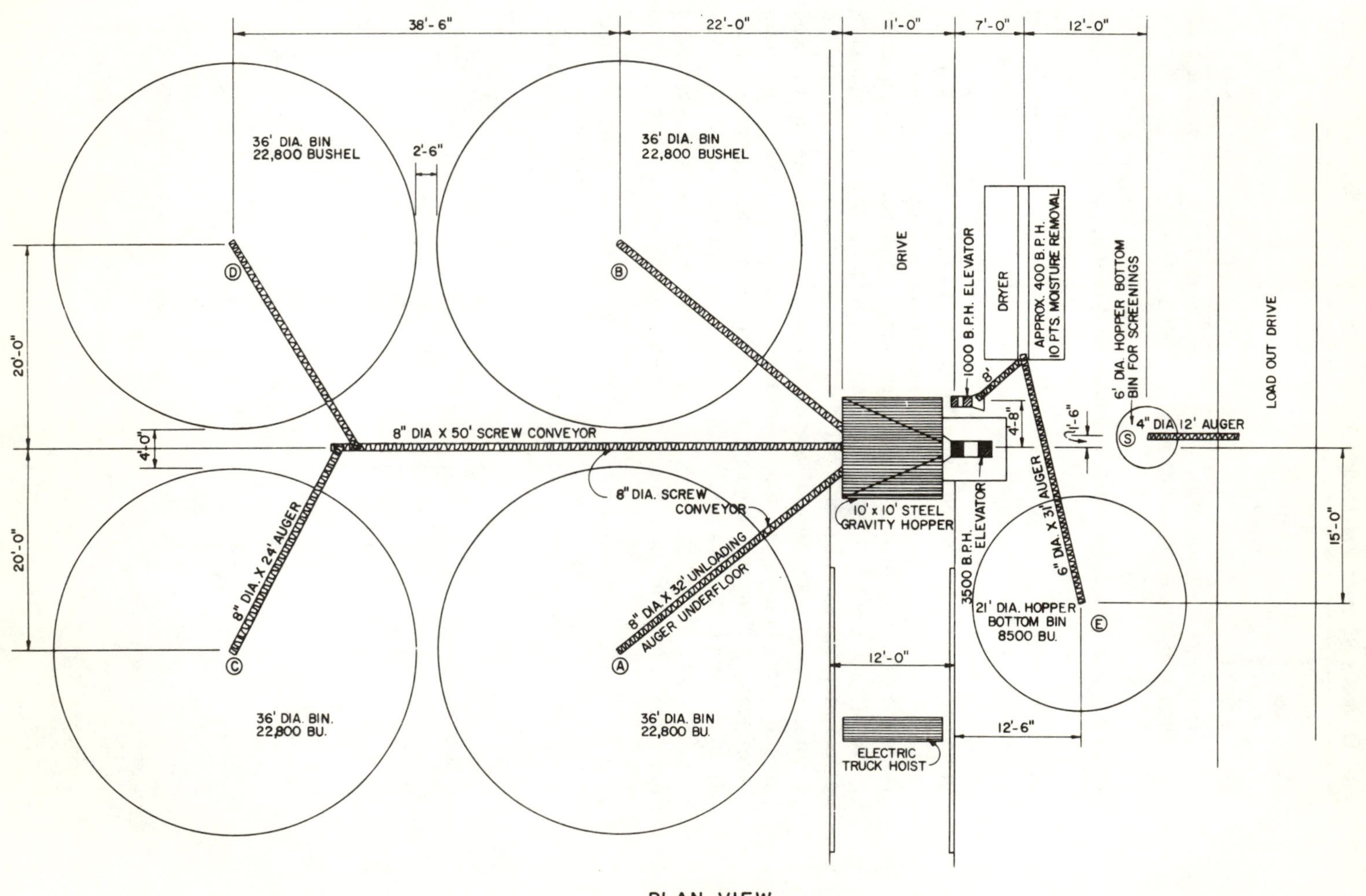

Figure 14-4. A large-volume, high-capacity system designed for the commercial grain producer. Although system design principles do not change for this large a system, it is important to provide for high-capacity components needed for rapid handling of material. (USDA 6294)

System layout and equipment sizing for your facility should be done by a person who is experienced in the design and operation of grain handling facilities. Different manufacturers produce equipment which may look similar, but not be compatible with what you have or want to do. Some guidelines on equipment sizing and capacity are included in Tables 14-2 through 14-4 to provide a general feel for some of the elements you will need.

Table 14-3. **Capacity and Average Horsepower Requirements for Screw Augers Used to Move Dry Shelled Corn**

Tube Size		Angle of Elevation			
		0°		45°	
Inches Diameter	Rpm	Bu/Hr	Hp/10 Ft of Auger	Bu/Hr	Hp/10 Ft of Auger
4	670	450	.27	320	.37
5	560	640	.35	575	.63
6	425	1,200	.75	900	.9
7	400	1,900	1.5	1,500	1.6
8	320	2,150	1.5	1,750	1.7
9	280	2,800	1.7	2,300	2.2
10	250	3,000	2.1	3,050	3.0

Table 14-4. **Capacity and Horsepower Requirements for Vertical Bucket Elevator**

Bucket		Capacity	Maximum Height for Given Hp			
Size	Spacing	(Bu/Hr)	3 Hp	4 Hp	7.5 Hp	10 Hp
6 in. x 4 in.	4.5 in.	800	80 ft			
6 in. x 5 in.	6 in.	1,350	60 ft	90 ft		
9 in. x 5 in.	9 in.	2,000	40 ft	60 ft	80 ft.	
9 in. x 5 in.	6 in.	3,000		45 ft	65 ft	85 ft
9 in. x 6 in.	8 in.	3,500		35 ft	55 ft	75 ft
10 in. x 6 in.	8 in.	4,000			45 ft	75 ft

Construction

The major difference between grain storage construction and other farm buildings is that grain storages must withstand much greater product loads in addition to the normal snow and wind loads. This means heavy duty foundations and, in the case of horizontal storages, paying close attention to sidewall design and construction.

Reinforced concrete is the most satisfactory material for grain storage foundations. If you purchase a vertical storage unit or bin and decide to install the foundation yourself, be sure to follow the manufacturer's plans with regard to the size and placement of reinforcing steel and bin anchors. Horizontal storages should have poured concrete floors 4 to 5 inches thick with a layer of 6 by 6 inch 10 gauge steel reinforcing mesh imbedded in the floor slab. If the depth of the grain in the horizontal storage will be more than 4 to 5 feet, you should seek help in designing anchorage for the wall to

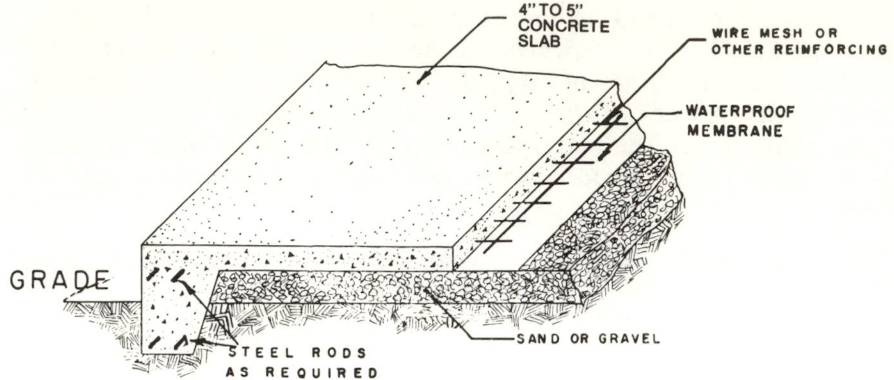

Figure 14-5. This drawing illustrates the general construction requirements of a foundation for a steel grain storage bin. If you are doing your own foundation work, the manufacturer of the bin you are purchasing should provide you with detailed foundation plans to fit the units you are purchasing. (Texas A&M University)

foundation connection.

The top surface of all storage floors should be a minimum of 6 to 8 inches above the surrounding ground level to provide some protection against moisture. Place at least 4 inches of gravel under the floor. Some bin manufacturers will also recommend placing a sheet of polyethylene plastic directly under the concrete floor to prevent moisture migration from the ground. This practice is of questionable value if you have provided good drainage and it does add to the difficulty in finishing the concrete floor surface.

Round storage bins are designed so that sidewall pressures are converted into tensile forces which are resisted by either hoops or the bin material itself. Hoops need to be tight and all fasteners used to secure metal sheets must be in place if the storage unit is to contain a full bin of grain. Grain stirring devices add extra loads to bin walls. If you are planning to use a grain drying system which uses stirring, make sure your storage has been designed for it.

Outward pressure on the sidewall of a horizontal grain storage increases nearly linearly with depth of grain. The highest pressure is at the bottom of the wall and the deeper the grain, the greater the pressure. For example, the outward pressure at the base of a wall holding back an 8 foot depth of shelled corn will be approximately 225 pounds per square foot. The size and spacing of conventional studs to withstand these loads can be found in Table 14-5. Good anchorage at both top and bottom of the walls is also required to insure that the storage will not fail.

Several manufacturers of post frame buildings now offer a grain storage option as an extra cost item for their buildings. This option usually provides some type of wall reinforcing or strengthening which will allow it to withstand outward pressure from stored grain. Almost all of these are limited to some specific depth of fill which is usually much less than full wall height. Before you purchase one of these options, make sure just how much storage you are buying.

Figure 14-6. Metal storage bins are assembled from the top down. Once the first ring is in place, the roof is assembled on it. The unit is then raised up and succeeding rings are installed at ground level. Some farmers have assembled metal bins, but it is generally a job that is best left to the people who do it for a living.

Table 14-5. **Size, Spacing, and Fill Limitations for Vertical Wall Studs in Horizontal Grain Storages***

Size	Spacing (Inches)	Maximum Depth of Grain (Feet)
2 in. x 4 in. x 8 ft	24	5
2 in. x 4 in. x 8 ft	16	6
2 in. x 4 in. x 8 ft	12	7.5
2 in. x 6 in. x 8 ft	24	8
2 in. x 6 in. x 10 ft	16	9

**Based on use of No. 2 Douglas Fir or Southern Yellow Pine*

Figure 14-7. Inclined augers make a good way to fill a grain storage unit for the farm that is starting out or is not large enough to justify a vertical leg. If bins are arranged in a semicircle, the auger can be pivoted from one to the next, making it possible to use a single dump site.

Processing Centers

All grain storage and handling facilities should be planned so that there is room available for feed processing. Even if feed processing is not in your immediate plans, the ability to add it without having to relocate storage units may be a real advantage at some future date. Fortunately, room for feed processing equipment can be easily incorporated into most layouts with little or no added cost.

A 20 by 30 foot building located at the central point of the handling system will provide enough room for drive through loading and unloading and feed processing equipment to handle needs of most farms. Provide a minimum clearance of 2 feet between this building and adjacent storage units.

Processing buildings are frequently pole frame construction. This allows use of relatively high sidewalls without having to change basic construction techniques. Minimum sidewall height on the processing building should be 14 to 16 feet to permit dumping of trucks into the receiving pit. If overhead holding bins are planned for the drive through, even higher walls may be needed.

The floor of the processing building will have to withstand heavy concentrated loads. It should be made of 6 inch thick poured concrete with 6 by 6 inch 10 gauge reinforcing mesh. The floor will need a well compacted gravel base to prevent settling. Pitch the surface of the floor

Figure 14-8. All good feed-processing buildings have high sidewalls and a drive-thru design. The high walls permit the use of a dumping truck or wagon and overhead storage bins for holding already processed feed.

away from the dump pit and toward the doors in the drive through alley.

Overhead bins present special construction problems in the feed processing center. If you know in advance exactly where they are, it may be possible to include a support system for them in the basic building design. In most cases, this is not possible and a separate supporting system is designed and constructed for overhead units. The design of support for overhead bins should be done by an engineer who is familiar with structural design and your needs for clearances under and around the bins.

Electrical wiring in the processing center needs special attention to insure safety. Grain dust is a highly explosive material. In order to prevent the possibility of igniting an explosion with an electrical spark, all switches and lights should be of the explosion proof or enclosed type. This will add extra cost to construction, but it will provide a measure of safety which should make both you and your insurance company happy.

CHAPTER **15**

Crop Growing Buildings: Greenhouses

The use of greenhouses to extend normal growing seasons and to produce "out of season" crops is a steadily increasing segment of American agriculture. At the present time, there are more than 8,000 acres of greenhouses in this country. They range in complexity from large glass covered structures with central heating and controlled light for flower production to simple plastic covered units used to grow bedding plants. The different types can be classified into the following general categories.

Quonset. This type unit is generally regarded as being the lowest cost type of greenhouse construction. Main support is provided by semi circular metal frames. End walls are often framed in with wooden studs and covered with rigid plastic. The quonset frames are usually covered with one or two layers of polyethylene film. Theoretically, a quonset can be constructed to any width. In actual practice, width is usually determined by the covering material used. Polyethylene is available in widths up to 40 feet. A 40 foot wide sheet can completely cover a quonset that is approximately 26 feet wide. The quonset unit is best suited to crops grown in or on the ground because of the sloping sidewall. Another major advantage is that the relatively light framing members admit a maximum of sunlight.

Rigid frame. This type construction is similar to quonset except that wooden members are used instead of the metal frames. It is relatively low in cost and can be easily fabricated using farm labor. Frames are usually spaced 4 to 6 feet apart. Wooden purlins between frames can provide support for rigid plastic covering. If polyethylene is used as a covering, frames are tied together at the ridge and eave points only. This type of construction is generally limited to buildings 30 feet wide or less. Wider units can be built; however, the increased size of required framing members

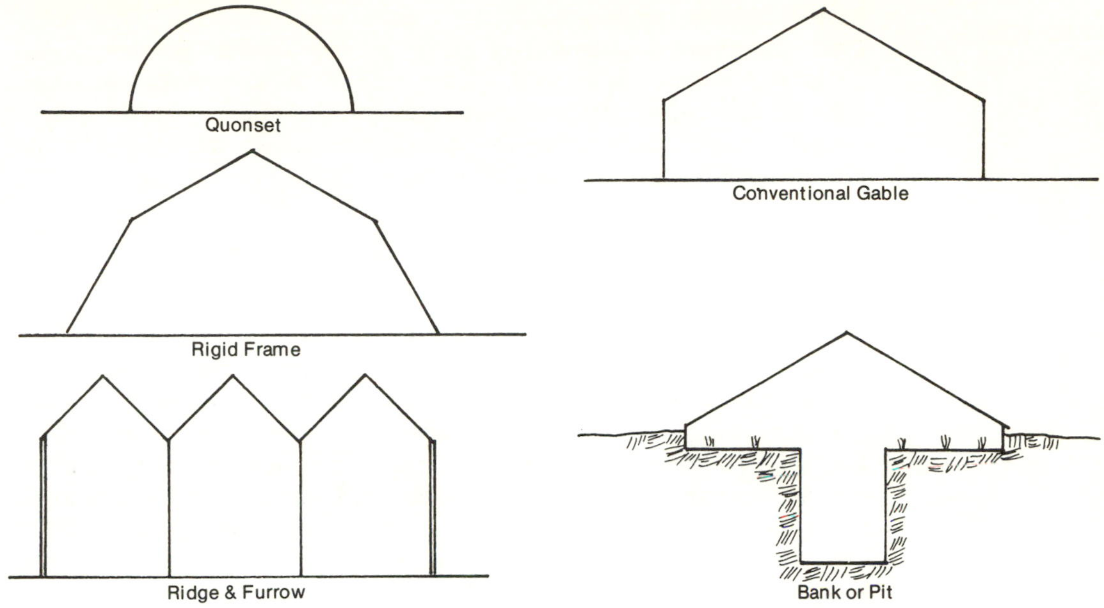

Figure 15-1. Commonly used cross-sectional shapes in greenhouse design.

will shade a considerable amount of the growing area.

Ridge and furrow. This type of building is a series of gable roof sections which are connected together at the eave or gutter line. The individual gable sections are usually between 10 and 25 feet wide. Framing is usually metal and the covering is either rigid plastic or glass. Ridge and furrow buildings are unlimited in size and offer the potential of covering large areas with a minimum of wall construction. The roof is supported by posts located under the eave connection. This type of roof profile tends to hold snow and special provisions should be made to both support and remove snow in northern parts of the country.

Conventional gable. A traditional "A" shaped roof with vertical sidewalls characterizes these buildings. They utilize a variety of construction techniques including pole frame, metal frame, and post and beam. These units are adaptable to a variety of coverings and costs vary widely depending on cover materials and type of framing. Minimum roof pitch is 6 inch rise per foot of run for glass covered units, with steeper slopes preferred for plastic covered units. The vertical sidewall will accommodate either floor or bench growing systems and different plant heights from wall to wall.

Bank or pit houses. Attempts to reduce greenhouse heating costs have led to the development of new designs which are partially recessed into the ground. The bank house is partially recessed into a south facing slope with the long dimension or ridge of the building running east-west. The design greatly reduces heat loss through the north wall and the close to the ground feature reduces leakage of outside air into the greenhouse. Pit type houses have excavated trenches which are used as walk ways and work alleys. Plants are grown at ground level and the greenhouse itself is simply a glass or plastic covered gable roof structure. The pit greenhouse eliminates sidewall construction and the below grade pit walls help to buffer some of the daily temperature extremes. Pit greenhouses are generally limited in size and are most often used for hobby units.

Construction

Greenhouses are designed to contain an environment favorable to plant growth. A major factor is natural light and most designs attempt to minimize shading through selection of small framing components. In many cases this leads to buildings which have much lower load carrying ability than is normally acceptable. It can be argued that snow will rapidly melt off a greenhouse and high design loads associated with conventional buildings are not needed. This is true; however, if you accept a design with less than the standard load for your area, you should be aware that you are also accepting some degree of failure risk.

Wood and steel used in greenhouse construction should be painted to protect it from the effects of moisture. Light colored paints reflect light and help minimize the effects of shading from framing members.

Greenhouses are relatively light weight structures and need to be constructed with foundations which can provide good anchorage as well as support. Traditional greenhouse foundations are made of poured concrete. A more recent innovation is the use of pressure treated poles and planks. The pole and plank foundation requires no form work and has proven to be an economical support system for some of the lower cost plastic covered greenhouses. Pressure treated wood used in greenhouses should be treated with water borne salts, not with creosote or pentachlorophenol (penta). Creosote and penta release vapors which are toxic to growing plants.

The main difference between greenhouse construction and other farm buildings is the covering material. The ideal greenhouse cover will provide maximum protection from the weather while transmitting nearly all available sunlight. Unfortunately, all materials being used today are less than ideal. Listed below are some of the more common materials and their features.

Glass. Glass is the number one material for greenhouse covering and is the material which all others are measured against for light transmission. Glass panels used in greenhouses will regularly transmit over 90% of the available light. Major objections to glass have included cost, available sizes, and breakage. The cost differential between glass and other materials is narrowing very rapidly as the cost of petroleum is causing rapid increases in cost of plastics. The size limitation is not now as great as it once was. Many manufacturers are now making large panes for greenhouses and new extruded aluminum frames make glazing much less of a chore than it once was. Breakage problems can be greatly minimized through use of high

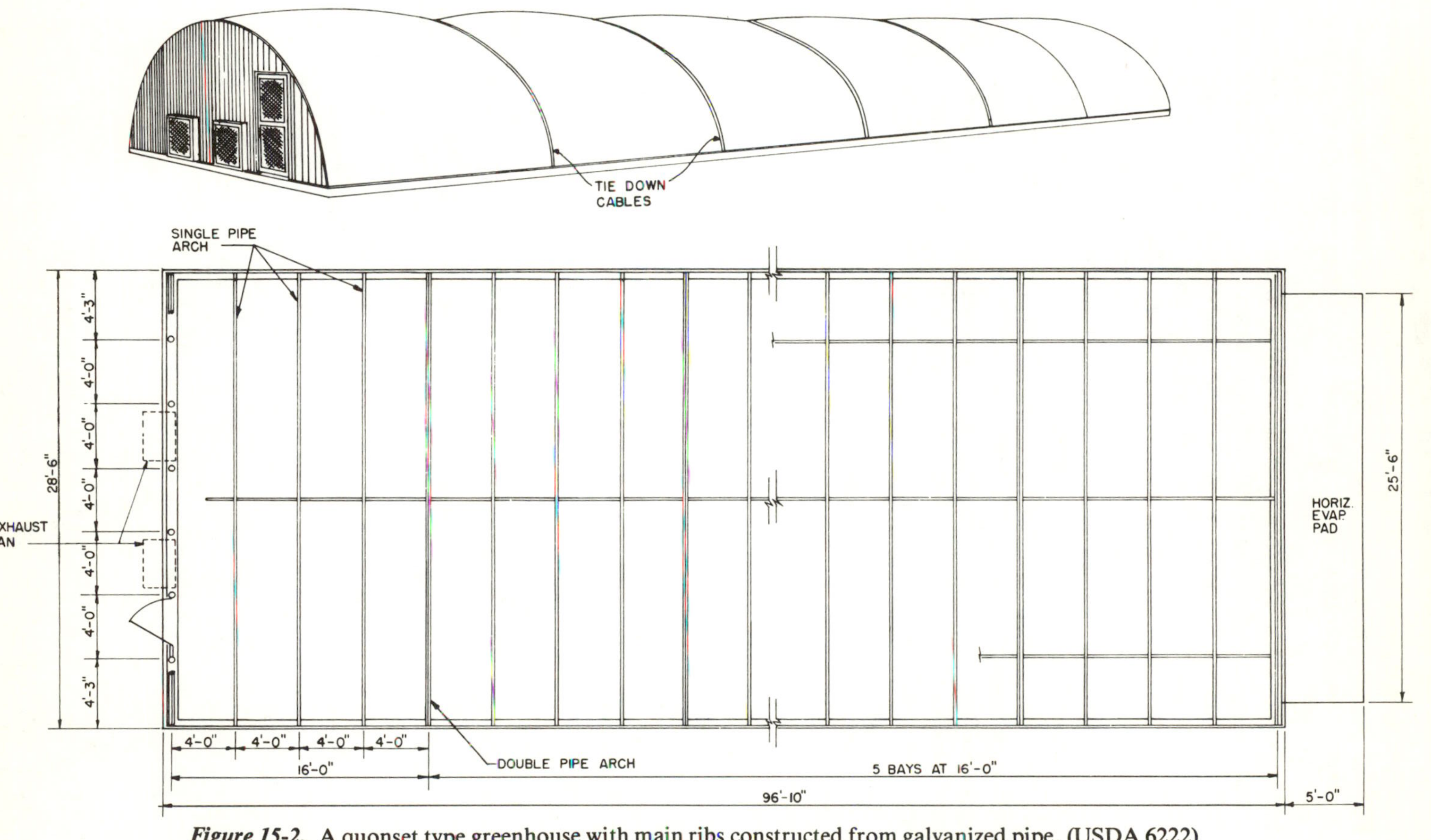

Figure 15-2. A quonset type greenhouse with main ribs constructed from galvanized pipe. (USDA 6222)

strength or tempered glass. The only problem with these is that they are difficult or impossible to cut on the job site. This makes alterations or "cut to fit" installation procedures hard to accommodate.

Polyethylene (PE). This economical plastic film has been used in large quantities by the greenhouse industry for the past several years. It has a light transmission capability which is only slightly less than glass and it will withstand some mechanical abuse without breaking. Its main drawback is that it breaks down rapidly under ultra violet radiation from the sun. Failure occurs in 6 to 9 months, depending on the particular part of the country in which it is used. This means recovering on a seasonal basis.

A technique of covering a greenhouse frame with two layers of PE and inflating the space between them reduces labor, conserves energy, and improves performance. The sheets of plastic are anchored around all edges and a small fan runs continuously to maintain a very low air pressure between the layers. The air inflated unit does not require the usual batten strips and withstands wind abuse much better than conventional installation methods.

Polyethylene film is available in thicknesses of 1 to 8 or more mils (1 mil equals .001 inch) and in widths up to 40 feet. The 4 and 6 mil thicknesses are normally used for greenhouses. It is also available with ultra violet radiation inhibitors, which will improve its durability. Don't expect it to last much more than 18 months even with these inhibitors.

Polyvinyl chloride (PVC). This plastic is available as either a film or a rigid sheet. PVC is also susceptible to ultra violet deterioration, although it is possible to get up to 4 years of service out of films treated with an

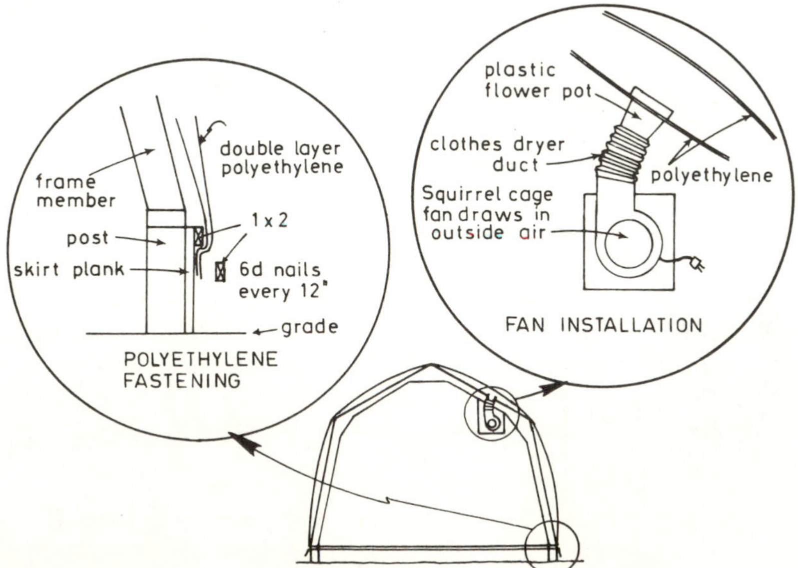

Figure 15-3. Details of the air-inflation method of covering with polyethylene plastic. (NRAES)

Figure 15-4. A 26' x 96' rigid frame building with air-inflated covering. This building was designed to be covered with two 40' x 100' sheets of polyethylene.

inhibitor. Films are available in 4 to 8 mil thicknesses and in widths of 3 to 5 feet. Rigid panels of PVC are relatively low cost and easy to install over a roof purlin system. Light transmission of this material deteriorates over time. In extreme cases, light transmission may drop to the point where plant growth is affected in as little as two years.

Mylar. This plastic is an excellent transmitter of light and is resistant to ultra violet radiation. It is relatively expensive and has not been well accepted as a greenhouse covering.

Fiberglass reinforced plastic (FRP). These panels are available in either corrugated or flat form and have very good light transmission characteristics. Light transmission will decrease over time due to surface erosion. This can be partially corrected by periodic application of a new surface treatment. Panels are available in widths from 2 to 5 feet and in a variety of lengths. FRP is stronger than glass and requires less framing to support it. It can also be quickly installed over roof purlins using nails or screws as fasteners. Be sure to specify "greenhouse grade" panels in order to obtain maximum light transmission and resistance to ultra violet deterioration.

Acrylic. This family of plastics is being developed into a number of glazings which have durability, strength, and maximum light transmission. Unfortunately, present cost of these materials is greater than that of glass. Also, experience in solar collectors has shown that the acrylics have a very high coefficient of thermal expansion. This means they will stretch and shrink by a large amount as they heat and cool. Expansion and contraction will cause problems in anchorage of the acrylics to the greenhouse structure.

Heating

Energy required for heating is one of the major costs in production of greenhouse crops, often as much as 30% of total cost. A major concern in the installation of heating systems is to obtain uniform distribution throughout the structure. Both central and distributed types of units have been used with success.

Glass covered houses frequently use centrally located steam boilers with finned pipe radiators to distribute the heat. These units are fairly expensive initially, but offer the advantage of a dependable system with low maintenance and uniform heating. The central unit will also be slightly more efficient in converting fuel into heat than the individual units. However, this gain can be easily lost in the distribution system if steam lines are not well insulated in places where they pass through unheated areas.

Individual heaters or small hot air furnace units are often chosen for greenhouses which are used only seasonally. These burners are considerably less expensive to install and can provide adequate heating if properly ducted. They do require more maintenance and management than the larger centrally located units. Any direct-fired burners used within the greenhouse must be properly vented to keep the products of combustion outside.

Sizing of heaters and fuel selection for greenhouses is the same as for other agricultural buildings and is discussed in greater detail in Chapter 29. Major heat loss is by conduction through the covering and by infiltration (leakage of cold air into the structure). Use of two layers of covering material instead of a single layer can reduce conductive loss by as much as 50%. Good construction practices and reduced ventilation during extremely cold weather will help reduce the infiltration losses.

Ventilation

All greenhouses require some type of ventilation system to provide temperature and humidity control. Hinged panels in sidewalls and at the ridge can provide this ventilation, but thermostatically controlled fans with properly designed inlet and distribution systems will do a better job with less labor.

In order to maintain satisfactory temperature control on bright, sunny days, the ventilation system should be capable of moving 7 to 12 cubic feet of air per minute (cfm) for each square foot of floor area in the greenhouse.

During late fall and early spring, a lower amount of air is required for temperature control (normally about 2 cfm per square foot of floor area). This amount can be easily provided and well distributed with a pressurized fan-tube ventilation system. This system uses a perforated polyethylene tube suspended under the ridge of the greenhouse and inflated by a fan. When temperatures become too high in the house, a thermostat opens a louver next to the fan, letting outside air in. During cold weather, these units can be run without introducing outside air to help control condensation and distribute heat in the building.

Evaporative cooling systems can be used to control extreme summer heat in greenhouses and are much more effective for this purpose than they are in animal shelters. They are especially effective if the relative humidity of the outside air is below 50%. A reasonable estimate of the cooling effect from an evaporative cooler is 75% to 80% of the difference between the dry bulb and wet bulb temperature of the outside air. Dry bulb temperature is what your regular thermometer measures. You can find out wet bulb temperature by calling your local weather station or by using an inexpensive instrument called a sling psychrometer, available from most greenhouse supply companies.

Evaporative cooling is accomplished by pulling or pushing ventilation air through a wetted pad into the greenhouse. Pads are usually constructed of excelsior or some other porous material. During operation, water is continuously run over the pad by a circulating pump. Evaporative cooling system design will depend on normal summer weather conditions expected in your location and the specifications of the equipment manufacturer. Cooling pads are rated in terms of cfm per square foot of pad. Depending on pad construction, values will range from approximately 140 cfm up to 230 cfm. If evaporative cooling is installed, summer ventilation rates can be designed using the lower end of the 7 to 12 cfm per square foot of floor area range. A 26 by 100 foot greenhouse with an installed summer ventilation rate of 26 by 100 by 7 = 18,200 cfm would need approximately 130 square feet of evaporative pad with a capacity of 140 cfm per square foot.

Saving Energy

A considerable amount of time and money has been and is being used for research into ways to reduce energy usage in greenhouse operation. Some of the findings are well enough documented that we have included them in a listing below.

Site selection. Heat loss from a greenhouse subjected to a 15 mph wind can be 10% to 15% higher than loss from a similar building located in a calm area. Selection of a site which is sheltered from prevailing winter winds can reduce season long heating bills by 5% to 10%.

Movable blankets. Transparent materials such as glass and plastic are very poor insulators. Several research projects have been carried out to show the effectiveness of placing a solid insulating blanket or curtain

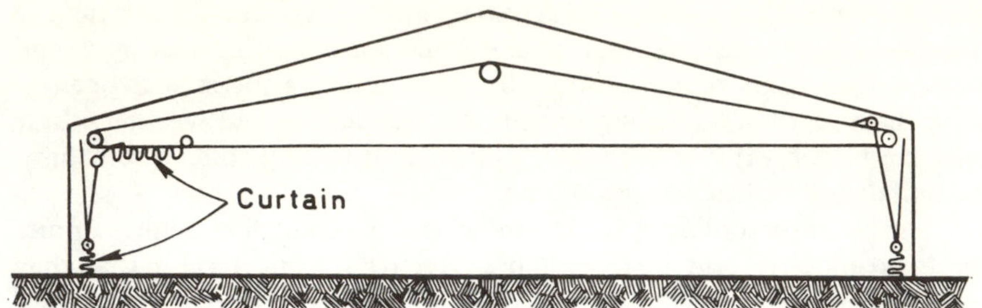

Figure 15-5. Blanket arrangements such as this one illustrated here can save considerably on nighttime heat losses from the greenhouse. (NRAES)

between the growing crop and the greenhouse covering during night time hours. Work in single covered glass houses has yielded energy saving of nearly 60% when using a dark colored shading system suspended above the crop at night. Blankets do a good job of keeping heat in the plant growth area. This means the area under the glazing material is much colder at night, leading to increased condensation. This condensation drips onto the insulating blanket and the plants below if the blanket is porous.

Insulation. A limited number of conventional insulation techniques can be used in greenhouses. One which is very effective is the use of perimeter insulation around the foundation. Methods of installing this are illustrated in Chapter 27. Perimeter insulation reduces heat loss through exposed portions of the foundation and from the relatively warm soil in the greenhouse. A layer of plastic foam insulation having a minimum R value of 8 is installed over all exposed areas of the foundation and extended into the ground for a depth of 24 inches. The above ground portion of this may need to be protected from mechanical damage if it is accessible to machinery contact.

Experiments with installation of permanent insulation in the north walls of greenhouses have given mixed results. Work at Cornell University

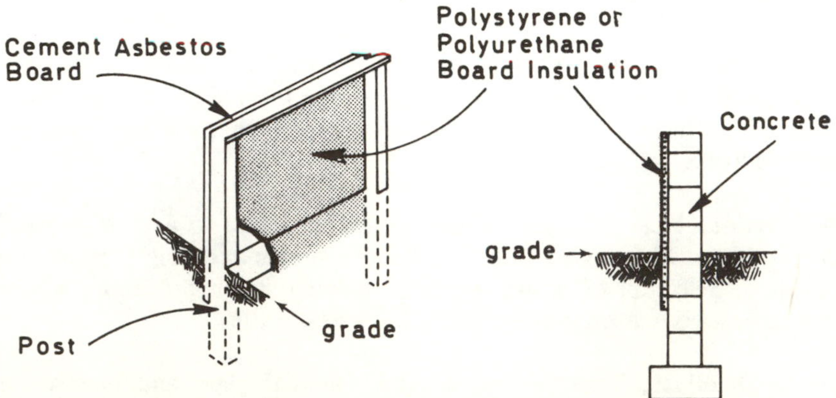

Figure 15-6. Perimeter insulation should be used to restrict heat loss from lower wall areas. (NRAES)

showed a 29% energy savings in a 36 by 36 foot glass covered greenhouse. However, most of the saving was due to the fact that the insulation helped reduce infiltration considerably. North wall insulation reduces light levels somewhat and leads to greater than normal temperature variation within the structure. Light reflecting surfaces on the interior of the insulated section help reduce the effects of lowered light levels.

Management. For any given building, there are certain things that the operator can do to significantly reduce energy usage.

Lowering operating temperatures in the greenhouse by 5° to 10° F will save 10% to 25% of the energy costs for northern states. Savings approaching 50% are possible in the southern states. *Caution:* Certain crops will require minimum temperatures in order to grow and reproduce. The December 1-March 1 period represents well over half the heating season. It is also the time of year many plants do not do well because of lowered light levels. Shutting down the greenhouse for these 3 months may be an economical choice for your particular operation. Before you shut down and leave for that winter vacation, make sure you drain the water pipes and arrange for someone to clear any heavy snow off the roof.

Some producers use only 60% to 70% of the available floor area in a greenhouse. Improvements in layout and installing narrower aisles can increase productive area to 70% to 85%.

Several solar collector storage systems have been developed for greenhouses. To date, some of these have shown promise for reducing energy costs, but most have not proven to be cost effective. It is expected that they will become more cost effective as energy costs continue to increase.

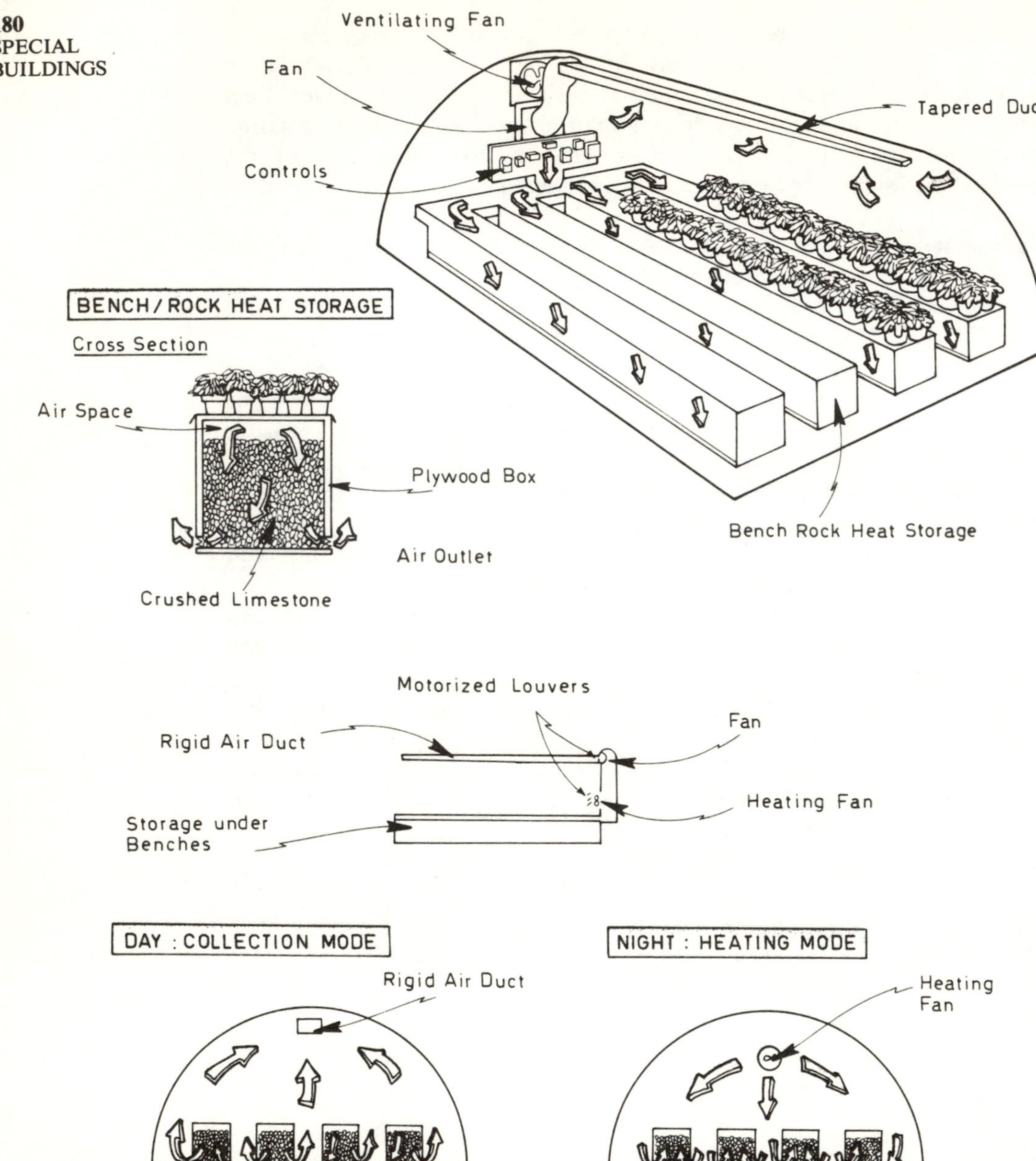

Figure 15-7. This is one of several solar energy systems that is currently being tested for use in greenhouses. The fan takes warm air from the ridge of the house during sunny days and forces it through the rock storages beneath the benches. At night, heat is extracted from the storages and used to offset some of the heating needs of the building. (NRAES)

Part III

Building Construction

CHAPTER **16**

Building with A Contractor

At one time, almost all farm construction was done by the farmer with the help of additional farm laborers or perhaps a few neighbors. This is no longer the case. The increased complexity of both farming and farm building construction often leaves little time available for farm labor to work on construction and makes employment of skilled building people an economical choice. The person skilled in construction of farm buildings is the farm building contractor. This chapter outlines some of the items you need to know and do in order to complete your new facility using a contractor.

Shopping For a Contractor

You are going to invest a lot of money in a complex facility that needs to be put together right and on time. Along the way, there will probably have to be some changes made in either the basic building or in materials selected. You need a contractor who is reliable, knowledgable in the type of construction, and with whom you can communicate. If you are lucky, this is not your first building and you already have had a good experience with a reliable contractor in your area.

The best way to start shopping for a contractor is to visit with people in your locality who have recently had new facilities constructed. Find out who their contractor was and if they were satisfied with his performance. Don't forget to ask about follow up. There has never been a building that didn't have a few minor errors or problems develop after it was put into use. A good contractor makes sure these items are taken care of promptly.

Most builders will advertise in local papers and farm magazines serving the area they work in. Use these ads to make a list of potential contractors for your building. When you make initial contact with these individuals or firms, there are four things you would like to know.

1. Does their firm have any experience in constructing the type of facility you are interested in. A firm that has specialized in machinery storages probably will not be able to handle the complexities of a milking center without spending extra time on the job. Extra time for them is extra cost for you.
2. Names of persons for whom they have recently built.
3. A list of business references. This would include their banker and some of the material suppliers with whom they do business.
4. The status of their current work schedule. Some contractors are booked up for several months in advance. If you need to be under construction within a few weeks, a contractor who can't get there for 6 months won't do you much good.

Once you have this information, follow up by contacting both customers and business references to find out just how good a contractor each one is. Rank the top four to five firms and then contact each to discuss your specific needs. During this discussion, provide each contractor with a set of plans and specifications, or a listing of your specific needs if you are asking for a building proposal. Ask for a firm bid price on your plans and specifications, along with a statement of any alterations or substitutions which the contractor might wish to propose. If you are working with a listing of your needs, ask for a complete building proposal from the contractor. This will include a set of plans and specifications, along with a bid price for construction. Also, be sure to have each firm include an estimated completion date. This can be expressed as a firm date or in terms of a specific number of days after awarding of the contract.

Set a deadline for delivery of bids and proposals to you. After these are received, you should make a specific appointment, to allow the contractor to fully explain his proposal and ask any questions you may have about the building he is proposing to erect for you.

When the final evaluation process is over, make your decision and award the contract. Price will undoubtedly be a primary consideration; however, you should be buying quality and performance and the low bidder may not always be the one who supplies these factors.

Building Specifications

Formal written specifications provide a way to elaborate on items which are not normally included in plans or blueprints for a building. For example, items such as equipment brand and model, color of siding, and required grades of lumber are not normally shown on plans. Specifications also help provide a greater understanding of exactly what is being furnished by the contractor.

Specifications may be prepared by the person who develops your specific plan or they may be included as a part of a formal building proposal submitted by a contractor in response to your request. Fill in the blank type specification forms which you can develop for yourself are often available through lending agencies, extension offices, or building supply dealers.

Specifications may be written to include some items which are often found in contracts. If this is done, it will greatly simplify the job of writing and interpreting the contract.

Items which you or the contractor are unsure of at the time you request bids can be specified as allowances. For example, suppose you have not made up your mind exactly what type of furnace you are going to install in your new farm shop. In the specifications you may indicate a heating system allowance of some amount, for example $1,500. After you make your decision, any cost over $1,500 will be added to the contract price; any amount less than $1,500 will be subtracted from the final payment.

Specifications take many forms, depending on who writes them. However, most tend to follow the general order of construction. Major sections and items which need to be included under each are as follows:

I. ***General information***

Name and address of owner
Type and size of building
Location of building

II. ***Incorporation statement***

Brief written statement indicating that the following specifications are a part of the overall plan for the building and that construction must conform to both the drawings and the specifications.

III. ***Site preparation***

Topsoil removal and disposal
Fill material to be used and compaction method
Any surface drainage work
Utilities which must be brought to site
Drainage lines to be installed from site
Allowance for unforeseen problems

IV. ***Building design loadings***

Roof load
Ceiling load
Wind load
Floor loads
Any unusual load carrying members

V. ***Wall construction***

Foundation
Concrete mix
Pressure treated material specifications
Mortar mix
Waterproofing

Footing drains
Anchorage
Exterior siding and finish
Interior surfacing and finish
Insulation type and R value
Vapor barrier material

VI. ***Roof construction***

Roofing material to be used
Insulation under roofing
Ceiling material and finish
Insulation type and R value
Skylights
Attic ventilation provided
Roof openings required
Gutters and downspouts

VII. ***Windows and doors***

Manufacturer and type if prefabricated
Description of construction and mounting hardware if contractor built
Flashing material

VIII. ***Interior walls***

Construction
Finish
Insulation type and R value

IX. ***Floors***

Fill material
Concrete mix
Surface finish

X. ***Electrical***

General statement on code compliance
Size and type of entrance panel
Number of outlets
Special equipment outlets
Light fixtures or fixture allowance
Type of switches
Minimum wire size if applicable

XI. ***Plumbing***

Size and type of supply lines
Size and type of waste lines
Water heater manufacturer and model
Water conditioning equipment
Fixture brands and models
Floor drains

Sewage disposal system description

XII. *Heating*

Size of system
Manufacturer and model number
Chimney or flue construction
Fuel storage

XIII. *Special equipment*

Description, manufacturer and model of any special equipment to be installed as part of the building contract.

XIV. *Exterior work*

Clean up of site
Finish grading and seeding
Driveway and sidewalk construction

Table 16-1. **Sample Set of Specifications for a Farm Shop**

SPECIFICATIONS
for
FARM SHOP
30 by 40 feet

I. *Owner:* Robert Farmer
Route 4
Crossroads, Kansas 65472
(732) 496-1084

Location of building: On farmstead at junction of hwys. 142 and 673.

II. *Specifications*

These specifications are hereby made a part of the overall plan for this farm shop and all construction must comply with both the formal drawings (Drawing No. 7329-1) and these specifications.

III. *Site preparation*

1. All topsoil to a depth of 10 inches is to be removed from the site and piled for later use in finish grading.
2. Fill material required to bring site to level is to be furnished by owner and hauled by contractor.
3. Fill shall be placed in 6 inch layers and well compacted with a 5 ton roller.
4. A 3 foot high surface water diversion shall be constructed on the North and East sides of the building site.
5. Owner will install one water supply line from well to site.
6. Contractor shall install drainage line to existing sewerage system for bathroom wastes. Floor drains to outlet on grade.
7. A $15.00 per cubic yard additional charge shall be allowed for excavation of any solid rock encountered.

IV. *Design loadings*

1. This building shall be designed and constructed with the following design loads.

   Roof: 25 psf total
   Ceiling: 5 psf
   Wind: 80 mph
   Floor: 75 psf

2. A 10 by 21 inch steel beam shall be installed as indicated to provide support for an overhead hoist.

V. Wall Construction

1. Concrete used to support and anchor posts shall be 2,500 psi mix.
2. Pressure treated posts shall be treated with pentachlorophenol to a retention of 8 pounds per cubic foot.
3. Wall purlins shall be No. 3 Fir or equal with treated members having 6 pounds per cubic foot of penta.
4. Exterior wall shall be covered with 28 gauge galvanized and prepainted steel manufactured by Acme Steel. Color: Brown.
5. Flashing and trim also by Acme. Color: White.
6. Interior walls to be covered with ½ inch thick gypsum board. All joints to be taped and sanded. Finish with 2 coats of ABC acrylic latex paint. Color: Mint green.
7. Walls to be insulated with 6 inch thick glass fiber batts (R = 19). Install 4 mil polyethylene vapor barrier over insulation.

VI. Roof Construction

1. Roof shall be covered with 28 gauge galvanized and prepainted steel manufactured by Acme Steel. Color: White
2. Ridge cap and trim also by Acme.
3. 2 by 4 nailing strips shall be attached to lower chords of the trusses (24 inches on center) and ceiling covered with ½ inch gypsum board. All joints to be taped and sanded. Finish with 2 coats of ABC acrylic latex paint. Color: White.
4. Ceiling to be insulated with 8 inches of blown in cellulose insulation treated with fire retardant material; R = 30. 4 mil polyethylene vapor barrier to be installed before applying finished ceiling material.
5. Install gable end ventilators at each end of building. Each ventilator shall provide 4 square feet of opening.
6. Install prefinished steel guttering and downspouts along eaves of roof. Four downspouts required. Color: White.

VII. Windows and doors

1. Shop windows to be sliding units with aluminum frames and double glazing. Tru-Vue Manufacturing Co. model #5976. Sizes as shown on drawings.
2. Overhead door to be Model #4421 by ODC Corporation.
3. Entry door to be prehung steel unit with polyurethane insulated core. Model #7932 by ODC Corporation.
4. All exterior wall openings shall be flashed with pre-finished stall flushing

material to match siding.

VIII. ***Interior walls—none***

IX. ***Floor***

1. Install 4 inch layer of 1-½ inch graded gravel over earth fill.
2. Floor to be 4 inch thick poured concrete with 6 by 6 inch 10 gauge welded wire reinforcing mesh. Floor shall slope uniformly to drains and shall have a steel troweled finish. Concrete shall be 3000 psi mix with 6% air entrainment.

X. ***Electrical***

All electrical work shall comply with provisions of the National Electrical Code and with requirements of the Crossroads Utility Company.

1. Furnish and install 150 Ampere capacity service entrance panel equipped with circuit breakers. ESE Company model #14-150.
2. Install 23 grounded duplex 110V outlets in locations shown.
3. Install 220V outlets for the following equipment:
   Welder
   Grinder
   Power hack saw
   Drill press
4. Lighting to be 40 watt twin tube fluorescent strip fixtures ceiling mounted in locations shown. 16 fixtures required. Switch as indicated.
5. Minimum wire size in this building shall be No. 12 AWG.

XI. ***Plumbing***

1. Supply lines shall be ½ inch CPVC plastic with solvent welded joints.
2. Waste lines shall be 1-½ inch and 3 inch PVC Schedule 40 with solvent welded joints.
3. Water heater shall be 30 gallon glass lined electric unit manufactured by Alpha Inc.; Model #4500-30.
4. Lavatory Model #C-125 by ASP.
   Water Closet Model #J-421 by ASP.
5. Floor drains shall be 12 inches deep box with steel grating (see detail on plans).
6. Lavatory and water closet waste lines shall be connected to existing house septic tank system.

XII. ***Heating***

1. Furnish and install 100,000 Btu per hour warm air, oil fired furnace. Shop Warmer Inc. Model #100K-HA.

   Chimney shall be 6 inch diameter prefabricated metal unit manufactured by Shop Warmer Inc.
2. Install 1,000 gallon capacity underground fuel oil storage tank for furnace.

XIII. ***Special equipment***

1. Contractor shall supply and install ventilated paint booth in the location shown. Paint booth and ventilating equipment to be Model #4792-10 as

manufactured by SPC Corporation.

XIV. Exterior work

1. Contractor shall remove all debris from the site as soon as construction is complete.
2. Finish grading, seeding, and driveway construction by owner.

The Contract

The contract is the legal agreement between you and the individual or firm who will be doing your construction work. It can be as simple as a spoken word over the telephone or as complex as a 30 to 40 page document. Both types are equally binding. However, if any problems ever develop, you can imagine the difficulty you might have in obtaining a court ruling on all points in a verbal contract.

All contracts for construction work should be written and signed by both parties. The contract should be prepared by an attorney and should include provisions to protect you against liens, excessive payments, and uncontrolled changes in plans. In some states, owners can protect themselves against mechanic's liens by obtaining waivers, in the contract, from the contractor himself. By recording the contract, the waiver can be held to protect against the mechanics' liens that might otherwise arise in favor of suppliers and subcontractors who deal with the contractor.

Construction contracts frequently provide for a reduction in price in the event that any materials or work are eliminated during the course of construction. It is also common to provide for increased charges in the event extra work or changes are involved. The contract should spell out that all changes from the original plans must be stated in writing, along with cost adjustments, and be signed by both you and the contractor *before* the change is made.

The contract should specify a completion date for the job. If it is essential that construction be done on time, you may want to include a penalty for failure to meet the deadline. Most contractors are reluctant to sign contracts with penalty clauses unless there is an escape for events which are beyond their control.

The contract should require that the contractor furnish proof of liability and workmen's compensation insurance. This coverage should be written in such a way that it protects both you and the contractor in the event of claims.

Other items which should be addressed by the contract include performance bonds, warranties, and payment schedules. These are discussed further in the following sections.

Performance Bond

A performance bond is a type of insurance policy which insures that the contractor will either complete the construction as agreed or you will be compensated by the company issuing the bond. Performance bonds are standard requirements in almost all government issued contracts and in many other large construction jobs.

Before requiring a bond, you should understand the following things. First, the contractor may be unable to obtain a bond. This may be due to present or past financial problems he may have had. Second, if he does obtain a bond, you can expect that the cost of the bond will be added to your cost of construction. Finally, if construction is covered by bond, be sure that the bonding agency is advised of any changes or adjustments in the project. Otherwise, the bonding company may use your failure to keep them advised as a lever to avoid payment.

Warranties

A warranty is a guarantee that the item or service you purchase will perform in a certain way. Warranties may be implied, verbal, or written. To illustrate the difference in these, let's suppose you are buying a new roof for your machinery storage. You go to the lumber yard and purchase enough roofing material to do the job. The fact that the material was called roofing and was sold as such "implies" that it will keep out rain and do those things normally expected of roofing material. The implied warranty is the weakest type of warranty and the hardest to get adjustment from in the event of failure. It has, however, been used successfully as an argument in some cases where a purchaser could not normally be expected to be able to evaluate a product in advance of purchase.

If you visited with the salesman at the lumber yard and he told you the roofing you bought would last at least 20 years, this is a verbal warranty. The verbal warranty is better than the implied warranty, but it is your word against theirs in the event of a claim.

Many items we purchase today come with a written warranty. The written warranty states a specific time period over which the product is guaranteed to perform without defect. It will frequently outline terms of replacement or adjustment in the event of failure. The written warranty will probably also contain a disclaimer which attempts to void any implied or verbal warranties. The written word provides the best basis for any legal action which might be needed to enforce a claim. You should insist on a written warranty covering construction of any facility on your farm. Also, you should require that the contractor provide you with any warranties supplied by manufacturers of equipment or components he installs in your building.

Payment Schedules

Unless you are involved in a small job or are dealing with a very large contractor, your contractor will require some type of intermediate payment schedule as work progresses. Schedules will vary between contractors and with different sizes of jobs. You can visit with your lending agency to find out what is common in your area and what is acceptable to them. The payment schedule should be included in the formal written contract.

Table 16-2. **Typical Payment Schedule Expressed as a Percentage of Total Contract Cost.**

Time Frame	Percentage
At signing of contract.	10
Building roof is on.	30
Plumbing and electric roughed in, insulation in place, and interior wall and ceiling material is on.	40
Building complete.	20
	100%

Mechanic's Liens

Most state laws provide for some form of mechanic's lien against real estate as a means of protecting contractors and suppliers who are unpaid for their work in improving that property. The lienholder normally has a specified time period following completion of the work within which to file a lien. He must then file suit to foreclose on the lien.

Laws generally treat contractors and suppliers differently, depending on whether they contracted directly with the owner or provided goods and services to the general contractor. You should be aware that a supplier can place a mechanic's lien against your property if your contractor failed to pay for something used in the construction of your building. This can be done even though you have paid him for the work. Require the contractor to secure partial or full lien waivers from each person or firm. If you are financing with a construction loan, the mortgage holder will probably require that lien waivers be provided as a condition for release of funds.

Insurance

Construction of a new building imposes some added risks which you may not be protected against. These fall generally into the categories of property loss and liability. Because of the wide variation in available insurance coverages and in state requirements, it would be nearly impossible to outline a definite program of coverage for all farm construction projects. You should plan to sit down with both your contractor and your insurance agent to discuss existing and needed coverage before you sign the contract.

Insurance is designed to protect you from financial loss in case of unexpected events. There is no way to list all the things that could possibly go wrong on a construction site. Some of the items you will want to ask your agent and the contractor about covering include the following:

Do we have insurance coverage if:

1. Wind blows down a partially finished building?

2. A neighbor's child is attracted to the construction site and is injured?
3. A laborer is injured while moving a piece of my equipment out of the way of the construction site?
4. Some of my livestock get out and walk through some recently finished concrete?
5. The neighbor's livestock get out and are injured at the construction site?
6. The contractor breaks an underground utility line while excavating?
7. My house or my neighbor's house is damaged by shock from blasting?
8. The building burns down while under construction?
9. Someone steals several hundred dollars worth of building materials from the construction site?
10. A contractor's employee or one of your employees sues both you and the contractor over an injury received at the construction site?
11. Shortly after it is complete and paid for, the roof collapses due to a construction error and kills several of the animals in your breeding herd?

Damage Awards

If the contractor fails to complete your building as agreed, the courts say you are entitled to a damage payment. The amount of payment will depend on the nature of the problem.

If the contractor abandons a partially completed project, you are generally entitled to recover any extra cost due to having another contractor complete the job, as well as any costs incurred or likely to occur from the delay in completion. If the contractor abandoned the job because of financial insolvency, you may have difficulty in collecting unless he was required to post a performance bond.

If there is a defect in the completed work or if plans were not followed, damage recovery varies among states. Generally, you can recover the cost of correcting the problem. But it has to be done without substantially destroying or dismantling construction already completed, the cost of which would vastly exceed the value of correcting the defect. If substantial destruction is required, the courts will probably allow the owner to recover only the difference in value of the structure resulting from the defect or omission.

CHAPTER **17**

Building It Yourself

Many farms have an excess of labor at certain times of the year. If yours happens to be one of these and the excess occurs when you are ready to build, you can save some money by building it yourself.

There are a number of options available for those persons who wish to do it themselves. These range from that of serving as general contractor to the individual who "does it all" with no additional outside labor. The potential for cost savings increases with the amount of responsibility and labor you have to contribute.

A general contractor is a person who takes responsibility for the overall building project. He hires and schedules sub-contractors to complete various parts of the overall project and is responsible for ordering much of the material used. He may or may not have one or more work crews of his own that do part of the construction. The general contractor's fee is normally about 10% of the total project cost.

Subcontractors

The subcontractor is a contractor who has specialized in some particular aspect of the construction process. Examples include electrical work, plumbing, concrete work, framing, roofing, and excavation. Subcontractors do most of their work for full time general contractors. This sometimes means that the individual doing his own general contracting will have a lower priority on the subcontractor's schedule than the contractor who can offer him another job next week.

Before you hire a subcontractor, review Chapter 16. The things covered there apply to subcontractors as well as general contractors.

Ordering Materials

One of the more time consuming jobs of the person serving as general contractor is the selection and ordering of materials. Unless you are in no hurry to complete your construction project, you will probably not have time to always check all potential suppliers for best price on each item you buy.

You can save some of this work and still be sure of getting a reasonably good price on materials by asking for materials only bids from building supply dealers. Before you start construction, take a complete set of plans and specifications to several dealers in your area. Explain to them that you will be doing the ordering of materials and what your planned construction schedule is. Ask each dealer to prepare a list of materials and give you a firm price on the materials delivered to your site on request during the expected construction period. Give the dealers a specific time to have their bids returned (usually about two weeks) and have them note any items they are unable to supply.

When all bids are in and you have selected the dealer you plan to do business with, let him know. This will give him time to order any material you need that he may not have in stock.

Make sure the successful bidder keeps a set of your plans and specifications in his files for future reference. This will enable you to call up and order "all the siding material" without having to sit down and figure out how many pieces of what size material you need.

It is highly unlikely that a single building supply dealer will be able to furnish all the materials you will be needing to complete your new building. You may want to repeat the above bidding and selection process with different types of supply firms or you might simply select individual firms to furnish specific items needed. No matter how you choose to proceed, do it well in advance of when you will need the material. This will allow time both for ordering of special items and to set up an account with each of the firms. Be sure to let each business know that you are serving as your own general contractor when setting up accounts. Most building supply firms offer special discounts to contractors which are not available to individual buyers.

Insurance

The risks don't change when you do it yourself, but the required insurance coverage probably will. Again, it's best to visit with your regular insurance agent to see that you are properly covered during all phases of construction. Coverages which you may need to add include contractor liability and workmen's compensation.

Contractor liability is a broad form type of coverage which defends the contractor against liability claims from anyone who suffers loss due to the construction activity. Although it is called "broad form" coverage, most policies contain a number of exclusions for specific occurrences. Study these carefully. It may well be that you will need specific coverage in addition to that provided by the general policy.

Most states require employers to pay into a state fund or to carry workmen's compensation insurance with a private insurance company.

Farm workers are frequently exempt from these requirements; however, this does not excuse the employer from liability in the case of negligence. If you plan to use hired labor in construction of your new building, check with both your attorney and your insurance agent. You will need an opinion on whether or not construction of your building will be classed as farm labor and how adequate any present insurance coverage may be.

Potential Savings

How much can I save by doing it myself? No one question is as easy to ask and as hard to answer. The cost of materials that go into a farm building represent 40% to 50% of the total contracted cost in most cases. You probably won't save anything on materials cost. In fact, they may cost you slightly more since you may not get full contractor discounts from all suppliers.

The 10% potential savings from serving as your own general contractor are not all savings. Some of it will have to go for extra insurance coverage and some should be allocated to cost of not getting done some things you would have done if you hadn't been working on the building. You will also have extra telephone costs and all those trips to town for things a regular contractor would have remembered to order.

Labor costs will usually equal materials cost for the professional builder. Farm labor costs are generally lower, but farm labor will take more hours and make more mistakes than the people who build every day. If you have salaried employees and are in a slack time of year, work on a building will help recover some of your overhead costs.

If you are absolutely truthful in allocating all of your costs, an upper limit on potential savings is probably in the range of 15% to 20%. You are the one who will have to decide exactly how much you can save and whether or not the effort is worth the cost.

CHAPTER **18**

Site Work and Foundations

Site Preparation

Very few construction sites are so perfect that they require no changes before building can begin. Site preparation should start with removal of topsoil from the entire building area. Topsoil contains organic matter which will decay over time. This gradual decay results in a settling which causes shifting and settling of parts of the building. As topsoil is removed, it should be piled somewhere close to the building so it will be available for use in finish grading around the outside of the completed structure.

Figure 18-1. Topsoil needs to be removed prior to starting construction in order to eliminate organic matter which will decay and cause settling of floors. It should be piled away from the building so that it will be available for final grading and landscaping work.

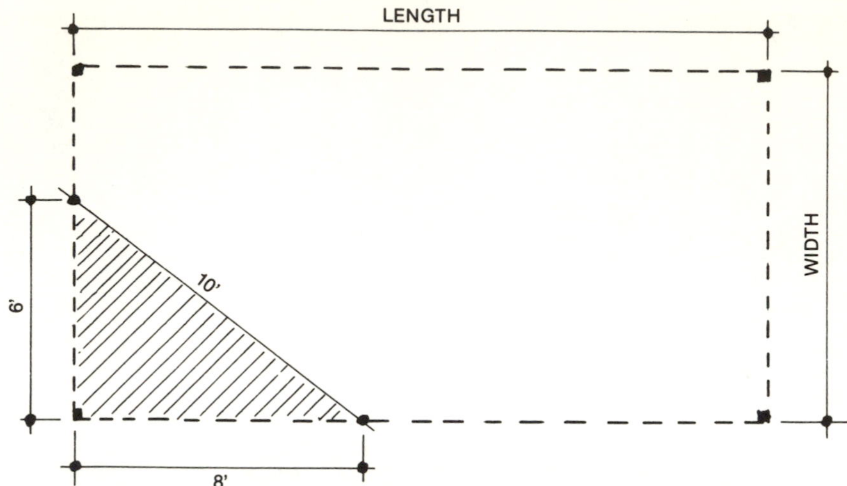

Figure 18-2. To get a square building, first set the two corner stakes for the long side of the structure. Then, using a tape measure, locate the line of the end walls using the measurements shown. This method is called the right triangle method because of the characteristic right triangle shape of the shaded area.

Use a tape measure and stakes to mark the approximate location of the building corners on the site. You can get the corners square using the right triangle method shown in Figure 18-2.

The next step is to determine how much grading or fill work is necessary to bring the site to a uniform level. Check elevations at the corners of the building with a builder's level or a transit and determine whether you will have to excavate, fill, or do a combination of both to get the desired level. If an excavation or cut is necessary, be sure it does not limit access to the building and that it is enough larger than the building to permit satisfactory water drainage. A cut area should be large enough to provide 15 to 20 feet of space between the outside of the finished building and any steep banks.

Fill needed should be placed over the site in thin layers (6 inches is suggested) and each layer should be well compacted before placing the next one. If you don't have access to a roller, a large rubber tired truck will do a good job of compacting fill. Fill material which is dry needs to have water added to it in order to get good compaction. An even better solution is to do the cut and fill work a year ahead of actual construction to allow plenty of time for natural settling. Fill should extend for a minimum of 10 to 15 feet beyond the walls of the finished building.

Buildings which will have concrete floors should have site preparation grade brought to a level 8 to 12 inches below the intended level of the finished floor of the building. This will allow for a layer of gravel under the concrete floor and a floor which is 6 to 8 inches above the level of the surrounding ground. Buildings which have no floors should have site preparation grade brought even with or slightly above the desired floor level.

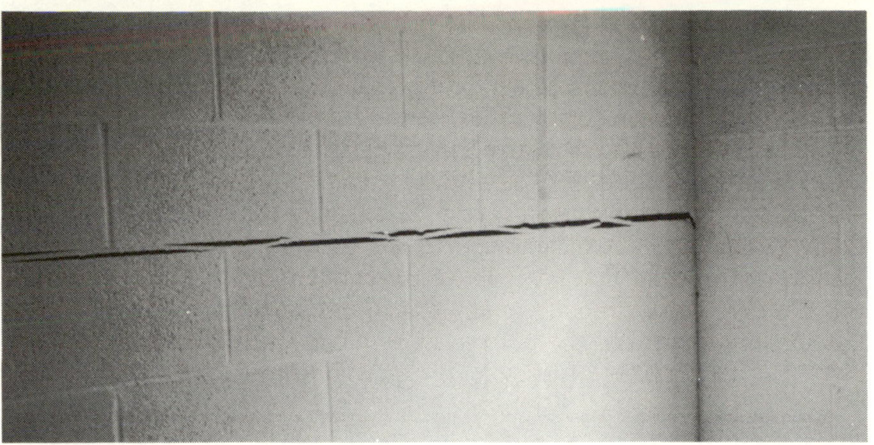

Figure 18-3. This wall was properly constructed. Failure to properly compact fill dirt allowed the footing and lower part of the wall to settle, leaving this crack.

Any diversions or waterways needed to control runoff around the building should be installed at the time of site preparation. This helps reduce water and mud problems during construction.

Utilities

Underground utility and drain lines are installed as soon as initial site preparation is complete. In order to locate the points where these lines terminate within the building, you will have to stake out and locate the building in its exact final position. Do this by setting batter boards and using string as illustrated in Figure 18-4. The right triangle method can be used to get corners square. As a final check for squareness, measure across the diagonals of the building. If the corners are square on a rectangular building, the diagonal measurements will be equal.

Extend all utility lines 2 to 3 feet above the level of the grade to prevent them from becoming covered up and lost during later construction. Plug the ends of water lines and drain lines so that they will not be filled with dirt during construction. It's also a good idea to place some temporary markers over the trenches that utility lines are buried in. This will remind you where they are when you are doing other excavation work.

Foundations

The foundation is the part of the building that is used to connect it to the soil. A good foundation must withstand all the loads on the building and transfer them to the supporting soil in such a way that there is very little movement or shifting in the building itself. At the same time, it must withstand soil movement due to changing moisture conditions, frost action in colder climates, and any horizontal soil pressure which may be present.

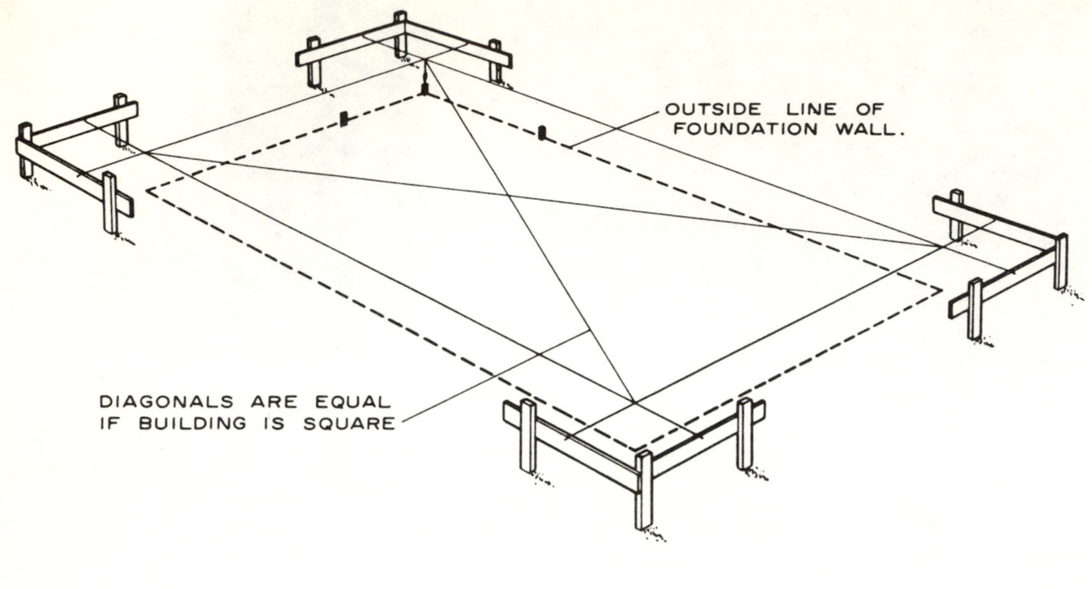

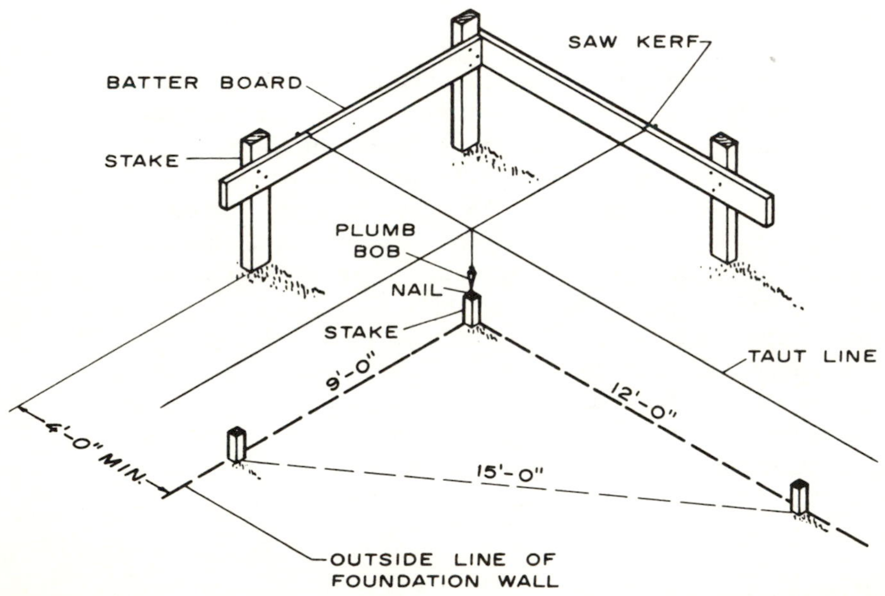

Figure 18-4. Building corners and footing lines are precisely located using batter boards, strings, and a plumb bob. (USDA)

The exact size of a foundation for a particular building is determined by the load carrying capacity (bearing strength) of the soil it is to rest on. Soil bearing strength depends on soil type and moisture capacity. In general, clay or silt has the poorest load carrying capacity, while gravel or coarse sand has the best. All soil types have lowered bearing strength when they are wet.

Table 18-1. **Allowable Bearing Strength for Different Soil Types**

Type	Capacity in Lbs per Sq Ft
Gravel or coarse sand	12,000
Dry, hard clay	8,000
Moderately dry clay	4,000
Ordinary clay and sand	3,000
Soft clay, loam, or silt	2,000

In northern parts of the country, foundations must be designed to resist frost action. Frost action or heaving is caused by the expansion of water in the soil as it freezes. Foundation designers typically avoid this problem by extending a solid foundation to a depth below the expected frost penetration line.

A footing is an enlarged supporting structure at the bottom of the foundation. It serves two purposes: to provide a firm level surface for constructing other parts of the foundation and to spread or distribute the building load over a larger area of soil. Most farm buildings are light weight enough that footings are not needed for load distribution. However, many contractors feel that the advantage of having a solid starting point for wall construction is well worth the cost of the footing. Footings should bear on firm undisturbed soil below the frost line. If it is not possible to excavate deeply enough to do this because of excessive fill at the site, you may want to consider a grade beam foundation which will provide bearing on undisturbed soil. Farm building footings are normally 8 to 10 inches deep and 16 to 20 inches wide. Two inch planks are used to form the edges of the footings. Footings are aligned using the strings which were used to outline the building during site preparation. The top edges of the footing forms should be leveled all around the building using a builder's level or transit. Two #4 reinforcing bars are frequently placed in footings to provide added strength. The outside edge of the footing should extend beyond the outside edge of the finished building wall a distance of 4 to 5 inches or one half the thickness of the foundation wall.

Conventional Foundations

This type of foundation is traditionally used in residential construction where there is a basement. The wall consists of either poured concrete or masonry block construction with sufficient reinforcing steel to withstand expected soil pressures. The exterior surface of these walls should have the below grade portion waterproofed to minimize any possible water seepage into the basement. Poured concrete walls are normally waterproofed with

Figure 18-5. This well-built foundation form is nearly ready to be filled with concrete. Note that the contractor has installed perimeter insulation in the form work. The concrete will adhere to this insulation, greatly simplifying a job that is often left until later in the construction process.

one or more coats of asphalt based waterproofing compound. Masonry block walls should be plastered with a cement based plaster and then coated with the asphalt based compound.

Farm buildings with slatted floors and under floor manure storage often use the conventional foundation wall. This type usage will result in higher than normal horizontal loads and requires special reinforcing steel in order to prevent failure. Do not fail to install reinforcing steel as shown on the plans for manure pit usage.

Forms for conventional poured concrete foundations can be farm constructed. However, it is usually less expensive and always easier to either rent prefabricated forms or hire a professional concrete contractor to set forms and pour the walls for you. One variation which has been used for manure pit sidewalls is to use a trenching machine to excavate the foundation wall to the proper width and depth. Reinforcing is then set into the trench and it is poured full of concrete. After the concrete is cured, the earth is removed from the pit area. This technique saves forming but it is much harder to correctly place reinforcing steel. The trenching method should not be used for manure pits that are more than 4 feet deep.

Curtain Walls

The curtain wall foundation is used with single story conventional frame construction buildings. It is very similar to the conventional founda-

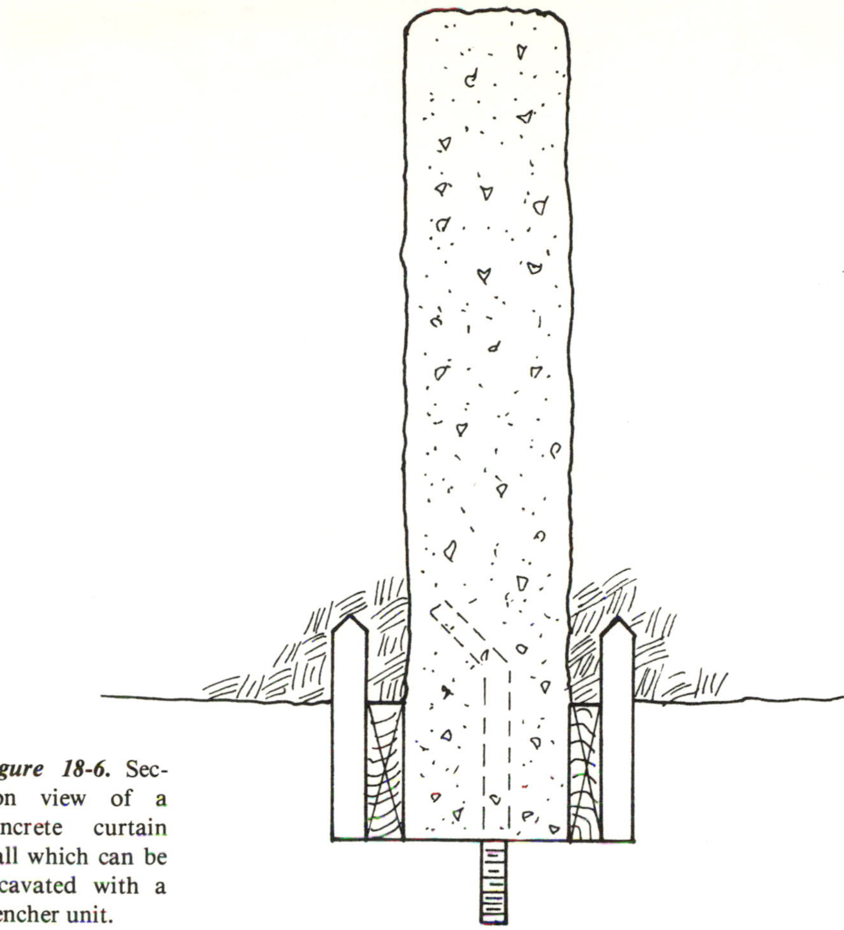

Figure 18-6. Section view of a concrete curtain wall which can be excavated with a trencher unit.

tion except that it is shorter and exterior waterproofing is not usually used. The wall itself is constructed of poured concrete or masonry block construction.

The curtain wall is supported on both sides by soil and does not normally require any reinforcing steel. It may or may not have a footing under it, depending on the type of building.

The trench and fill method of construction works very well for curtain walls on light weight buildings. A 6 to 8 inch wide trencher is used to excavate the perimeter wall to a depth below frost. Two inch planking is used to form an 8 to 10 inch high above-ground portion of the wall. The entire trench and formed section are poured full of concrete.

Curtain wall foundations used with rigid frame buildings may require special design. Rigid frames produce a large amount of outward thrust at the point where they connect to the foundation wall. Depending on the particular frame design, the foundation may need to be tied to the floor, equipped with supporting buttresses, or increased in size.

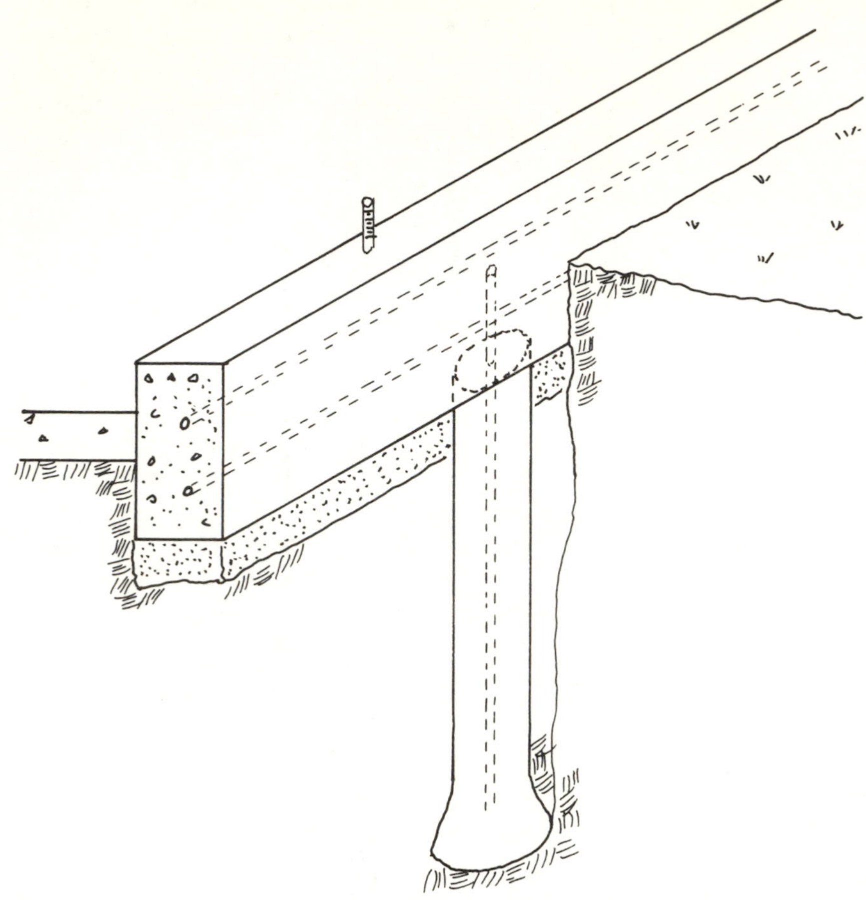

Figure 18-7. Schematic view of a grade beam type of foundation.

Grade Beam

In extremely cold climates or on building sites which require extensive fill, the grade beam foundation can provide an economical way to reach down to undisturbed frost free soil with a foundation. The grade beam is a reinforced concrete beam 6 to 8 inches wide and approximately 20 inches deep. It is used around the perimeter of the building to provide a base for above ground construction. The beam is supported by concrete piers which extend down to undisturbed soil below the frost line. Piers may be reinforced and are usually spaced 6 to 8 feet apart. The beam is imbedded in the ground at least 12 inches, with a 6 inch layer of gravel under it to provide drainage.

The foundation is constructed by first excavating a trench wide enough to accommodate forms for the beam and about 18 inches deep. A post hole digger or auger is used to dig holes for the piers at the required interval in the bottom of the trench. A 6 inch layer of gravel is placed in the bottom of the trench and the beam is formed and poured on top of the columns. Use high quality (6 sack or 3,000 psi mix) concrete in both beams and piers.

A variation of the grade beam foundation uses pressure treated wood poles and planks to form a wooden support for a building. The wood version is not as strong as the reinforced concrete unit and its use is generally restricted to light weight buildings such as greenhouses. Depending on the post size and spacing and the size of the building, footings may be required under the supporting poles.

Floating Slab

The floating slab foundation combines the building floor and foundation into a single unit. It is the easiest type of foundation to construct and it performs very well with light weight buildings, in well drained soils, and in areas where frost is not a problem.

The concrete floor and slab are formed and poured together. The major difference between this and a normal floor slab is that the edge of the slab is thickened and reinforced to form a type of grade beam which bears directly on the ground. The slab edge is normally thickened enough so that it extends 10 to 12 inches below the outside ground level to prevent washouts and rodent burrowing.

Wood Foundations

A relatively new development in the area of foundations is the use of pressure treated wood to construct both conventional and curtain wall type foundations. The system uses conventional stud frame construction techniques to fabricate wooden wall assemblies which replace the more traditional concrete. This eliminates the need for form work and can be constructed at any time of year without having to be protected from either cold or heat. The system also lends itself to prefabrication at an off-site location.

Treated lumber used in construction of foundations should be treated with a preservative approved for foundation use (usually Chromated Copper Arsenate (CCA)). All cuts made in either treated lumber or plywood should have treatment material brushed on them before they are assembled into the structure. It is recommended that all nails used below grade in assembly of wood foundations be made of stainless steel.

An easy to follow design manual on wood foundations is available from: *The American Plywood Association, Tacoma, Washington 98411.* It contains information on how to size members for different building conditions and has a well illustrated section on installation.

A wooden foundation presently costs about the same as a poured concrete unit. It does offer the advantages of being easier to work with and easier to insulate. A properly designed and constructed wood foundation should last just as well as other types of foundations.

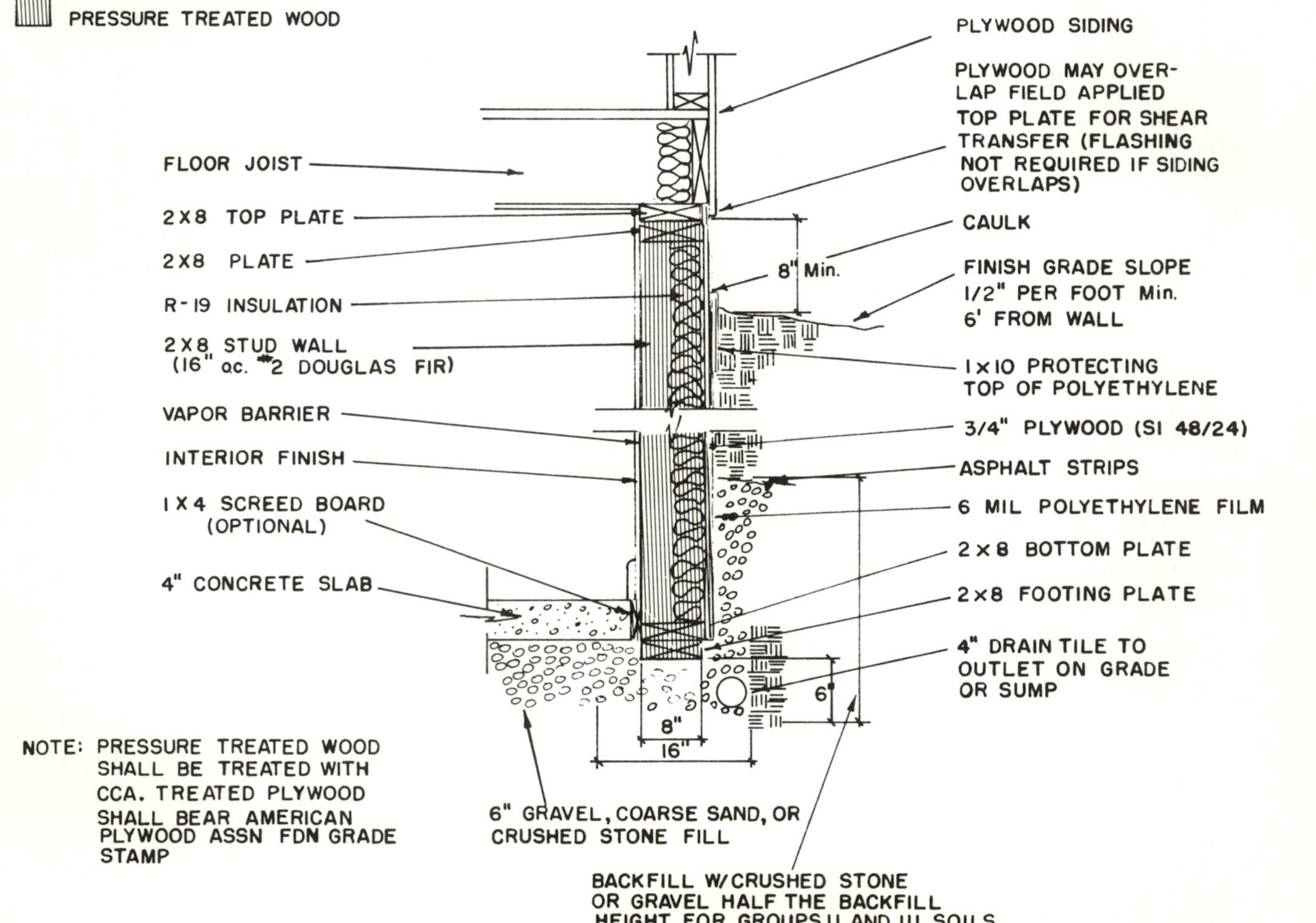

Figure 18-8. Construction detail for a wooden foundation. Member size and spacing for this type foundation will depend on building size and depth the foundation is placed in the ground. This same construction technique can also be used to build manure storage tanks. (University of Missouri)

Pole Footings

Pole frame buildings support nearly the entire load of the structure on the relatively small ends of their poles. A typical 48 foot wide clear span building at design load will place a load of nearly 6,000 pounds on each of its poles. If these poles are 6 by 6 inches, the load they place on the soil will be more than 20,000 pounds per square foot, well above the load carrying capacity of any common soil type. If this load is not spread out or distributed, the building will settle to the point where it is carried by the sidewall instead of the poles.

A concrete pad or footing placed under each pole will distribute the downward load over a larger soil area and prevent settling of the building. Footings should be sized to hold the design load in the particular type of soil that is expected at the site. A concrete pad that is 6 to 8 inches thick and 18 inches in diameter will provide adequate support for most buildings.

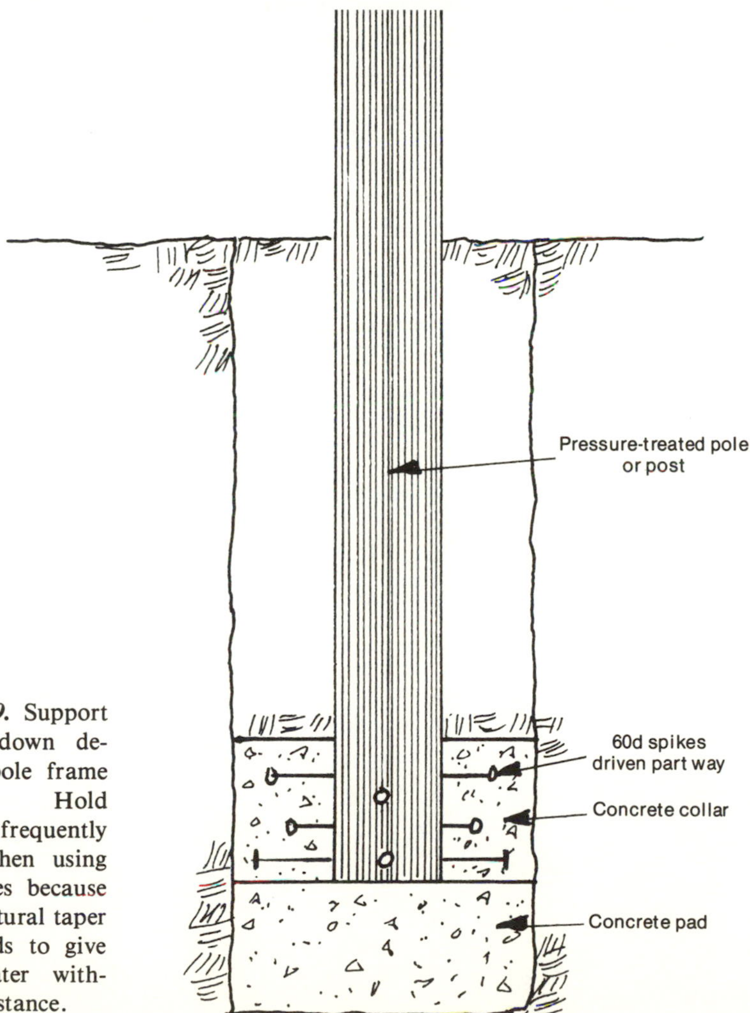

Figure 18-9. Support and hold-down details for pole frame buildings. Hold down is frequently omitted when using round poles because of their natural taper which tends to give them greater withdrawal resistance.

Concrete pads may be precast and placed in the bottom of the pole holes as they are dug. Other builders will have a ready mix truck come by and pour concrete in the bottom of each hole as it is dug. Another method is to pour a sack of dry ready mix concrete in the bottom of each hole when setting the pole. There will be enough soil moisture to harden the dry mix long before the building is complete.

Anchorage

Unless you live in an area where there is no wind, your building foundation needs to be able to hold the building down as well as up. With masonry or concrete foundations, this is done by locating anchor bolts in the foundation wall. Anchor bolts are "L" or "J" shaped rods with threaded ends. They are mortared in or imbedded into the top of the foundation wall as it is constructed. The threaded portion is used as a bolt to tie down the building to the foundation wall. Anchor bolts are usually ½ to 5/8 inch in diameter and 12 inches or more long. They are placed at intervals of 6 to 8 feet in the foundation wall.

Buildings are tied down to wooden foundations using either metal framing anchors or overlapping construction techniques. Framing anchors are described in more detail in Chapter 33.

Round poles have a natural taper which tends to provide good anchorage for buildings they are used in. Square poles do not have a taper and must be anchored. An easy way to do this is to drive several spikes part way into the sides of each pole near the end which goes in the ground. After the pole is placed in the hole, aligned, and braced, a 6 inch layer of concrete can be poured in the hole around it. The spikes will tie the concrete to the pole, providing a good anchor against uplift.

CHAPTER **19**

Concrete Floors and Paving

Concrete is by far the number one material for use in floors for farm buildings and for paving of outside yard areas. It provides an easily cleaned, durable surface and can be formed to almost any grade or shape.

Subgrade Preparation and Forming

Concrete has good wearing ability, but very little flexural strength. This means it must be supported by a firm, well drained base or cracks will develop from settling or frost action. All topsoil and organic material which was not removed in initial site preparation should be removed. Any manure or other organic material will decay over time, causing voids under the concrete which will lead to undesirable cracks. Soil under the concrete needs to be well compacted. Pay particular attention to areas over and around ditches that may have been dug to bring in utility lines.

A 4 to 6 inch layer of sand, gravel, or other well drained material should be placed over the soil immediately under where the concrete is to be placed. As material is placed and leveled, try to bring its top surface in line with the desired slope of the concrete surface. Slopes for outside paved areas should be a minimum of 1% to 2% to provide for positive water drainage. Maximum slope should probably not exceed 10% to 12%. Interior floor slopes will depend on the use of the particular building or room.

Concrete flat work is easier if it is placed in strips 10 to 12 feet wide. The 10 foot width is easier to level and finish and is preferred unless ready mix trucks have to maneuver in the strips. In this case, the 12 foot width is better.

Use 2 by 4 inch or 2 by 6 inch lumber to form the edges of paving strips. Stake them in place with 1 by 4 inch stakes located about 4 feet apart. Drive the stakes in first and then fasten the form boards to them as

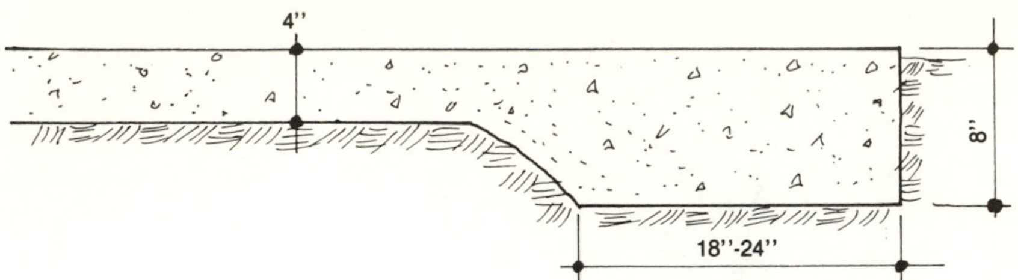

Figure 19-1. A thickened edge on a concrete slab helps to keep the slab from breaking up due to vehicle traffic on and off of it and also helps prevent washing out of subgrade material.

you establish the desired slopes. A coating of used motor oil brushed on the form boards will make them easier to remove after the concrete has hardened.

Thickness

A four inch thickness of concrete is satisfactory for all types of livestock and normal machinery traffic. In areas of heavy loads such as large liquid manure spreaders or semi-trailers of feed, increase thickness to 6 inches.

Where vehicles enter and leave paved areas, thicken the slab to 8 inches for a distance of 18 to 24 inches back from the edge. This reduces the incidence of edge failure.

One cubic yard of concrete will pave 80 square feet 4 inches thick or 54 square feet if paving is 6 inches thick. To estimate the amount of concrete you need, calculate the square footage to be paved and divide it by the appropriate value. Be sure to make some extra allowance for any thickened edge areas.

Joints

Isolation joints prevent concrete from sticking to walls, feed bunks, or other immovable objects it is poured against. The slab is free to move or settle slightly without cracking or damaging other structures. Isolation joints are made with asphalt impregnated strips or 55 pound asphalt building paper.

Control joints help prevent random cracking of concrete due to shrinking or settling. They are made with a grooving tool which forms a groove about ¼ to ⅓ the depth of the slab. Grooves are made after the concrete has partially set up, but before final finishing. Control joints may also be cut into the slab with a masonry saw after the concrete has hardened. Locate joints about 10 to 12 feet apart in both directions. Control joints are often omitted from outdoor paving where random cracks are not particularly objectionable.

Reinforcing

Loads in and around farm buildings are usually light enough so that reinforcing is not needed in floors or outside paving. If you do wish to include reinforcing in floors or paving, the easiest method is to use welded wire mesh. Welded mesh comes in a variety of sizes and is packaged in rolls 4 to 6 feet wide and 100 feet long. Farm paving can be adequately reinforced with a 6''x6''x10 gauge mesh. Cut the mesh to fit and place it inside the formed area on top of the fill. As the concrete is poured, occasionally lift up the mesh to a position near the center of the slab.

Concrete Specifications

Floors and outside paving should be done with a six bag mix. A six bag mix contains 6 sacks of cement per cubic yard of concrete. It can also be specified by asking the ready mix plant to send a 3,000 psi mix.

Milk room floors and any other paving subjected to acid base cleaners or other corrosive material should be paved with a 7 bag or 4,000 psi mix.

Concrete used should be of the air entrained type. Air entrained concrete contains millions of tiny air bubbles which help resist both acid and freeze-thaw damage. Specify a 6% air mix.

Placing and Finishing

Concrete should be placed in the formed area as soon as possible after it is mixed. When poured, it should be placed as near as possible to its final position in order to avoid separation of coarse and fine materials caused by

Figure 19-2. A 2''x6'' board known as a screed is used to strike off the concrete as soon as it is placed. Note that the mix is fairly stiff, not sloppy or runny. The stiffer the mix, the stronger the concrete will be after it cures.

moving concrete around. As soon as forms are full, the surface should be struck even with the top of the form boards using a board or a mechanical screed.

A wooden float is used to remove any surface imperfections immediately after screeding. Further finishing may not be necessary if surface texture is satisfactory.

As soon as surface water has evaporated and the concrete has started to harden, cut in any desired control joints. Final smoothing is done with a steel or magnesium trowel as soon as the concrete is hard enough to walk on. A rougher texture can be obtained by brushing the surface with a stiff bristled broom instead of using the steel trowel. After finishing, keep concrete continuously damp for 5 to 7 days to insure a good cure.

Slip Proofing

Providing a skid resistant walking surface for livestock is an important aspect of concrete paving. The broom finish described above has been the traditional recommendation for achieving a skid proof surface. Unfortunately, the acid action of manure and mechanical abuse from scrapers and other cleaning tools will wear away the roughness of a broom finish in relatively few years. As a result, many farmers are adopting roughening techniques which produce much more severe surfaces.

How much roughness you can stand will be a compromise between skid resistance, possible foot problems, and cleanability of the floor surface. Large grooves or extremely rough floors may cause foot or leg

Figure 19-3. This milking parlor floor received a broom finish to give it this rough-textured surface. Broom finishes are made by brushing the surface of the concrete with a stiff-bristled broom at the time the concrete has hardened enough to walk on.

problems with small animals. They will also be difficult to clean, which may cause a problem in areas such as milking parlors which are subject to inspection.

One device we have seen used successfully is called a jitterbug. It is a tool made of expanded metal which is used to tamp concrete into position in the forms. It is used immediately after screeding and leaves a rough diamond patterned surface which provides skid resistance and a reasonable degree of cleanability.

A smooth floor and skid resistance can be obtained by using aluminum oxide grit. The grit is sprinkled over the finished floor at a rate of ¼ to ½ pounds per square foot before the concrete sets. Select a fairly coarse grade of grit and use a trowel to tamp it into place in the concrete surface. Aluminum oxide is a very abrasive material and will cause accelerated wear on scraping tools and animal hooves. Rapid hoof wear has reduced hoof trimming and has not been a problem.

Concrete Slats

Reinforced concrete is one of the more popular materials for construction of slats used in slotted floor housing buildings. Since concrete is fairly heavy, shipping costs for factory built concrete slats are high and it is frequently more economical to cast slats on location. Forms for slats can be home built or purchased ready made from livestock equipment dealers.

Concrete for slats should be a 7 bag or 4,000 psi mix. It should be placed in the forms as dry as possible to insure maximum strength and

Figure 19-4. These concrete floor slats were factory made or "precast" and delivered to the construction site ready for installation. The notched crossbeams hold the slats in alignment and maintain the proper slot width.

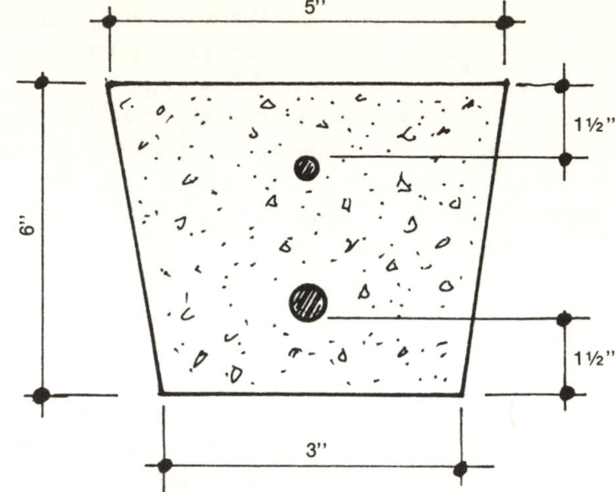

Figure 19-5. Cross section of a typical concrete slat. Actual dimensions for a given slat will depend on span, spacing, and required design load.

vibrated to obtain good contact with reinforcing steel.

Slats are normally about 2 inches wider at the top than at the bottom. This helps reduce the problem of manure sticking to sides of the slats and plugging up the floor slots. A cross section of a typical slat is shown in Figure 19-5. Dimensions and size of reinforcing required depend on design load for the particular housing unit floor and the length of the individual slats. Design load is usually expressed in terms of pounds per foot of length

***Table 19-1.* Design Loads for Floor Slats Used in Livestock Housing**

Animal	Slat Load (Pounds per Foot of Length)
Swine	
Nursery buildings	50
Finishing buildings	100
Gestation & farrowing	170
Sheep	120
Calves	150
Beef and Dairy	250

***Table 19-2.* Typical Slat Dimensions* and Reinforcing Required for Concrete Slats**

Design Load Lbs./Foot of Length	Slat Length Between Supports								
	4 ft			6 ft			8 ft		
	B in.	D in.	Bar Size	B in.	D in.	Bar Size	B in.	D in.	Bar Size
50	4	4	#3	4	4	#3	4	4	#4
100	4	4	#3	4	4	#4	4	5	#4
120	4	4	#3	4	4	#4	4	5	#4
150	5	4	#3	5	4	#4	5	6.5	#4
170	5	4	#3	5	4.5	#4	5	4	#5
250	6	4	#3	6	5.5	#4	6	4.5	#5

**There is a wide variety of possible slat dimensions to meet a particular design load.*

for individual slats. Table 19-1 presents some typical values. Table 19-2 gives sizes frequently used for concrete slats.

The upper reinforcing bar in each slat is a #3 bar used to provide strength for handling the slat. If slats were cast in place this bar would be unnecessary.

CHAPTER **20**

Wall Construction

Three general types of framing systems are used in the majority of the farm buildings constructed in the United States today. They are the conventional stud-frame (sometimes referred to as western platform framing), the post or pole frame, and the rigid frame system. Masonry wall construction is discussed in Chapter 26.

Stud Frame Construction

This system is used in almost all residential buildings and in many specialty type or processing buildings such as milking centers or grain and feed handling buildings. It is the only framing system which is easily adapted to multi story buildings.

Basic elements of the stud frame system are illustrated in Figure 20-1. They include the following:

Sills. The wooden member located at the top of the foundation wall. The sill is usually 2 to 4 inches wide. Agricultural buildings which are subjected to large amounts of moisture often use sills made of preservative treated wood to reduce the possibility of decay.

Joists. These are the horizontal wooden members which rest on the sills and are used to support a wood floor system. Joists are normally spaced 16 or 24 inches apart and sized according to the size of the design load they must carry. A table of joist sizes can be found in the appendix. Buildings more than 16 to 18 feet in width usually have a center beam with supporting posts to support the joist system. A newer construction technique is the use of parallel chord trusses instead of joists to support the floor system. These trusses are capable of spanning the entire width of a building and eliminate the need for a support under the center of the floor.

Joists are not used in single story buildings with concrete floors which

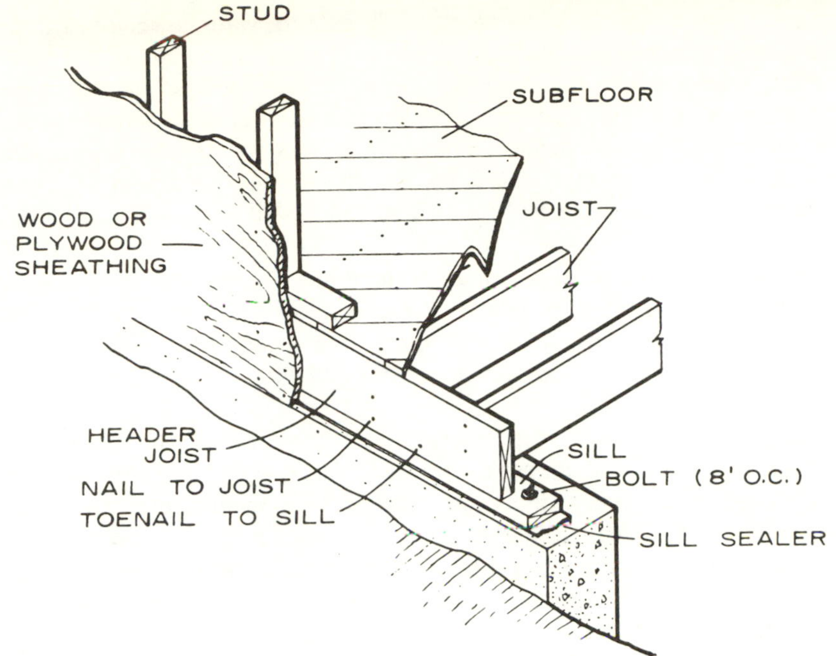

Figure 20-1. Typical stud frame construction illustrating component parts. (USDA)

are poured directly on a fill layer.

Sub flooring. A layer of wood or plywood fastened to the top edge of the floor joist system. If wooden boards are used, they are usually 1 inch thick and are frequently laid at a 45° angle to the joists to provide extra strength. A second layer of finish flooring or underlayment is fastened to the sub-flooring after the building is nearly complete. The American Plywood Association has developed a combination system which replaces the two layer system of flooring. It calls for a single layer of underlayment grade plywood with tongue and groove edges to be nailed and glued directly to the floor joists. The glue and nail assembly provides a rigid floor assembly and eliminates both materials and labor cost for floor systems which do not require a second layer of hardwood strip flooring.

Sole. A 2 inch thick member which forms the base of the stud wall. Width of the sole member will be the same as the wall studs, usually 4 or 6 inches.

Studs. Vertical members which provide the main structural support for the wall system. Traditional wall systems used 2 by 4 inch studs placed 16 inches on center. Buildings more than two stories high or buildings with extremely heavy upper floor loads would use 2 by 6 inch studs for the lower level walls.

The major problem with 2 by 4 inch stud walls is that they limit the amount of insulation which can be placed in exterior walls. Because of this, there is now a movement toward the use of 2 by 6 inch studs in the construction of exterior walls. In order to minimize the cost of the extra lumber, the 2 by 6 inch studs are usually placed on 24 inch centers rather than the traditional 16 inches. There is no loss in structural strength when this is done; in fact, the 2 by 6 inch assembly provides an even stronger wall than the more traditional 2 by 4 inch wall.

Top Plate. The horizontal member or members at the top of the wall stud assembly. The plate member is 2 inches thick and equal to the stud width. Double plates are frequently used as a means of stiffening wall assemblies and tying them together at corners and with interior partitions.

Sheathing. The first layer of materials placed over the exterior face of the studs. A wide variety of materials are used for sheathing. These include foam plastic insulation, asphalt impregnated fiber board, and plywood. Many farm buildings will use either metal, exterior grade plywood or other sheet material as a combination sheathing and exterior finish. The choice of a particular system will depend on the intended use of the building and the cost of various alternatives.

The normal progression of steps in assembly of the stud frame wall is as follows:

1. Drill holes in sill members to match location of anchor bolts in the foundation wall. Then place sill pieces over the anchor bolts and use a builder's level or transit to check for levelness completely around the building. Do this by locating the high point and shimming the remainder of the sills up to equal elevations. Wooden shingles make convenient shims. If you have to do an excessive amount of shimming, you may want to use a cement mortar mix to bring the top of the foundation wall into better alignment around the building.

   After the sill pieces are aligned and level, and any mortar used to fill gaps has set, install flat washers and nuts on the anchor bolts and tighten.

2. If used, floor joists or trusses are installed next. Make their locations on the sill members and install with the crown side up. Almost all floor joists will be slightly bowed or crowned. Floor trusses will have a slight crown (often referred to as camber) built into them. By placing the crown side up, the floor will tend to settle back toward a level position when the weight of flooring and building contents are placed on it.

   Joist members are fastened to the sills by toenailing with 8d to 10d nails. Use 4 to 6 nails at each joint.

   Many builders use a header or ribbon joist along the outside of the building. This helps keep joists in alignment and will strengthen the overall assembly.

3. Install subflooring or combination subfloor-underlayment. If using 1 inch boards, fasten them to the floor joists at a 45° angle with 8d nails. Plywood subflooring is installed with the face grain perpendicular to the floor joists. Joints in the plywood should be staggered so they do not all occur at the same joist. Do this by starting every other row of plywood sheets with a half sheet.
4. The easiest way to assemble the wall stud system is to lay it out and nail it together on the surface of the subfloor and then tilt it up into place. Assemble the sole plate, studs, headers, corners, and a single top plate using 16d nails. Two men can usually handle a 20 foot long wall section. Tip the assembled section up into place, brace it with temporary braces, and nail securely to the sill or joist assembly using 16d nails.
5. After the exterior wall studs are all in place, use the same method to put together any interior partitions. When all the stud walls are in place, install the top plate. Make sure all walls are straight and plumb as the top plate is secured.
6. Install any needed diagonal bracing and the wall sheathing. Continuous sheets of sheathing should extend from the studs down over the sill plates. This provides a mechanical tie which holds the framing components together. If this cannot be done or if the sheathing has no mechanical strength, metal strapping or framing anchors should be used every 4 to 6 feet to tie components together.

The stud frame assembly is not a particularly stable unit. Before the sheathing is on, you can grab a stud almost anywhere and shake the entire building. Bracing is required to achieve stability which will enable the building to withstand wind loads without failure. All of the following methods have been used successfully to brace stud frame walls.

Let in bracing. This technique uses 1 by 4 inch wooden members to brace corners and occasionally along the sidewall of long buildings. Studs, plates, and sole members are notched out so that the 1 by 4 inch members can be let in flush with the stud faces at an angle of 45°.

Metal bracing. Prefabricated metal strips are used in the same way as the diagonal let in 1 by 4 inch bracing. The metal is thin enough so that it can be nailed directly to the surface of the studs, eliminating the labor involved with "letting in" the 1 by 4 inch bracing. The metal bracing also has the advantage of not occupying any space between studs so that insulation is not compressed.

Plywood. The alternating layers of wood in plywood make it extremely resistant to the type of forces associated with building racking. A stud frame unit which is sheathed with plywood does not need additional bracing. In fact, many builders who use other types of sheathing will install

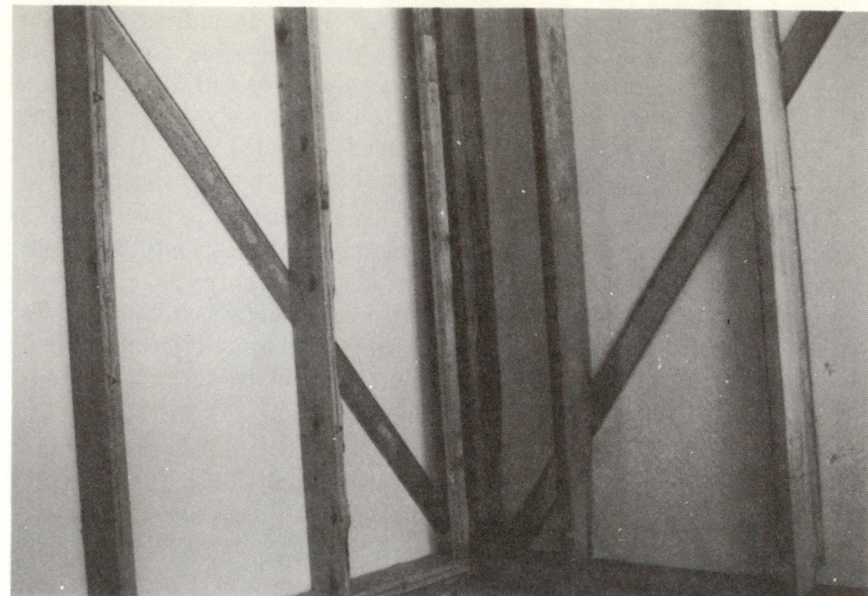

Figure 20-2. The use of metal straps as diagonal bracing has become popular since the introduction of foam plastic insulating sheathing materials. These plastic foams greatly improve the energy efficiency of a structure but have essentially no structural strength at all.

plywood sheathing at the corners of a building to provide the required bracing.

Diagonal sheathing. When individual boards are used for sheathing, they can be made to do double duty of sheathing and bracing by installing them at a 45° angle to the studs.

Pole Frame Construction

The main structural member in the sidewall of this type of building is the pole. It provides the vertical support for the roof system and also furnishes the main structural members to which any siding is attached. Basic elements of the pole frame wall system include the following.

Poles or posts. Main structural support members for pole frame buildings are made of wood which has been pressure treated with a preservative to prevent decay. Poles are available in standard sizes ranging from 4 by 4 inch up to 6 by 10 inch and in lengths up to 24 feet. Longer and larger poles may be available at extra cost. Round poles are normally specified in terms of minimum top diameter and length. Top diameters of 4 to 8 inches are typical for farm construction. Lengths up to 30 feet are readily available. Lengths of 60 to 80 feet can be special ordered at a much higher cost.

The particular size of pole will depend on post spacing, overall build-

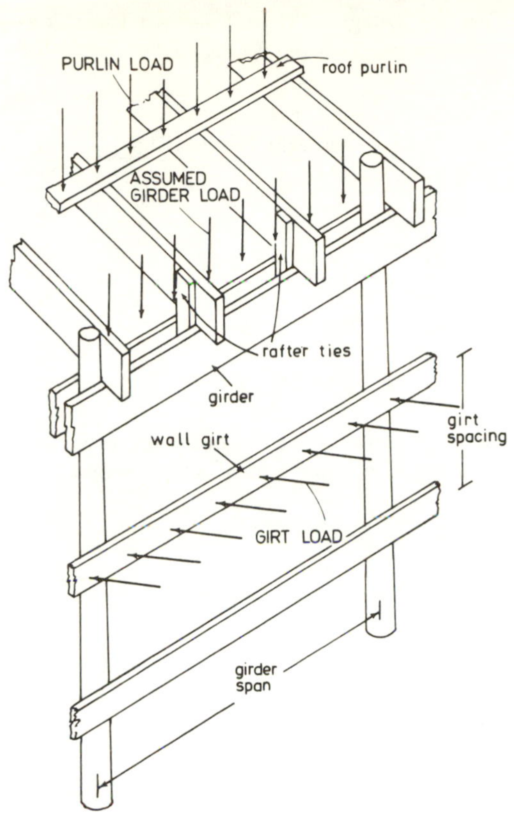

Figure 20-3. This sketch shows the framing components of a pole frame building, along with an indication of how building loads are supported by them. (NRAES)

ing height, and the design wind load. Tables 20-1 and 20-2 present typical sizes used in farm building design.

Splash boards. Horizontal board or boards nailed to the outside of poles at ground level. Splash boards are of treated material 2 inches in thickness. They provide a decay resistant surface which can be back filled against and a nailer for the lower edge of building siding. Splash boards are located on

Table 20-1. **Maximum Spacing in Feet for Douglas Fir or Southern Pine Construction Grade Round Poles to Withstand 75 Mph Winds on Gable Roofed Buildings**

	Effective* Building Height (Feet)				
Top Diameter (Inches)	**9**	**10.5**	**12**	**14**	**20**
4.5	18	14	11	11	8
5.5	16	13	10	9	6
6.0	20	17	14	13	9
7.0	20	20	18	16	11

**Effective building height is equal to eave height for buildings with roof slopes of 4 in 12 or less. For steeper roofs, effective height equals eave height plus ½ the roof height.*

Table 20-2. **Maximum Spacing in Feet for Douglas Fir or Southern Pine Construction Grade Posts to Withstand 75 Mph Winds on Gable Roofed Buildings**

	Effective** Building Height (Ft.)				
Nominal* Post Size (In.)	**9**	**10.5**	**12**	**14**	**20**
4x4	5	4	3	2	1
4x6	9	7	5	4	2
6x6	15	11	8	6	3
6x8	20	20	16	12	6
8x8	20	20	20	17	8

**Actual sizes will be approximately ½ inch smaller. If poles are full sized, spacings can be increased somewhat.*

***Effective building height is equal to eave height for buildings with roof slopes of 4 in 12 or less. For steeper roofs, effective height equals eave height plus ½ the roof height.*

the inner side of the poles and extended 2 to 3 feet up from the ground if a manure pack is to be allowed to build up in the barn.

Girt. Horizontal members nailed to the exterior face of the poles to provide support for exterior siding. Girts are 2 inches thick with width being determined by spacing of the poles. Two by fours are normally used for pole spacings up to 6 feet apart. Two by sixes are used for spacings up to 12 feet. Vertical spacing between girts will depend on the type of siding used. Most common spacing is 24 inches on center.

Girder. Horizontal member or members located at the top of the pole and used as a support for roof framing members which terminate between poles. Buildings which have trusses or rafters located only at the poles may not have a girder.

Once the holes are dug and the supporting pads are in place, construction of the pole frame building may proceed as follows:

1. Select 4 of the straightest poles to be used for the corners of the building. Set all poles in the holes and allow them to tip toward the inside of the building. Then replace string lines used to mark the outside edge of the building and plumb and brace all poles. Remember that the outside face of the poles should be 1-½ inches inside the string to allow for thickness of the wall girts. Install braces toward the inside of the building so that they will be out of the way of later construction.

   As soon as poles are aligned and braced, backfill the holes with a concrete collar and earth, or earth only, as required. Place backfill in 6 inch layers and tamp well as you go.
2. Fasten splash boards to the poles using 16d nails. Use a builder's

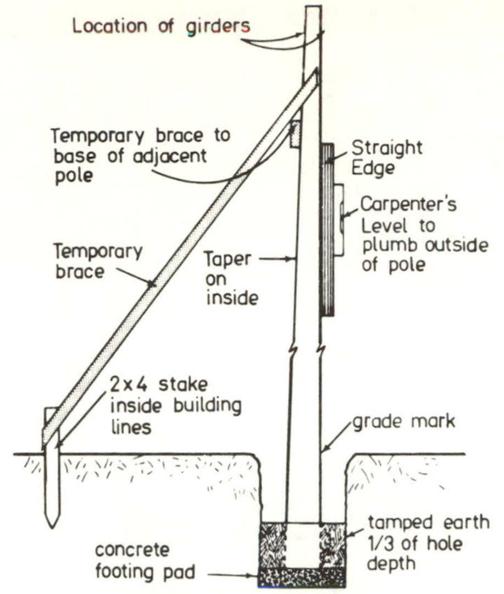

Figure 20-4. Probably the single most critical factor in the construction of a pole frame building is the proper alignment and plumbing of the poles themselves. If even one pole is crooked or out of line, it makes all the subsequent steps just that much harder. This figure illustrates plumbing of the outside of a round pole. (NRAES)

level or transit to make sure the top edges of splash boards are level all around the building. You will be using this point as a reference for measurements during later construction.

3. Install nailing girts using 16d nails. Stagger joints so that they do not all occur at the same pole. Frame in any openings required for windows and doors as you go.
4. Install girder members at the top of the pole. Girder support will be improved if the member on the inside of the pole is let into the pole.
5. Cut off poles 4 to 6 inches above the top of the girder. The 4 to 6 inch stub will provide a convenient tie down for the roof truss system.
6. Windows, doors, and siding may be installed at this point or you may wish to wait until later. Waiting to install siding until after the roof is on will greatly simplify later work.

Pole frame structures depend on the rigid imbedment of poles in the ground to provide bracing required to withstand wind loads. Diagonal wall bracing such as that used with stud frame buildings is not required in pole frame buildings. They do, however, require knee bracing to stiffen the connection between the girder and the roof framing system.

Knee braces are framing members (usually 2 by 6 inches) placed at a 45° angle to tie the roof and sidewall structure together. They should connect to the pole at a distance of at least 2 feet below the top of the girder and extend upward to the rafter. They must be securely nailed to the pole, the ceiling joist or lower rafter chord, and the rafter itself if they are to develop full strength. Knee braces are not needed at each pole or in all buildings. However, if the person who designed the plans for your building included knee braces, do not omit them.

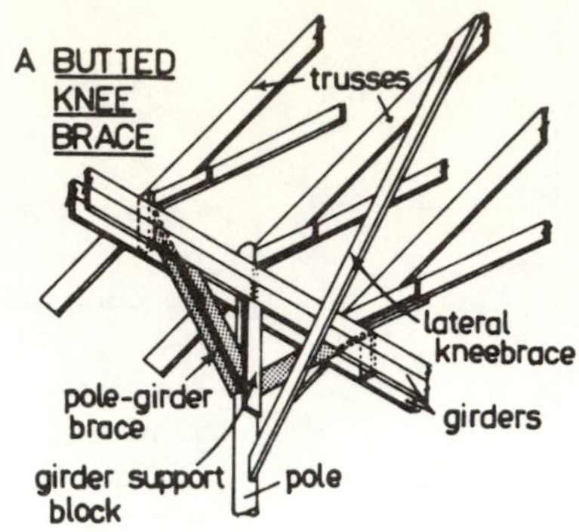

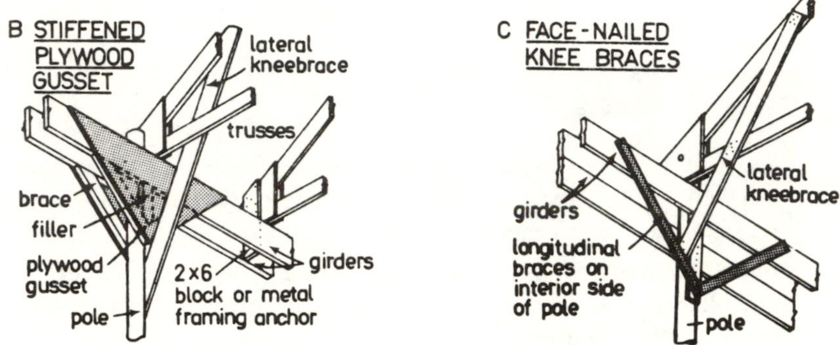

Figure 20-5. Three different methods of bracing pole to girder and rafter connections to withstand building loads. If the person who designed your building indicated the use of bracing, don't assume you can get along without it. (NRAES)

Another bracing system which is sometimes used in pole frame buildings is the pole-girder brace. This brace is placed at a 45° angle between the bottom or side of the girder and the pole. Its function is to provide extra support and increased load carrying capacity for the girder. Again, if it is shown on the plan, don't leave it out of the construction process.

Rigid Frame Construction

Sidewall construction in the rigid frame building is similar in many ways to that of the pole frame unit. Major structural support is provided by the rigid frame unit, not by the framing used to enclose the wall.

Splash boards may or may not be used, depending on the particular type of foundation used. Buildings using conventional or grade beam types of foundations will normally extend the concrete far enough above the ground to provide protection similar to that of the splash board assembly. A wooden sill plate is then used to provide an anchor point for the lower edge of the exterior siding. Buildings using piers to support the rigid frames will sometimes use pressure treated planking as a splash board to provide solid connection between sidewall and ground. Others will use a short nonsupporting concrete wall poured between individual piers to serve the same function.

Sidewall girts may be either wood or formed sheet metal. Wood is more common for frame spacings up to 10 to 12 feet. Sheet metal girts are used in most commercial buildings and with wider frame spacings. Siding material is fastened to the metal girts using self tapping metal screws.

The frame members themselves are designed to be the load carrying members of this type building and all roof and wall loads are transferred directly to the frames by the connecting members. Because of this, girders are not used in rigid frame buildings. The only exception would be if a frame member had to be cut off in order to accommodate a wide opening in the building sidewall.

Rigid frame members terminate at the foundation and do not have the basic rigidity of the pole frame building. Because of this, some type of diagonal bracing is usually used to provide wind resistance. In the case of wood frames, plywood sheathing or let in diagonal bracing is commonly used. Metal frame buildings frequently use metal rods or straps in an "X" bracing arrangement between two or more adjacent frames. These can usually be found in the two end bays of the building and sometimes at other locations, depending on building length and the particular design.

CHAPTER 21

Roof Construction

All types of farm buildings except the rigid frame structures have to have some type of separate framing system to support the design roof load. There is a wide variety of shapes available and two types of framing systems: conventional and trussed rafters. Several shapes commonly used on farm buildings were illustrated in Figure 21-1. A brief description of each of these shapes follows.

Shed roof. This type roof is generally acknowledged to be the least costly to construct. It is most adaptable to structures less than 20 feet wide. Wider buildings will require some type of internal support or the use of trusses, either of which increase the cost. Another problem associated with wider shed roofed buildings is the increased wall height and construction costs associated with it.

Gable. This is the most commonly used roof shape in farm buildings today. It is relatively easy to construct at a reasonable cost and offers low wind resistance when slopes are kept at 4 in 12 or less. Buildings up to 24 feet wide can be conventionally framed without interior support. Wider structures will require trusses or supporting members inside the buiding.

Combination. Sometimes referred to as offset gable or salt box. This roof shape is primarily associated with residential construction and has not been generally used on farm buildings. It has gained some attention and use recently because of its adaptability to solar heat collection. The relatively steep short side of the gable can be pitched at an optimum angle for roof mounted solar collectors. Widths up to 24 feet can be conventionally framed without interior supports.

Gambrel. This roof system was developed many years ago as a means of obtaining more overhead storage in two story barns. It also provided a way to use more or less conventional framing techniques to obtain wider buildings without interior supports. Gambrel roofed barns up to 36 feet

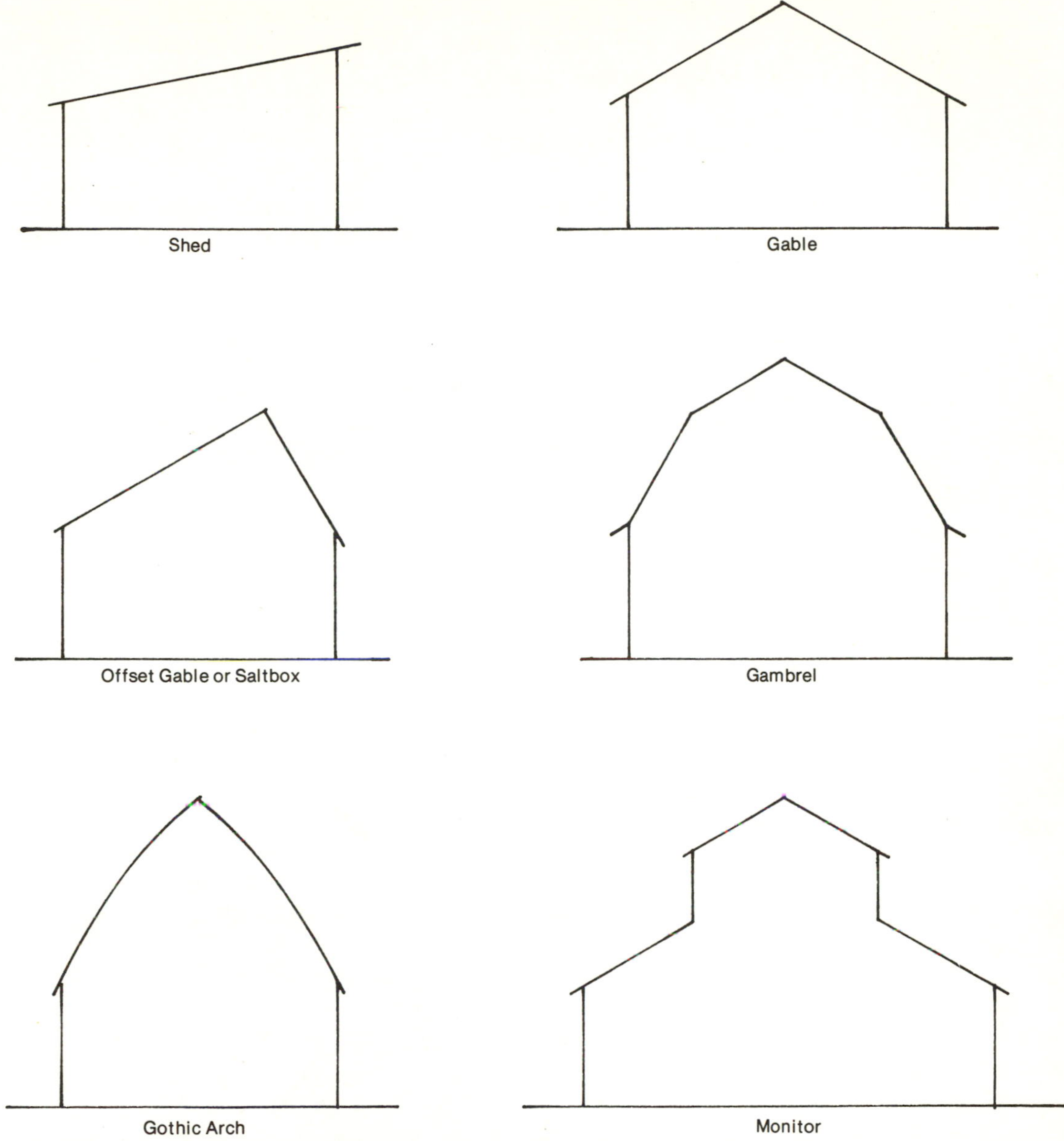

Figure 21-1. Commonly used barn roof shapes.

wide were commonly used on dairy barns in the northern United States. Gambrel roof construction is fairly costly and today we see it used mainly where someone is trying to achieve a special visual effect.

Gothic arch. This is a type of rigid frame which provides storage space advantages similar to those of the gambrel design. It too is fairly costly to construct and has failed to gain widespread acceptance on farm buildings. Widths to 100 feet are possible.

Monitor. This roof system might best be described as a gable roof with two shed type lean-to sections added. It provides head room for a second floor and overhead storage.

Conventional Framing

Major components of the conventional roof framing system for a gable roof are illustrated in Figure 21-2. They include the ridge board, collar tie, rafter and ceiling joist.

Ridge board. This 1 to 2 inch wide by 6 inch deep board is an optional feature in conventional roof construction. It provides a convenient means of holding rafters in place and aligning them until the roof sheathing or purlins are in place. Once the roof assembly is complete, the ridge board contributes essentially nothing to the structure of the roof.

Collar tie. This cross tie located 12 to 18 inches below the ridge helps prevent the roof assembly from sagging. It is usually built with a 1 by 6 inch board. It is not uncommon for collar ties to be located only on every other rafter assembly.

Ceiling joist. These 2 inch wide framing members are designed to counteract the outward thrust of the rafters at the top of the sidewall. They also serve as convenient supports for the ceiling of the room below. If no ceiling is used, joist depth will be 4 to 6 inches and they will normally be located at every other or sometimes every third or fourth rafter. In buildings with ceilings, joists will be at each rafter and their size will depend on the building width and type of ceiling supported. Normal ceiling design loads will be 5 to 10 pounds per square foot with the higher value reserved for plastered ceilings with high levels of insulation. Ceiling joists must be

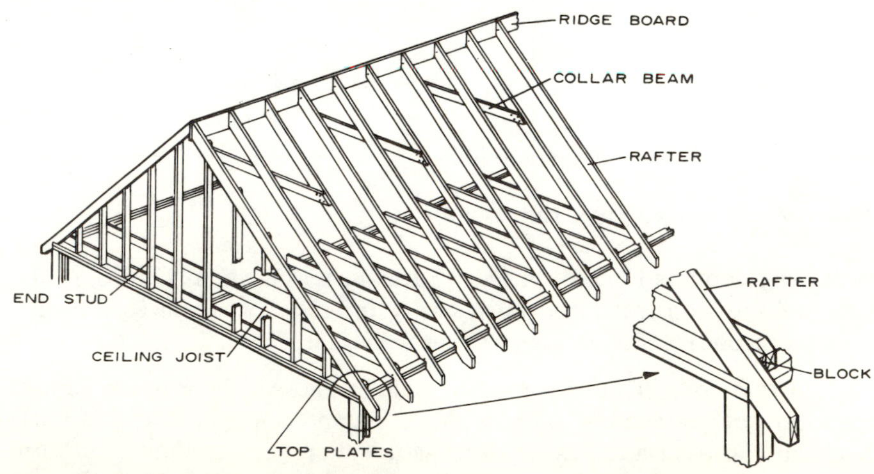

Figure 21-2. Conventional roof framing system and its parts. (USDA)

securely nailed to both the adjoining rafter and the top plate or girder in the supporting wall. Failure to do this can result in uplifting of the roof under high wind loading or spreading of the sidewalls and sagging of the roof under snow and ice loads.

Rafter. The rafter is the main structural member of the conventional roof assembly. It is usually constructed of 2 inch thick lumber with the depth being determined by roof design load and the span and spacing of the rafter. Rafter span is determined from the horizontal distance it covers. For example, a gable roof over a 24 foot wide building would require two sets of rafters, each with a 12 foot span. Most lumber dealers will have a set of load-span tables which will enable you to select the proper size and grade of lumber for your application. A typical table for a 30 pound per square foot roof load is shown in Table 21-1.

Table 21-1. **Maximum Spans for Rafters Subjected to a 30 Pound per Square Foot Roof Load***

	Rafter Spacing (Inches)			
Nominal Size	**16**	**24**	**36**	**48**
2x4	9 ft 6 in.	8 ft 3 in.	6 ft 9 in.	5 ft 10 in.
2x6	14 ft 9 in.	12 ft 6 in.	10 ft 3 in.	8 ft 10 in.
2x8	19 ft 8 in.	17 ft 1 in.	13 ft 11 in.	12 ft 1 in.
2x10	24 ft 0 in.	21 ft 8 in.	17 ft 8 in.	15 ft 4 in.
2x12	—	24 ft 0 in.	21 ft 5 in.	18 ft 6 in.

**No. 2 Douglas Fir or Southern Pine.*

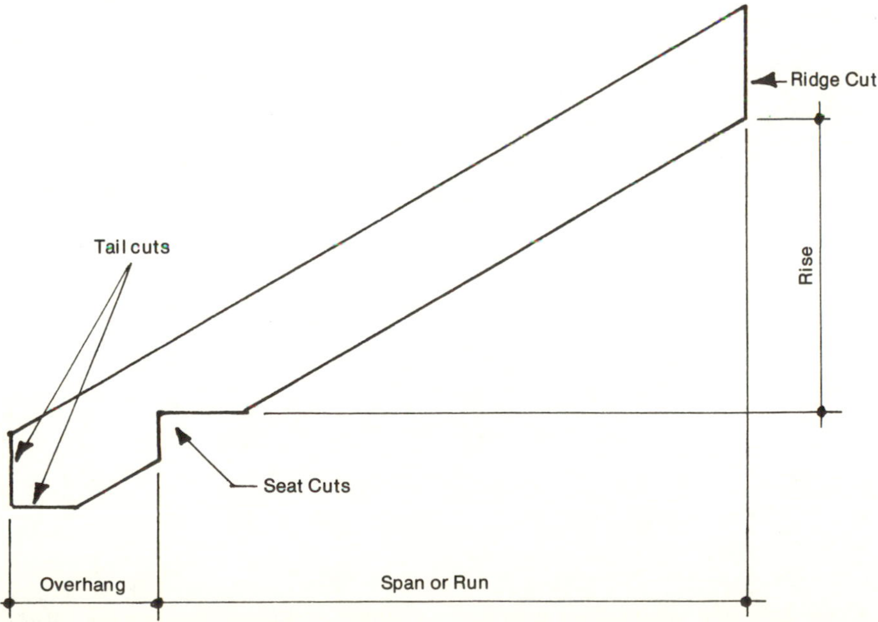

Figure 21-3. Nomenclature used in the design and construction of a common rafter.

Typical rafter spacing for residential construction is 16 inches on center. For farm buildings, a 24 inch spacing is used when solid decking and shingled roofing are planned. Spacings of 36 and 48 inches are sometimes used if a purlin and metal roof coverage are planned.

The parts of the common rafter are illustrated in Figure 21-3. The *rise* of a rafter is the vertical distance from the top edge of the rafter immediately over the outside corner of the plate to the top of the ridge. The *run* of a rafter is the horizontal distance from the outside edge of the plate to a point directly below the ridge of the building. Pitch is defined as follows:

$$\text{Pitch} = \frac{\text{Rise}}{2 \times \text{run}}$$

An even pitch gable roof has a span which equals the run multiplied by two. A more useful way to refer to the rise-run relationship in a rafter is to refer to it as slope and specify it as inches of rise per foot of run. Following is a listing of commonly used slopes and their equivalent pitches.

Slope	*Pitch*	*Slope*	*Pitch*
3:12	1/8	6:12	1/4
4:12	1/6	12:12	1/2

The strength of the roof system depends on having rafters which are properly cut so that there are tight joints at both the ridge and the plate. Rafters are laid out using a framing square as illustrated in Figure 21-4.

Rafters are fastened to the wall plate or girder using toenailing with 8d to 10d nails. In addition, at least every other rafter should be tied down to the wall using either a length of plumber's strap or a metal framing anchor.

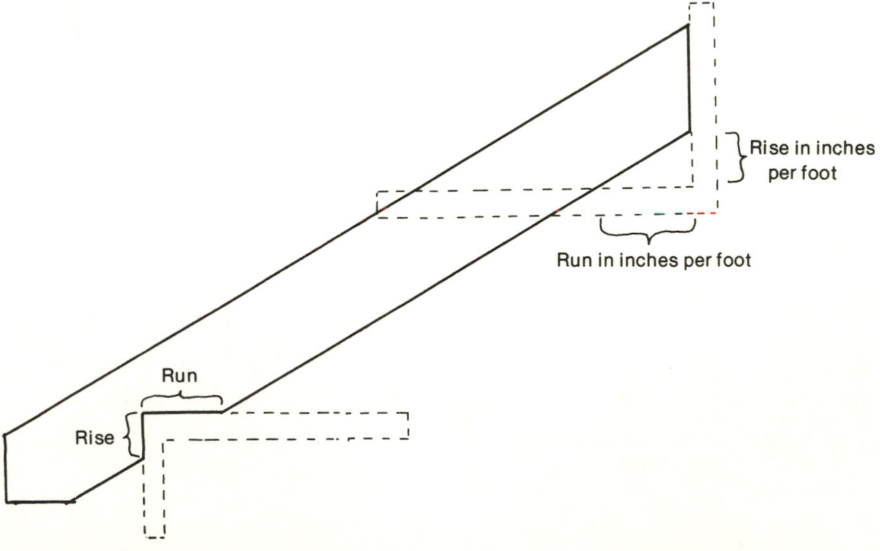

Figure 21-4. Use of the framing square to determine cuts in the common rafter. The square can also be used to "step" along the rafter to locate the proper horizontal distance (run) between the ridge cut and the seat cut.

Figure 21-5. Wooden blocks are being used here to tie down ends of the rafters to the girder of this pole frame building. Tie down is necessary to prevent wind from lifting the roof off the building.

Trussed Rafters

The triangle is one of the most rigid shapes that can be incorporated into a building. We see it used routinely for all types of both temporary and permanent bracing. A roof truss is nothing more than a series of triangles put together in an assembly designed to fit the desired shape and load carrying requirements of a roof. Trusses can be designed to fit almost any desired roof shape. Several different arrangements of the internal members which form the triangles are possible. Some of the shapes and arrangements frequently seen in farm buildings are illustrated in Figure 21-6.

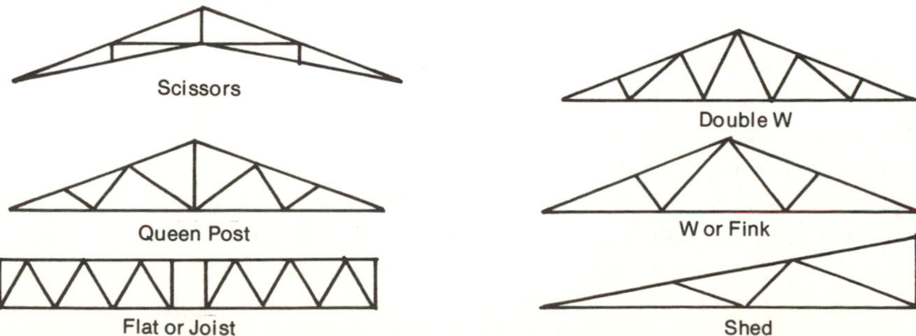

Figure 21-6. Trusses are named both by their general shape and the arrangement of their interior members or diagonals. These six are frequently used in the construction of farm buildings.

Although trusses have been in common use for many years, it was not until the late 1950's that they started to gain acceptance and use in farm buildings. Some of the reasons for this acceptance are among the basic advantages of using trusses.

These include:

- Trusses can be easily fabricated in a factory type assembly plant and transported to the site ready for use.
- They can span buildings up to 60 feet wide at a cost competitive with any other type of framing system.
- Interior support for the roof system is not required. This means complete flexibility within the building both for present management systems and any future changes which might be desired.

Most trusses used in farm buildings today are assembled in a factory and delivered to the building site ready for erection. Manufactured trusses are usually assembled using toothed metal connector plates (referred to as truss plates) which are pressed into the wood with hydraulic presses or large rollers. When ordering trusses you will need to specify the following items.

Shape or type. Figure 21-6 illustrates some of the commonly used shapes. If you need a gable design with an offset and different roof slopes, this needs to be specified to the fabricator.

Span. This is specified as the horizontal distance from outside to outside across the building in the direction the trusses will be placed. Although trusses can be made to span any distance, building dimensions which are in even multiples of 2 feet will result in faster delivery of lower cost trusses.

Roof slope. Commonly used slopes in farm trusses are 3:12, 4:12, and 5:12. Slopes lower than 3:12 will require special attention in selecting and installing roofing to insure against leakage. In general, the higher the slope, the lighter the truss members can be. However, higher slopes make for higher buildings which must withstand higher wind loads. The 4:12 or 5:12 slope provides a good compromise for most buildings.

Spacing. Normally used truss spacings are 24 inch, 48 inch and 96 inch on center. The 24 inch spacing is used in buildings with a high degree of ceiling finish, such as residences and milking centers. Forty-eight inch spacing has been the traditional interval used on most farm buildings. The 96 inch spacing has been adopted by many builders who specialize in buildings without ceilings. This spacing reduces the total amount of lumber involved in the roof truss system and places a truss at each pole along the sidewall of a pole frame building, eliminating the need for a supporting girder. Although the presently used design methods appear adequate for trusses spaced on 96 inch centers, there is some question as to building reliability with widely spaced trusses. No matter how well a building is designed and constructed, there is always some possibility of a particular part failing somewhere. If the part happens to be a critical member in a truss spaced 24 inches on center, chances are excellent that the two adjacent trusses will carry the increased load without any particular problem. When the same failure occurs in a 48 inch on center spaced truss, there is better than an even chance that the same thing will occur. With the 96 inch spacing, chances are pretty good that failure at a critical point in a single truss is going to bring down the entire building. During the winter of 1978-79, high snow loads in the Midwest caused a large number of farm building failures. In most cases, design techniques were adequate, but poor fabrication or poor selection of lumber at a critical point caused a truss to fail. This resulted in a domino effect which led to roof collapse. The majority of the failures occurred in buildings which used truss spacings wider than 48 inches on center. Until we learn more about designing to increase building reliability, we would suggest that you consider limiting truss spacings to a maximum of 48 inches on center.

Number Needed. Divide the total length of the building by the truss spacing and add one. Some fabricators build a special gable end truss which has internal members located so that ventilators can be easily installed and siding or sheathing can be nailed directly to the truss. If these are available and you wish to use them, order two gable end trusses and a number of other trusses equal to building length divided by spacing, minus one.

Overhang. Specify in inches the amount of overhang you want on each side of the truss, if any. Commonly used overhangs are 6 inches, 12 inches, 18 inches and 24 inches. Occasionally, a wider overhang may be used to shelter a feeder running along the front edge of a building.

Tail Cut. Specify either a rafter cut or a plumb cut for the tail of the trusses. A rafter cut is perpendicular to the upper chord member and is used when no eave trough or finish is planned for the roof edge. The plumb cut is a cut which is perpendicular to the ground. It provides a convenient surface for attaching a fascia board and eave trough.

Roof Load. Specify the required design load in pounds live load per square foot. If the dealer requires a specification for total roof load, add 5 pounds per square foot to the live load.

Ceiling Load. For buildings with ceilings, specify a ceiling design load in terms of pounds per square foot. Normally applied ceilings with insulation will impose a load of approximately 5 pounds per square foot. If there are any unusual ceiling loads such as hanging cages, hoists, or heavy equipment, be sure to specify how much weight is to be supported and where it will be attached to the ceiling.

Plans. Be sure to specify that the dealer provide you with a set of plans for the trusses. These plans should contain basic dimensions, design loads, and the stamp of the registered professional engineer responsible for the design. In the event that there is ever any question about the truss design, the stamped plan will be an invaluable asset to you.

Some builders or farmers who have time available prefer to construct their own trusses. If you choose to do this, we suggest that you consider using a design which involves plywood gusset plates which are both glued and nailed in place. Plans for this type truss are available through county extension centers or from the Midwest Plan Service. Basic steps in truss construction are as follows:

1. Use the plan to carefully lay out the entire truss assembly on a flat work surface. A wooden floor is an ideal work place.
2. Cut out all the pieces for one truss and locate them in their proper places on the assembly floor.
3. Tack the gusset plates in place using nails partially driven and check all joints for fit.
4. Use scrap pieces of 2 by 4 to block around all parts of the truss. This makes an assembly jig to be used in putting together all the trusses.
5. Take apart the original truss and use the parts as patterns to cut out all the remaining truss parts.
6. Assemble trusses using glue and nails as specified on the plans. Be extra careful to do a good job in gluing and nailing of gusset plates. More than half the truss failures we have seen over the past 20 years have been due to poor joint fabrication.

Before you start to erect trusses, make sure the sidewalls of the building are parallel and adequately braced to prevent them from tipping

Figure 21-7. This contractor rented a crane to erect these 50-foot trusses. Since he was paying the crane by the hour, he neglected to fully brace the trusses as they were erected. Fortunately, not many of the trusses were broken by the fall. A trussed rafter roof system is one of the most rigid assemblies in construction—once it is in place and braced. Until that time, it must be carefully secured, or results like this are bound to occur.

out at the top. This is particularly important with stud frame construction since it lacks the natural rigidity of the pole frame building.

Lightweight trusses up to 30 feet long can usually be lifted and placed by hand. Place them upside down on top of the building walls and rotate them up into place. Heavier or longer trusses are best erected using a crane. The crane can lift and place 2 to 3 trusses at a time with a minimum of effort and maximum safety. A series of 2 by 4s or 2 by 6s temporarily nailed to the end wall of the building can be used to support the end wall truss until the second truss is in place. As each truss is put into place, it must be securely anchored to the plates at each sidewall and braced to the truss next to it. Bracing helps hold trusses in alignment and will prevent failures of the roof system before the roofing and ceiling materials are in place.

Purlins and Corrugated Roofing

As soon as all rafters are in place, the roof covering system can be installed. One of the more commonly used systems is the roof purlin with metal covering. Roof purlins are members which are placed at right angles to rafters or rigid frames and used to anchor roofing sheets. The majority of farm buildings use wooden purlins, although some of the metal framed buildings are using purlins fabricated from formed sheet metal.

Purlin spacing and size will depend on the distance between rafters or frames and the particular type of roofing to be used. The most common spacings for steel and aluminum roofing are 24 inches and 30 inches. Two by four purlins are laid flat for rafter spacings up to 48 inches. They should be secured to each rafter with 2 to 10d ring shank nails or 2 to 16d common nails.

Use 2 by 4 members placed on edge for rafter spacings up to 96 inches. These can be secured by driving a single 60d ring shank nail through the 2 by 4 into the rafter or by using metal framing anchors at each connection point.

Two by six, two by eight or formed sheet metal purlins are used for frame spacings in excess of 8 feet. These are usually secured to the frames with metal anchors, wood anchor blocks, or by bolting.

If rigid insulation is used under metal roofing for control of radiant heat, it should be fastened directly to the roof purlin system. Use only enough nails to hold it in place until the roofing is applied. Fasteners used to hold down the roofing will also secure the insulation. *Caution:* If you are going to use aluminum roofing, do not use steel nails to hold down the insulation. An electrical (galvanic) reaction between the steel nail heads and the aluminum roofing will eventually lead to holes in the roofing.

Three different types of formed or corrugated roofing materials are available for use over roof purlins. They are steel, aluminum, and an asphalt composition board.

Steel. Steel roofing is by far the most popular material used on farm buildings today. It is available in a variety of widths, lengths, and in thicknesses of 26, 28, and 29 gauge. (Twenty-six gauge is the thickest.) Thickness of the steel is not as much of a factor in determining durability as is the coating which is applied to the steel. Standard corrosion protection is provided by a thin coating of zinc known generally as galvanizing. The industry standard is 1.25 ounce per square foot, which represents .62 ounce of zinc applied per square foot to each side of the sheet. This coating is commonly referred to as complying with standard G-90 of the ASTM (American Society for Testing and Materials). A heavier 2 ounce coating is available and is suggested if a plain galvanized surface treatment is all that is used.

Much of the steel used today has an additional coating of baked on enamel applied over the galvanizing. Available in a wide variety of colors, this coating adds durability and provides an attractive finish for the metal roofing. It will also add about 50% to the cost of materials.

Steel roofing is applied with steel nails or steel screws. Nails are available with ring shanks and heads which are either lead covered or provided with a neoprene washer to seal the hole where the nail is driven through. Self tapping screws also come with a sealing washer. Screws and the neoprene washer nails are available in color to match roofing finishes.

Aluminum. Formed aluminum roofing is corrosion resistant and lighter in weight than steel. It too is available in a variety of widths and lengths. It also can be purchased in rolls which are usually 4 feet wide and can extend the entire length of the building.

Aluminum has a high coefficient of thermal expansion which causes it to "stretch and shrink" with changes in temperature. This has caused some problems with enlargement of nail holes and leakage, particularly when using longer sheets.

Aluminum roofing is secured to purlins with aluminum nails having neoprene washers. Because of galvanic action which can occur, aluminum should never be installed in direct contact with steel. If aluminum roofing is used on a steel frame building with steel purlins, a layer of insulation or other protective material should be used to prevent direct contact between aluminum and steel. Stainless steel fasteners can be used to secure aluminum roofing to steel purlins.

Asphalt composition board. This material is a relatively new product to the American farm building market. It is a corrugated sheet material composed of asphalt and fiber. It offers the advantage of being extremely corrosion resistant and having a relatively low coefficient of thermal expansion. The sound deadening characteristics of this material will also reduce noise level in buildings during rain or hail storms and it possesses a somewhat higher insulation rating than either steel or aluminum.

This material is secured to purlins with either ring shank nails or screws with neoprene washers.

The fewer the number of joints in corrugated roofing, the less apt you are to have leaks. Manufacturers have recognized this factor and are continuing to increase the sizes of available sheets. You should plan to purchase the largest sheet size you think you can handle. If at all possible, select a sheet long enough to reach from ridge to eave of your building.

Start installation of corrugated sheet material on the edge of the roof which is farthest away from the prevailing wind. This will help keep the wind from blowing water through the roof at the edge overlaps.

There is a wide variety of accessories available to finish your corrugated roof. These include such things as ridge caps, edge closure strips, flashing, and preformed sealers to fill in spaces under corrugations at the eave line. Before you spend time trying to figure out how to handle a particular problem, check with your dealer to see what accessories are available. Chances are the manufacturer has already thought of you and has made a piece to solve your problem; and it will probably be colored to match the rest of the roof.

Solid Decking and Shingles

A solid roof deck covered with composition shingles is the traditional roof covering system for many farm structures, particularly residences. It offers a durable, attractive finish with less probability of leakage than the corrugated roofing system. It is also more costly in both labor and materials than other roofing systems.

Plywood is the most frequently used roof decking material today. It is applied directly over the rafters with the face grain running perpendicular to the direction of the rafters. Joints should be staggered so that all vertical joints between sheets do not occur over the same rafter.

Plywood can be applied directly to rafters spaced up to 48 inches on center. Wider spacings will require the use of purlins to support plywood. For spacings over 24 inches on center some method of supporting plywood edges between rafters is suggested. This can be done by installing edge blocking, the use of tongue and grooved plywood, or with plyclips. Plyclips are small "H" shaped metal clips about 1 inch long which are slipped over the edges of two adjacent plywood sheets to keep them in alignment.

Plywood thickness will depend on rafter spacing, type of plywood, and the design roof load. Chapter 28 contains information on plywood selection. In general, thicknesses less than ½ inch are not used unless it is planned to apply shingles with a staple gun. Plywood sheathing which is ½ inch or less in thickness is nailed to rafters with 8d nails. Space nails 6 inches apart along edges of the plywood sheet and 12 inches apart along other supports. Use the 6 inch spacing for all nails if rafters are 48 inches on center.

Several different types of composition roofing can be applied over solid decking. The more commonly selected ones are listed below.

Asphalt shingles. These are made of asphalt with a fiber or felt reinforcing material. The exposed surfaces are usually coated with a colored gravel finish which adds to the appearance and protects the asphalt material from rapid deterioration by the ultra violet rays of the sun.

Shingles are sold by the square (100 square feet of roof coverage) and

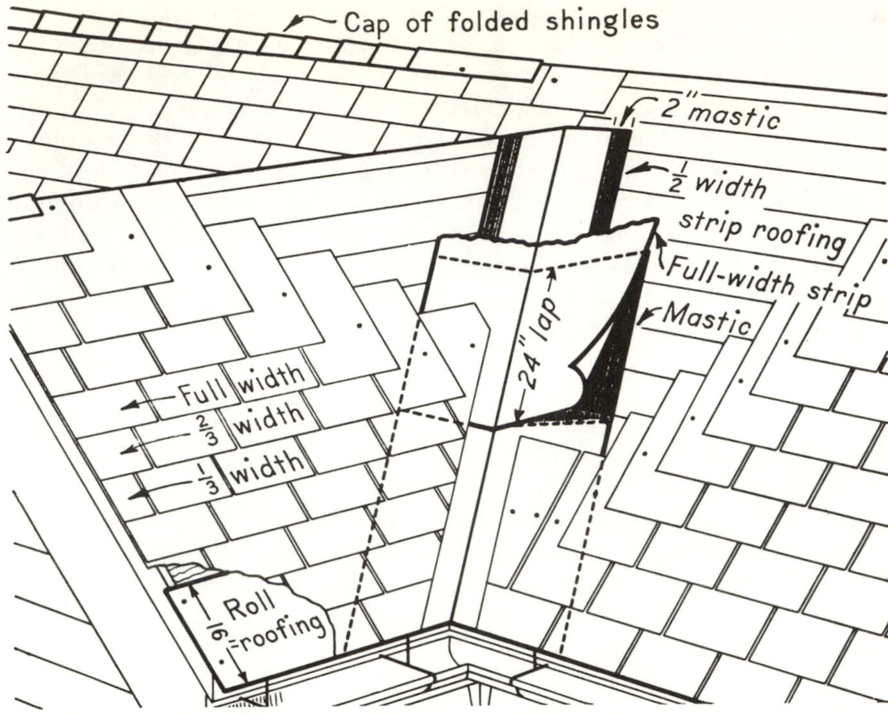

Figure 21-8. Installation procedure for standard asphalt-base shingles. Also illustrated is the proper procedure for roofing an intersecting roof or valley. (USDA)

weight per square is an indicator of quality. A shingle weighing 235 to 240 pounds per square should give 20 years of service without any major problems.

Shingles are generally not recommended for roof slopes below 3:12. Some manufacurers will warrant their shingles for lower sloped roofs provided you follow very explicit installation instructions.

Most manufacturers have available a "seal down" shingle which provides extra resistance against wind damage. The feature uses spots of asphalt on the surface of the shingle which stick to the shingle that overlaps from above. These stick points help hold down the shingle in the event that a strong wind blows toward the down slope edge.

Roll roofing. As the name implies, this material comes in rolls, usually 36 inches wide. It is composed of the same material as asphalt shingles and is available in several different weights per square.

Standard roll roofing is suitable for roof slopes of 3:12 and higher when installed with a 2 inch overlap. Overlaps are sealed by covering with a layer of liquid asphalt before nailing in place. Standard roll roofing should provide 5 to 10 years of service without major repair.

Double coverage (also known as selvage edge or 19 inch overlap roofing) roll roofing provides much longer life than standard material. It

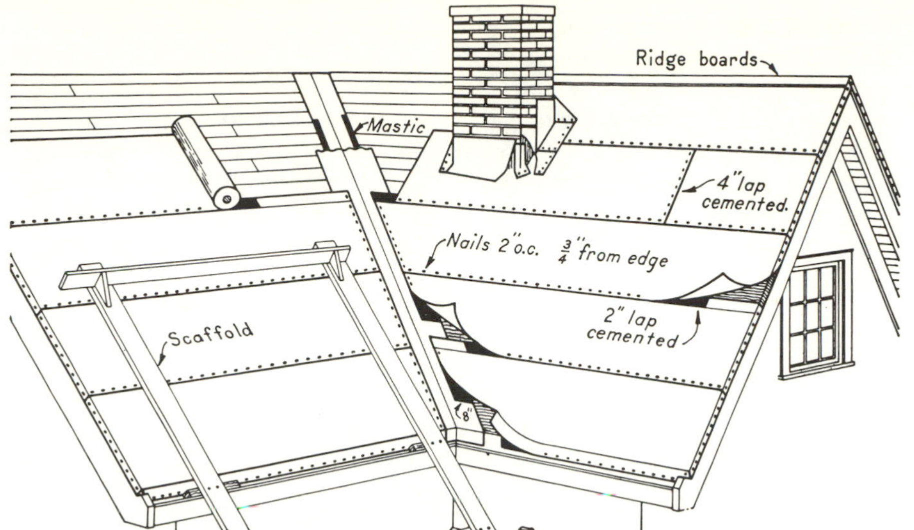

Figure 21-9. Standard roll type asphalt roofing is about the lowest cost type of roofing that can be installed over a solid roof deck. It also has one of the lower life expectancies. (USDA)

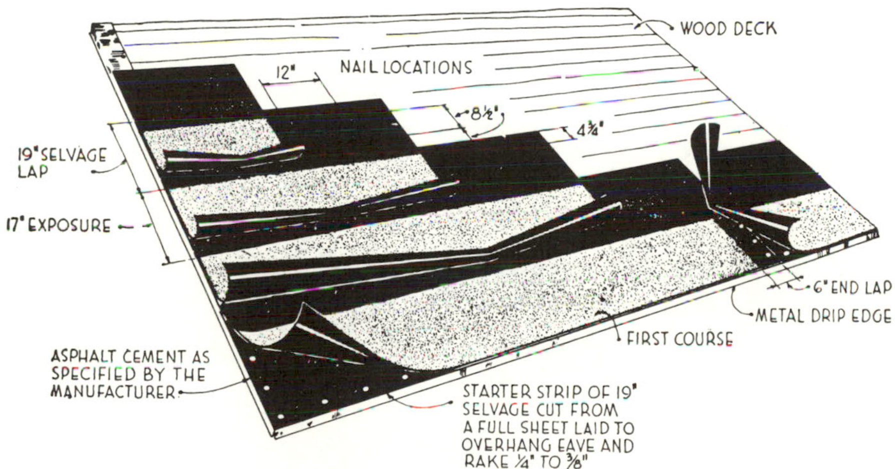

Figure 21-10. Selvage edge roofing was once a very popular roof covering for farm buildings. Its use declined rapidly with the introduction of pole frame construction and improvements in type and application of metal roof coverings. It is still one of the better coverings for very low sloped roofs. (USDA)

can also be used on roof slopes as low as 1:12.

Built up roofing. Built up roofing consists of alternate layers of roofing felt and hot asphalt. It is topped with a layer of gravel to reduce deterioration by sunlight.

The major advantage of this roof system is that it can be applied to an essentially flat roof. It does, however, require professional applicators and is a fairly expensive roof system.

Built up roof systems may be sold by the number of plies or by warranty bond. The number of plies refers to the layers of felt with higher numbers being associated with longer-lived roofs. A warranty bond specifies that the roof will remain intact for the indicated number of years. One problem that has occurred frequently over the years is that the company installing or warranting the roof is no longer in business when problems develop.

Although the built up roof is capable of giving good service, it is a complex type of roof covering and its use on farm buildings should be avoided if at all possible.

CHAPTER 22

Basic Wiring

Electricity is a basic input for much of today's agricultural production and electric wiring is an integral part of most farm buildings. Any well planned wiring system must be safe, adequate, expandable, and efficient.

The requirement for safety is directly addressed by the National Electric Code (NEC). This code outlines requirements considered necessary if the wiring system is to function safely throughout the life of the structure. You should insist that all wiring done in your new building be in compliance with the NEC. If you live in an area subjected to building codes and inspections, your wiring system will probably be subjected to an inspection to see if it complies with the NEC. In other areas, you may be able to schedule such an inspection through your local power supplier.

We would like to emphasize that most power suppliers throughout the United States have service representatives who are more than willing to work with you in planning the electrical needs for a new building. In most cases, this service is free of charge and we would encourage you to make use of it. It is beyond the scope of this book to provide anything but a few basics in the design and installation of an electrical service system.

Circuits

Electrical distribution within a building is accomplished by one or more distribution circuits. A circuit is nothing more than a fuse protected wire which carries electricity to the points of use. There are three general types of circuits in use in farm buildings. They are lighting circuits, general purpose outlet circuits, and special purpose circuits. The total number of circuits needed in a particular building will depend on the type of structure and the activities which will take place within it. A hay barn or machinery storage may require only a single circuit, while a milking center frequently has 10 or more.

No.	Symbol	Description
1.0		**Lighting Outlets** **Ceiling**
1.1		Surface or pendant incandescent or similar lamp fixture
1.3		Surface or pendant individual fluorescent fixture
1.5		Surface or pendant continuous-row fluorescent fixture
1.10	B	Blanked outlet
1.11	J	Junction box
		Wall
		To indicate wall installation of above outlets, place circle near wall and connect with line as shown
2.0		**Receptacle Outlets**
2.1		Single receptacle outlet
2.2		Duplex receptacle outlet
2.3		Triplex receptacle outlet
2.5		Duplex receptacle outlet – Split wired
2.7		Single special-purpose receptacle outlet
2.8		Duplex special-purpose receptacle outlet
2.9	R	Range outlet
2.12	C	Clock hanger receptacle

No.	Symbol	Description
3.0		**Switch Outlets**
3.1	S	Single-pole switch (SPST)
3.2	S_2	Double-pole switch (DPST)
3.3	S_3	Three-way switch (SPDT)
3.4	S_4	Four-way switch (DPDT)
3.6	S_p	Switch and pilot lamp
3.9	S	Switch and single receptacle
3.10	S	Switch and double receptacle
3.11	S_d	Door switch
3.12	ST	Time switch
3.15	S	Ceiling pull switch
		Power, Fusing, Ground
(46.3)	MOT	Electric motor
(46.2)	GEN	Electric generator
(86.1)		Power transformer
(48)	WH	Electric watthour meter
(11.1)		Circuit breaker
(36)		Fusible element
(13.1)		Ground

No.	Symbol	Description
6.0		**Panelboards, Switchboards and Related Equipment**
6.2		Surface-mounted panelboard and cabinet
6.7		Motor or other power controller*
6.8		Externally operated disconnection switch*
6.9		Combination controller and disconnection means*
8.0		**Remote Control Stations for Motors or Other Equipment**
8.1		Pushbutton station
8.2	F	Float switch – Mechanical
8.3	L	Limit switch – Mechanical
8.4	P	Pneumatic switch – Mechanical
8.5	T	Thermostat
		Low-Voltage and Remote-Control Switching Systems
1.12	L	Outlet controlled by low-voltage switching when relay is installed in outlet box
3.7	S_l	Switch for low-voltage switching system
3.8	S_{lm}	Master switch for low-voltage switching system

*Use number or letter either within the symbol or as a subscript alongside the symbol, keyed to an explanation in the drawing list of symbols, to indicate **type** of receptacle or usage. Use supplemental symbol schedule, below.

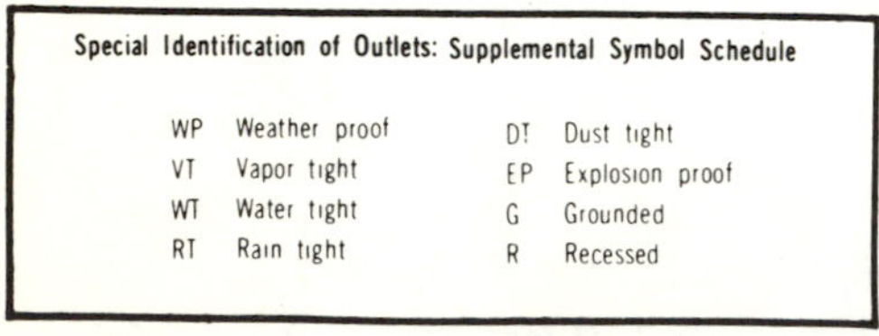

Special Identification of Outlets: Supplemental Symbol Schedule

WP	Weather proof	DT	Dust tight
VT	Vapor tight	EP	Explosion proof
WT	Water tight	G	Grounded
RT	Rain tight	R	Recessed

Figure 22-1. Listing of standard electrical symbols used on plans and architectural drawings. (AGRICULTURAL WIRING HANDBOOK published by Food and Energy Council (FEC))

Lighting

Circuits used for lighting are generally 120 volt circuits and are fused at 15 amperes each. This results in a total capacity per circuit of approximately 1,800 watts of light. The total number of lighting outlets which can be served by one circuit can vary widely, so long as the total wattage does not exceed 1,800. For example, a single lighting circuit could serve 9-200 watt lights or as many as 72-25 watt bulbs. In residential buildings, a general rule of thumb is to provide one lighting circuit for every 600 square feet of floor space. Some farm buildings, such as poultry housing units, may need only one circuit for every 1,500 to 1,800 square feet, while others may require much more light than a residence. Lighting circuits in residences are usually wired with No. 14 wire, which has a capacity rating of 15 amperes or 1,800 watts at 120 volts. Farm buildings tend to be much larger than residential buildings and the length of the individual circuits increases accordingly. In order to keep voltage drop due to line losses at a minimum, it is generally recommended that No. 12 wire be the smallest size allowed in farm wiring circuits.

General purpose outlet circuits

These circuits are usually 120 volt circuits fused at 20 amperes and used to connect a series of duplex receptacles. They are wired with No. 12 copper wire or its equivalent and serve these kinds of needs.

1. Portable equipment such as trouble lamps, clippers, drills, motors of ⅓ horsepower or less and other appliances which are not in continuous service.
2. Portable electric heaters of 1,500 watts or less.

The number of outlets located on an individual circuit should be based on the probable usage of the circuit, with a maximum limit of 10. If you know that the circuit will be used regularly to supply a 1,500 watt heater, one or possibly two outlets may be sufficient.

Special purpose circuits

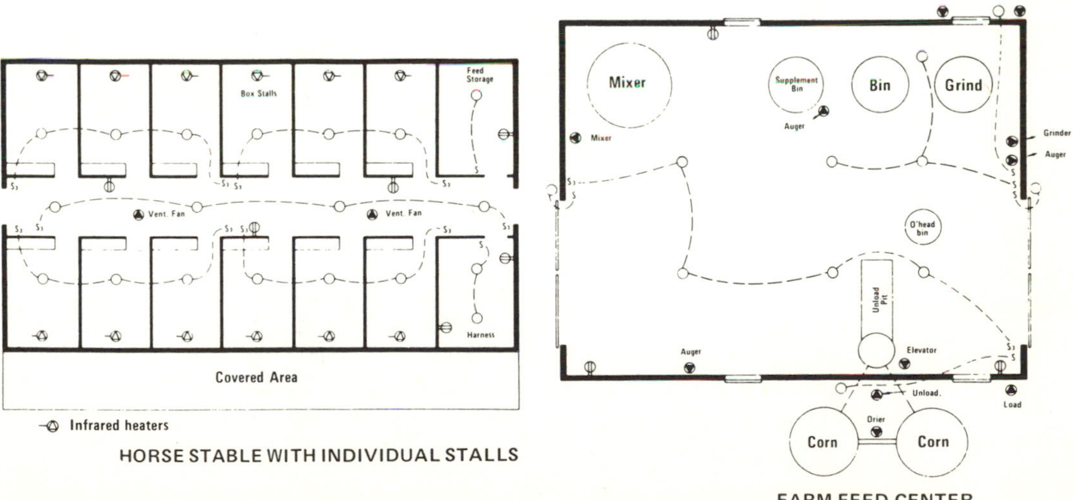

Figure 22-2. Electrical layouts for two different farm structures. (FEC) (AGRICULTURAL WIRING HANDBOOK)

These are designed to serve and protect individual pieces of electrical equipment which are major users of electrical power. Examples include motors of ½ horsepower or larger, stationary equipment using 1,500 watts or more, and all 240 volt appliances. These circuits may be 120 volt or 240 volt and are protected with fuses which are sized to the particular load served. Wire should be sized to keep voltage drop to less than 2% with No. 18 being the smallest size allowed.

Materials

Farm buildings provide a wide variety of environmental conditions, almost all of which are bad for components of electrical wiring systems. Among these are high moisture, dust and the presence of corrosive materials such as fertilizers, chemicals and manure. Standard wiring materials used in residential construction are not designed for use in farm buildings. Materials which can be used safely include the following.

Type TW wire. A single conductor covered with a single layer of plastic insulation which can be easily stripped. The insulation does not have much mechanical strength. Therefore, this wire should be used inside a conduit. Do not confuse this wire with type T, which does not have a moisture resistant covering.

Cable. A cable is an assembly of two or more insulated wires into a single unit. Size designations are based on the number and size of conductors contained. A cable with No. 12 wires would be designated as 12-2. One with three No. 12 wires, as 12-3, and so on. If a bare ground wire is also enclosed in the assembly, the size is listed as with ground (i.e., 12-2 w/gnd). The individual wires in cables have color coded insulations to aid in the wiring process. Black and white are used in two wire cables; black, white and red in three wire units.

1. Type NMC—A non metallic covered cable designed for use in damp and corrosive locations. This cable is ideal for most agricultural locations.
2. Type UF—Similar to type NMC wire in its ability to perform under damp and corrosive conditions, UF cable is also suitable for direct burial in the ground.

Conduit. Conduit is a pipe like material used to provide mechanical protection for electrical wiring. Traditionally, conduit has been thin walled steel tubing protected from corrosion with a layer of galvanizing. Today plastic conduit made of polyvinyl chloride (PVC) is also available. The PVC is easier to work with, less expensive than steel, and completely resistant to the corrosive effects of agricultural environments.

Composition boxes. Electrical boxes made of plastic or other non-corrosive material. They are used to house switches, outlets and wire junctions. These boxes are usually less expensive than the conventional metal boxes and will provide much better service in farm buildings.

Dust and moisture proof components. Switches, lighting fixtures, controllers, and motors are all available in enclosures or assemblies which are designed to protect them from the environment they must operate in. Use of these components will add to the overall cost of the electrical system. It will also add to its life and reduce the risk of failure.

Electrical Grounding

Electricity will always flow from where it is to the ground, if you give it a path to follow. If it has two paths to follow, it will always take the one with the least resistance. The purpose of grounding is to provide a low resistance path between anything likely to be charged with electricity and the ground. Without a planned grounding path, equipment which becomes electrically charged due to some type of short circuit or perhaps even a lightning strike is likely to discharge to ground through a path which may involve you or one of your animals.

The NEC requires more grounds for a farm installation than it does for an ordinary residential installation. If the service originates at a meter pole, a ground must be located at the pole and an additional ground located at each building served. The only exception is for buildings which contain only one circuit, do not contain equipment which must be grounded, and do not house livestock.

According to the NEC, an acceptable ground may be obtained by

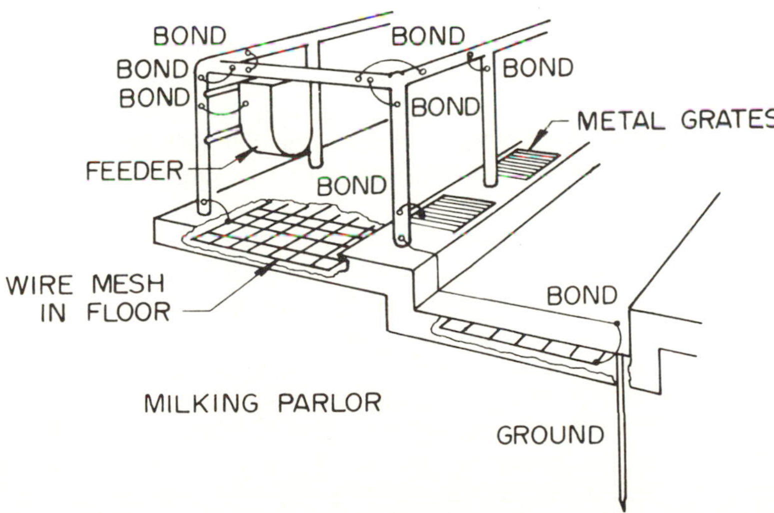

Figure 22-3. Naturally wet areas used by animals must have all metal parts electrically bonded together and grounded to prevent leakage of electric current. Animals will react to voltages that are well below what can be felt by a human. The illustration shows proper grounding technique for a milking parlor. (University of Minnesota)

driving a copper coated steel grounding rod at least 8 feet into the ground. The grounding rod must be at least ½ inch in diameter. An even better ground can be obtained by driving two rods, separating them by at least 6 feet, and connecting them together with grounding wire. Do not locate ground rods in areas where manure seepage is likely or rapid deterioration of the ground rod will result. A ground wire is connected to the rod(s) with a grounding clamp and then to the neutral or ground terminal on the distribution panel.

Each piece of electrical eqiupment is then grounded by running a wire (the grounding wire in supply cables) from the equipment to the grounding terminal at the service box. The grounding wire must be of the same size as the wire used to supply power to the equipment.

In normally wet places with several electrically powered devices (such as milking centers), it is desirable to provide an electrical ground for all metallic parts in the building. This is done by electrically bonding (connecting) together such things as feeders, auger tubes, stalls, floor grating and pipelines and connecting them to an electrical ground. Animals are considerably more sensitive to electrical currents than are people. An electric current which a human cannot normally detect can cause cows to fail to properly let down milk or to drink water from a "hot" waterer. Many suppliers of electric powered equipment designed for contact with livestock provide specific grounding instructions to be followed with their equipment. Make sure you follow these when the equipment is installed.

Sizing the Service to a Building

Wires leading from the main service or metering point to the individual building and the service panel within the building must be capable of handling the maximum anticipated electrical load. Electrical equipment is sized in amperes (amps) of capacity at a specific voltage (120 or 240 in the United States). Motors will have the amps which they require printed on the nameplate. Amperage requirements for other loads can be calculated by dividing their respective wattages by the service voltage.

One way to determine the size of service required would be to merely total up all the possible connected load for a building and use the value you obtain as a basis for sizing service equipment. However, not all equipment will be operating at the same time in most buildings and this method would result in the purchase of equipment much larger than would be needed at any one time. For example, an electric heater and an air conditioner would probably never be running at the same time in the same building. The NEC recognizes this and allows service entrance sizes to be calculated using a technique which provides for diversity of load.

Almost all farm buildings today will be served by a 120/240 volt service. This means that service sizes are based on amperage requirements at 240 volts, even though some of the actual loads will be operating at 120 volts.

The following steps are used to arrive at a size.

1. Add up amperages at 240 volts for all loads that are likely to be operating at any one time.
2. If step 1 includes the largest motor in the building, calculate 25% of its amperage. If you have two or more motors that are the same size, assume one of them is the largest.
3. If the largest motor was not included in step 1, calculate 125% of its amperage.
4. Add results from steps 1, 2, and 3.
5. Total up the amperage at 240 volts for all other connected loads in the building. (You may use a value of .75 amperes per outlet for light fixtures and convenience outlets for calculation purposes.)
6. Add results from 4 and 5.

Determine service size from the following:

a) If the total from step 6 is 30 amperes or less and not more than two circuits are needed, specify a 30 ampere service. If more than two circuits are needed, specify a 60 ampere service.

b) If step 6 is between 30 and 60, specify a 60 ampere service.

c) If step 4 is less than 60 and step 6 is more than 60, minimum service size is:

100% of the first 60 amps,
plus 50% of the next 60 amps,
plus 25% of the remainder.

d) If step 4 is over 60, minimum service size is:

100% of step 4,
plus 50% of the first 60 amps from step 5,
plus 25% of the remainder of step 5.

Example: The following illustrates use of this procedure for sizing a service for a dairy milking center.

Step 1: Amperage of all loads likely to be operating together:

5 hp compressor motor	26.5
3 hp vacuum pump	17.0
2-4500 watt water heaters	37.5
milk room lighting 1000 w	4.2
parlor heater 3000 w	12.5
milk transfer pump	3.0
crowd gate	5.0
parlor lights	3.3

Step 2: Largest motor is the compressor at 26.5 amps.

$$26.5 \times .25 = 6.6 \text{ amps}$$

Step 3: Largest motor already calculated

Step 4: 109 + 6.6 = 115.6 amps

Step 5: All other loads in building

milk truck pump circuit	5.0
duplex receptacles	15.0
ventilating fans in parlor & milkroom	7.0
lights in utility area 200 w	.8
milk room heater 3000 w	12.5
high pressure washer	7.0
bulk tank washer pump	5.0
	52.3

Step 6: 115.6 + 52.3 = 167.9

Use D to calculate entrance size since loads expected to operate simultaneously exceed 60 amps.

100% of 115.6 = 115.6
50% of 52.3 = 26.2
141.8

The minimum service required for this building is 150 amperes.

Underground Cable

For many years, the standard method of distributing electricity has been through pole mounted overhead wires. The use of underground distribution offers several advantages for the farmstead.

1. It eliminates the possibility of direct storm damage to wires.
2. You do not have to worry about overhead wire clearances when moving large equipment or loads.
3. Farmstead appearance is improved.
4. When used for the main service entrance, it allows the power company to locate transformers closer to the point of use.

Wires and cables approved for underground service usually cost more than other wire types. However, if trenching can be done with farm labor, the total installation cost may not be much different than for overhead lines.

There are two types of wire which are approved for direct burial. They are type UF cable and type USE cable. UF is available in two or three conductor cables and can be used to run a single circuit to a building with low electrical demand. Type USE is a service entrance cable used in construction of main distribution lines from the central meter to entrance panels in individual buildings.

Some amount of care must be used in installation of underground cable to insure against the possibility of mechanical damage. General rules which should be followed include the following.

1. Place cable at least 24 inches below ground level to avoid contact with any tillage tools.
2. Place sand under and around cable buried in rocky soil to reduce possibility of stone damage when backfilling the trench.
3. Do not pull cable tight in trenches. Allow it to "snake" back and forth from one side of the trench to the other. This will help take any strain due to settling or shifting soil.
4. Place cable in conduit at the point where it exits from the ground in order to protect it against contact with vehicles such as lawn-mowers.
5. If the cable must penetrate a foundation wall: (a) protect it with conduit, (b) allow enough slack to accommodate settling of backfill, and (c) be sure to seal the hole against leakage of water into the basement.

Sizing Wire

Electrical wire must be sized to the intended load if the system is to perform with maximum efficiency and economy. A wire that is too small for the load results in high voltage drops which can damage motors and other appliances connected to it. It can also overheat, melting insulation and eventually leading to a short circuit or even a fire.

The carrying capacity of an electrical wire is specified in amperes. It is a function of wire size, material the wire is made of, and the length of the wire. The larger the wire, the more electricity it can carry safely. Materials which are better conductors of electricity can carry more than those that are not so good. Copper and aluminum are the two materials most often used to make electrical wire. Copper is a better conductor than aluminum and is rated accordingly. When using aluminum it is not uncommon to have to select a wire that is at least one size larger than you would need if copper had been chosen. The longer the wire, the larger it has to be to carry a given load with a minimum line loss.

Building wires are normally sized to carry the designed power load with a minimum of 2% voltage drop. Tables 22-1 through 22-4 show the required wire sizes for various loads and distances for copper and aluminum conductors.

Three-Phase Service

The decision to use single or 3-phase power for a particular application should be based on both electrical and economic evaluations. A 3-phase motor may cost less to purchase and may operate longer with less maintenance than a single phase motor. However, a 3-phase service will usually cost more to install and there may be a monthly service premium charged to offset the added cost to the power company. Your power

Load in Amps	Minimum Allowable Size of Conductor: In Cable, Conduit, Earth — Types R, T, TW	Types RH, RHW, THW	Overhead in Air* — Bare & Covered Conductors	Copper up to 200 Amperes, 115-120 Volts, Single Phase, Based on 2% Voltage Drop — Length of Run in Feet (Compare size shown below with size shown to left of double line. Use the larger size.) 30	40	50	60	75	100	125	150	175	200	225	250	275	300	350	400	450	500	550	600	650	700
5	12	12	10	12	12	12	12	12	12	12	10	10	10	10	8	8	8	8	6	6	6	6	4	4	4
7	12	12	10	12	12	12	12	12	12	10	10	8	8	8	8	6	6	6	6	4	4	4	4	4	3
10	12	12	10	12	12	12	12	10	10	8	8	8	6	6	6	6	4	4	4	4	3	3	2	2	2
15	12	12	10	12	12	10	10	10	8	6	6	6	4	4	4	4	4	3	2	2	1	1	1	0	0
20	12	12	10	12	10	10	8	8	6	6	4	4	4	4	3	3	2	2	1	1	0	0	00	00	00
25	10	10	10	10	10	8	8	6	6	4	4	4	3	3	2	2	1	1	0	0	00	00	000	000	000
30	10	10	10	10	8	8	8	6	4	4	4	3	2	2	1	1	1	0	00	00	000	000	000	4/0	4/0
35	8	8	10	10	8	8	6	6	4	4	3	2	2	1	1	0	0	00	00	000	000	4/0	4/0	4/0	250
40	8	8	10	8	8	6	6	4	4	3	2	2	1	1	0	0	00	00	000	000	4/0	4/0	250	250	300
45	6	8	10	8	8	6	6	4	4	3	2	1	1	0	0	00	00	000	000	4/0	4/0	250	250	300	300
50	6	6	10	8	6	6	4	4	3	2	1	1	0	0	00	00	000	000	4/0	4/0	250	250	300	300	350
60	4	6	8	8	6	4	4	4	2	1	1	0	00	00	000	000	000	4/0	250	250	300	300	350	400	400
70	4	4	8	6	6	4	4	3	2	1	0	00	00	000	000	4/0	4/0	250	300	300	350	400	400	500	500
80	2	4	6	6	4	4	3	2	1	0	00	00	000	000	4/0	4/0	250	300	300	350	400	400	500	500	600
90	2	3	6	6	4	4	3	2	1	0	00	000	000	4/0	4/0	250	250	300	350	400	500	500	500	600	600
100	1	3	6	4	4	3	2	1	0	00	000	000	4/0	4/0	250	250	300	350	400	500	500	500	600	600	700
115	0	2	4	4	4	3	2	1	0	00	000	4/0	4/0	250	300	300	350	400	500	500	600	600	700	700	750
130	00	1	4	4	3	2	1	0	00	000	4/0	4/0	250	300	300	350	400	500	500	600	600	700	750	800	900
150	000	0	2		2	1	1	0	000	4/0	4/0	250	300	350	350	400	500	500	600	700	700	800	900	900	1M
175	4/0	00	2		2	1	0	00	000	4/0	250	300	350	400	400	500	500	600	700	750	800	900	1M		
200	250	000	1		1	0	00	000	4/0	250	300	350	400	500	500	500	600	700	750	900	1M				

*Conductors in overhead spans must be at least No. 10 for spans up to 50 feet and No. 8 for longer spans.

Table 22-1. Copper wire size selection for 115 to 120-volt applications. FEC (AGRICULTURAL WIRING HANDBOOK)

	Minimum Allowable Size of Conductor			Copper up to 400 Amperes, 230-240 Volts, Single Phase, Based on 2% Voltage Drop																					
	In Cable, Conduit, Earth		Overhead in Air*	Length of Run in Feet. Compare size shown below with size shown to left of double line. Use the larger size.																					
Load in Amps	Types R, T, TW	Types RH, RHW, THW	Bare & Covered Conductors	50	60	75	100	125	150	175	200	225	250	275	300	350	400	450	500	550	600	650	700	750	800
5	12	12	10	12	12	12	12	12	12	12	12	12	12	12	10	10	10	10	8	8	8	8	8	6	6
7	12	12	10	12	12	12	12	12	12	12	12	10	10	10	10	8	8	8	8	6	6	6	6	6	6
10	12	12	10	12	12	12	12	12	10	10	10	10	8	8	8	8	6	6	6	6	4	4	4	4	4
15	12	12	10	12	12	12	10	10	10	8	8	8	6	6	6	6	4	4	4	4	4	3	3	3	2
20	12	12	10	12	12	10	10	8	8	8	6	6	6	6	4	4	4	4	3	3	2	2	2	1	1
25	10	10	10		10	10	8	8	6	6	6	6	4	4	4	4	3	3	2	2	1	1	1	0	0
30	10	10	10	10	10	10	8	6	6	6	4	4	4	4	4	3	2	2	1	1	1	0	0	0	00
35	8	8	10	10	10	8	8	6	6	4	4	4	4	3	3	2	2	1	1	0	0	0	00	00	00
40	8	8	10	10	8	8	6	6	4	4	4	4	3	3	2	2	1	1	0	0	00	00	00	000	000
45	6	8	10	10	8	8	6	6	4	4	4	3	3	2	2	1	1	0	0	00	00	00	000	000	000
50	6	6	10	8	8	6	6	4	4	4	3	3	2	2	1	1	0	0	00	00	000	000	000	4/0	4/0
60	4	6	8	8	8	6	4	4	4	3	2	2	1	1	1	0	00	00	000	000	000	4/0	4/0	4/0	250
70	4	4	8	8	6	6	4	4	3	2	2	1	1	0	0	00	00	000	000	4/0	4/0	4/0	250	250	300
80	2	4	6	6	6	4	4	3	2	2	1	1	0	0	00	00	000	000	4/0	4/0	250	250	300	300	300
90	2	3	6	6	6	4	4	3	2	1	1	0	0	00	00	000	000	4/0	4/0	250	250	300	300	350	350
100	1	3	6	6	4	4	3	2	1	1	0	0	00	00	000	000	4/0	4/0	250	250	300	300	350	350	400
115	0	2	4		4	4	3	2	1	0	0	00	00	000	000	4/0	4/0	250	300	300	350	350	400	400	500
130	00	1	4	4	4	3	2	1	0	0	00	00	000	000	4/0	4/0	250	300	300	350	400	400	500	500	500
150	000	0	2				1	0	0	00	000	000	4/0	4/0	4/0	250	300	350	350	400	500	500	500	600	600
175	4/0	00	2			2	1	0	00	000	000	4/0	4/0	250	250	300	350	400	400	500	500	600	600	600	700
200	250	000	1			1	0	00	000	000	4/0	4/0	250	250	300	350	400	500	500	500	600	600	700	700	750
225	300	4/0	0				0	00	000	4/0	4/0	250	300	300	350	400	500	500	600	600	700	700	750	800	900
250	350	250	00				00	000	4/0	4/0	250	300	300	350	350	400	500	600	600	700	700	750	800	900	1M
275	400	300	00				00	000	4/0	250	250	300	350	350	400	500	500	600	700	700	800	900	900	1M	
300	500	350	000				000	4/0	4/0	250	300	350	350	400	500	500	600	700	700	800	900	900	1M		
325	600	400	4/0					4/0	250	300	300	350	400	500	500	600	600	700	750	900	900	1M			
350	600	500	4/0					4/0	250	300	350	400	400	500	500	600	700	750	800	900	1M				
375	700	500	250					250	300	300	350	400	500	500	600	600	700	800	900	1M					
400	750	600	250					250	300	350	400	500	500	500	600	700	750	900	1M						

*Conductors in overhead spans must be at least No. 10 for spans up to 50 feet and No. 8 for longer spans.

Table 22-2. Copper wire size selection for 230 to 240-volt applications. (FEC AGRICULTURAL WIRING HANDBOOK)

	Minimum Allowable Size of Conductor			Aluminum up to 200 Amperes, 115-120 Volts, Single Phase, Based on 2% Voltage Drop																					
	In Cable Conduit, Earth		Overhead in Air*	Length of Run in Feet. Compare size shown below with size shown to left of double line. Use the larger size.																					
Load in Amps	Types R, T, TW	Types RH, RHW, THW	Bare & Covered Conductors Single Triplex	30	40	50	60	75	100	125	150	175	200	225	250	275	300	350	400	450	500	550	600	650	700
5	12	12	10	12	12	12	12	12	10	10	8	8	8	8	6	6	6	6	4	4	4	4	3	3	3
7	12	12	10	12	12	12	12	10	10	8	8	6	6	6	6	4	4	4	4	3	3	2	2	2	1
10	12	12	10	12	12	10	10	8	8	6	6	6	4	4	4	4	3	3	2	2	1	1	0	0	0
15	12	12	10	12	10	8	8	8	6	4	4	4	3	3	2	2	2	1	0	0	00	00	00	000	000
20	10	10	10	10	8	8	6	6	4	4	3	3	2	2	1	1	0	0	00	00	000	000	4/0	4/0	4/0
25	10	10	10	8	8	6	6	4	4	3	2	2	1	1	0	0	00	00	000	000	4/0	4/0	250	250	300
30	8	8	10	8	6	6	6	4	3	2	2	1	0	0	00	00	00	000	4/0	4/0	250	250	300	300	350
35	6	8	10	8	6	6	4	4	3	2	1	0	0	00	00	000	000	4/0	4/0	250	300	300	350	350	400
40	6	8	10	6	6	4	4	3	2	1	0	0	00	00	000	000	4/0	4/0	250	300	300	350	350	400	500
45	4	6	10	6	6	4	4	3	2	1	0	00	00	000	000	4/0	4/0	250	300	300	350	400	400	500	500
50	4	6	8	6	4	4	3	2	1	0	00	00	000	000	4/0	4/0	250	300	300	350	400	400	500	500	600
60	2	4	6	6	4	3	3	2	0	00	00	000	4/0	4/0	250	250	300	350	350	400	500	500	600	600	700
70	2	2	6	4	4	3	2	1	0	00	000	4/0	4/0	250	300	300	350	400	500	500	600	600	700	700	750
80	1	2	6	4	3	2	1	0	00	000	4/0	4/0	250	300	300	350	350	500	500	600	600	700	750	800	900
90	0	2	4	4	3	2	1	0	00	000	4/0	250	300	300	350	400	400	500	600	600	700	750	800	900	1M
100	0	1	4	3	2	1	0	00	000	4/0	250	300	300	350	400	400	500	600	600	700	750	900	900	1M	
115	00	0	2		1	1	0	00	000	4/0	300	300	350	400	500	500	600	600	700	800	900	1M			
130	000	00	2	2	1	0	00	000	4/0	250	300	350	400	500	500	600	600	700	800	900	1M				
150	4/0	000	1		0	00	00	000	250	300	350	400	500	500	600	600	700	800	900	1M					
175	300	4/0	0		0	00	000	4/0	300	350	400	500	600	600	700	750	800	900							
200	350	250	00		00	000	4/0	250	300	400	500	600	600	700	750	900	900								

*Conductors in overhead spans must be at least No. 10 for spans up to 50 feet and No. 8 for longer spans

Table 22-3. Aluminum wire size selection for 115 to 120-volt applications. (FEC AGRICULTURAL WIRING HANDBOOK)

Load in Amps	In Cable Conduit, Earth: Types R, T, TW	In Cable Conduit, Earth: Types RH, RHW, THW	Overhead in Air*: Bare & Covered Conductors Single	Overhead in Air*: Bare & Covered Conductors Triplex	50	60	75	100	125	150	175	200	225	250	275	300	350	400	450	500	550	600	650	700	750	800
5	12	12	10		12	12	12	12	12	12	12	10	10	10	10	8	8	8	8	6	6	6	6	6	4	4
7	12	12	10		12	12	12	12	12	10	10	10	8	8	8	8	6	6	6	6	4	4	4	4	4	4
10	12	12	10		12	12	12	10	10	8	8	8	8	6	6	6	6	4	4	4	4	3	3	3	2	2
15	12	12	10		12	12	10	8	8	8	6	6	6	4	4	4	4	3	3	2	2	2	1	1	1	0
20	10	10	10		10	10	8	8	6	6	6	4	4	4	4	3	3	2	2	1	1	0	0	0	00	00
25	10	10	10		10	8	8	6	6	4	4	4	4	3	3	2	2	1	1	0	0	00	00	00	000	000
30	8	8	10		8	8	8	6	4	4	4	3	3	2	2	2	1	0	0	00	00	00	000	000	000	4/0
35	6	8	10		8	8	6	6	4	4	3	3	2	2	1	1	0	0	00	00	000	000	000	4/0	4/0	4/0
40	6	8	10		8	6	6	4	4	3	3	2	2	1	1	0	0	00	00	000	000	4/0	4/0	4/0	250	250
45	4	6	10		8	6	6	4	4	3	2	2	1	1	0	0	00	00	000	000	4/0	4/0	250	250	250	300
50	4	6	8		6	6	4	4	3	2	2	1	1	0	0	00	00	000	000	4/0	4/0	250	250	300	300	300
60	2	4	6	6	6	6	4	3	2	2	1	0	0	00	00	00	000	4/0	4/0	250	250	300	300	350	350	350
70	2	2(a)	6	4	6	4	4	3	2	1	0	0	00	00	000	000	4/0	4/0	250	300	300	350	350	400	400	500
80	1	2(a)	6	4	4	4	3	2	1	0	0	00	00	000	000	4/0	4/0	250	300	300	350	350	400	500	500	500
90	0	2(a)	4	2	4	4	3	2	1	0	00	00	000	000	4/0	4/0	250	300	300	350	400	400	500	500	500	600
100	0	1(a)	4	2	4	3	2	1	0	00	00	000	000	4/0	4/0	250	300	300	350	400	400	500	500	600	600	600
115	00	0(a)	2	1			2	1	0	00	000	000	4/0	4/0	250	300	300	350	400	500	500	600	600	600	700	700
130	000	00(a)	2	0		2	1	0	00	000	000	4/0	250	250	300	300	350	400	500	500	600	600	700	700	750	800
150	4/0	000(a)	1	00			1	00	000	000	4/0	250	250	300	300	350	400	500	500	600	600	700	750	800	900	900
175	300	4/0(a)	0	000			0	00	000	4/0	250	300	300	350	400	400	500	600	600	700	750	800	900	900	1M	
200	350	250	00	4/0			00	000	4/0	250	300	300	350	400	400	500	600	600	700	750	900	900	1M			
225	400	300	000					000	4/0	250	300	350	400	500	500	500	600	700	750	900	1M	1M				
250	500	350	000				000	4/0	250	300	350	400	500	500	500	600	700	750	900	1M						
275	600	500	4/0					4/0	250	300	400	400	500	500	600	600	750	900	1M							
300	700	500	250					250	300	350	400	500	500	600	600	700	800	900	1M							
325	800	600	300					250	300	400	500	500	600	600	700	750	900	1M								
350	900	700	300					300	350	400	500	600	600	700	750	800	900									
375	1M	700	350					300	350	500	500	600	700	700	800	900	1M									
400		900	350					300	400	500	600	600	700	750	900	900										

Minimum Allowable Size of Conductor — Aluminum up to 400 Amperes, 230-240 Volts, Single Phase, Based on 2% Voltage Drop. Length of Run in Feet: Compare size shown below with size shown to left of double line. Use the larger size.

*Conductors in overhead spans must be at least No. 10 for spans up to 50 feet and No. 8 for longer spans.

Note (a) For three-wire, single-phase service and sub-service circuits, the allowable current-carrying capacity of RH, RH RW, RHH, RHW, and THW aluminum conductors shall be for sizes No. 2-100 amp, No. 1-110 amp, No. 0-125 amp, No. 00-150 amp, No. 000-170 amp and No. 4/0-200 amp.

Table 22-4. Aluminum wire size selection for 230 to 240-volt applications. (FEC AGRICULTURAL WIRING HANDBOOK)

company service representative can help you evaluate the costs and potential savings from a 3-phase service. Study these costs carefully before making a final decision.

Lightning Protection

Lightning is nothing more than uncontrolled electricity which exists in nature. Each year in the United States lightning kills about 400 persons, injures 1,000, and causes more than two million dollars in property damage. Lightning strikes somewhere on earth an average of 100 times each second.

Lightning can cause property damage in two ways. First, by directly striking an object, resulting in fires, personal injury, and livestock losses. Lightning rods and grounding systems are designed to protect against direct strikes. The second type of damage occurs when lightning strikes power lines, causing surges of high voltage electricity through the wiring system of a building.

Lightning protection is a form of insurance. Whether or not you decide to purchase it should be based on an evaluation of risk and possible loss. Such things as frequency and severity of storms in your area, the nature of the building and its contents, the exposure of a building (is it on top of a hill or in a protected valley), and the hazards to people or livestock should all be carefully weighed before deciding to purchase.

Lightning Rod Systems

The lightning rod and ground system is designed to intercept the electrical charge of lightning and lead it through a safe path to ground. It does this by providing contact points which are higher than the item they are protecting and a path which is both large enough and of lower resistance than normal building components.

The three general components of the lightning rod system are: 1) Air terminals, 2) down conductors, and 3) ground rods. Materials used in their construction must be resistant to corrosion over long periods of exposure to outdoor weather conditions. Most systems are made of either copper or aluminum. Aluminum systems must use a ground system which is constructed of some type of metal which will not corrode under exposure to soil.

The installation of a lightning rod system should be done by a professional who is familiar with proper design and construction. A good system includes the following design features:

- Properly spaced air terminals or points.
- Down leads should not have turns sharper than 90°.
- All metal parts in contact with the building should be electrically bonded to the lightning rod down lead system. This includes guttering, down spouts, TV antennas, metal roofing, metal

MASTER LABEL NO.
Underwriters' Laboratories, Inc.
®
LISTED
LIGHTNING ROD EQUIPMENT
INSTALLED-DATE
NOTICE
ADDITIONS TO THIS BUILDING MAY RENDER PROTECTION AFFORDED BY THIS EQUIPMENT INEFFECTIVE. NOTIFY THE COMPANY MAKING INSTALLATION WHEN ADDITIONS TO BUILDING ARE CONTEMPLATED OR WHEN EQUIPMENT HAS BEEN DAMAGED IN ANY MANNER.

Figure 22-4. Master label used to designate lightning-protection systems that are installed in accordance with requirements of Underwriters' Laboratories, Inc. (University of Missouri)

chimneys, water or drain pipes and vents, and the main electric service conduit.

- Ground rods must be driven into the ground a minimum of 10 feet. Use at least 2 rods for each building, located at opposite corners. Rods are driven 2 feet away from the foundation of the building.
- Buildings with a perimeter of more than 250 feet need one additional down lead and ground for each 100 feet of perimeter distance.
- Nearby water towers, silos, flag poles, or tall trees should have their own protective system.
- If lightning rod grounds are driven within 6 feet of any other electrical or telephone ground, they must be bonded to it to prevent side flashes.
- Down conductors should be protected from mechanical damage for a distance of 5 feet above ground level. Use metal conduit or tubing.

You can be sure of obtaining a quality system if you insist on *Master Label* installation. Such a system is approved by the Underwriters Laboratory upon receipt of a special application form signed by the owner, installer, and equipment manufacturer. If all materials and workmanship meet UL specifications, the Master Label is issued to the owner. UL will make periodic unannounced inspections of selected Master Label systems to insure compliance with their standards.

Lightning Arresters

Lightning arresters are devices which are designed to intercept surges of high voltage electricity and lead them safely to ground before they can enter a building and damage any connected electrical equipment. Most arresters are smaller than a baseball and are designed for 120/240 volt single phase systems. They are connected to the electrical supply line at the point where the service enters the building. Connectors between the arrester and the service leads should be as short as possible.

Lightning arresters should also be installed ahead of specialized

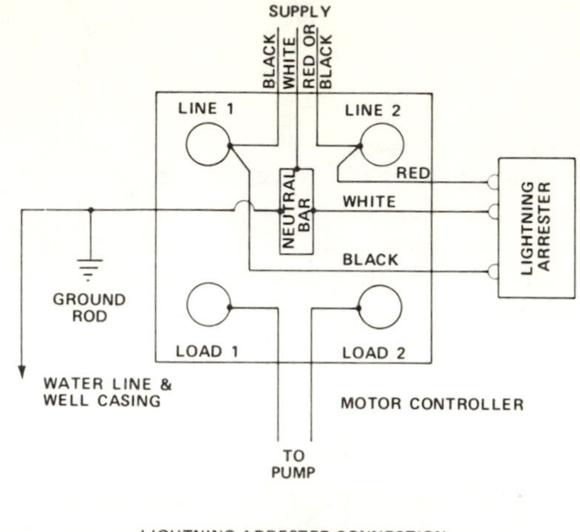

Figure 22-5. Submersible water pumps are among the most likely pieces of equipment to suffer lightning damage on the farm. The above diagram shows the proper way to protect these pumps using a lightning-arrester unit. (University of Missouri)

electric loads which are located away from or outside an arrester protected building. Examples include submersible pumps and motors used on outside overhead feed auger systems.

The NEC specifies that for electrical systems of 1,000 volts or less, the grounding conductor of the lightning arrester must be conducted to one of the following:

a) The grounded wire of the service conductor.

b) The grounding electrode conductor.

c) The service ground.

d) The equipment grounding terminal in the service box.

The conductor between the arrester and the ground should be as short and as straight as possible and at least No. 6 copper or its equivalent.

CHAPTER 23

Plumbing and Sewage Disposal

This chapter is designed to provide you with some of the basics on selection of water supply lines and systems for disposal of domestic sewage. We are assuming that your farmstead already has an adequate supply of potable water under pressure at some central point.

If you need information on development of a water supply, pumps, or water treatment, we recommend that you obtain a copy of PRIVATE WATER SYSTEMS, published by Midwest Plan Service. This booklet costs about $4.00 and is one of the most complete references available on water systems for rural locations.

Determining Pipe Size

There is probably nothing so frustrating as turning on a faucet to wash up some equipment and getting out only a trickle of water because some animal happens to be drinking. Problems of this type can be avoided by choosing the right size of supply line from your water source to the building being served.

Proper line size is a function of flow rate (expressed in gallons per minute or gpm) and the distance from the supply to the building. Maximum flow rate is determined by adding up the flow rates for individual outlets which are likely to be operating at the same time. Table 23-1 presents some typical flow rates for different outlets found on the farm.

Let's use an example to illustrate how we might use the values in Table 23-1 to arrive at a required flow rate for a combination farrowing house and swine nursery. One room holds 20 sows in farrowing crates. The other end of the building has six nursery pens. There is an office complex in the middle with a shower and bathroom. Hose outlets in the two rooms are

Table 23-1. **Flow Rates Required for Optimum Service for Various Water Outlets**

Use	Desired Flow Rate (Gpm)
Stock waterers	
Large animals	1.5
Poultry	.5
Hose outlet	5.0
Manure wash down hose	10.0
Outdoor hydrant for fire fighting	10.0
Water softener regeneration	5.0
Flush toilet	3.0
Shower	5.0
Lavatory	2.0
Wash sink	3.0

used to wash down floors and clean animals when necessary.

Flow rate requirements are as follows:

1. Sow waterers (20). There probably won't ever be more than two in operation at one time. $2 \times 1.5 = 3.0$
2. Nursery Waterers (6). Assume that about half could be operating simultaneously. $3 \times 1.5 = 4.5$
3. Hose Outlets (2). Assume one operating. $1 \times 5.0 = 5.0$
4. Bathroom. Only one outlet will be operating at any one time. The shower requires the most water at: 5.0
5. Total flow rate needed 17.5 gpm

Whenever we push water through a pipe there is resistance due to friction between the flowing water and the inside surface of the pipe. The amount of friction depends on how fast the water is moving, the roughness of the pipe, and the length of the pipe. In order to keep energy costs for pumping at a minimum and system performance high, we try to select a pipe size which will allow for the desired flow rate while keeping friction losses to 5 pounds per square inch (psi) or less. Tables 23-2, -3, and -4 give friction losses per 100 feet of pipe for different flow rates.

Suppose in our example above, it is 200 feet from the well to the building and we want to use copper pipe. Looking at Table 23-2 under 18 gpm, we find that 1-½ inch copper has a friction loss of 1.6 psi per 100 feet. For 200 feet, the friction loss would total 3.2 psi, well within our maximum allowable of 5 psi. It is also interesting to compare what would happen with plastic. Looking at Table 23-3, we find that 1-¼ inch plastic has a friction loss of 2.1 psi per 100 feet or a total of 4.2 psi for the 200 foot run, well within our 5 psi limit. The fact that plastic is smoother inside reduces the friction loss enough so that we can use one size smaller pipe for this particular case.

Table 23-2. **Friction Loss in Psi per 100 Feet of Pipe for Copper Pipe**

Flow Rate	Pipe Size (Inches Diameter)					
(Gpm)	½	¾	1	1-¼	1-½	2
1	1.1	.2				
2	3.8	.7	.2			
4		2.3	.6	.2	.1	
6		5.0	1.4	.5	.2	
8			2.3	.8	.4	
10			3.5	1.3	.5	.1
14			6.5	2.3	1.0	.3
18				3.7	1.6	.4
20				4.5	1.9	.5
30					4.1	1.1
40						1.8

Table 23-3. **Friction Loss in Psi per 100 Feet of Pipe for Plastic Pipe**

Flow Rate	Pipe Size (Inches Diameter)					
(Gpm)	½	¾	1	1-¼	1-½	2
1	.5	.1				
2	1.8	.4	.1			
4	6.4	1.6	.5	.1	.1	
6		3.4	1.1	.3	.1	
8		5.8	1.8	.5	.2	
10			2.7	.7	.3	.1
14			5.1	1.3	.6	.1
18				2.1	1.0	.3
20				2.6	1.2	.4
30					2.6	.8
40						1.3

Table 23-4. **Friction Loss in Psi per 100 Feet of Steel Pipe**

Flow Rate	Pipe Size (Inches Diameter)					
(Gpm)	½	¾	1	1-¼	1-½	2
1	.9	.2				
2	3.3	.8	.3			
4	11.8	3.0	.9	.2	.1	
6		6.4	2.0	.5	.2	
8		10.9	3.3	.9	.4	
10			5.1	1.3	.6	.2
14			9.4	2.5	1.2	.3
18				3.9	1.9	.6
20				4.8	2.3	.7
30					4.8	1.4
40						2.4

The same principle in pipe sizing can be followed to determine how big pipes serving individual appliances inside the structure should be. However, it is more conventional to merely select a certain size pipe which experience has shown will do the job for the relatively short interior runs.

Table 23-5 presents recommended minimum sizes for plumbing supply lines. If a single line serves two fixtures which are not likely to be operating at the same time, a pipe sized to the larger of the two can adequately serve both. For example, a ½ inch pipe could serve both a shower and a lavatory in the same bathroom.

Table 23-5. **Minimum Recommended Sizes for Plumbing Distribution Lines Within a Building**

Fixture Served	Pipe Size (Inches Dia.)
Livestock waterer	1/2
Outside hydrant	3/4
Water heater	3/4
Toilet	3/8
Shower	1/2
Hose faucet	1/2
Sink	1/2
Lavatory	3/8

Pipe Selection

There are three types of pipe available for use in water supply systems. They are galvanized steel, copper and plastic. Advantages and disadvantages of each type, along with recommendations on usage are discussed in the following sections.

Galvanized steel. Galvanized pipe is available in all standard sizes and comes in standard lengths of 21 feet. The pipe must be cut to fit and cut ends threaded to fit standard connectors during installation. Galvanized steel has greater mechanical strength than either plastic or copper pipe. Materials cost is between that of copper and plastic. However, labor required will generally make steel pipe the most expensive type on an installed basis. Steel has a greater tendency to corrode and mineral deposits tend to build up more rapidly than in other types of pipe.

Copper. Copper is the most commonly used material for water supply lines, although plastic is gaining rapidly in many areas of the country. It is available in three grades or types, depending on the strength. They are designated as types "K," "L" and "M." Types "K" and "L" are available in flexible coils. All three types are available in rigid lengths of 10 and 20 feet.

Copper pipe is cut to length and fitted together with either solder type or mechanical fittings. Soldered fittings are known generally as "sweated" connectors and make a low cost, durable joint. They are also a fairly permanent joint which is difficult to disassemble unless all water is out of the pipe and it is completely dry. Mechanical connectors are known collectively as compression type fittings. They are made by flaring the end of the pipe to fit the center portion of the connector. The flared end is then "compressed" or clamped to the connector with a threaded collar section.

Type "K" pipe is the heaviest of the three copper pipes. It is used primarily for underground supply lines.

Type "L" is a medium weight copper used for general interior work. Type "L" can be used for exposed plumbing runs which are not subjected to extreme mechanical abuse.

Type "M" is the lightest weight of the three types of copper. It is used primarily in residential applications where it can be protected within wall partitions or between floor joists. Its use is generally not recommended for farm buildings.

Plastic. The use of plastic pipe for both plumbing supply and drain lines is growing rapidly. This is due both to its generally lower cost and the ease with which it can be installed.

Plastic pipe is available in both flexible and rigid forms. It can be purchased in different sizes, wall thicknesses, and even colors. When you purchase plastic, there are three things you should look for: pressure rating, recommended use, and the seal of the National Sanitation Foundation (NSF). Most plastic pipe will have pressure ratings from 80 pounds per square inch (psi) on up. Although 80 psi will be sufficient for most farm water systems, there may be some particular applications where a higher rating will be required. These would include farms which are connected to a municipal water system or locations which have long uphill supply lines. Some plastics lose strength rapidly when they are heated. Because of this, they cannot be used for hot water supply lines. Plastic which can withstand temperatures of hot water and still maintain strength will be labeled for use with either hot or cold water. The NSF label is your assurance that plastic pipe is made of new material and is not going to release toxic materials into water passing through it. The types of plastic generally used for piping are:

Polyethylene (PE). This is the lowest cost of the plastics and is most commonly available in coils of 100 to 400 feet or more. It loses strength rapidly upon heating and is restricted to cold water only applications. Normally available pressure range is 80 to 160 psi. Connections between pipes or to fixtures are made with tapered connectors which are inserted into the pipe and clamped in place with stainless steel hose clamps.

Polyvinyl Chloride (PVC). Rigid type pipe designed for use with cold water supply or waste disposal lines. Pressure ratings range from 50 to 300 + psi. Pipe is available in 20 foot lengths and is easily cut to fit with a standard hack saw. Connections are made with solvent welded (glued) connectors. Long runs of drain lines subjected to alternating warm and cold water should be provided with a slip type connector at periodic intervals to accommodate normal expansion and contraction.

Chlorinated Polyvinyl Chloride (CPVC). Rigid plastic similar to

PVC except that it will withstand temperatures associated with hot water. Some manufacturers make CPVC in different colors to aid in installation and identification of hot and cold lines.

Polybutylene (PB). Similar to CPVC in that it can be used for both hot and cold water lines.

Acrylonitrile Butadene Styrene (ABS). Semi rigid plastic available in 20 foot lengths. Pressure ratings range from 80 to 160 psi. Joints are solvent welded. ABS is normally used for drain and sewer lines.

Sewage Disposal Systems

Connection to a public or municipally operated sewage system is the most satisfactory and trouble free method of sewage disposal. Unfortunately, very few farms are fortunate enough to be located where this can be done.

Domestic waste or waste containing human sewage must be disposed of in a system which is separate from other farm waste handling in order to minimize the possibility of transmitting disease. There are three types of systems available for handling these wastes in an acceptable manner. They are the septic tank-absorption field, the aerobic lagoon, and the small treatment plant.

Septic Tank Systems

The septic tank system consists of two major components—the septic tank and the absorption field. A septic tank is a large buried container which reserves raw sewage from the plumbing drains. It provides a place where solids settle out of the raw sewage and are broken down by bacteria. The absorption field is a subsurface leaching area which receives effluent from the septic tank and spreads it out over an area where it can seep into the soil. The filtering action of the soil, along with further bacterial action, complete the treatment process.

A septic tank should be located at least 50 feet from any well, water supply, or stream and at least 10 feet from any building or property line. The absorption field should be 100 feet from any well and at least 25 feet from any building or property line.

Septic tanks are constructed of many materials, the most common of which is probably reinforced concrete. No matter what type you select, the tank should be water tight and properly sized. Size will depend on intended use.

The number of bedrooms in a home is frequently used as a measure of sewage production. A 1,000 gallon tank should be the minimum size tank for a 3 bedroom home used on a year-round basis. This minimum should be increased by 250 gallons for each additional bedroom. A 500 to 750 gallon tank will be adequate to handle wastes from bathrooms located in other buildings on the farmstead. Tanks which are larger than the minimum

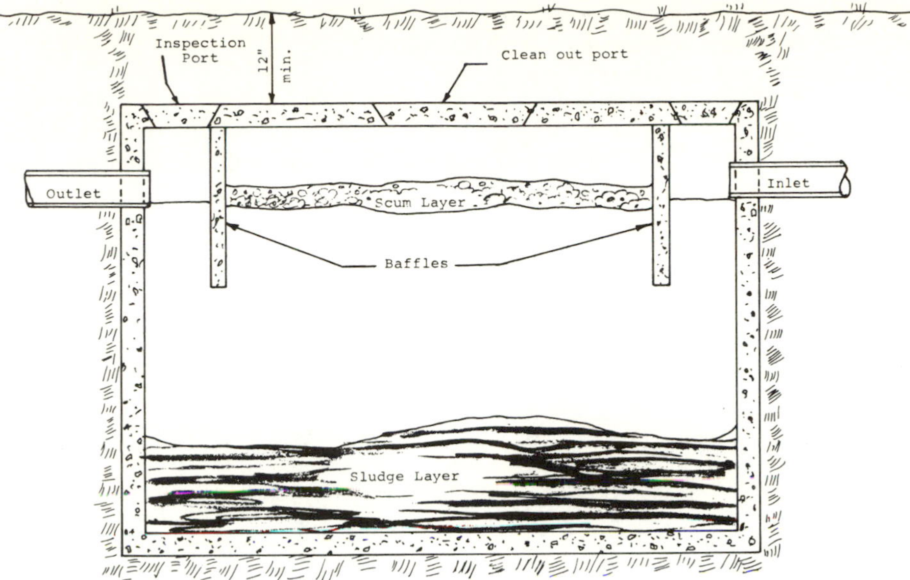

Figure 23-1. Sectional view of a typical precast concrete septic tank illustrating the essential components and locations of solids and scum accumulation. (University of Missouri)

required size usually do not add much to initial cost and will increase the interval between required cleanings.

Tanks must have baffles at both ends to prevent solid particles in raw sewage from flowing directly through the tank into the disposal field and to prevent the scum layer from flowing out of the tank. Baffles are illustrated in the septic tank shown in Figure 23-1.

The required size of the absorption field is determined by testing the ability of your soil to absorb water. The test used is known as a percolation test and it is conducted as follows:

1. Dig a minimum of two, preferably four or six holes 6 inches in diameter and 30 inches deep spaced over the area where the field is to be located.
2. Carefully roughen any smoothed areas of the hole sides and bottom and add a 2 inch layer of coarse sand to the bottom of each hole.
3. Fill and maintain a 12 inch depth of water in each hole for at least 4 hours, preferably overnight. This will saturate the soil and simulate conditions existing at the wettest time of the year. Percolation rate is determined 24 hours after water is first added to the hole.
4. To measure percolation rate:
   a) Adjust water depth in the holes to 6 inches.
   b) From a fixed reference point, measure the drop in water at 30 minute intervals for 4 hours. Refill the holes to the 6 inch mark as required.

c) The water drop during the last 30 minutes is used to determine the percolation rate in minutes per inch.

The required area of the absorption field is determined from the percolation rate using values in Table 23-6. Use values for one bedroom when planning a field for a system serving a farm building not used as a residence.

Table 23-6. **Absorption Area Required in Square Feet per Bedroom for Soils With Various Percolation Rates**

Percolation Rate (Minutes per Inch)	Absorption Area (Sq Ft per Bedroom)
2 or less	85
2 to 4	115
5 to 10	165
11 to 15	190
16 to 30	250
31 to 45	300
46 to 60	330
Over 60	not suitable for conventional field

One of the most satisfactory and least expensive absorption areas is the absorption trench. The trench is 18 to 36 inches wide and a minimum of 24 inches deep. Trenches are filled to a depth of 6 inches with ½ inch to 2-½ inches graded gravel. Perforated pipe or agricultural drain tile, 4 inches in diameter, is placed on the gravel and an additional 6 inches of gravel is placed in the trench. A layer of hay or light weight building paper is placed over the gravel and the trench is backfilled with soil.

All trenches in an absorption field should be excavated to the same level and the pipe should be laid level. A good field distributes waste water uniformly over the entire area and keeping it level permits this uniformity. In some cases, the site will not permit constructing a level field. If you have this problem, you should seek help in planning a field acceptable for your particular location.

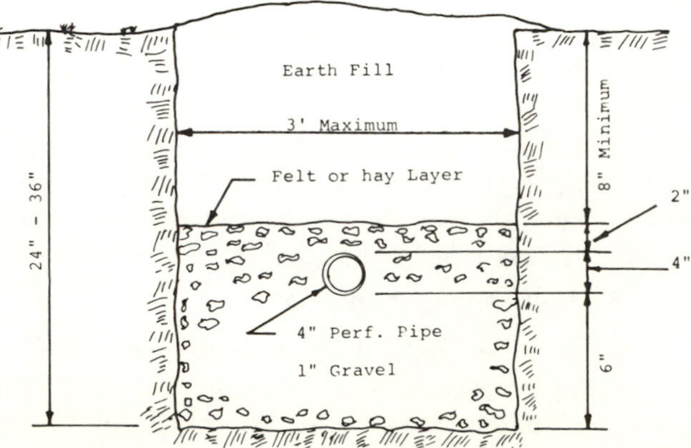

Figure 23-2. Cross section of a properly constructed absorption trench. (University of Missouri)

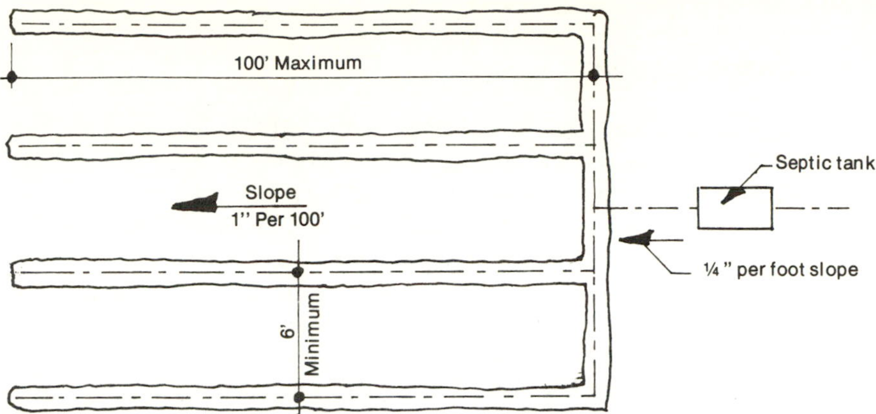

Figure 23-3. Plan view of an absorption trench system. There are a number of different layouts that can be used to accommodate varying site conditions. If your site is unusually steep or limited in physical size, you can get absorption-system design help through either the extension service or the SCS.

The total length of trench required can be determined from the width of trench and the total area determined by the percolation trench. Divide the total area required by the trench width in feet to get total trench length. Individual trenches should not exceed 100 feet in length. Adjacent trenches should be separated by at least 6 feet.

Even well designed and properly constructed absorption fields will occasionally fail after extended use. For this reason, it is a good idea to lay out your original field in an area where there is room to construct another one of equal size in the event of failure.

Soil absorption fields should not be constructed during periods when soil is wet. Construction equipment working in wet or muddy soil will tend to destroy natural soil structure which can lead to early failure of the field. If a handful of soil does not crack or crumble when you squeeze and release it, it is too wet to be worked.

A properly designed and constructed septic system is capable of handling all domestic wastes, including those from garbage disposal units. A separate system is not required for laundry wastes.

Paper towels, disposable diapers, newspaper, rags, and other items not considered as sewage should not be placed in the septic system. These items do not decompose rapidly and will quickly fill the tank. This ultimately leads to early failure of the system.

Additives such as enzyme products are not necessary to make a septic system function properly. Over 1,200 different products have been placed on the market for use in septic tanks. To date, none of these have proven to be effective in controlled testing programs.

Septic tanks should be inspected periodically to determine how much sludge has accumulated. Pump the tank when the bottom of the scum layer is within 3 inches of the bottom of the baffle or the top of the sludge layer is less than 6 inches below the outlet baffle. Sludge and scum depths can be determined by probing the tank with a stick.

Sewage Lagoons

Many states will permit the use of a small aerobic lagoon for disposal of domestic waste. In areas where this is possible, the lagoon provides an economical, low maintenance solution to handling of wastes.

An aerobic lagoon is simply a small pond of a uniform 3 foot depth. Size is determined by the amount of sewage entering it and the appropriate state or local regulations. A 900 to 1,000 square foot surface area is considered to be minimum in many places. Sewage is delivered to the lagoon by a tile line and released at the bottom near the lagoon center. The sewage is decomposed by bacteria which inhabit the lagoon. Oxygen in the water is necessary for these bacteria to work. In a properly constructed lagoon, it is not likely that solids will ever build up to the point where the lagoon will need to be cleaned out.

A lagoon is best located so that wastes can be carried to it by gravity. It is also desirable to locate it in a non-conspicuous place 100 feet or more from the dwelling or any water supply. There will be some overflow from the lagoon. Consideration must be given to the flow of this effluent so that it will be of the least nuisance.

A bulldozer is the best equipment for building a lagoon. Side slopes should not be steeper than 2:1, with flatter slopes preferred for easier maintenance. Provide a top width of 4 feet on the berm and a free board of about 24 inches. Construct shallow diversions around the lagoon to keep any surface run off out of it. Construct a fence around the lagoon as soon as it is complete.

Small Treatment Plants

Small or individual package treatment systems are a relatively new development in waste handling. Most units available today have been on the market less than 15 years. In spite of some claims made for these systems, the following general comments can be made about all units available today.

1. Effluent (discharged fluid) from these systems is not clean water. It is a potential pollutant and must be handled as such.
2. Each system has some mechanical parts which will require periodic observation, maintenance and repair. There is no such thing as a completely trouble free, maintenance free sewage system.
3. Individual package treatment units cost more to install and operate than other types of systems.

All small treatment plants use an aerobic process to treat sewage. In this process, oxygen using (aerobic) bacteria attack and break down organic portions of the sewage into simpler inorganic compounds. Aerobic treatment is preferred because it is rapid, relatively odor free, and provides

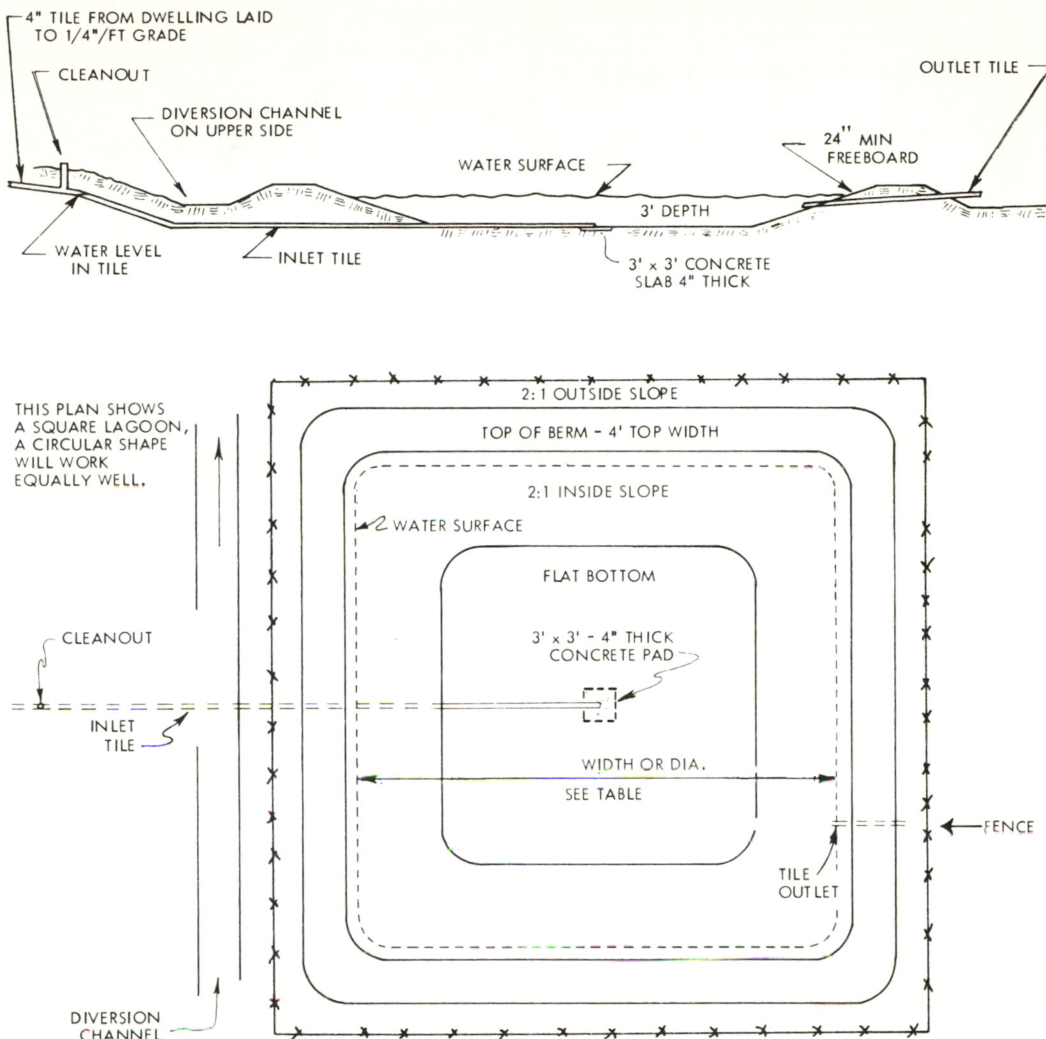

Figure 23-4. Sewage lagoons are one of the most economical and trouble-free methods of handling domestic sewage for those locations where there is room to construct one and it is approved by local regulatory authorities. (University of Missouri)

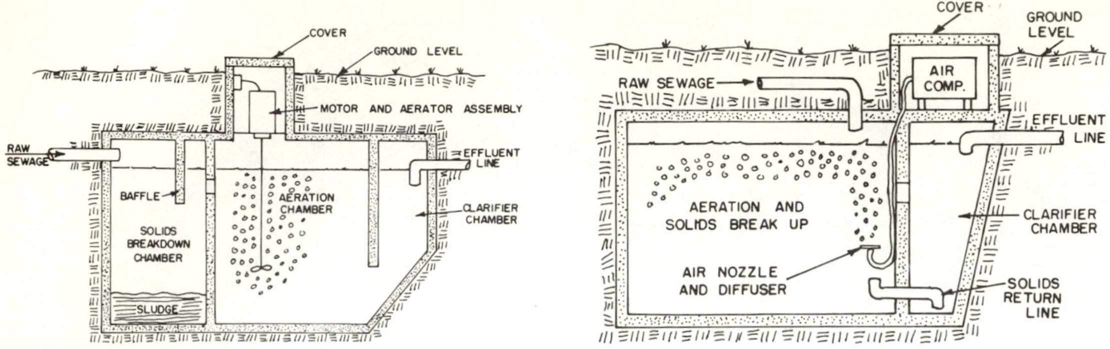

Figure 23-5. Two different styles of aeration tanks (package treatment plants). The primary difference in the two designs is the manner in which air is introduced to the liquid sewage in the tank. Both types function equally well. (University of Missouri)

greater solids reduction. Septic tanks use the anaerobic (without oxygen) process which is less efficient and produces the characteristic "septic" odor.

Treatment plants maintain aerobic conditions by mixing air with sewage in the treatment tank. This is done in two ways. Some manufacturers use an external air compressor to force air into the tank. Others draw air into the sewage by using a pump or a stirring device.

Treatment in the sewage plant is accomplished in three stages. In the first stage, raw sewage enters the system and larger particles are settled out or broken up mechanically to increase their surface area and make them more accessible to bacteria. The second phase is the aeration process. Air is mixed and blended with sewage, allowing the aerobic bacteria to reduce it to simpler compounds. The final stage is settling or clarification. Treated sewage from the aeration process is emptied into a chamber where heavier solids remaining in the sewage are allowed to settle. There solids are returned to the aeration chamber for further processing. The clarified liquid from this chamber either flows or is pumped out of the treatment plant.

Treatment plants are sized based on expected loading, their ability to mix oxygen with sewage, and a designed retention time. Most manufacturers specify capacity in terms of either people or number of bedrooms served.

The most satisfactory methods of effluent disposal are underground disposal through an absorption field or controlled application to a soil plant filter. Absorption field design should follow the same criteria as for a septic tank system. A soil plant filter is a level area well covered with growing crop which can filter and purify sewage effluent. A well sodded, level terrace is a good example of a soil plant filter which can be used. Design information on soil plant filters is available through offices of the Soil Conservation Service.

The NSF has developed a series of standards for the construction and performance of small treatment plants. It is recommended that you consider only systems which meet or exceed NSF standards.

Waste Line Plumbing

Plumbing fixtures are connected to the sewage disposal system using pipes which are approved for DWV (drain, waste and vent) service. The smallest line used should be 1-½ inches in diameter. The 1-½ inch pipe is used to connect sinks, lavatories and showers or tubs to the main waste line. A 3 inch line is used as the main disposal line within the building and can be connected directly to the toilet. All waste lines leaving the building should be 4 inches in diameter. Plastic pipe may be used except where prohibited by code or exposed to excessive loads.

Drain pipes should have a minimum pitch of ¼ inch per foot towards the sewage treatment facility. Less pitch than this allows solids to settle out of the sewage, which tends to plug drains.

Clean out ports should be placed at regular intervals in all drain pipes. A maximum distance of 50 feet between clean outs is suggested. Clean outs should also be placed wherever a change in direction greater than 45° occurs in the pipe.

CHAPTER **24**

Fire Resistant Construction Practices

Each year fire costs American farmers millions of dollars in lost facilities and productive capacity. This loss is not completely preventable, but could be substantially reduced through better selection of building materials and use of some simple fire stopping techniques.

Fire normally starts within a single room or area. It then spreads over surfaces and penetrates combustible coverings, moving to adjacent areas either directly or through natural openings in the building construction.

Buildings collapse when fire has progressed to the point where structural members are weakened either by direct burning or by excessive heat.

Risk of loss is reduced whenever we use construction practices that are designed to slow or prevent the normal progression of fire.

Fire Stopping

Fire stops are obstructions placed in concealed passages within buildings which slow or halt the movement of flames, heat and hot gasses from one area to another. They are used most often to block wall stud spaces or areas between floor joists on multi-story buildings. Solid wood blocks, 2 inches thick, make effective fire stops. Wall cavities which are completely filled with noncombustible insulation do not require fire stops.

One area of modern agricultural buildings which can benefit from fire stopping is the area above the ceiling and under the roof. This relatively open space provides a natural tunnel for fire to move throughout the building, once it has penetrated the ceiling.

An easy way to provide fire stops for this area is to cover both sides of a truss with ½ inch thick gypsum board. The gypsum should cover the area between ceiling and roof completely. There should be one of these fire stops

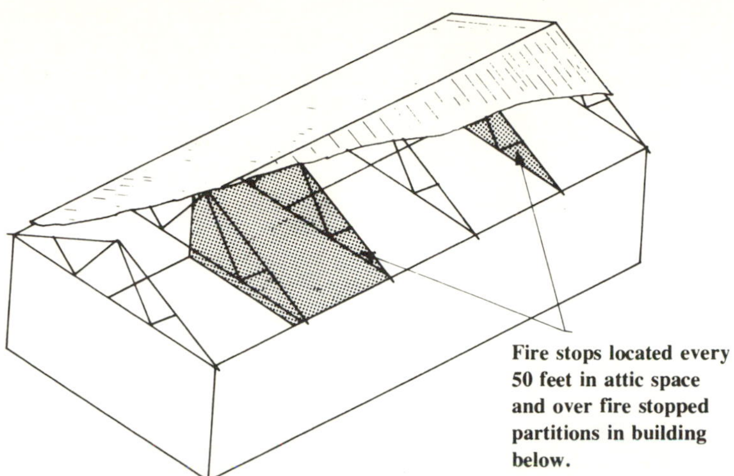

Figure 24-1. Fire stops are cheap insurance that can give the fire department a few extra minutes to get there and save at least a portion of your investment. A particularly important area in large, clear span farm buildings is the area above the ceiling. Even the simple practice of periodically covering both sides of a truss with ½'' sheet rock will greatly delay the spread of fire down the length of the building. (University of Missouri)

over each cross partition in the buildings with large rooms.

Properly constructed walls can be used as fire stops in buildings where it is desirable to provide positive control over fire spread between adjacent areas. These partitions (referred to as fire walls) can provide time to remove animals or equipment from a portion of the building.

Consider using a fire wall whenever areas with different risk levels are contained within a single building. For example, a shop constructed in one end of a machinery storage building should be separated from machinery storage with a fire wall. Other examples include separation of utility rooms or heating plants from other areas of the building.

Fire walls need not be elaborate. In many cases, more careful selection of materials, combined with conventional construction, can provide valuable protection. A standard 2 by 4 inch stud wall, covered both sides with ½ inch gypsum board, provides a 40 minute fire rating. Ratings for other types of wall construction can be found in Table 24-1.

Flame Spread Ratings

Fire moves through a room at a rate which depends on the material used to cover interior surfaces. Many building materials carry a flame spread or fire rating which is indicative of their ability to resist burning.

Flame spread or fire ratings are obtained by comparing the burn rate for a material with the burn rates obtained from the standardized materials, red oak lumber and asbestos cement board. Flame spread ratings for these are given values of 100 and 0, respectively. Tested materials are given values which represent how they compare with these. For example, a material which burns twice as fast as red oak would receive a flame spread rating of 200.

Flame spread ratings are sometimes grouped into classes, providing a general indication of flammability. Table 24-2 lists classes and their associated flame spread ratings.

Table 24-1. **Fire Resistance Ratings for Various Types of Wall Construction**

Construction	Fire Rating in Minutes
Wood framing covered both sides with:	
1/2 in. Fiberboard	10
1/4 in. Plywood	10
3/4 in. T & G boards	20
3/8 in. Gypsum wallboard	25
1/2 in. Gypsum wallboard	40
5/8 in. Type X Gypsum wallboard	60
3/16 in. Asbestos cement board	10*
3/8 in. Gypsum board + 3/16 in. Asb. cement brd.	60
Masonry construction:	
4 in. Blocks plastered both sides	60
6 in. Blocks	60
6 in. Concrete	240

**Even though asbestos cement board will not burn, it will conduct heat very well. This will result in fire development in the wall cavity even though there is no direct flame contact.*

Table 24-2. **Fire Classification, Flame Spreads, and Suggested Usage for Interior Building Materials**

Class	Flame Spread	Usage Suggested
A	0 to 25	Farm shops, heating plants, fuel storages, high risk areas
B	26 to 75	Confinement buildings without heating systems
C	76 to 200	Low risk buildings such as hay storages
D	201 to 500	Do not use without protective covering
	500 +	Do not use without protective covering

Protective Coverings

Some urethane and styrene plastic foam insulations commonly used in farm buildings have extremely high flame spread ratings. To minimize risk when using these materials, it is suggested that they be protected from fire with fire resistant coatings. Materials which provide satisfactory protection include the following.

1. ½ in. thickness of cement plaster
2. Fire rated (type X) gypsum board
3. ¼ in. to ½ in. thickness of sprayed on magnesium oxychloride
4. ¼ in. asbestos cement board

Caution: If foam plastic insulations are not adequately protected, your insurance company may refuse coverage on the structure.

Fire Retardant Treatment

There are two methods of treating wood to improve its resistance to fire: pressure treatment with special chemicals and using fire retardant paints.

The pressure treating process is similar to that used to prevent decay, except different materials are used. Special water borne salts are used which limit the amount of combustible products released when wood is exposed to flame. Some of the more commonly used materials include monammonium and diammonium phosphate, ammonium sulphate, zinc chloride, sodium tetraborate, and boric acid.

Fire retardant treatment does not prevent wood from burning, nor does it slow up the penetration of fire into structural members. Its main benefit is to slow the rate of surface spread. It is very questionable if the cost of fire retardant treatment can be justified in most farm buildings.

Fire retardant paints have low surface flammability and tend to expand or "foam" when exposed to fire. This expanded layer acts as an insulation to keep heat away from the flammable surface under the paint. Properly applied coatings can reduce the flame spread rating for wood to 25 or less, and they are being routinely applied to some factory finished building products.

Metal Frame Buildings

Many farmers have purchased metal frame buildings because they believe them to be fireproof. The flame spread rating of metal is 0; however, when a fire occurs, the unprotected metal frame will fail much more rapidly than a wooden structure. This is particularly true in the case of machinery and other storage buildings where fire is more likely in the stored product than the building itself.

Temperatures build up very quickly in the early stages of a fire, particularly if the building happens to be insulated. Heat often spreads through the entire building even more rapidly than fire itself. As soon as metal structural members get hot, their strength decreases rapidly. The result can be complete structural collapse long before flames have spread throughout the building.

Metal frames can be protected from heat by encasing them in concrete, by constructing an insulated firewall around them, or by spray-on insulating coatings. A one inch thickness of sprayed on asbestos fiber provides a one hour fire rating for an eight inch steel I-beam. An unprotected beam has a 10 minute rating. In most cases, protective coatings are probably not warranted for farm buildings. An exception might be the farm shop, which is a high risk area which frequently contains high value equipment.

First Aid for Fires

Nearly all fires start small and grow big. A good fire extinguisher in the hands of a person who knows how to use it can often prevent a small fire from becoming a major catastrophe.

Fire extinguishers are designed and sold by size and type of fire for which they are to be used. Table 24-3 lists the three general classes of fire likely to occur on the farm and indicates the type of extinguisher most often used on each.

Fire extinguishers are tested and rated by Underwriters Laboratory (UL). For multipurpose use around the farm, select an extinguisher with a minimum rating of 1A-5 B:C for use on all types of fires. A more desirable rating would be 2A-10 B:C.

Locate extinguishers near exits and always make sure you are between the fire and an exit when using the fire extinguisher. Make sure you read and understand operating instructions when you install the extinguisher. Chances are you won't have time when a fire breaks out.

Table 24-3. **Fire Classifications and Methods of Extinguishing**

Class	Description
A	Ordinary combustibles such as wood, cloth, paper, hay. Water is the best extinguisher.
B	Flammable liquids such as oil, paint, or grease. Best extinguished by excluding oxygen or flame interruption.
C	Electrical fires. Use carbon dioxide, dry chemical or some other non conductive extinguishing material.

Part IV

Materials Selection And Use

CHAPTER **25**

Concrete

Concrete is a mixture of portland cement, sand, aggregates and water. It is one of the most versatile of all construction materials. When first mixed, it is plastic and can be formed into almost any shape. Once cured, it provides a durable, long lasting, easily cleaned surface. The two major problems with concrete are its poor insulating property and the fact that it is extremely weak in tension.

Portland cement is the "glue" which holds the sand and aggregate together in concrete. It is manufactured by heating together lime, aluminum, iron and silica in controlled portions. The resulting mixture has the ability to combine with water (hydrate) to form a product which will adhere to sand and aggregate and will become very hard over time. Cement is sold in bulk to ready mix plants and is available in 94 pound sacks at building supply dealers. One 94 pound sack is equal to 1 cubic foot of cement. Five types of portland cement are available.

Type I. Standard general purpose cement used for nearly all farm construction mixes. It is available as regular, white, and air entrained (type I-A).

Type II. This type releases heat more slowly during the curing process. It is also resistant to sulphate attack and is sometimes used to construct drainage structures in areas where surface waters contain large amounts of sulphates.

Type III. High early strength cement used where it is important to gain strength soon after the concrete is placed (1 to 3 days instead of 5 to 7 for other types). Type III is sometimes used when placing concrete in cold weather.

Type IV. Low heat cement designed to reduce the total amount of heat generated during curing. This type is used in construction of large massive structures such as dams.

Type V. Sulphate resistant cement is used for concrete which will be exposed to soils or water of high sulphate or alkali content.

Air Entrainment

A foaming agent can be added to cement which causes the formation of millions of tiny air bubbles in the concrete during mixing. These bubbles are less than .02 inch in diameter and cannot be seen without the aid of a magnifying device. This captured or entrained air improves the weathering ability of concrete by a factor of several hundred percent. It also makes the concrete easier to work and finish. Air entrainment should be specified for all concrete used in outside paving applications and for concrete exposed to livestock wastes.

The entraining agent may come already pre-mixed into the cement or it may be added at the time of mixing the concrete. The desired amount of air in concrete will range from 4% to 8.5%, depending on the size of aggregate used. In general, the smaller the aggregate, the larger the volume of air. A 6% air content is satisfactory for just about all farm construction applications.

Mixing Your Own

Anyone can make good concrete if he selects the proper materials, proportions them correctly, and does a good job of mixing them together.

Sand. Material used in making concrete which will pass through a ¼ inch screen is designated as sand. Sand is used to fill in the spaces between the larger particles in the mix. It should be clean, hard, and have a variety of particle sizes. The two most common faults with sand are silt and organic matter. Silt coats particles and prevents cement from adhering to them. This results in weak porous concrete. Sand can be tested for silt content in the following manner.

1. Place 2 inches of sand in the bottom of a pint jar. Make sure to get a representative sample from the sand you are planning to use.
2. Fill the jar nearly full with water, cover, and shake vigorously. Then set the jar aside until the water over the sand clears.
3. Measure the layer of silt that settles out on top of the sand. If it is more than 1/8 inch thick, the sand is not suitable for making concrete unless it is washed first.

Too much organic material in sand can prevent concrete from properly hardening or may result in reduced strength. A simple test for organic matter can be performed as follows:

1. Dissolve a heaping teaspoon of lye in ½ pint of water in a clear 1 pint jar.

2. Add a ½ pint representative sample of sand to the lye water.
3. Cover the jar and shake well for 1 to 2 minutes.
4. Set the jar aside for 24 hours.
5. If the water remained clear or colored not more than cider vinegar, the material is suitable for use in concrete. If the color is darker, the material will need to be washed before using.

Aggregates. Particles which are too large to pass through a ¼ inch screen are referred to as gravel or aggregates. Aggregates should also be clean and hard to insure good concrete. If there is any question about silt or organic matter, tests which are used on sand can also be used to test aggregates.

The larger the aggregate, the less cement and sand needed. Remember when the old timers used to fill the concrete forms with rocks as they poured concrete? Unfortunately, too large an aggregate makes concrete difficult to place and work, and they can lead to a honeycombed porous structure which is not nearly as strong as it might have been. The largest practical size for an aggregate will depend on what you are making. For vertical walls, select an aggregate not larger than 20% of the wall thickness (for an 8 inch wall, this means about 1.5 inch aggregate). Aggregates for paving or flat work should be limited to about ⅓ the thickness of the slab. Reinforced concrete should have an aggregate size of not more than 75% of the distance between reinforcing bars or between bars and the surface of the concrete.

Bank run gravel. Bank or creek gravel that can fill the requirement for both sand and aggregate is sometimes available for farm construction. Most gravel banks contain an excess amount of sand in proportion to the aggregate. This means that more cement must be used to paste together all the particles.

To determine if bank run gravel is suitable, screen a 2 cubic foot sample through a ¼ inch screen. The proportion of sizes should be nearly the same as those specified in the mix chart (Table 25-1). If they are not, separate the sand and gravel with a screen and use them in the correct proportion in the mix. This will result in stronger concrete, and will save enough cement to offset the labor for screening.

Light weight aggregates. Conventionally made concrete weighs about 150 pounds per cubic foot. This weight can be reduced considerably by using lightweight aggregates in the mix. These aggregates consist of expanded materials such as cinders, shale, slag, pumice, or expanded mica. Use of cinders will reduce weight to 120 to 130 pounds per cubic foot and it is possible to get it as low as 50 pounds per cubic foot with expanded mica or pumice.

The main advantage of lightweight concrete is its improved insulating qualities. This leads directly to greater fire resistance and improved fire ratings for components. The major disadvantage is the loss of overall strength and wearing ability.

Water. Mixing water should be clean and free of either acid or alkali material. Salt water should not be used in concrete. In general, if water is not fit to drink, don't use it to make concrete.

Additives. Several materials are available which can be used to alter or change the basic properties of a concrete mix. A few of the more commonly available ones are listed below.

Hydrated lime. Used to improve workability of concrete. It will result in a loss of strength. A better way to improve workability is to add more cement or vary the sand-aggregate ratio slightly.

Air entraining agents. Materials designed to capture air bubbles during mixing. They must be carefully measured to insure proper amounts of air. A better solution is to purchase cement with the agent already added.

Calcium chloride. Used to accelerate setting and hardening of concrete, particularly in cold weather. Do not add more than 2 pounds per sack of cement. Add as the concrete is being mixed.

Mineral oxides. Coloring agents used to give concrete a specific color. Three to six pounds per sack of cement are usually used. Longer mixing time is required to get uniform coloring.

Mixes. The proportions of cement, sand and aggregate used in a particular sequence of 3 numbers referring to the volumes of the respective components (a 1:3:5 mix would have 1 part cement, 3 parts sand, and 5 parts aggregate). Different mixes are used for different applications as shown in Table 25-1. These proportions may have to be varied slightly to get a workable mix.

Table 25-1. **Concrete Mixes Used in Farm Construction**

Use	Mix Cement	 Sand	 Aggregate	Gallons* of Water per Sack of Cement
Floor slats	1	2	2	4.5
High strength and water tight work	1	2	3	5.5
Floor slabs	1	2.5	3.5	6.5
Footings & foundation walls	1	3	5	7

**Assuming all components are dry.*

The single most important factor in achieving strong, high quality concrete is the amount of water which is used per sack of cement (water-cement ratio). Given two mixes with equal workability, the one with the lower water-cement ratio will make stronger and more water tight concrete. The amount of water which should be used for dry ingredients is given in Table 25-1. If the sand and gravel are not dry, these amounts must be reduced by 1 to 2 gallons per sack. It is extremely important that concrete be made with only enough water to obtain a mix which can be properly placed and worked. The amount required to get a workable mix will always be greater than the amount required for proper setting (hydration) of the cement.

Always make a trial batch of concrete to find out if the recommended mix proportions work well with your particular materials. Mix the concrete thoroughly, then stop the mixer and test the mix by working it with a float. A workable mix is smooth and plastic. It is not so dry that it crumbles or so wet that it runs. If the mix is too wet, add small amounts of sand and aggregate until it becomes workable. If it is too stiff, add small amounts of cement and water. Never add water without adding cement or you will dilute the existing cement paste mix and weaken the concrete. Once you have obtained the proper mix, make note of the exact proportions used so that future batches will be made as nearly the same as possible.

Estimating materials. Table 25-2 lists the volume of materials required to make 1 cubic yard of concrete using several different mixes. Order some extra sand and aggregate because these amounts can vary by as much as 10% depending on the particular material.

Table 25-2. **Materials Required per Cubic Yard of Concrete**

Mix	Cement Sacks	Sand Cu Yds	Aggregate Cu Yds
1:2:2	8.2	.6	.6
1:2:3	7	.52	.78
1:2.5:3.5	5.9	.55	.77
1:3:5	4.6	.51	.85

Buying Ready Mix

Most concrete used in farm construction today is proportioned at a ready-mix plant and delivered to the site ready for use. Ready-mix concrete offers the advantage of better quality control and much more rapid mixing and placement than is possible with farm mixed concrete. In many cases it will also be nearly the same cost as the farm mixed product.

When you buy ready mix, there are several things the plant operator will need to know in order to fill your order properly.

Amount. Ready-mix is sold by the cubic yard. You will need to calculate the total volume of concrete needed to complete your job and then convert it into cubic yards. One cubic yard equals 27 cubic feet. A cubic yard of concrete will pour 81 square feet of 4 inch thick paving or 40.5 square feet of an 8 inch thick foundation wall. Be sure to order a little extra in case your forms are not exactly set. It is less expensive than having another truck bring less than a yard to finish your job.

Mix. Ready-mix is commonly specified by the number of sacks of cement used in a cubic yard of concrete. Table 25-3 lists mixes and example uses.

Table 25-3. **Typical Mix Specifications and Applications for Ready-Mix Concrete**

Sacks of Cement per Cu Yd	Use
5	Building footings
5.5	Mild exposure
6	Livestock paving
6.5	Building walls
7	Floors in milk parlors

Aggregate size. Follow the same rules given for mixing your own. The plant operator will be able to help select a size if you tell him what you are making.

Water. Specify a number of gallons per sack of cement. Normal range for farm work is 5 to 7 gallons with the lower amount being used with higher strength mixes.

Delivery time. The ready-mix plant makes money by keeping its trucks as busy as possible. They are not interested in sitting around waiting for you to finish your farm work. In fact, you will probably be charged for any excessive waiting periods. Many plants allow a total wait and unload time of 6 to 7 minutes per cubic yard delivered. It is important that you specify exactly when your concrete is to be delivered. If more than one truck load is ordered, leave enough time between trucks to allow for some preliminary finish work.

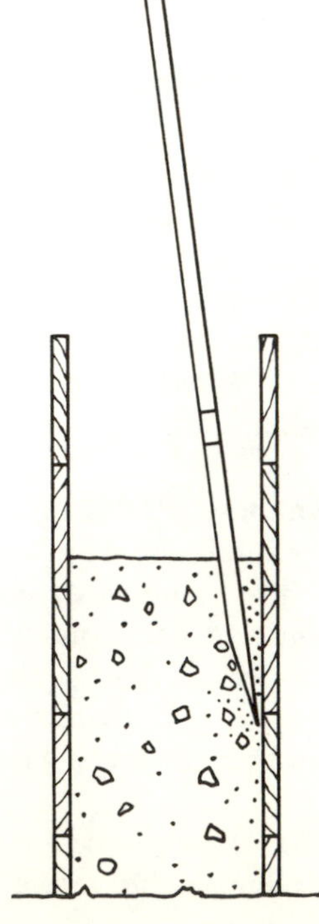

Figure 25-1. Concrete needs to be worked, or spaded, along form surfaces to prevent surface voids or honeycombing. Large honeycombed areas are a weak spot in concrete, which can be a point of water leakage in foundation or tank walls. (USDA)

Placing and Finishing

Concrete should be placed as close as possible to its final position in the forms soon after mixing is complete. It should not be placed on frozen ground, mud, or soil that is covered with water. If you are placing concrete paving over extremely dry ground, dampen the surface before pouring concrete to prevent the ground from absorbing too much of the mixing water from the concrete.

Concrete should be spaded or worked as it is placed to completely fill the forms. If reinforcing is used, the concrete should be vibrated slightly to insure good contact between the concrete and the steel. Avoid working any more than is absolutely necessary since it tends to cause a separation of aggregates, resulting in honeycombed weak concrete.

After forms are filled, strike off the surface with a straight edged board. This operation is called screeding and is done by pulling the board back and forth in a saw like manner while moving it along the top edge of the forms.

The next operation is called floating and is done as soon as screeding is complete. A long handled wood or metal floating tool is used to remove major surface imperfections left by the screed board. Float the surface only enough to give a reasonably level appearance. In some cases, floating will be the only finishing operation needed. The additional operations described below are done only to achieve a particular type of surface finish or appearance.

Brooming is used to obtain a rough textured surface with a high degree of slip resistance. It is done by brushing the surface with a stiff

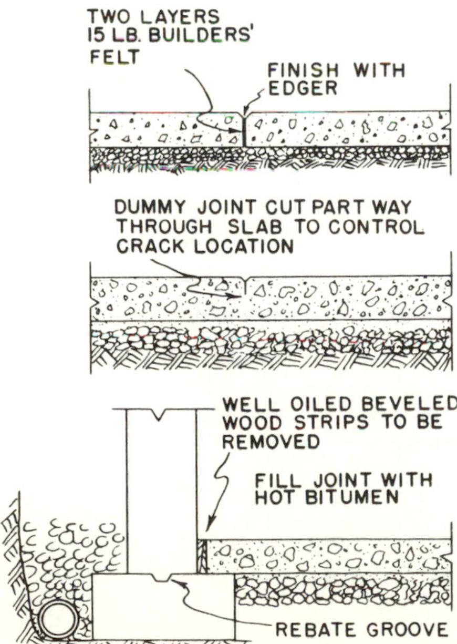

Figure 25-2. Three different types of joints commonly found in concrete flat work. Joints are used to control the location where cracks develop and to provide room for expansion and contraction of the slab with temperature changes. (USDA)

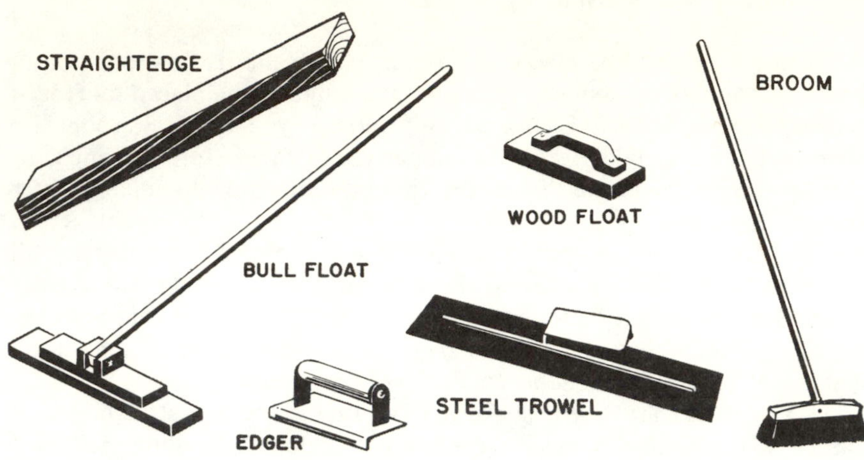

Figure 25-3. Commonly used concrete placing and finishing tools. When using air-entrained concrete, magnesium trowels are preferred, since the air-entrained mixes tend to stick to steel tools. (USDA)

bristled broom about the time when the concrete is starting to set. The stiffer the broom and the more vigorous the brushing, the rougher the surface will be.

Steel troweling provides a smooth easily cleaned surface. Troweling can be started as soon as the concrete has set enough to prevent the trowel from bringing water to the surface. If done with a power trowel, the concrete will be set enough to walk on before it is ready for troweling. Troweling too soon causes cement and sand particles to be worked up to the surface of the concrete. This results in rapid wear of the surface and a series of alligator like cracks in the surface.

Curing

Concrete sets and gains strength because of the chemical reaction between water and cement. If it is allowed to dry out before this reaction has taken place, it will not develop maximum strength. Proper curing is aimed at keeping moisture in concrete until the hydration process has developed a high percentage of the final strength in the concrete. This normally takes 5 to 7 days.

There are several methods of curing concrete, all of which work well. One of the following may work best for you.

1. Leave forms on walls for at least a week to keep moisture in.
2. Cover the concrete with polyethylene plastic to retain moisture.
3. Cover with hay or straw and soak thoroughly with water as needed to keep the surface of the concrete wet.
4. Sprinkle the surface with water several times a day.

5. Coat the surface with a chemical curing compound. Curing compounds are designed to keep water from evaporating from the surface of the concrete.

Weather Extremes

Concrete is easiest to mix, place, and finish when temperatures are between 50° and 80°. Colder temperatures slow the setting process and if too cold, freezing will damage fresh concrete. High temperatures increase the set rate to the point where there may not be enough time to properly finish concrete before it gets too hard.

During cold weather:

1. Do not place concrete on frozen ground.
2. Use type III high early strength cement to cut down on curing time. If using type I cement, add up to 2 pounds of Calcium Chloride per sack of cement to speed curing.
3. Use warm water (not over 180°F) to warm up the mix. If it is very cold, use heated aggregate. Aim for a fresh mix temperature of 50° to 70°.
4. Keep concrete at 50° for 7 days (4 days when using type III cement).
5. Concrete paving can be kept warm by covering with insulation or a 6 to 12 inch thickness of straw topped with a tarpaulin. Concrete walls can be kept warm with insulated forms. Work areas can be enclosed with plastic and heated. *Caution:* Never use an unvented burner to heat a space containing fresh concrete. The fumes from the burner will react with the concrete and weaken the surface.

During hot weather

1. Dampen the subgrade under paving to lower its temperature before placing concrete.
2. Use cold water to mix concrete.
3. Keep aggregates in the shade until you are ready to add them to the mix.
4. Place concrete late in the day to take advantage of lowering temperatures and increasing humidity.
5. Start curing promptly to avoid premature drying out of concrete surfaces.

Reinforcing

Concrete has essentially no strength in tension. This means it is useless in places which are subjected to loads which either bend or pull on the concrete. In order to overcome this problem, steel reinforcing material is added to concrete to carry any tension loads.

Prestressed concrete is a technique of reinforcing which takes advantage of the high compressive strength which concrete has. A prestressed concrete beam has steel members which are stretched or placed under tension before the concrete is placed. After curing, the force is released and the steel tends to shrink back to its original length, compressing (prestressing) the beam as it does. When the beam is placed into service, tensile loads act to relieve or unload the prestressing which was placed in the beam at the time of fabrication.

Design of reinforced concrete is a complex process which should be done by a registered professional engineer, preferably one who does it on a regular basis. If your plans call for reinforcing steel, follow them very closely. Proper selection and placement of steel are essential to the performance of reinforced concrete.

Reinforcing steel is available in two forms, steel rods or bars (commonly referred to as rebars) and welded wire mesh. Bars used in farm construction are usually 20 feet long and are manufactured in two different types of steel. Type 40 has a minimum yield strength of 40,000 psi. Type 60 has a minimum yield of 60,000 psi. Bars are sized by numbers which represent their diameter in eighths of an inch (i.e., a number 5 bar is 5/8 inch in diameter). You will purchase bars by the total length you need but the selling price will be based on the weight of steel you get. The cross sectional area of a bar is directly related to its strength and is an important property for the designer. Some properties of rebars commonly specified for farm construction can be found in Table 25-4.

Table 25-4. **Properties of Steel Reinforcing Bars**

Bar Size	Diameter (Inches)	Weight (Lbs/Ft)	Cross Sect. Area (Sq Inches)
3	.375	.376	.11
4	.500	.668	.20
5	.625	1.043	.31
6	.750	1.502	.44
7	.875	2.044	.60
8	1.0	2.670	.79

Welded wire fabric or mesh is manufactured from either smooth or deformed wire which is machine welded into a rectangular grid pattern. It is available in a variety of wire sizes and spacings as indicated in Table 25-5. Wire mesh can be used almost any place reinforcing is needed; however, most designers will confine its use to reinforcement of flat slabs. Mesh is packaged in rolls. The usual size is 4 to 5 feet wide by 100 feet long. Mesh should be lapped a minimum of 1 square where two pieces come together in the concrete.

All reinforcing steel should be clean and relatively free of rust in order to develop its full strength in concrete. If you are not able to use reinforcing as soon as it is delivered, store it in a dry place out of the weather. When placed, reinforcing steel must be completely surrounded and covered with concrete. A minimum concrete cover of 1 inch to 1-½ inches is usually specified by designers.

Table 25.5. **Properties of Steel Reinforcing Fabric (Mesh)**

Style* Size Wire Gauge	Wire Spacing (Inches)	Wire Diameter (Inches)	Wt. (Lbs/100 Ft²)
6x6 — 10x10	6x6	.135	21
6x6 — 8x8	6x6	.162	30
6x6 — 6x6	6x6	.192	42
4x4 — 10x10	4x4	.135	31
4x4 — 8x8	4x4	.162	44
4x4 — 6x6	4x4	.192	62

**A new style designation has been developed which specifies wire size in hundredths of a square inch of cross sectional area instead of by gauge. We have found, however, that most suppliers still use the older designation which we have included here.*

CHAPTER 26

Concrete Masonry

Concrete masonry units, or concrete blocks as they are more commonly known, have been a popular form of construction for certain types of farm buildings for many years. They provide a structure that is resistant to both fire and decay at a cost which is comparable to conventional stud frame techniques. Blocks also can be used to replace concrete walls without the problem of forming. The main disadvantages of block construction are its poor insulating ability and its low resistance to horizontal loads.

Sizes and Types

Blocks are available in 5 general types:

1. Hollow load bearing
2. Solid load bearing
3. Concrete brick
4. Concrete building tile
5. Hollow non load bearing

The so called "hollow load bearing" unit is most commonly used in farm construction. It has a hollow core area which is usually equal to 40% to 50% of the total cross sectional area of the block.

Blocks are available with both regular and lightweight aggregates. Lightweight units use such things as cinders (cinder blocks), slag, volcanic rock and other light materials. A lightweight block will weigh 40% to 50% less than a standard block of the same size. Lightweight blocks are easier to handle and have a somewhat better insulating value. They are also more porous and tend to weather more rapidly unless adequately sealed.

The standard size block is the 8 inch or 8 by 8 by 16 inch block. Other commonly found units are 6 by 8 by 16, 4 by 8 by 16, and 12 by 8 by 16. These sizes refer to the size of the space which the block will fill when it is in place in the wall system. Actual dimensions of the blocks will

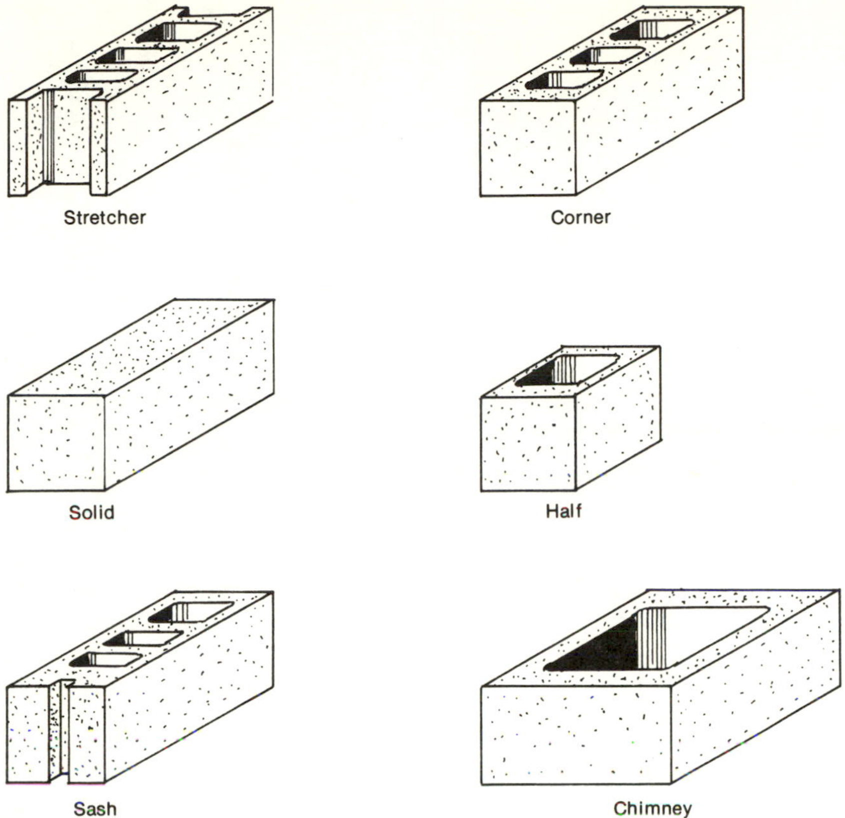

Figure 26-1. Several of the commonly used shapes of masonry units used in farm construction.

be approximately 3/8 inch less than the nominal dimensions to allow for the thickness of mortar joints and surface finishes.

Different shapes are available in each of the standard sizes to accommodate openings, control joints, corners, and other standard features in construction. Several are illustrated in Figure 26-1.

Construction Planning

The old adage of plan ahead is particularly important in masonry construction. While it's easy to take a power saw and cut a board to fit, shortening a concrete block takes time and does not result in a particularly attractive wall. The standard module for block construction is 8 inches. If all lengths, heights, and wall opening locations are based on this module, you can eliminate much of the cutting and fitting work from your construction job. Prefabricated door and window units are available which conform to this 8 inch module. Check with your dealer early in the planning process to see exactly what sizes he normally stocks.

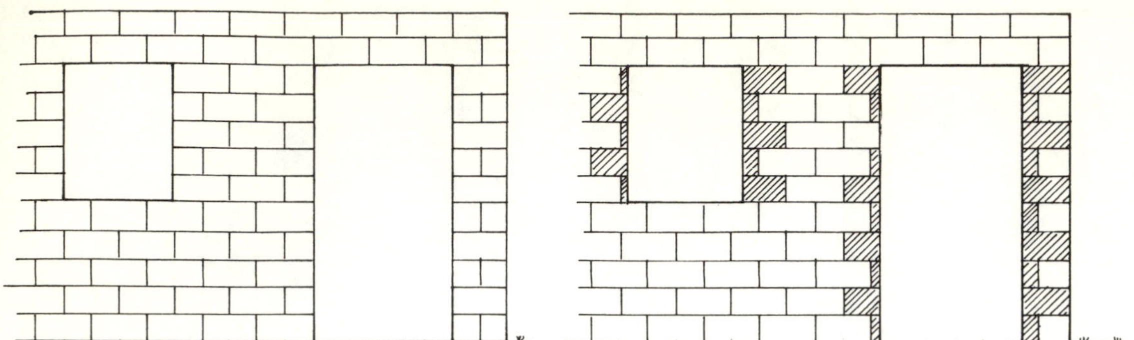

Figure 26-2. A well-planned wall on the left and, on the right, one that will require extra labor and materials. Openings were not planned with masonry unit length as a major consideration in the wall on the right. All shaded blocks require cutting.

Mortar

Cement based mortar is the glue used to stick concrete blocks together into a solid wall unit. Good mortar must be workable, adhere well, and have good water retention ability. Mortar is normally made with a masonry cement, sand, and clean water. Masonry cement is portland cement (usually type II) to which material such as hydrated lime has been added to improve workability. Regular cement can also be used in combination with hydrated lime to make a mortar mix. Sand should be clean, sharp, and well graded. Many sand and gravel suppliers sell masonry sand which has been washed, sieved, and selected for properties desirable in making mortar. If available, it is recommended that you purchase enough of this to complete your job.

Table 26-1. **Standard and Heavy Duty Mortar Mix Proportions**

Service	Cement	Hydrated Lime	Sand
Standard	1-Masonry cement	—	2-¼ to 3
	or		
	1-Portland cement	½ to 1-¼	4-½ to 6
Heavy Duty	1-Masonry plus		
	1-Portland cement	—	4-½ to 6
	or		
	1-Portland cement	0 to ¼	2-¼ to 3

Calcium chloride is sometimes added to mortar to accelerate the setting process, particularly during winter months. The maximum amount added should not exceed 1% of the weight of the masonry cement in the mortar mix. For mixes with regular portland cement, limit calcium chloride to 2% or less of the weight of cement. The use of any other materials to provide freeze protection is not recommended. Masonry walls should be kept above freezing until mortar has developed its primary strength (5 to 7 days).

Mortar which stiffens during use because of evaporation may be retempered by adding small amounts of water to it and remixing. If stiffening is due to setting, discard the mix and make a new one. Mortar should be used within 2-½ hours of mixing if air temperature is above 80°. For lower temperature, use it within 3-½ hours of mixing.

Reinforcing

Several different methods are used to improve the horizontal load carrying ability of block walls. The more common ones include horizontal wire grids, vertical rebars, and pilasters.

Several manufacturers fabricate a wire reinforcing grid which is designed to be imbedded in the horizontal mortar joint between courses of blocks. These grids are welded assemblies constructed of ¼ inch steel wire and are designed so that they can be imbedded without changing the standard size of the mortar joint.

Vertical steel rebars can be placed in the core spaces of blocks to improve wall strength. Size and spacing will depend on the particular load carrying capacity needed. Bars should be continuous from top to bottom of the wall for maximum strength and the core spaces they pass through should be completely filled with mortar.

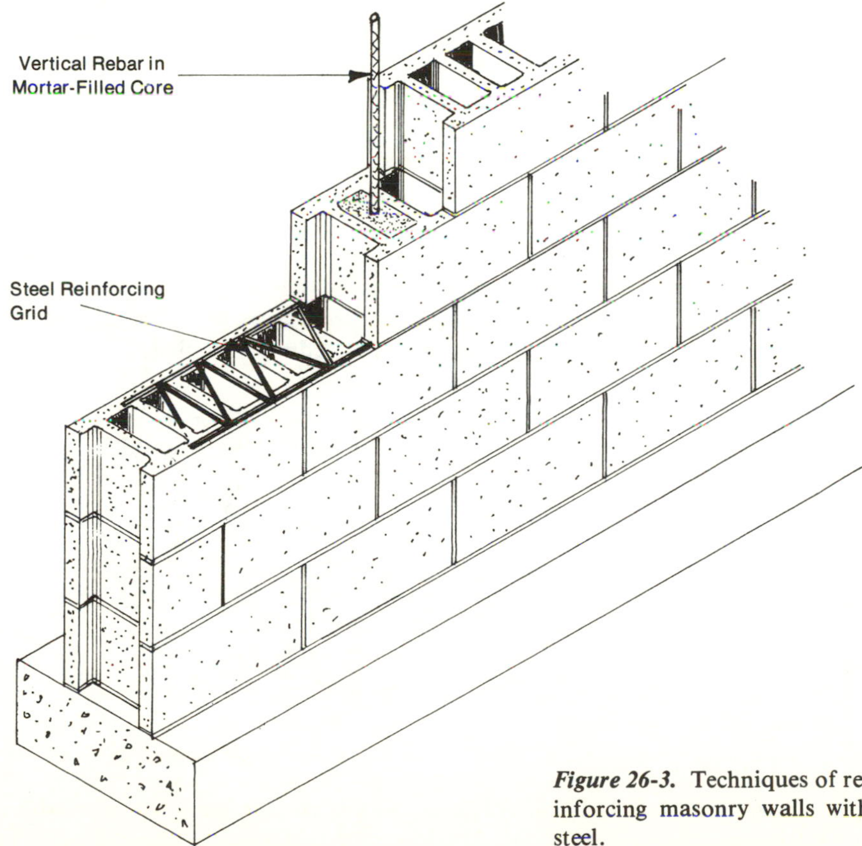

Figure 26-3. Techniques of reinforcing masonry walls with steel.

Pilasters or buttresses are thickened sections of a block wall. They are constructed by adding a second row of blocks, by turning two blocks sideways in the wall, or by using a special pilaster block. Placement of vertical rebars in pilasters will add considerably to their strength. Pilasters are normally spaced at intervals not exceeding 18 times the wall thickness along walls which have no intersecting partitions to support them.

Construction Practice

Blocks must be dry when used or mortar joints will not develop full strength. Keep blocks inside or covered with plastic to prevent wetting by rain or snow. If they do accidently become wet, they must be dried out before use.

Block walls are normally constructed on poured concrete footings which conform to the shape of the building. The first layer or course of blocks is placed on the footing in a full block width bed of mortar. It is absolutely essential that the first course be both level and plumb. A very small error in the first course can turn into a big mistake by the time you reach the top of the wall.

After the first course is in place, most masons will lay up 4 to 5 courses at each corner of the wall they are working on. Mortar for blocks above the first course is placed only along the edges of the blocks, a technique known as face shell bedding. Corners must be checked for alignment, levelness, and plumb as they are constructed. A line stretched between corners can then be used to align the top outside edge of each course of blocks. Corners are kept 4 to 5 courses ahead of the center section of the wall until full height is reached.

Mortar which is squeezed out of joints is removed with the trowel as blocks are laid. After mortar has started to set, joints should be smoothed or tooled using a special tool which compresses the mortar into the joint. Tooling increases the density of mortar at the joint edge. This improves both the water tightness of the wall and its ability to withstand freeze-

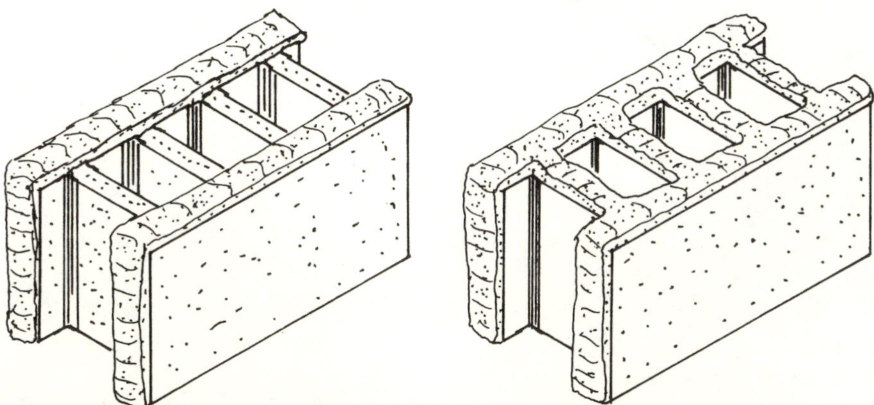

Figure 26-4. Face shell bedding (left) and full bedding of masonry units with mortar (right).

thaw cycles.

Control joints are used in block walls to prevent random cracking associated with minor shifts in the building footings. A control joint is a continuous vertical joint in the blocks for the full height of the wall. After mortar has started to set in the control joint, it is partially removed or raked out to a depth of about ¾ inch. When the mortar has completely cured, this raked area is filled with a caulking material which can expand and contract to fill any crack which develops. Special Z-shaped metal tie bars or control joint blocks are used to maintain stability of the wall on the two sides of the joint. Metal tie bars should be placed in every other course when used. Control joints are located as follows:

1. At distances equal to 2-½ times the wall height for walls without openings.
2. At intersections of old and new construction.
3. Above any joints in foundation or steps in the footing.
4. Above major wall openings.

Anchor bolts for securing wood or metal framing to block walls are located in the core space of the top course of blocks. Bolts should be long enough to extend downward into the top two courses of blocks and the core spaces they are placed in should be filled with mortar.

Waterproofing

Below grade block walls can be waterproofed after construction by plastering them with two coats of ¼ inch thick cement plaster. The same mix used for mortaring can be used for plastering. The wall surface should be dampened slightly before applying plaster. Allow at least 24 hours between coats. The second layer should be shaped out over the edge of the footing to direct any water toward the footing drain. Keep plaster damp for at least 48 hours to insure a good cure. After plaster has completed setting and is dry, apply a coating of asphalt sealer to the below ground portion of the wall.

Above ground walls, particularly those made with lightweight or porous block can be sealed against normal weather with a waterproofing masonry paint. These are available in several types and colors and should be applied with a stiff brush or long napped roller to get good penetration into the open pore spaces in the blocks.

Surface Bonding

Surface bonding is a relatively new construction technique where blocks are stacked up dry without mortar and bonded together by applying a layer of material to both sides of the wall. This system of building offers several advantages over conventional masonry work.

1. Less time is required to construct.

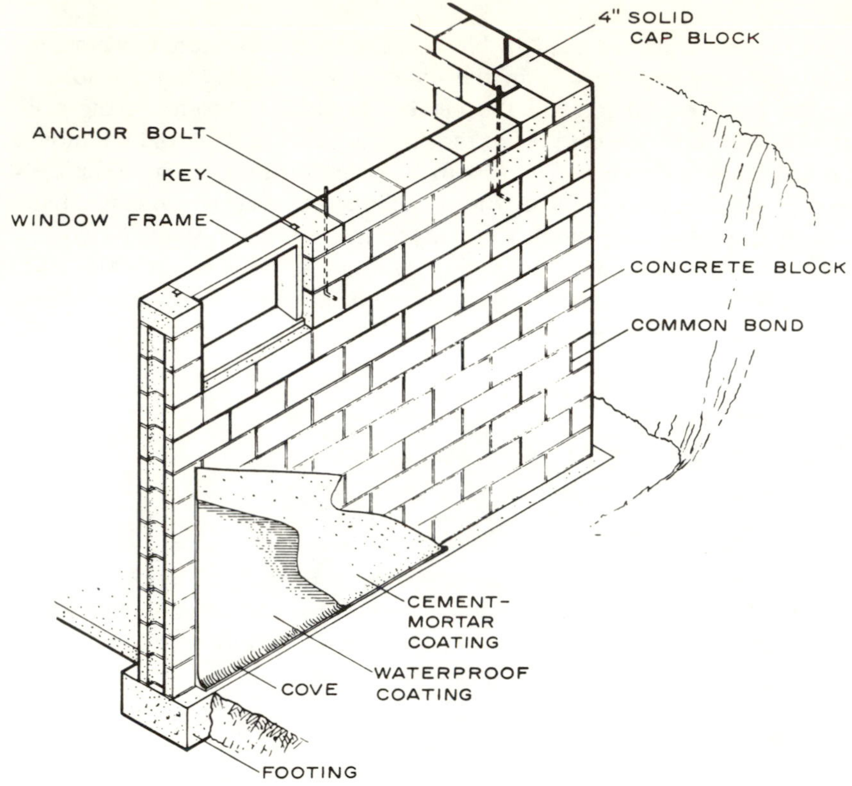

Figure 26-5. Waterproofing a masonry wall requires complete plastering with a mortar mix and then coating with an asphalt-based compound. Note how both the plaster layer and the waterproofing material completely cover the joint at the base of the wall and extend over the footing. (USDA)

2. Unskilled labor can be used to place blocks.
3. Walls are actually stronger than conventional mortar assembled walls.
4. The bonding mixture serves as a waterproofing as well as a bonding agent.
5. Walls can be colored by adding pigment to the bonding mix.

Since mortar joints are not used, dimensions of walls will be off both vertically and horizontally by 3/8 inch for each block. This requires some extra calculations in locating wall openings in order to avoid cutting too many blocks. Another problem is the fact that blocks are seldom exactly square and surfaces are not always level. This can cause some problems in keeping walls in alignment during the stacking process. Some block manufacturers are now making special full sized blocks with ground surfaces which eliminate both of these problems.

Bonding material can be purchased in a pre-mixed dry form or you can assemble materials and mix your own. The mix recommended by

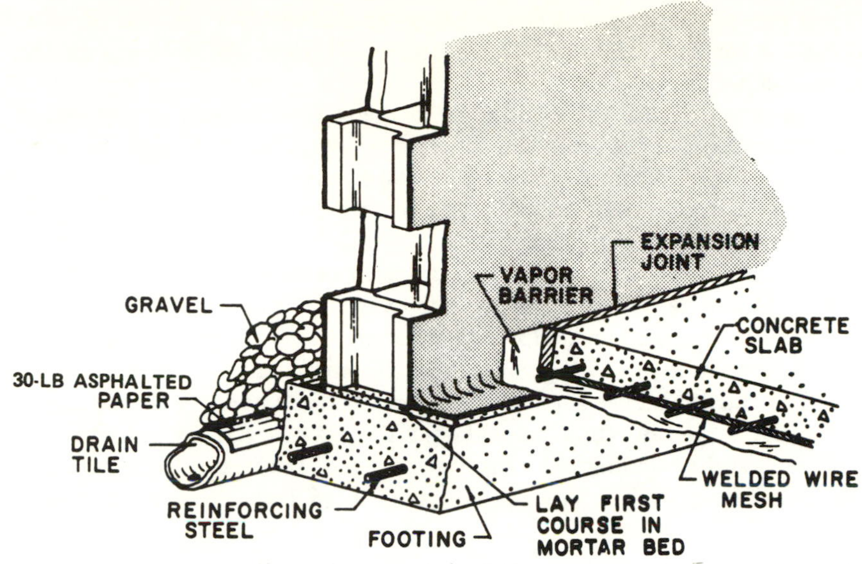

Figure 26-6. Wall-footing-floor detail for a surface-bonded wall section. The drain tile and gravel are an essential part of any dry, below-grade construction, whether it is concrete, masonry, or treated wood. (USDA)

USDA researchers to make 25 pounds of mix is as follows:

19.5	lbs	type I portland cement
3.75	lbs	hydrated lime
.5	lb	calcium chloride
.25	lb	calcium stearate
1	lb	type E glass fibers chopped to ½ inch length.

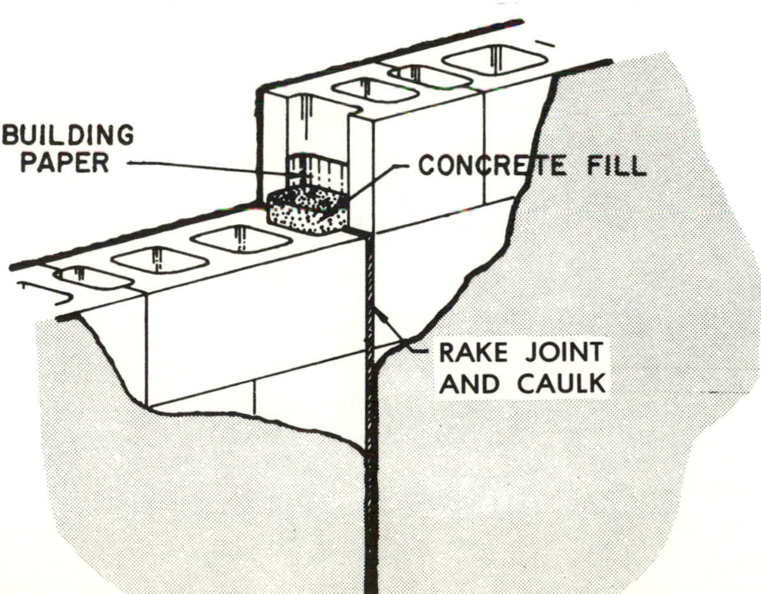

Figure 26-7. Control joint construction in a surface-bonded wall. (USDA)

Twenty-five pounds of dry mix is combined with 1-½ gallons of water to make a workable solution. This amount will cover about 44 square feet of wall on both sides.

Anchor bolts for the wood plate at the top of the wall should extend through the core space from the concrete footing (full height of the wall). Anchors are spaced a maximum of 8 feet on center.

The first course of block is full bedded in a standard mortar mix placed on the footing. This mortar is allowed to set up before stacking blocks. Use a level and chalk lines to keep stacked blocks aligned and plumb. Minor variations in block shape or size can be worked out by shimming or spacing blocks up to ¼ inch apart. Try to keep spacing to an absolute minimum as it will weaken the wall somewhat.

The stacked blocks should be thoroughly clean and wet before applying bond material. Bonding mix will not stick to a dusty or dirty block.

Trowel the bonding mix onto both sides of the wall using a standard plasterer's trowel. A layer approximately 1/16 inch thick is sufficient.

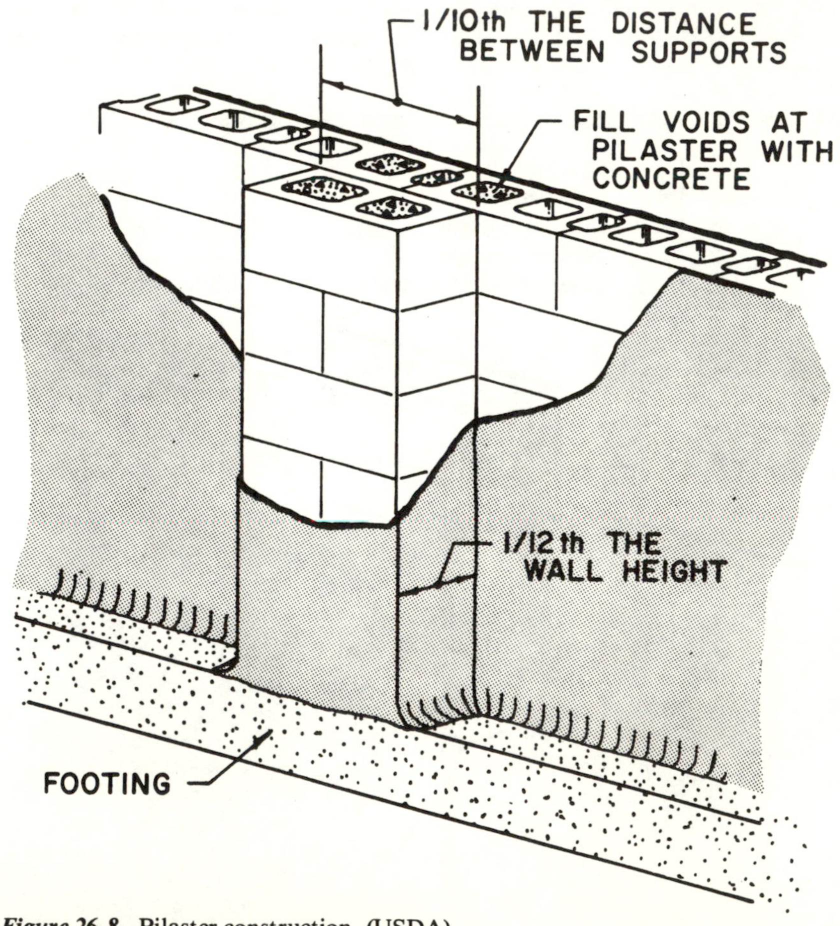

Figure 26-8. Pilaster construction. (USDA)

Figure 26-9. This surface-bonded partition wall has withstood the punishment of market hogs without effect for several years. The lower portion of the exterior wall is also of surface-bonded construction.

Trowel only enough to get a reasonably smooth surface and to work the mix into cracks and pore spaces. Too much troweling weakens the mix. Do not apply bonding mix when temperatures are below 40° or above 90°.

Proper curing is essential for good bonding. If the mixture dries too rapidly, cracks will develop. As soon as the mixture has set enough so that it cannot be washed off with a fine spray of water, start wetting it with a hose. Keep it continuously damp for at least 48 hours.

CHAPTER 27

Wood

Lumber made from wood is without question the most widely used of all building materials. This is just as true today as it was 100 years ago when there was not much in the way of other choices. There are many reasons for this popularity. Wood is an abundant, renewable resource, it is easily worked, structurally sound, and a reasonably good insulator. On the other hand, wood burns easily, is subject to decay, and makes good food for termites. In spite of these limitations, chances are pretty good that you will be using some wood in just about any structure you choose to erect on your farm.

The Language of Wood

There are about 60 different kinds of woods grown in the United States which are used commercially. In addition, we import another 30 varieties to satisfy our needs throughout the construction and manufacturing industries.

All varieties of wood have one thing in common, their composition. Wood contains cellulose, lignin, ash, and cellular extracts. Variations in the different varieties are due to different proportions of these four components and variations in individual cellular structure.

The wood and lumber industry has a language of its own when it comes to describing its product. Some of the terms you need to know are found in the following paragraphs.

Hardwoods and softwoods. These are the two major divisions of wood varieties. The division is made on the basis of whether a species is deciduous (loses its leaves in the fall) or a conifer (evergreen). Deciduous trees provide hardwood lumber, conifers yield softwood. The physical characteristics of the wood itself have nothing to do with the classification. In fact, there are several hardwoods such as basswood and aspen which are much "softer" than softwoods such as pine and fir.

Heartwood. This is the wood which is located near the center of the tree. The cells in heartwood are less active in the growth process and often contain deposits which give heartwood a darker color and better resistance to decay.

Sapwood. The outer portion of the wood in a tree, located directly below the bark. Sapwood is actively involved in the growth process and contains cells which conduct fluids needed to sustain life in the tree. Sapwood is generally less resistant to decay than heartwood. Both sapwood and heartwood have about equal strength.

Growth Rings. If you look at the end of a log or piece of lumber, you will see lines or rings which represent annual growth pattern for the particular tree. These are referred to as growth rings and are caused by variations in growth rate at different times of the year. In the spring when growth is rapid, cells are larger and new wood is more porous. These layers or rings are referred to as springwood or earlywood. Wood formed in summer and fall has smaller cells with thicker walls and is referred to as latewood or summerwood. Areas of the country or world which have long uniform growing seasons tend to produce trees with less variation between springwood and summerwood. The more uniform the wood is, the stronger the lumber it will produce. This is one reason why the West Coast and southeastern areas of the United States have become prime suppliers of structural lumber.

Plainsawed and quartersawed lumber. Lumber can be cut from a log in two different ways, tangent to the annual rings or perpendicular to the rings. Lumber sawn tangent to the rings is referred to as *plainsawed* lumber. This method of sawing offers these advantages:

1. Lumber is easier to saw and a log may yield more lumber.
2. It shrinks and swells less in thickness.
3. Figure patterns due to annual growth rings are enhanced.
4. Knots are usually round or oval and have less effect on strength of the board.
5. Cracks between growth rings (shakes) extend through fewer boards.

Quartersawn lumber is cut perpendicular or nearly so to the annual growth rings. Boards which are *quartersawn* offer the following advantages:

1. They shrink and swell less in width.
2. They have less tendency to twist and cup.

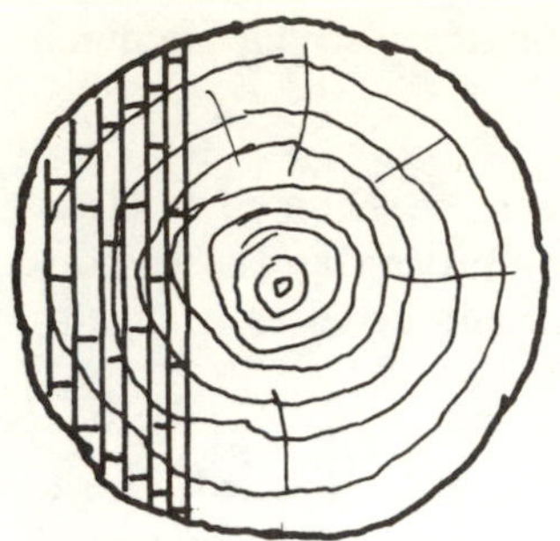

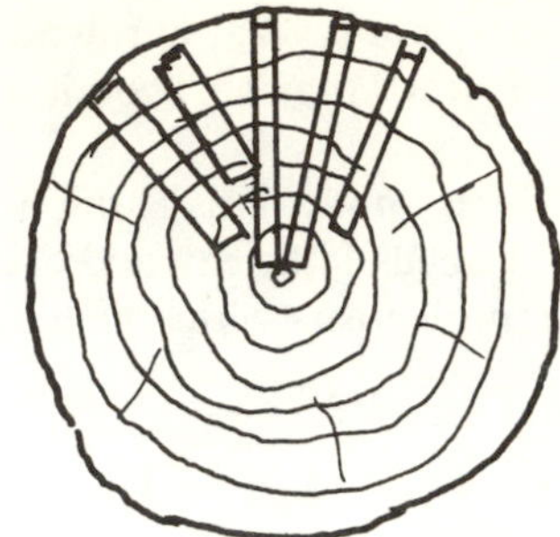

Figure 27-1. End view of two logs showing cuts required for plainsawed (left) and quartersawed (right) lumber.

3. Wear is more even.
4. The paint holding ability is improved for some varieties.
5. Surface cracks and splits which develop over time are reduced.

Knot. A knot is part of a branch which extends into the trunk of the tree. A knot affects the strength and other mechanical properties of the wood surrounding it because it disrupts the main grain pattern. Wood members which are loaded in tension are more affected by knots than are members in compression. In a simple beam such as a floor joist or roof rafter, the bottom edge of the member is in tension, the top in compression. Because of this, knots located near the edge of a particular board should be placed toward the top or compression side when building.

Defects. In addition to knots, wood has several other common defects which can affect its strength, ease of use, or both.

Cross graining. The grain in a particular board runs at a sharp angle to the long dimension. Cross graining can be caused by large knots or sawing lumber from a crooked log. It greatly reduces strength of lumber.

Pitch pockets. These are small pockets or holes which contain pitch. They are usually not large enough or numerous enough to affect overall strength. Pitch will gradually weep out of these pockets, making lumber with them almost impossible to paint.

Check. Cracks which run perpendicular to the growth rings.

Shakes. An area on a piece of lumber which has bark left on it or where bark has dropped off. This results in an undersized board with a reduction in load carrying ability.

Warp. Twisting or bending of a board due to unequal shrinkage during drying. As lumber loses moisture, it shrinks. The amount of shrink will vary in each of the three directions: parallel to the grain, perpendicular (radial) to growth rings, and along (tangential) the growth rings. Parallel to the grain or longitudinal shrinkage is not usually a major factor. It will range between .1% and .2% for all species of wood. Tangential and radial shrinkage vary between species. Several of the commonly used species are listed in Table 27-1.

Table 27-1. **Radial and Tangential Shrinkage in Lumber From Green to Oven Dry Condition**

	Shrinkage in Percent	
Species	**Radial**	**Tangential**
Basswood	6.6	9.3
Cherry	3.7	7.1
Cottonwood	3.6	8.6
Oak-Red	4.4	11.1
Oak-White	5.6	10.5
Douglas Fir	4.8	7.6
Hemlock-Western	4.2	7.8
White Pine	2.1	6.1
Redwood	2.6	4.4
Loblolly Pine	4.8	7.4

Strength

The ability of a piece of lumber to support or resist a load is referred to as strength. Strength depends on species, moisture content, defects, load duration, and treatment.

Species. Varieties which are straight grained, dense, and which grow uniformly tend to have greater natural strength. Strength variations may exist within a particular variety, depending on where it grows. For example, Douglas Fir grown along the West Coast is generally considered superior to fir grown further inland.

Moisture content. Wet wood is not as strong as dry wood. As wood dries from its fresh cut or ‘‘green’’ state it shrinks and individual cell walls become stiffer, resulting in greater load carrying ability or strength. The allowable design loads for wood are always expressed at a given moisture content—usually the moisture content to which wood naturally air dries in a structure. If wood is to be used in a damp location or if it is subjected to alternating wet and dry cycles, an allowance for strength reduction should be made when selecting member sizes.

Defects. All the defects which we described earlier have a negative effect on the strength of wood. No two pieces of lumber are exactly alike with regard to defects and therefore no two pieces will have exactly the same strength. The lumber industry has established grading rules for various species which grades each piece of lumber based on a maximum number and size of defects which it possesses. An allowable design load is then assigned to each grade based on the worst possible piece of lumber which can be assigned to the grade.

Load duration. Wood is the only material in general construction use which has a strength that depends on duration of load. When a load is placed on a wood beam, the beam deflects or bends slightly. If this load is left on the beam, it will continue to bend very slowly over time. If the load is heavy enough, failure will eventually occur. A wood member under continuous load for several years will fail under a load which is slightly more than half the load the same beam can support for a few minutes. This property allows us to plan for short time overloads (snow and wind in particular) and still meet the long time load capacity with economical construction. It also explains why wooden structures often withstand unusually high short time loads due to events such as earthquakes.

Treatment. Wood is frequently treated with chemicals to improve its decay resistance or to retard fire. Depending on the particular chemical used, the strength may be reduced slightly. A value of 10% to 15% is often used by designers to account for this reduction.

Wood is classified as an orthotropic material. This means that it has mechanical or strength properties which vary depending on the direction of load with respect to the grain and on whether the load is a tensile or a compressive load. In general, wood will withstand higher loads in compression than it will in tension and has greater load capacity when loads are applied parallel to the grain than when applied across the grain.

Sizes

Lumber is sawn to full dimensions—usually 1, 2, or 4 inches thick and in widths of 2 to 12 inches in 2 inch increments. It is then planed or surfaced to remove saw marks and provide smooth straight working surfaces. The final size of the lumber is dependent on whether surfacing is done when the wood is green or dry. Lumber surfaced when green is finished slightly oversized to allow for shrinkage during curing. Table 27-2 lists finished sizes for lumber surfaced green and dry. The extent of surfacing is indicated by a sequence of letters and numbers.

- ***S1S:*** Surfaced one side (side is the larger dimension of the board, i.e., for a 2 by 4 S1S would mean one of the 4 inch sides was surfaced.
- ***S2S:*** Surfaced both sides
- ***S1E:*** Surfaced one edge
- ***S2E:*** Surfaced both edges
- ***S1S1E:*** Surfaced one side and one edge
- ***S4S:*** Surfaced on all sides

Length of lumber varies from 8 to 24 feet by increments of 2 feet. A premium is usually charged for lengths of over 20 feet.

When you purchase lumber it will be priced by the board foot. The board foot is a volume measurement and is equal to the amount of wood in a piece which is 1 inch thick, 1 foot long, and 1 foot wide. Board foot calculations are based on nominal dimensions. For example, a 2 by 6 contains 1 board foot per foot of length even though the actual cross sectional dimensions are only 1-½ by 5-½. The number of board feet per foot of board length is also listed in Table 27-2.

Table 27-2. **Nominal and Finished Sizes for Softwood Lumber**

Nominal Size (Inches)	Actual Size: Surfaced Green (Inches)	Actual Size: Surfaced Dry (Inches)	Board Feet per Lineal Foot of Board
1 x 4	25/32 x 3-9/16	3/4 x 3-1/2	.33
1 x 6	25/32 x 5-5/8	3/4 x 5-1/2	.50
1 x 8	25/32 x 7-1/2	3/4 x 7-1/4	.67
1 x 10	25/32 x 9-1/2	3/4 x 9-1/4	.83
1 x 12	25/32 x 11-1/2	3/4 x 11-1/4	1.00
2 x 4	1-9/16 x 3-9/16	1-1/2 x 3-1/2	.67
2 x 6	1-9/16 x 5-5/8	1-1/2 x 5-1/2	1.00
2 x 8	1-9/16 x 7-1/2	1-1/2 x 7-1/4	1.33
2 x 10	1-9/16 x 9-1/2	1-1/2 x 9-1/4	1.67
2 x 12	1-9/16 x 11-1/2	1-1/2 x 11-1/4	2.00
4 x 4	3-9/16 x 3-9/16	3-1/2 x 3-1/2	1.33
6 x 6	5-1/2 x 5-1/2	—	3.00

Softwood Lumber Grades

Much of the lumber purchased for farm construction is softwood which is produced either in the northwest or southeastern parts of the United States. This lumber is sorted or graded under a set of rules published by the U.S. Department of Commerce. The current rules are known as the American Softwood Lumber Standard PS 20-70 (ASLS). The standard classifies softwood according to intended use into lumber for construction and lumber for remanufacture. Lumber for remanufacture is intended for use in furniture, ladders, poles, pencil stock, laminated assemblies, and numerous other purposes. Construction lumber is further divided into the following classifications.

Dimension lumber: Lumber that is 2 to 4 inches thick and 2 or more inches wide. Used for sills, joists, studs, rafters, and most other components of light frame construction.

Boards: Less than 2 inches thick and 2 or more inches wide. Used for subflooring, sheathing, and wood paneling.

Timber: Material with minimum dimension of 5 or more inches. In farm construction it is most often found in pressure treated poles.

Finish or select: Up to 1-½ inches thick and 2 or more inches wide. This lumber is graded solely on the basis of appearance and is used primarily in finish work.

The different classifications are further subdivided into specific

Table 27-3. **Classification, Grades, and Description for Softwood Lumber**

Classification	Grade	Description
Dimension	*Structural Light Framing* Structural Select No. 1 No. 2 No. 3	Used in general construction where strength is an important factor.
	Light Framing Construction Standard Utility Economy	Used in applications where strength and appearance are less critical.
	Studs	Suitable for studs only.
	Structural Joists and Planks Structural Select No. 1 No. 2 No. 3	Similar to structural light framing except this grade is limited to members 2 to 4 inches thick and 6 inches or wider.
	Appearance Framing A	Used in exposed locations where appearance is an important factor.
Timbers	*Select Structural* No. 1 No. 2 No. 3	Material that is 5 inches or more in least dimension.
Boards	*Sel. Mer. or 1* Const. 2 Std. 3 Util. 4 Econ. 5	1 inch material used for paneling, shelving, and sheathing.
Finish or select	*B & Btr* C D	Graded solely on appearance. For exposed applications.

grades which reflect both quality and intended use. Typical grades and uses within each classification are listed in Table 27-3.

The actual grading and enforcement of ASLS standards is done under the direction of independent regional associations. These associations supervise grading at individual member mills, arbitrate disputes over grades, and authorize grade stamping of lumber. The three organizations which do the majority of the grading work are the West Coast Lumber Inspection Bureau (WCLIB), the Southern Pine Inspection Bureau (SPIB), and the Western Wood Products Association (WWPA). Typical grade stamps authorized by these associations are illustrated in Figure 27-2.

Each of the grades is assigned design values, based on species, by the National Design Specification for Wood Construction. These design values are used by engineers and architects to arrive at the specific lumber sizes which they indicate on individual plans. Because of the wide variation in

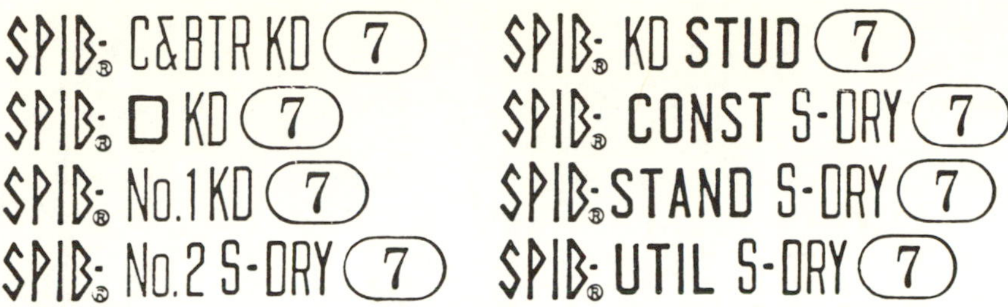

Figure 27-2. Shown in this illustration are several of the grade stamps used by one of the softwood grading agencies. The letters SPIB stand for the grading agency (Southern Pine Inspection Bureau). Next is the grade name abbreviation; i.e., C&BTR indicates that the lumber so stamped would meet the standard required of C or better. Following the grade designation is an indicator of the condition of seasoning at manufacture (KD is an indication that the lumber was kiln-dried). The circled number at the end identifies the mill that has approval to use the grade stamp. (Southern Pine Inspection Bureau)

allowable loads which can occur with grade changes, you should never substitute a lower than specified grade for any highly loaded member in a building.

Hardwood Grades

Hardwood lumber is graded according to intended use into three general classifications: factory lumber, dimension parts, and finished market products. Factory lumber and dimension parts classes are aimed at fulfilling requirements of industry and are seldom, if ever, encountered by the farm construction industry.

There is no centrally organized or published set of grading rules for hardwoods used in the finished market products area. Instead, grading rules are developed, adopted, and enforced by associations of manufacturers within specific industries. The largest single user of hardwood is the flooring industry. Two associations regulate grading in this industry. They are the Maple Flooring Manufacturers Association and the National Oak Flooring Manufacturers Association.

An example of the types of grades typical to hardwood can be found in the plainsawed and quartersawed classes of the oak flooring grades. Plainsawed oak flooring has four grades—clear, select, No. 1 common, and No. 2 common. Quartersawn has two grades—clear and select. Since hardwood is not often used in major load bearing components of a building, almost all grading is done on an appearance basis.

Native Lumber

Many farmers have access to locally grown or "native" lumber which is often available at a much lower price than the graded softwoods. Native

The following components may appear in various combinations on official WWPA gradestamps:

This is the official Association certification mark. It denotes that the product was graded under WWPA supervision. The symbol is registered with the U.S. Patent Office and may be used only when authorized by the Western Wood Products Association.

Each mill is assigned a permanent number. Some mills are identified by mill name or abbreviation instead of by mill number.

2 COM — This is an example of an official grade name abbreviation, in this case 2 Common Boards as described in the WWPA 1970 Grading Rules. Its appearance in a grade mark identifies the grade of a piece of lumber.

This is a species mark identifying the tree species from which the lumber is sawn, in this case Douglas Fir.

S-DRY
MC 15
S-GRN

These marks denote the moisture content of the lumber when manufactured. "S-DRY" indicates a moisture content not exceeding 19 percent. "MC 15" indicates a moisture content not exceeding 15 percent. "S-GRN" indicates that the moisture content exceeded 19 percent.

When an Inspection Certificate issued by the Western Wood Products Association is required on a shipment of lumber and specific grade marks are not used, the stock is identified by an imprint of the Association mark and the number of the shipping mill or inspector.

12 SEL STR
WWP ® S-GRN DOUG. FIR-L

Douglas Fir—Larch

12 1 S-DRY
WWP ® HEM FIR

Hem-Fir (California Red Fir, Grand Fir, Noble Fir, Pacific Silver Fir, White Fir and Western Hemlock)

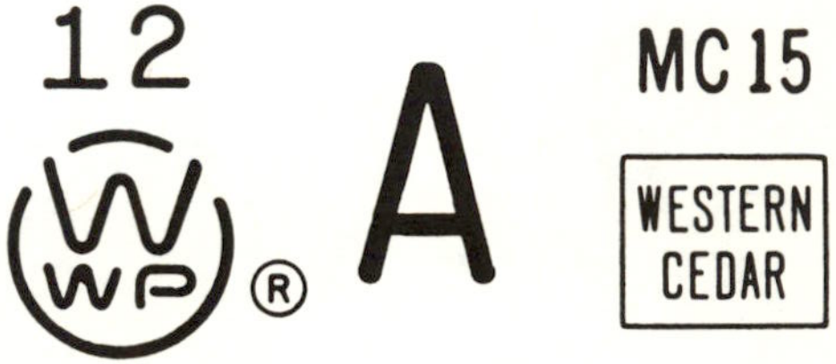

12 A MC 15
WWP ® WESTERN CEDAR

Incense Cedar—Western Red Cedar (or Inland Red Cedar)

Figure 27-3. Examples of official gradestamps of the Western Wood Products Association (WWPA).

lumber can be highly variable in both quality and strength, even within a single species. By paying careful attention to selection of individual pieces it is possible to directly substitute native lumber in critical parts of a building. If you are not willing, or don't feel qualified, to make this selection, you should confine the use of native lumber to noncritical parts of your building. Places where it can be easily used include studs, purlins, siding, sub-flooring, pen partitions, and fencing.

One of the more frequent requests we get is to compare the strength of a particular species of native lumber with a common softwood such as Douglas Fir or Southern Pine. It is almost impossible to do this because of the variation in growth patterns. We can, however, get an idea of relative strengths among different species by comparing clear, straight grained samples of each. Table 27-4 compares several kinds of wood in terms of relative bending strength. Douglas Fir and Southern Pine are rated at 100 and the other species are ranked against them.

***Table 27-4.* Relative Strength in Bending for Samples of Clear, Dry Lumber**

Species	Relative Strength
Douglas Fir—Coast type	100
Southern Pine	100
Cottonwood	50
Elm	73
Hemlock—West Coast	86
Hickory	127
Silver Maple	30
Hard Maple	100
Oak: Red and White	93
Spruce	50
Yellow Poplar	66
Sweetgum	91
Sycamore	79
Black Locust	125
Black Walnut	100

CHAPTER **28**

Plywood

Plywood is one of the more versatile materials used in farm construction. It combines the strength and durability of wood with the convenience of a sheet material which is much larger than the normal wooden member.

Plywood is manufactured by gluing together large thin sheets of wood known as veneers. Logs known as "peeler logs" are selected and cut to lengths of just over 8 feet. These logs are then mounted in a large lathe like device and a sharp knife is used to "peel" off a continuous thin sheet of wood as the log is rotated. This thin sheet is cut into smaller pieces, dried, and laminated together into plywood.

The standard size for individual sheets of plywood is 4 feet by 8 feet. Longer sheets (4 by 9 and 4 by 10) are also manufactured and can be ordered through most dealers at a slightly higher cost. Sheets are made in thicknesses from 3/16 inch up to one inch or more. The thicknesses most commonly used in farm construction are 1/4 inch, 3/8 inch, 1/2 inch, 5/8 inch, and 3/4 inch.

Some 70 different species of wood are used in the manufacture of plywood. Most plywood used for construction and industrial use is manufactured under a voluntary product standard (PS 1-74) published by the National Bureau of Standards (NBS) of the U.S. Department of Commerce. Implementation and enforcement of the standard is carried out by trade associations, the largest of which is the American Plywood Association (APA). The APA currently represents industries producing over 80% of United States plywood output.

Veneer Grades

Veneers made from peeler logs are separated into several grades on the basis of the number and size of defects which they contain. The categories defined by PS 1-74 are reviewed in the following paragraphs:

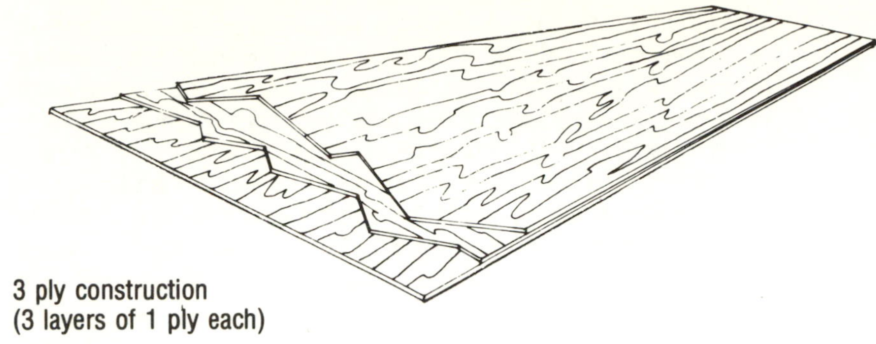

3 ply construction
(3 layers of 1 ply each)

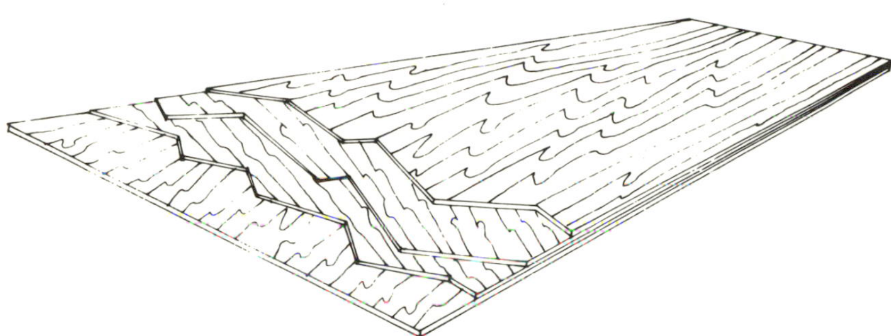

4 ply construction
(3 layers: Plies 2 and 3 have grain parallel)

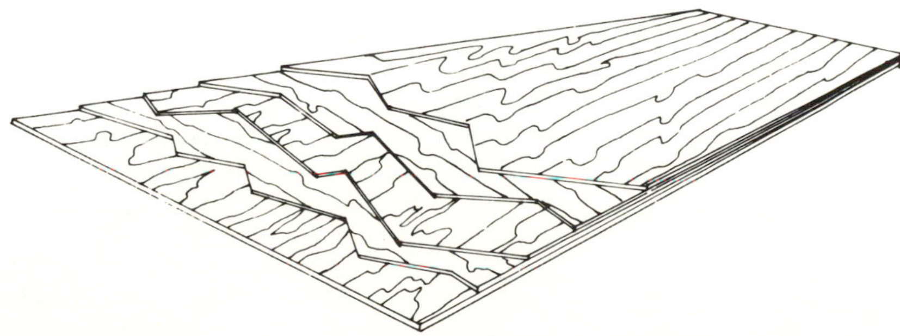

5 ply construction
(5 layers of 1 ply each)

Figure 28-1. Plywood is constructed of layers of thin wood veneer glued together. Direction of wood grain for each layer is dependent on the total number of layers or plies in the particular piece. (American Plywood Association)

N: The N grade of veneer is intended for use in plywood which will receive natural finish. It has to be either completely heartwood or completely sapwood. It must be free of knots, knot holes, pitch pockets, splits, and stain. Fillers may be used to fill small cracks or checks not over 1/32 inch wide and other small defects. Repairs are limited to a maximum of six per 4 by 8 sheet and must be neatly made. A maximum of 3 patches (maximum size 1 inch by 3-1/2 inch) may be used per sheet. Plywood with type N veneer is not generally stocked by most dealers and has little application in farm construction.

A: The A veneer is designed to provide a surface that is suitable for painting. It is firm, smoothly cut and free of open defects. When used in exterior panels, small defects may be patched with fillers. For interior panels, openings up to 3/16 inch wide and 2 inches long, small cracks and checks are allowed. Discolorations are permitted. Patches up to 2-1/4 inches wide are permitted. Surface of the veneer must be smooth.

B: Solid and free from open defects. Minor sanding and patching defects shall not exceed 5% of the total surface area. Knots of 1 inch in size (measured across the grain) are permitted if sound and tight. Splits are limited to 1/32 inch. Vertical holes up to 1/16 inch are permitted if there are not more than 1 per square foot.

C: Defects which will not impair the strength or serviceability of the panel are permitted. Open knot holes of up to 1 inch measured across the grain, with an occasional hole up to 1-½ inches are permitted. Splits of ½ inch wide by ½ panel length are permitted. C veneer provides a serviceable surface suitable for many uses in

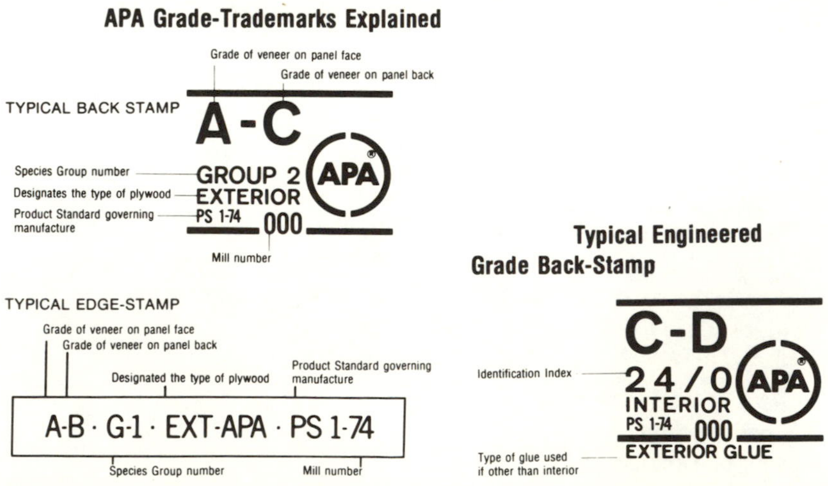

APA Grade-Trademarks Explained

TYPICAL BACK STAMP

Grade of veneer on panel face
Grade of veneer on panel back
A-C
Species Group number — GROUP 2
Designates the type of plywood — EXTERIOR
Product Standard governing manufacture — PS 1-74
000
Mill number
APA

TYPICAL EDGE-STAMP

Grade of veneer on panel face
Grade of veneer on panel back
Designated the type of plywood
Product Standard governing manufacture
A-B · G-1 · EXT-APA · PS 1-74
Species Group number
Mill number

Typical Engineered Grade Back-Stamp

C-D
Identification Index — 24/0
INTERIOR
PS 1-74
000
Type of glue used if other than interior — EXTERIOR GLUE
APA

Figure 28-2. Grade stamps and how to decipher them, as explained by the trade association. (American Plywood Association)

farm construction.

C Plugged: A C veneer which has been repaired to limit the number and size of defects. Open holes not larger than ¼ by ½ inch are permitted. Knots up to 1-½ inches are allowed if they are solid and tight.

D: This is the lowest grade of veneer and is used in applications where it will not be exposed and where strength is not a major factor. Open knots of 2-½ inches are permitted, with an occasional knot up to 3 inches allowed.

Types of Plywood

Veneer layers are bonded (glued) together into two general types of plywood—interior and exterior.

Interior. Plywood of this type is bonded with a moisture resistant, but not water proof glue. It is intended for use only in applications where moisture content will not exceed 18%. It should not be used in livestock housing or other applications subject to high moisture conditions.

A special type of interior plywood is fabricated with exterior glue. This is sometimes referred to as "CDX" and will have the fact that it has exterior glue indicated on the grade stamp. This particular type of plywood was designed to be used in applications where it would be exposed to weather conditions for a longer than normal period before it could be protected with roofing or siding. It is not an exterior plywood and should not be used in continuously wet conditions or delamination (separation of the veneer plies) will occur.

Exterior type. All plywood which is continuously exposed to weather or high moisture conditions should be of the exterior type. Exterior type plywood is bonded with a waterproof glue and all inner veneer layers are restricted to C or better grade. Exterior plywood is the generally recommended type for most farm applications.

Marine plywood is a kind of exterior plywood which has interior veneer layers selected for strength characteristics. Marine plywood is also limited to fabrication from either Douglas Fir or Larch species of wood. It is a premium priced product designed to meet both waterproof and strength needs of the marine industry. It is not a material which has much application in agricultural construction.

Species Groups

PS 1-74 separates the species of wood used in plywood manufacture into 5 different groups. Groupings are intended to represent the general strength of the basic wood. The lower the group number, the higher the strength of the wood. Table 28-1 provides a partial listing of species groups designated by PS 1-74.

The species of face and back veneers may be from any of the 5 groups. If more than one piece of veneer is used in making a face or back ply, the entire ply shall be made of the same species. Inner plies of panels labeled as group 1, 2, 3, or 4 may be from any species listed in groups 1, 2, 3, or 4. In other words, it is permissible for a group 1 panel to have group 1 species front and back plies and group 4 inner plies. It is not permissible to use a group 5 species for inner plies unless the panel is designated as a group 5 panel.

Table 28-1. **Species Classifications for Plywood Veneers**

Group 1	Group 2	Group 3	Group 4	Group 5
Beech	Cypress	Black Maple	Red Alder	Basswood
Birch	Fir	Pine, Virginia	Hemlock, Eastern	Balsam Fir
Douglas Fir	Hemlock, Western	Red	Jack Pine	
		Western White		
Larch, Western			Redwood	
		Red Spruce	Black Spruce	
Sugar Maple				
		Sitka Spruce	White Spruce	
Southern Pine			Aspen	

Grades—Engineering

Plywood panels designed with special structural requirements in mind are grouped into a classification known as engineering grades. Appearance is not usually a major factor in the application of engineering grades. Uses for engineering grade plywood would include roof and sidewall sheathing, subflooring, truss plates, plywood box beams, concrete forms, gussets, and treated wood foundations. Engineering grades normally include only C and D veneers.

Several different panels within the engineering grade classification are designated for use over different framing member spans by manufacturer members of the American Plywood Association. The "span index" is indicated on the grade stamp as two numbers separated by a slash mark (i.e., 32/16 or 24/0). The first number represents the maximum recommended roof framing spacing in inches when using the panel for sheathing. The second number is the maximum recommended spacing in inches for floor framing when the panel is used for subflooring. These recommendations are based on running face grain in the panels across the framing members. Span indexes are determined by the structural needs of residential construction which are often much greater than for farm construction. If you order or specify plywood in terms of a span index number, be sure you also include a thickness specification. It is possible to get plywood panels of different thicknesses which have the

	Use these terms when you specify	Description and Most Common Uses	Typical Grade-trademarks	Veneer Grade Face	Back	Inner Plies
APPEARANCE (1)	A-A EXT-APA (2) (4)	Use where the appearance of both sides is important. Fences, built-ins, signs, cabinets, commercial refrigerators, tanks and ducts	AA G3 EXT APA PS 1 74	A	A	C
	A-B EXT-APA (2) (4)	For use similar to A-A EXT panels but where the appearance of one side is less important	AB G1 EXT APA PS 1 74	A	B	C
	A-C EXT-APA (2) (4)	Exterior use where the appearance of only one side is important. Sidings, soffits, fences, structural uses, truck lining and farm buildings. Tanks, commercial refrigerators	A-C GROUP 2 APA EXTERIOR PS 1-74 000	A	C	C
	B-B EXT-APA (2) (4)	An outdoor utility panel with solid paintable faces for uses where higher quality is not necessary	BB G1 EXT APA PS 1 74	B	B	C
	B-C EXT-APA (2) (4)	An outdoor utility panel for farm service and work buildings, truck linings, containers, tanks, agricultural equipment	B-C GROUP 1 APA EXTERIOR PS 1-74 000	B	C	C
ENGINEERED	C-D INT-APA w ext glue (2)	A utility panel for use where exposure to weather and moisture will be limited	C-D 32/16 APA INTERIOR PS 1-74 000 EXTERIOR GLUE	C	D	D
	C-C EXT-APA (2)	Unsanded grade with waterproof bond for subflooring and roof decking, siding on service and farm buildings. Backing, crating, pallets and pallet bins	C-C 32/16 APA EXTERIOR PS 1-74 000	C	C	C
	C-C PLUGGED EXT-APA (2)	For refrigerated or controlled atmosphere rooms. Also for pallets, fruit pallet bins, tanks, truck floors and linings. Touch-sanded	C C PLUGGED GROUP 4 APA EXTERIOR PS 1-74 000	C Plgd	C	C
	STRUCTURAL I & II C-D INT & C-C EXT-APA	For engineered applications in farm construction. Unsanded. For species requirements see (4)	C-C 32/16 APA 000	C	C or D	C or D
SPECIALTY	HDO EXT-APA (2) (4)	Exterior type High Density Overlay plywood with hard, semi-opaque resin-fiber overlay. Abrasion resistant. Painting not ordinarily required. For concrete forms, signs, acid tanks, cabinets, counter tops and farm equipment	HDO AA G1 EXT APA PS 1 74	A or B	A or B	C (5)
	MDO EXT-APA (2) (4)	Exterior type Medium Density Overlay with smooth, opaque resin-fiber overlay heat-fused to one- or both panel faces. Ideal base for paint. Highly recommended for siding and other outdoor applications. Also good for built-ins and signs	MDO BB G4 EXT APA PS 1 74	B	B or C	C
	303 SIDING EXT-APA	Proprietary plywood products for exterior siding, fencing, etc. Special surface treatment such as V-groove, channel groove, striated, brushed, rough-sawn and texture-embossed MDO. Stud spacing (Span Index) and face grade classification indicated on grade stamp.	303 SIDING 6-S GROUP 1 24 oc SPAN EXTERIOR PS 1-74 000 APA	6	C	C
	T 1-11 EXT-APA	Special 303 panel having grooves 1/4" deep, 3/8" wide, spaced 4" or 8" o.c. Other spacing optional. Edges shiplapped. Available unsanded, textured and MDO.	303 SIDING 6 S/W T 1 11 GROUP 2 16 oc SPAN EXTERIOR PS 1-74 000 APA	C or B&R	C	C
	PLYRON EXT-APA	Hardboard faces both sides, tempered, smooth or screened.	PLYRON EXT APA PS 1 74			C

(1) Sanded both sides except where decorative or other surfaces specified.
(2) Can be manufactured in Group 1, 2, 3, 4, or 5 unless otherwise noted.
(3) Standard 4 × 8 panel sizes, other sizes can be manufactured.
(4) Also can be manufactured in STRUCTURAL I (all plies limited to Group 1 species) and II (limited to Groups 1, 2 and 3)
(5) Or C Plugged.
(6) C or better for 5-plies; C Plugged or better for 3-ply panels.
(7) Stud spacing is shown on grade stamp.

Table 28-2. Types of plywood adaptable to agricultural construction. (American Plywood Association)

same span indexes.

A special panel designated as B-B Plyform is also included in the engineering grades. This panel has sanded face veneers and comes with either a mill oiled or a high density overlay finish to provide a high degree of reusability for concrete form work. It is available in either 5/8 or 3/4 inch thicknesses.

Grades—Appearance

Panels in this classification have veneers or other treatments which are intended to provide some type of desired surface appearance. A listing of products found in both engineering and appearance grades can be found in Table 28-2. A few of the specialty items are listed with their descriptions and use below.

Decorative panels. Rough sawn, brushed, grooved, or striated finishes intended for use as interior paneling, accent walls, displays, or exhibits.

MDO and HDO. Plywood panels which are overlaid with medium density (MDO) or high density (HDO) surfaces designed to provide a smooth finish. MDO surfaces are designed to take paint and are often used for highway signs. HDO does not require painting. Both can be used for exterior siding, cabinets, and displays.

303-siding. Specialty finishes such as unsanded, grooved, rough sawn, and textured, which are designed specifically as exterior siding. Texture 1-11 is a 303 panel which has grooves 1/4 inch deep, 3/8 inch wide and spaced 4 or 8 inches apart. 303 siding material can be used as a combination sheathing and siding material provided framing supports are properly spaced.

Plyron. Panels are overlaid on both sides with hardboard faces. It is used whenever a smooth surface is required. Examples includes doors and cabinet work.

FRP coated. Fiberglass reinforced plastic coatings used on one surface to provide an easily cleaned durable finish. These panels are frequently used in the food processing industry and have become popular interior finishes for on farm milking centers.

Buying Plywood for Farm Use

Plywood is an important material in farm construction; however, it is even more important to the commercial and residential construction industry. Because of this and the wide variety of plywoods available, it is not unusual to find a dealer who stocks only for the residential market and who has little knowledge of selecting plywoods for farm use. Table 28-3 summarizes some of our recommendations for farm buildings.

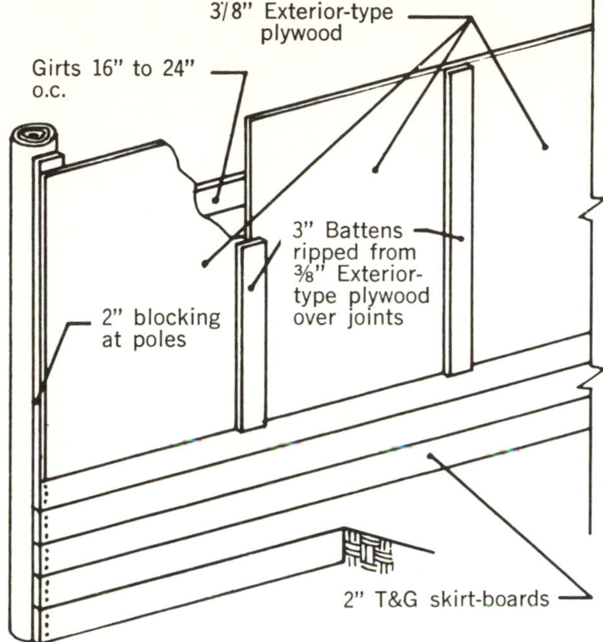

Figure 28-3. Plywood siding used on a pole frame building. (American Plywood Association)

Fastening Plywood

Plywood is usually nailed or nailed and glued to supporting framing members. Common nails are recommended for sheathing and subflooring. Finish or casing nails are used with paneling and siding. Ring shank or screw shank nails provide additional withdrawal resistance for underlayment and where extra strength is required. Nails selected for use in siding or other locations subjected to moisture should be either galvanized or made of stainless steel.

Recommended nail sizes are 4d for 1/4 inch thick plywood, 6d for 3/8 to 1/2 inch and 8d for 5/8 to 3/4 inch panels. Space nails 6 inches apart along panel edges and 12 inches apart over interior supports. If supporting members are 48 inches on center, space all nails 6 inches on center. Nails should be spaced 3/8 inch back from the panel edges to avoid splitting of veneer layers.

Several different types of adhesives are available for use with plywood. Adhesives will improve the structural strength and rigidity of the overall building assembly. Most adhesives have specific requirements for application and service in order to develop maximum strength. When selecting an adhesive, be sure to read and follow the label. Pay particular attention to temperature requirements at the time of application and whether or not the adhesive is designed for high moisture conditions.

Installation Practices for Plywood

1. Plywood will expand and contract due to seasonal changes in

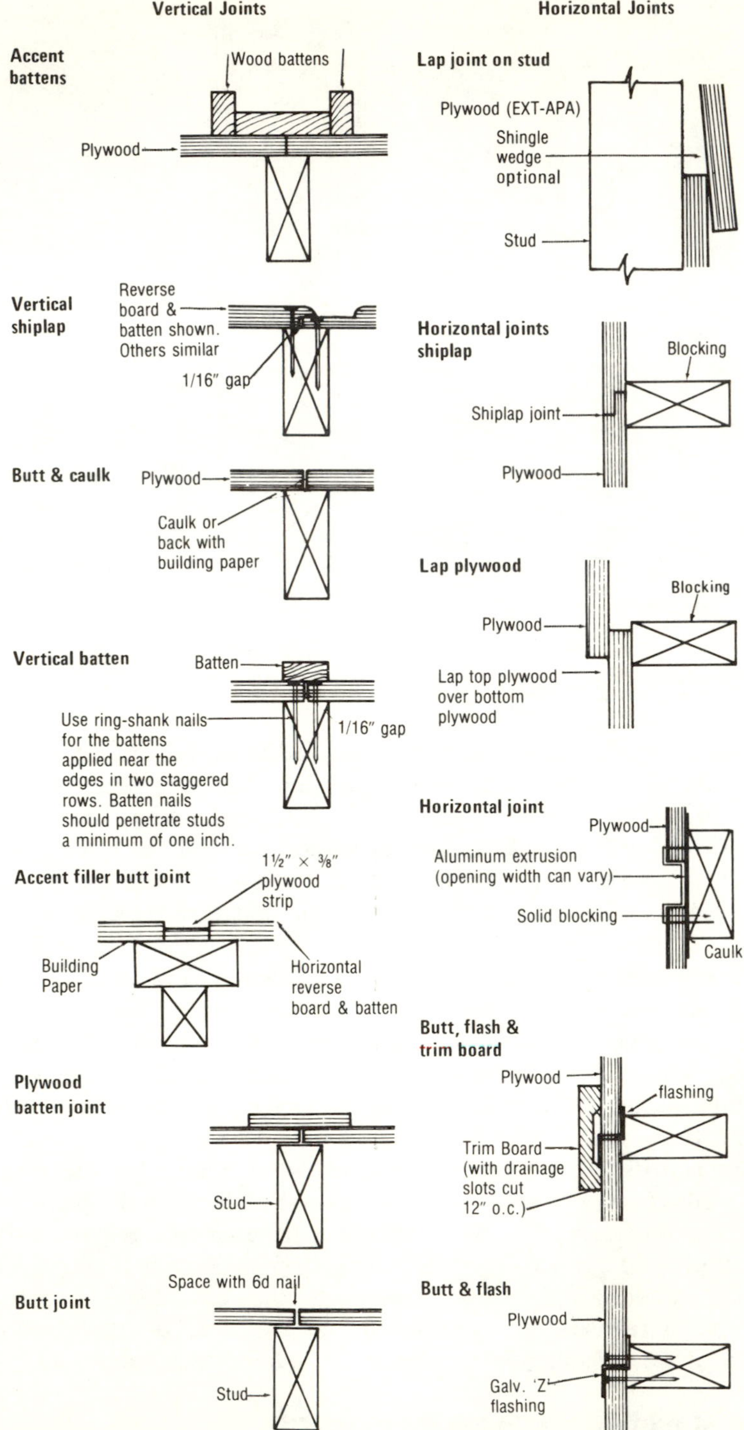

Figure 28-4. Construction joint details recommended for use with plywood. (American Plywood Association)

moisture. Panels should be spaced 1/16 to 1/8 inch apart to prevent buckling.

2. Butt joints between plywood sheets should be staggered so they do not all occur at the same supporting member.
3. If supporting members are more than 32 inches apart, use edge blocking to support adjacent sheets of plywood. Plyclips (small H shaped pieces of metal) can be used to tie edges of adjacent panels together in ceiling and roof sheathing applications.
4. Always run face grain of top and bottom veneers perpendicular to support for maximum strength.
5. Select plywood sheathing which is at least ½ inch thick if a covering material such as roofing is to be nailed directly to the sheathing. Thinner panels can be used if covering is to be stapled rather than nailed to it.

Table 28-3. **Suggested Plywood Types and Grades for Selected Farm Building Use**

Use	Type and Grade
Wall or roof sheathing	(1) C-D interior with exterior glue (2) CC-exterior
Exterior siding	(1) C-C exterior if knot holes are OK and stain finish is planned (2) MDO-exterior best for painted finish (3) 303-siding for special effects
Ceiling covering	(1) C-C exterior for livestock buildings or high moisture areas (2) C-D interior in dry buildings such as shops or grain processing
Flooring	(1) C-C exterior for moist areas (2) C-D interior for dry buildings (3) B-C exterior (wet areas) or B-D interior (dry areas) for combination subfloor-finish floor use
Partitions, gates, livestock equipment	(1) C-C exterior
Structural elements such as grain bins, truss gussets, bracing	(1) As specified on plans (2) C-D interior with exterior glue (3) B-C exterior

CHAPTER **29**

Preservative Treatments for Wood

Wood has only two principle disadvantages as a construction material; it can be destroyed by insects or fungus growth and it burns. The builder or contractor has four choices to make with regard to these disadvantages.

1. Ignore the problem and let the owner worry about building repair when wood failure occurs.
2. Use construction techniques which minimize the exposure of wood to potential destruction.
3. Use masonry or steel construction techniques.
4. Buy and use preservative treated wood in locations where hazards exist.

An entire industry exists today for the main purpose of applying preservative treatments to wood which are intended to eliminate its two disadvantages. As a result of its efforts, wood can be treated to meet almost any situation in which it needs to be used. It can be made to resist decay, insects, and fire for an indefinite period.

Decay

Four factors are necessary for decay to occur. They are oxygen, moisture, favorable temperature, and a food supply. The fungi which cause decay cannot exist if any one of the four is missing.

In construction it is not possible to control either the oxygen supply or temperatures. We can and do control moisture and food supply. Moisture is controlled by restricting the use of wood to locations where its natural moisture content will not exceed 18% to 20%. When wood must be used in wet locations, we can make the food supply unavailable to decay organisms through the use of treatments.

Decay is caused by fungus organisms. They feed on wood, causing both physical and chemical changes in the cellular structure. Most fungi attack wood only after the tree has been cut or has died. Wood destroying fungi are divided into two groups, white and brown rot producers. White rot fungi attack the material which cements the cells of the wood together (lignin). Brown rot fungi attack the cellulose which makes up the cell wall itself. The two types leave behind white and brown rotted residues, respectively.

Insects

Three general classes of insects destroy wood in farm structures. They are beetles, termites and carpenter ants.

Beetles. Bark beetles, Ambrosia beetles, roundhead, and flathead borers all attack freshly cut logs. To avoid damage by these beetles, wood is cut during dormant times of the year (late fall-early winter).

The powder post beetle does the most damage of all beetles. It attacks both hardwoods and softwoods. Eggs are laid in the pores of the wood. When the larvae hatch, they burrow into the wood and destroy its overall structure. Beetles are controlled by treating wood with a material which is toxic to them.

Termites. Subterranean termites live in groups or colonies buried in the ground. Although they are very common in areas with warmer climates, there is a substantial amount of termite damage done each year in many of our northern states.

Termites must maintain contact with their underground colonies in order to secure moisture needed to maintain life. Because of this, they usually damage wood which is either in contact with the ground or located close to it. Termites will frequently build mud tunnels or shelter tubes which extend from their below ground colonies up the inside or outside of a foundation to the nearest source of wood. Once they enter wood, most damage is done from the inside, leaving an outward appearance that everything is fine. Because of this, termite damage is often not discovered until it has reached the point where structural failure starts to occur.

Termites are controlled by two general methods. Wood located close to the ground is treated with a toxic material or the ground itself is treated with long lasting poisonous material. Mechanical barriers such as termite shields have also been used to prevent termites from gaining access to wooden portions of a structure. These have been only marginally effective because they are not usually absolutely tight. Termites can get through openings which are as small as 1/32 of an inch.

Carpenter ants. The carpenter ant relies on wood as a source of shelter, not as a food supply. They usually prefer soft wood or wood which has been softened by decay. These ants frequently gain entrance to a structure by being carried in on firewood. The first evidence that carpenter ants are at work is usually a small pile of sawdust located below the member being attacked. Carpenter ants will not attack preservative treated wood and can be controlled after they are present by surface applications of oil base preservatives.

Treatment Processes

There are several methods or processes used to introduce preservative material into wood. These vary widely in their degree of difficulty, cost, and effectiveness. Some processes can be used for both green or wet wood and dry wood; others are restricted to use on dry wood. Several of the more popular methods are described below.

Pressure treatment. The pressure process is the most desirable of the treatment processes. It can be used on either green or dry wood and results in the greatest penetration and thus the most protection of all methods.

The full cell pressure treatment method is used to achieve maximum retention of preservative in the treated wood. It is used as the standard method for treating marine timbers with creosote and for all treatments with water borne preservatives. The steps in treatment are as follows:

1. Wood is placed in a sealed chamber called a retort.
2. Vacuum is applied to remove air from the wood.
3. Preservative is added to the chamber while vacuum is maintained.
4. Pressure is applied until the desired retention of preservative is obtained.
5. Excess preservative is drained from the chamber.

The so called "empty cell" process is used when deep penetration and relatively low retention rates are desired. It differs from the full cell process in two major ways. First, the initial vacuum is not drawn. Second, after treatment pressure is released, a vacuum is drawn to help remove or recover as much liquid preservative as possible.

One variation on the empty cell process is the use of LP-gas as the liquid in which preservative is dissolved. When pressure in the retort is released, the LP turns to gas and escapes, leaving the preservative behind in the wood. The resulting treated wood is both clean and dry and can be easily painted. It is a fairly costly process and is not widely used.

Brushing or spraying. This is the least expensive and least effective process. Penetration is never good and retention of preservative is low. Any mechanical damage to the wood surface during construction is likely to break through the preservative layer and leave an opening for decay organisms or insects. Brush on treatments will add 1 to 3 years of life to wood which is in contact with the ground.

Dipping. Similar to brushing or spraying in that poor penetration and low retention is a common problem. This method is used most often for factory millwork where a limited amount of preservative, usually combined with waterproofing, is desired to protect wood until it can receive a protective paint coat.

Soaking. Wood which is either green or dry is immersed in a tank or preservative solution and allowed to soak for 7 to 10 days or more. If the soaking period is long enough, it is possible to get penetration and retention similar to that obtained with pressure treatment. Penetration into sapwood is much better than into heartwood.

Hot and cold soak. Dry wood is soaked for several hours in a hot solution of preservative, then for several more hours in a cool or cold solution. The hot bath warms and expands air in the wood cells. The cold bath causes the air to contract, creating a partial vacuum which draws preservative into the wood. This process has been used extensively for butt treatment of poles.

Preservatives

Material used to preserve wood must be able to easily penetrate wood, be poisonous to both fungi and insects, and remain in place for the useful life of the wood. It must also be able to kill any existing organisms in wood at the time of treatment. Chemicals which fulfill these needs have been separated into two general classifications: oil borne preservatives and water borne preservatives. The distinction is based on the type of carrier material which is used.

Oil borne preservatives. The two most commonly used oil borne materials are creosote and pentachlorophenol (penta). *Creosote* is black to dark brown in color and is produced by a distillation process from several different sources.

Advantages of creosote:

1. Relatively low cost.
2. Penetration can be determined by color change.
3. Does not leach out easily.
4. Highly toxic to wood destroying agents.

Disadvantages:

1. Unpleasant odor.
2. Burns easily.

3. Can be irritating to workers' skin.
4. Cannot be painted over.

Penta is normally dissolved in a lightweight oil and used in pressure or surface treatment processes. The color of the preservative is dependent on the type of oil used as a carrier. *Penta* is probably the number one preservative used in material for farm construction, although its use appears to be declining with the rapid increase in petroleum prices.

Advantages of penta:

1. Highly toxic.
2. Colorless.
3. Good penetration and resistance to leaching.
4. Can be painted over with proper selection of carrier oil.

Disadvantages:

1. Toxic and irritating to workers and animals.
2. Long lasting odor.

Both creosote and penta give off vapors which are highly toxic to living plants. For this reason, they should not be used in the construction of plant growth structures, such as greenhouses. There are two oil borne preservatives which are not toxic to plants. These are *copper napthenate* and *zinc napthenate.* These are not generally available for use in pressure treated material and most applications are made by brushing or soaking. When purchasing these materials, look for solutions with at least 2% metallic content.

Advantages of copper and zinc napthenate:

1. Not toxic to plants.
2. Can be used to treat rope and fabrics.

Disadvantages:

1. Copper Napthenate is difficult to paint over and leaves a green surface.
2. Zinc is easily painted over but is not as good a preservative.
3. More costly than creosote or penta.
4. Strong persistent odor.

Water borne preservatives. These materials until recently were used primarily in treatment of wood for use in locations where their cleanliness, paintability and lack of odor were important factors. They have been higher cost than the oil borne preservatives; however, increased oil costs have had a greater effect on oil borne than on water borne preservatives. As a result, we are now experiencing a rapid increase in the use of water borne preservatives in farm construction.

Water borne preservatives must be applied with the pressure treatment process to be effective. Surface applied material quickly leaches out, leaving unprotected wood. After treatment, wood must be dried to remove the water.

Commonly used materials for water borne preservatives include the following.

1. *Acid Copper Chromate* (ACC)
2. *Ammoniacal Copper Arsenite* (ACA)
3. *Chromated Copper Arsenate* (CCA)
   Type I or A
   Type II or B
4. *Chromated Zinc Chloride* (CAC)
5. *Flour Chrome Arsenate Phenol* (FCAP)
   Type I or A
   Type II or B

Retention

In order to perform its protective function, preservative must be present in a certain minimum amount. The amount of preservative present in treated material is measured in pounds per cubic foot (pcf) and is referred to as retention. The amount required will depend both on the type of preservative and the type of exposure to which the wood will be subjected. In general, below ground or earth contact exposures require the greatest retentions; above ground, the least. Table 29-1 lists recommended retention rates. Sometimes rates are expressed in terms of solution retention instead of preservative retention. A 6 pcf retention of a 5% penta solution gives a .3 pcf (6x.05) retention of preservative.

Fire Retardant Treatments

Whenever wood is subjected to a temperature of slightly over 500°F, it will spontaneously ignite. It has been found that certain chemicals when added to wood are able to insulate the surface so that its temperature will stay below the ignition point for a period of time when exposed to a heat source or fire. These chemicals include chromated zinc chloride, ammonium salts, borates, and boric acid. All are water soluble and are combined with wood using the full cell pressure treatment process. After treatment, moisture content of the wood has to be reduced to less than 19%.

Fire retardant materials do not prevent wood from burning. They do slow the rate of burning and prolong the amount of time available to move building occupants or contents to safety and increase the chances of being able to bring the fire under control before complete destruction of the building.

When temperature of a retardant treated piece of wood approaches 500°F, the treatment chemicals react with one another to produce non flam-

Table 29-1. **Recommended Retention Rates for Wood Preservatives**

Use	Creosote	Penta	ACC	ACA	CCA Type I	CCA Type II	CAC	FCAP
Building poles								
Southern Pine	9.0	.45	—	.60	.75	.45	—	—
Douglas Fir	16.0	.80	—	.60	.75	.45	—	—
Fence posts	6.0	.30	.50	.40	.75	.45	—	—
Lumber								
Above ground	8.0	.40	.25	.25	.35	.25	.45	.25
Soil contact	10.0	.50	.50	.40	.75	.45	—	—
Plywood								
Above ground	8.0	.40	.25	.25	.35	.25	.45	.25
Soil contact	10.0	.50	.50	.40	.75	.45	—	—
Plant structures								
Above ground	—	—	—	.25	.35	.25	—	.25
Soil contact	—	—	—	.40	.75	.45	—	—

mable gasses and water vapor. These are released at a slow rate and act as an insulating layer to protect the wood surfaces. The gasses also contribute to surface charring which helps further insulate the surface.

Wood which has been treated with fire retardant is rated in terms of flame spread rather than in pcf retention. An explanation of flame spread can be found in chapter 24.

Advantages of fire retardant treatments:

1. Colorless and odorless
2. Also provides some resistance to decay and insects.
3. Controls flame spread.
4. Easily handled and completely paintable.
5. May reduce fire insurance rates.

Disadvantages:

1. Most retardants are easily leached out of wood, and must be protected in exposed areas.
2. Treatment material is hard on wood working tools. Carbide tipped saws are recommended.
3. Laminated wood components must be glued with waterproof glue (exterior) in order to be treated.

CHAPTER **30**

Wall Covering Materials

The variety of materials available to cover, protect, and decorate building walls is almost endless. This chapter reviews some of the more commonly used materials, with emphasis on their advantages or limitations in agricultural construction. We cannot possibly cover all the options, and even if we did, there will undoubtedly be several new products on the market between the time we write this and the time you read it.

Exterior Coverings

Materials selected for outside wall coverings (sidings) on all buildings must be capable of withstanding the effects of weather over long periods of time with a reasonable amount of upkeep. Sidings used on farm buildings may also have to withstand loads from within the building, animal manure, an occasional bump from a piece of farm equipment, or direct contact by animals. In fact, this extra abuse may make far greater demands on the siding than any amount of weathering.

Vertical boards. At one time, 1 inch thick vertical board siding was the single most popular type of exterior siding for farm buildings. It provided a durable siding which could be expected to last for many years, with or without paint.

Advantages of vertical boards:

1. Makes good use of local or native grown lumber.
2. High mechanical strength.
3. Relatively good insulating ability.
4. Easily worked and fastened with ordinary carpentry tools.

Figure 30-1. Vertically applied 1-inch thick native boards make a durable and attractive finish for many farm buildings. They need not be painted, unless it is desired for appearance.

5. Does not need to be painted if natural weathered appearance is acceptable.

Disadvantages:

1. High labor requirement for installation.
2. Requires horizontal framing members in the wall which means extra cost with some types of construction.

Plywood. Exterior grade plywood panels combine the high strength characteristics of wood with larger piece size, which will reduce installation labor. It is also available either plain or in a variety of surface woods and patterns. Several manufacturers are also making plywood sidings available with factory applied finishes, which show good potential for long maintenance free life.

Advantages of plywood sidings:

1. Can be used as a combination sheathing and siding without need for diagonal bracing.
2. Sheet size reduces installation labor.
3. Wall framing can be either vertical or horizontal.

Disadvantages:

1. Medium to high cost material, depending on finish selected.
2. Standard length is 8 feet with 9 and 10 foot panels available at extra cost. This means that some type of horizontal joint has to be used in buildings with high sidewalls.
3. Edge blocking may be required when applying over horizontal framing members.

Hardboard. This is a man-made material constructed by bonding together wood fiber or cellulose into sheets. There is a wide variety of sheet sizes and surface finishes available for use as exterior siding material.

Advantages of hardboard:

1. Generally lower cost than plywood sidings.
2. Reasonably good structural strength, but not as good as wood in this respect.
3. Either horizontal or vertical wall framing can be used.

Disadvantages:

1. Is more sensitive to moisture than some other materials.
2. Manufacturer's recommendations with regard to thickness of siding, spacing of support members, and installation must be closely followed to obtain a ripple free exterior surface.
3. Must be protected from the weather with a good quality paint.
4. Product quality can vary considerably among different manufacturers.

Particle board or chip board. This material is manufactured by bonding together particles or chips of wood into panels. Standard panel size is 4 by 8 feet with larger sizes available (up to 8 by 28 feet) on special order. Panel thicknesses available range from ¼ inch up to ¾ inch.

The majority of particle boards on the market today are not intended for exterior use and will deteriorate very rapidly if exposed to outside conditions. If you purchase this material for exterior use, make sure it is a product designed for exterior application. Most particle boards are grade stamped with a label which will indicate whether or not they are exterior panels. If it is not stamped, don't buy it.

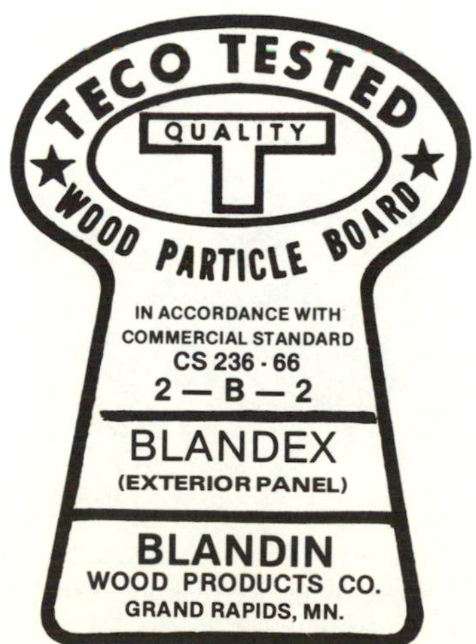

Figure 30-2. Typical grade stamp used on a particle board panel. Note that this stamp is intended for use on panels designed for exterior use. (USDHUD)

Advantages of particle board:

1. Low cost material.
2. Available in large sheets.
3. Material properties are not directional dependent. This means sheets can be installed over framing members running in any direction with the same result.

   Note: Research work is now in progress which will probably lead to production of a particle board panel which has oriented fibers and will have directionally dependent properties.

Disadvantages:

1. Material will not withstand mechanical abuse as well as wood and may be damaged by animals.
2. Will not hold fasteners as well as other materials.
3. Requires protective coating of paint or stain for maximum durability.
4. Will not withstand high sidewall pressures.

Metal sheets. Corrugated or ribbed metal is rapidly becoming the most common type of siding for farm buildings. It is the same product that is being used for roof covering and is available in several thicknesses and a variety of sheet sizes. It is applied with the corrugations or ribs running across the framing members and can be used with either vertically or horizontally framed walls. Factory applied color finishes are available, as is a wide variety of trim pieces and closure strips to complete the job.

Although metal is available in both steel and aluminum for roof

Figure 30-3. Prepainted metal makes a durable, attractive finish for the exterior of many farm buildings. Contrasting colors can be used to improve appearance, and a variety of closure strips are available to provide a professional finish.

covering, aluminum is not a good siding material for farm buildings because of its relatively low strength and its tendency to corrode rapidly when exposed to manure and other acids.

Advantages of metal sheets:

1. Low cost material.
2. Wide variety of sizes, shapes, and colors available.

Disadvantages:

1. Requires special tools for cutting and fitting if labor is to be kept at a minimum.
2. Will not withstand high wall pressures from stored product.
3. Is easily damaged by contact with farm machinery.

Asbestos cement. This is a masonry panel constructed of cement reinforced with asbestos fibers. It is usually manufactured in 4 by 8 foot sheets and thicknesses ranging from 1/8 to 3/8 inch. It has also been manufactured in patterned shingles for use as exterior siding.

Advantages of asbestos cement:

1. Hard, durable, easily cleaned surface.
2. Makes good protective cover for perimeter insulation.

Figure 30-4. One of the disadvantages of using metal siding on farm buildings is its susceptibility to mechanical damage from tractors or other equipment.

3. May be placed in contact with soil.

Disadvantages:

1. Material is extremely brittle and is easily broken both during construction and when struck by machinery.
2. Requires back up sheathing or other solid material to support it if it is accessible to large animals.
3. Carbide tipped masonry saw must be used to cut it and holes for nails must frequently be drilled to prevent breakage when installing.

Masonry. This provides the most durable of all exterior coverings. It also tends to be the most expensive if used only as a siding and not as the complete wall construction. Bricks, stone and concrete blocks are all available in a variety of sizes and surface finishes for exterior application. With the exception of blocks, which are usually used as the complete wall section, masonry has not been used much in farm construction.

Advantages of masonry:

1. Durability and resistance to most acids and chemicals found in the farm environment.
2. Requires little or no maintenance after construction.

Disadvantages:

1. High cost.
2. Poor insulating qualities.

Beveled siding. Horizontal, beveled, or clapboard siding can also be used on many farm structures. It is available in a wide number of materials including wood, hardboard, vinyl, aluminum, and steel. In general, the manufactured products (vinyl, aluminum, steel and hardboard) must be applied over some type of solid wall sheathing. Wood can be applied directly to vertically oriented wall framing members, if they are not spaced more than 24 inches apart.

Advantages of beveled siding:

1. Easily applied attractive siding.
2. Available in low maintenance types (vinyl and prefinished metals).
3. Some types are available with insulating backer strips.

Disadvantages:

1. Requires separate structural bracing to provide racking strength.
2. Is applied only over vertically oriented framing members.
3. Some types can be high cost.
4. Vinyl and prefinished metals do not have particularly good resistance to mechanical abuse.

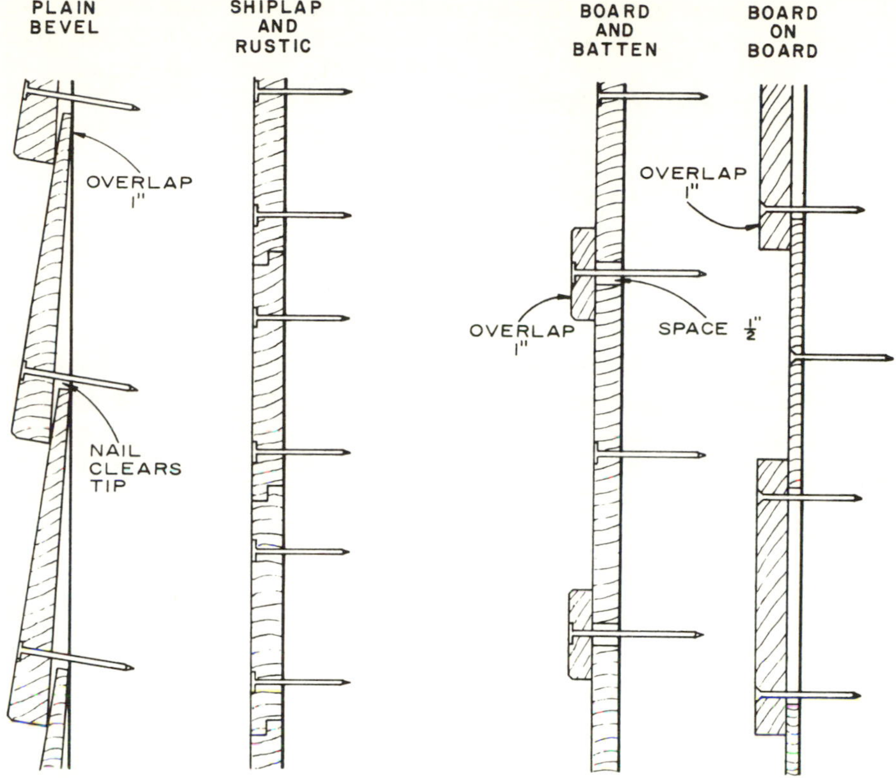

Figure 30-5. Types and recommended fastening system for wood sidings. (USDA)

Interior Coverings

Because of their built in resistance to moisture and their natural durability, many of the materials used for exterior siding make excellent interior surfaces as well. Exterior plywood, corrugated metal, hardboard and asbestos cement board have all been used successfully as linings for farm buildings. In addition there are several materials which have been specifically designed as interior surfaces.

Plastic coated paneling. These are usually hardboard panels which have been surfaced with a melamine plastic material. They are manufactured primarily for use in residential buildings; however, their easily cleaned surfaces have made them popular in farm buildings which have to be cleaned and sanitized frequently. These panels are available in 4 by 7 foot and 4 by 8 foot sizes and in thicknesses of 1/8 to 1/4 inch. The 1/4 inch panels can be applied directly to studs spaced up to 16 inches on center, provided there is no direct contact with large animals. Thinner panels, wider stud spacing, or animal contact all require a solid backing to provide adequate support.

Panels are usually nailed or glued and nailed in place. Plastic trim strips are available to seal joints between panels and to close both inside and outside corners. To provide an even better seal, these strips can be bedded with silicone caulking as they are installed.

Advantages of plastic coated paneling:

1. Highly cleanable surface.
2. Surface requires no additional finish work.
3. Available in a variety of colors and patterns.

Disadvantages:

1. Relatively high in cost.
2. Panels are brittle and require backing to provide added strength.

Rigid insulations. Both the polystyrene and polyurethane industries manufacture rigid insulation boards with surfacing materials laminated to them. For the most part, these surfaces have been polyethylene coated paper or aluminum foil, although it is possible to obtain panels with heavier metallic surfaces. The main advantage of these materials is that they provide a one step insulation and interior finish application. Since they are applied over the face of the framing members, they also offer a more continuous insulation than do other systems.

Panels are usually available in 4 foot widths and lengths up to 16 feet. They are relatively light in weight and can be easily handled by one man. The plastic foam is easily cut to fit with a knife and the panels are nailed to framing members with large headed nails. The finished surface provides a vapor barrier. Nail holes and joints between panels must be taped to prevent the escape of water vapor.

There has been a considerable controversy between manufacturers and the insurance industry over the use of these panels in any exposed application. Most of them will burn at a rapid rate and produce a heavy toxic gas while doing so. There have been some rather dramatic fire losses in buildings using some of these materials. Recent changes in product formulation have reduced the fire spread ratings considerably. However, you should contact your insurance company before deciding to purchase and install one of these products. Otherwise, you may find yourself with a structure which cannot be insured.

Advantages of rigid insulation:

1. One step insulation and finish.
2. Lightweight, easily installed material.

Disadvantages:

1. Essentially no mechanical strength. This means it must be covered with a more durable finish in areas where exposed to animals or equipment traffic.
2. Problems with insurability.

3. It is difficult to get extremely high levels of insulation needed in buildings requiring supplemental heat.
4. More costly than other insulation-finish systems, especially at higher R values.

FRP panels. Fiberglass reinforced plastic (FRP) provides an interior surface with many of the characteristics of the plastic coated panelings. They also offer much greater strength and a higher impact resistance than some of the other easily cleaned surface covering. Because of this, this material is rapidly replacing asbestos cement board as an interior surface in milking centers and food processing areas.

FRP is available either factory laminated to exterior plywood panels or as a separate covering. The laminated material can be cut with a carbide tipped saw and is nailed or glued and nailed directly to framing members. Corrosion resistant nails should be used in areas exposed to high moisture.

The plain panels are available in thicknesses up to approximately .2 inch and in either cut sheets or rolls up to approximately 9 feet high. Because of its thinness, this material must be applied over a solid backing. Particle board has been satisfactorily used as a backing in milking center construction.

FRP is an inert material not damaged by moisture, cleaning compounds, manure, or acid. In milking centers, it can cover the full wall height and be extended down into the concrete floor, providing a completely cleanable wall surface.

FRP is applied to backing with special fasteners available from the manufacturer. Connectors are used to provide a tight seal at joints and corners. Connectors should be set with silicone caulking for complete water resistance.

Advantages of FRP panels:

1. Cleanable and durable surface.
2. A single panel can be ordered to cover a complete wall in many buildings.
3. Provides a vapor barrier and complete moisture protection for wall components.

Disadvantages:

1. Relatively high cost.

Gypsum board. This panel material is manufactured using a gypsum core surrounded with a paper cover. Although used primarily in residential construction, it can be used for many surfaces in agricultural buildings.

Gypsum board is produced in several thicknesses (3/8, 1/2 and 5/8 inch are the most common ones) and in panels which are 4 feet wide by 8, 10, 12 or 14 feet long.

A primary feature of gypsum board is its high degree of resistance to fire. It is commonly specified and used to construct fire walls and to

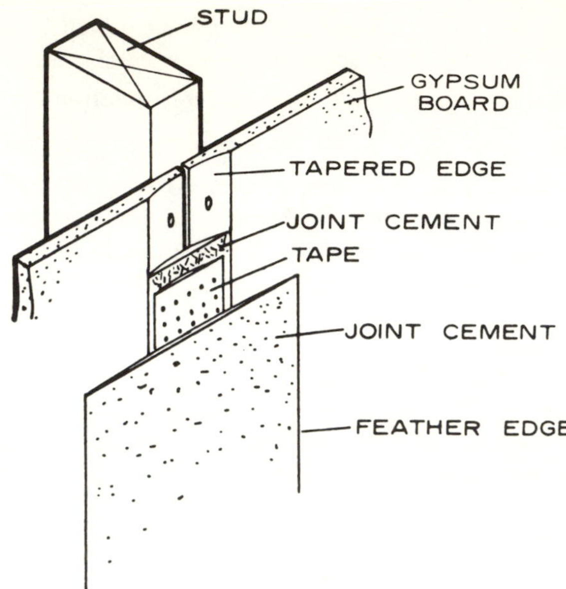

Figure 30-6. Joint finishing method for exterior or interior gypsum board material. Nails are covered with layers of joint cement only. (USDA)

cover exposed surfaces in farm shops and boiler rooms. A special kind of gypsum board known as Type X is specifically designed to give even more fire resistance than the standard board.

Gypsum board is available with a special paper covering which is moisture resistant and rated for use under certain exterior conditions. This is the type which should be used in all agricultural applications except fire wall construction.

Gypsum board is nailed or nailed and glued to framing members spaced up to 24 inches on center. Nails should be ring shank to reduce the incidence of popping and are spaced 6 to 7 inches apart along all framing members when no adhesive is used. Joints between panels and nail heads are covered with a special joint compound, reinforced with a paper tape. Properly applied joint finish results in a completely smooth interior surface. Gypsum board should be protected from moisture in agricultural buildings with at least two coats of a high quality alkyd enamel.

Advantages of gypsum board:

1. Low cost material.
2. Good fire resistance.
3. Easy to install.

Disadvantages:

1. Low structural strength and low resistance to impact. Must be protected in areas of animal contact.
2. Application of joint finish requires some degree of skill.
3. Cannot be used where there is any possibility of prolonged contact with water.

CHAPTER 31

Paints and Caulking

Paints and caulking are often referred to as the carpenter's best friends. When properly applied, they seal and hide minor imperfections in construction and provide a protective coating to resist the effects of weather.

There are literally hundreds of different paints on the market today. Each of these is carefully formulated and manufactured to accommodate a specific application. We can cover some of the basic information on paints; however, when you are ready to buy, there is no substitute for reading and following the label instructions provided by the manufacturer.

All surface coatings, whether they are called paints, stains or varnishes, consist of two components—pigment and vehicle. The pigment is the solid portion of the coating which provides the wearing surface and color. The vehicle is the liquid in which the solids are dissolved. Vehicles are normally made up of a solvent, which evaporates as the paint dries, and resins and oils which help bind together the pigment particles into a solid coat.

One of the basic choices in coating selection is the surface finish desired. Coatings are manufactured in gloss, semi-gloss, and flat finish. The gloss finish provides a slick surface which is easy to wash. It also reflects light and this tends to make any minor surface defects much more visible. At the other extreme, flat finishes hide defects well, but tend to be somewhat softer and are not as easily cleaned.

A good paint job will consist of an application of a primer, followed by one or more finishes or top coats. A primer is designed to accomplish two things. First, it provides a base which is designed to improve the adherence of the top coat. Second, it seals porous surfaces to prevent penetration of the top coat. This insures that the top coat will remain on the surface where it will provide maximum protection. Some paints may be self priming, others require a specific type of primer for different surfaces. It is always a good idea to select a primer and top coat from the same manufacturer in order to reduce the possibility of incompatibility.

Coating Types and Uses

Following is a brief description of several of the more common surface coatings available for use on farm structures.

Oil base paints. These paints use linseed oil and turpentine as the primary ingredients of the vehicle. At one time, lead was the primary pigment ingredient; however, its use has been discontinued by most manufacturers because of toxicity problems. Oil base paints are manufactured for exterior application on wood and composition sidings. Their popularity for other use has diminished greatly due to the development of the alkyd bases.

Alkyd base paints. Alkyd base vehicles are produced by blending vegetable oils with alcohols. Depending on the particular blend used, they can be designed for a wide variety of surface applications. Alkyd base paints are available in primers and top coats for metals, wood, composition materials, and for both interior and exterior application. Most paints manufactured today which are referred to as "oil base" are actually alkyd base paints. Alkyd formulations are not compatible with strong alkali materials. For this reason, they are not acceptable for use on fresh plaster or concrete surfaces.

Latex base paints. These paints are formulated using acrylic or vinyl plastic resins and water as the vehicle. They are also formulated to accommodate a wide range of surfaces. Unlike the alkyds, latex paints can withstand alkaline conditions and are regularly used as primers and top coats for plaster and concrete. Latex paints tend to retain their color well and the "soap and water clean up" feature has made them popular with the occasional painter. Latex paints provide a surface coating which is reasonably permeable to water vapor. This has made them popular as a house paint for homes which have experienced paint failures due to high moisture conditions. This may be a way to reduce a paint failure problem, but should not take the place of a more permanent solution to the moisture problem. Excessive moisture in a structure can do far more harm than paint failure. Latex paints typically do not cover as much area per gallon as do alkyd paints. The difference can be 25% to 50% and should be considered when comparing materials cost.

Urethane. This is a type of plastic which is being used in an increasing number of coating formulations. It provides a surface which is harder and wears better than the alkyd based coatings. Urethane finishes are available in clear or pigmented versions and for interior or exterior applications.

Epoxy paints. This family of coatings cures or hardens due to a chemical reaction rather than by evaporation of solvents from the vehicle. They require a fairly specific temperature range (usually about 70°F) for application. Too cold a temperature results in failure of the paint to properly set; too warm a temperature causes a rapid set which limits the amount of time available for application. Epoxies have been used in agriculture to provide acid resistant, easily cleaned surfaces for milking parlors, feed mangers, and interior surfaces for silage storages. They are usually more expensive than other coatings. They tend to chalk excessively when exposed to sunlight and weather, and some types form a surface which cannot be painted over.

Varnish. Varnish is best described as a paint without a pigment. It relies on the resins included in the vehicle to provide a transparent protective coating. Since is has no pigment to strengthen the surface, varnish does not perform as well as paint under exposure to weather and sunlight. Varnish is primarily intended for use as a finish coating for wood.

Stains. Stains are designed to provide some coloring without completely hiding the grain or texture of the wood they are protecting. They are formulated as transparent, semi-transparent, and opaque, depending on the amount of pigment and surface hiding which is built into them. Stains can be designed to penetrate into the wood surface, providing a more lasting color. Stains do not provide a continuous surface film as do paints. Because of this, they will not last as long under exterior exposure (usually 3 to 5 years as compared to 6 to 8 years). Stains are recommended for use on exterior plywood siding because of its tendency to crack or surface check.

Lacquer. A coating designed for quick drying. Lacquers are available with or without pigment and are normally applied with a sprayer or aerosol can. Lacquers are normally used in factory applied finish operations because of their quick drying feature.

Shellac. A quick drying transparent finish used primarily as a spot sealer to help prevent wood resins contained in knots from bleeding through primers and top coats. Shellac uses an alcohol solvent and is subject to water spotting when used as a finish coating material.

Cement paints. Portland cement can be used as a low cost durable finish for concrete and masonry construction. It must be applied to damp surfaces and properly cured to obtain maximum performance. Cement paint is made by mixing 1 part hydrated lime with 5 parts of portland cement (white cement is usually used). Add enough water to obtain a brushable mixture. Pigments used to color cement can be added, if desired. Add 2 parts of fine sand to the mix if you want to fill in pores of a rough cinder block surface.

Asphalt coatings. These are designed primarily for use as roof coating materials. Some formulas will contain aluminum which floats to the surface and forms a reflective finish which helps keep heat gains to a minimum. Asphalt coatings will break down under exposure to sunlight and usually require renewal every 3 to 4 years.

WRP. Water repellent preservative coatings are usually formulated with paraffin and pentachlorophenol. These transparent finishes are designed to provide limited protection for exposed wood until a more permanent finish can be applied. Millwork manufacturers frequently apply WRP to their products to provide protection during the construction process. *Caution:* Do not use material containing silicone as a temporary protective coating. Silicone coatings cannot be painted over.

Application

Surface coatings can be applied with brushes, sprayers, rollers or pads. The choice is usually based on what the painter is familiar with and the type of surface being coated.

Sprayers, either compressed air or the newer airless units, have the ability to accommodate nearly any type of surface at maximum speed. They do require some thinning of most coating materials and usually use more material for a given job than other application methods. Spraying is best adapted to large surface areas which do not have excessive amounts of trim work.

The brush has been the standard application tool for surface coatings for many years. It adapts well to a variety of surface conditions. Brushes should be selected for the particular material you are using in order to obtain best performance. Many of the natural bristle brushes which give excellent results with oil type paints will not work well with latex base materials. And some of the synthetic bristle materials may dissolve when used in certain solvents used in epoxy paints.

Rollers are adaptable to a wide variety of flat surfaces. When purchasing, select a roller nap length designed for the surface you are painting. Rollers do not adapt well to irregular surfaces such as beveled or board and batten siding.

Pads are a sponge material covered with a short nap designed for painting flat surfaces which are relatively smooth. They do not work well on rough surfaces such as concrete blocks.

Painting new wood.

1. Apply WRP to all surfaces before priming. WRP should dry for at least two full days before additional coatings are applied.
2. Apply primer in a layer thick enough to cover the grain of the wood. Primer should be selected according to the top coat which you are planning to use.

3. For maximum life, use two top coats over the primer. A single top coat will last approximately 3 years on an exposed surface, the second coat can extend the life of the paint job for up to 8 to 10 years.

Repainting wood.

Wood needs repainting when the existing coating has weathered to the point where wood fibers are starting to be exposed.

1. Use a scraper or sander to remove any loose paint.
2. Wash the entire surface with a solution of Trisodium Phosphate (TSP) and water to remove loose dirt, paint chalk and any mildew. Rinse thoroughly with water after washing.
3. Spot prime any bare wood with a primer compatible with the top coat selected.
4. Apply two top coats.

Painting iron and steel.

1. For new material, remove oil or mill finish using a solvent designed to prepare new metal for painting.
2. Remove any loose rust or welding slag with a wire brush.
3. On previously painted metal, brush or scrape off any loose paint and roughen the surface of the remaining paint to help improve the adherence of the new paint.
4. Prime with a material designed for metal use.
5. Apply two top coats.

Painting galvanized steel.

Galvanized steel should be painted before it has weathered to the point where rust is starting to appear.

1. If the galvanized surface has not been exposed to weathering for at least 6 to 12 months, treat the surface with a pre-primer to remove mill oil and prepare the surface for painting.
2. Apply a metallic zinc primer coat.
3. Apply one or two top coats of a metallic zinc dust paint. It can be used as both a primer and a top coat.
4. If a different color is desired, use a good quality exterior paint as the final top coating.

Painting aluminum.

1. Wash down bare aluminum with a solvent and rinse thoroughly.
2. Prime with a zinc based primer.
3. Top coat with 2 coats of paint designed for application to metal surfaces.
4. For repainting prefinished aluminum siding, sand glossy areas to

improve paint adhesion, then proceed with steps 1 through 3 above.

Painting masonry.

1. Clean surfaces thoroughly using a stiff wire brush and a solution of TSP and water. If the paint manufacturer requires an etched surface, wash with a solution of 1 part muriatic acid to 6 to 10 parts water before using the TSP solution. *Caution:* When mixing water and acid, always add acid to the water, never water to the acid. Rinse well after using the TSP.
2. Patch any cracks or defects in the surface with mortar.
3. Apply primer and/or top coats in accordance with manufacturer's instructions for the type of paint you are using. If you are using an epoxy paint with a specific temperature requirement, the concrete surface temperature (not necessarily the air temperature) must be within the specified ranges.

Paint Problems and Their Causes

Many paint problems are the result of poor application techniques or failure to read and follow the manufacturer's instructions for his product. Others are the result of basic problems within the building itself.

Blistering and peeling. Well over 90% of the blistering and peeling problems are caused by excessive moisture in the wood or composition material on which the paint is installed. Outside water may be leaking into the wall or a poor vapor barrier may be allowing moisture from inside to penetrate and condense within the wall.

Blistering and peeling caused by moisture is prevented by eliminating the moisture source. Make sure all wall openings are properly flashed and that there are no roof leaks. Crawl spaces should be covered with a plastic vapor barrier to keep ground moisture from moving up into the structure. If the building does not have an adequate vapor barrier, the interior surface of all outside walls should be painted with a good vapor resistant paint.

Cross grain cracking. Usually caused by too thick a paint layer on the structure. After many years and many coats of paint, the paint layer becomes so thick and brittle that it no longer can withstand the normal expansion and contraction of the base material and it develops cracks. This problem is prevented by waiting until each layer of paint is nearly worn away before repainting. For a structure that already has cross grain cracking, all paint must be removed back to bare wood in order to solve the problem.

Mildew. Mildew is a dark colored fungus growth which occurs on the surface of paint. The mildew fungus requires a warm, moist place with an adequate food supply in order to exist. Many of the commonly used paints provide a good food supply for mildew. It is usually found in areas which do not dry rapidly following a heavy dew or rain. Common locations are under roof overhangs, behind foundation plantings, and in the shade of a porch or large tree. Mildew can be removed by scrubbing with a solution of TSP and water. Pruning shrubbery or anything else which will speed up evaporation of surface moisture will help prevent mildew. Use of a mildew resistant paint or paint additive will help prevent its growth.

Intercoat peeling. This is peeling of one or more layers of paint due to poor adhesion with the existing paint layer. It is usually caused by poor surface preparation or an incompatibility between paint types. Using primers and top coats from the same manufacturer will help prevent intercoat failures. After failure has occurred, there is little that can be done except to remove the peeling layer of paint and start over again. Repainting without removing the offending layer will be a waste of time and money.

Excessive chalking. Most exterior paints are designed to chalk or wear away at a slow uniform rate. This chalking helps keep the paint surface clean and improves the overall appearance of the structure. Occasionally a paint will chalk too rapidly, leading to streaking or discoloration. This is usually due to either poor quality paint or excessive thinning of the paint.

Caulking

Caulking material is designed to fill in cracks or other small openings which are too large for paint to bridge over and seal. The maximum size of a crack which caulking can seal is generally considered to be about ¼ inch wide.

Caulking is commonly used in the following locations to provide a weather resistant seal.

1. Around window openings.
2. Where changes in siding material occur (i.e., between bricks and wood siding).
3. Where water or electrical lines penetrate the structure.
4. Around and over door framing.
5. Joints between walls and floor.

Caulks should be selected on the basis of weather resistance, flexibility, and paintability. Caulking is sold in cans for use in hand or air powered caulking guns and in cartridge type tubes for use in open frame type guns.

Oil base. This is the lowest price and poorest quality caulking material. It will give only a few years service at best before it will dry out and pull away from the cracks it is supposed to be filling.

Latex. One step above the oil base materials, the latex caulks are probably the most widely used caulking compounds today. They are easy to use, non toxic, and residue can be cleaned up with soap and water. There are several types of latex caulking on the market today. The best quality is obtained with acrylic latex materials.

Butyl rubber. This material is a relatively low cost, flexible caulking material which does not lose its flexibility during curing. It is priced about the same as high quality acrylic latex caulks. It is not as good as some of the more expensive materials for joints which are subject to movement.

Polysulphide rubber. A high quality and high performance flexible caulking designed for the professional user.

Silicone rubber. Excellent quality flexible caulking that is widely available and relatively easy to use. It cures by a chemical reaction with moisture in the air. Silicone gives the best long time performance of all the caulking materials. It is fairly expensive and some types cannot be painted over. They have attempted to get around the paintability problem by manufacturing the silicone in several different colors.

CHAPTER 32

Plastics

Man-made plastics are without question the most versatile materials used in the construction industry today. Plastics are used as roofing, flooring, insulation, vapor barriers, water lines, and even for plumbing fixtures. They have gained this widespread usage and acceptance primarily because they have been able to adapt to a wide variety of working conditions at an economical price.

Types of Plastics

There are two types of plastics used in construction. They are known as thermoplastics and thermosets. Thermoplastics soften when they are heated and harden up again when they are cooled. Their strength is temperature dependent and they can be worked or reworked and formed many times. Polyethylene (PE) and Polyvinyl Chloride (PVC) are the two most commonly used thermoplastics in construction. Thermoset plastics do not soften when heated. Once they are shaped and set, they cannot be reworked. Melamine plastic paneling is an example of a thermoset material.

Additives

The plastics industry uses a variety of different additives to improve or change the characteristics of a particular plastic to meet the needs of its intended use.

Fillers. Additives used to extend or dilute the plastic material. Unless they are used to excess, fillers normally do not affect the basic properties of the parent plastic material.

Reinforcing. Plastic by itself is not a particularly strong material. How-

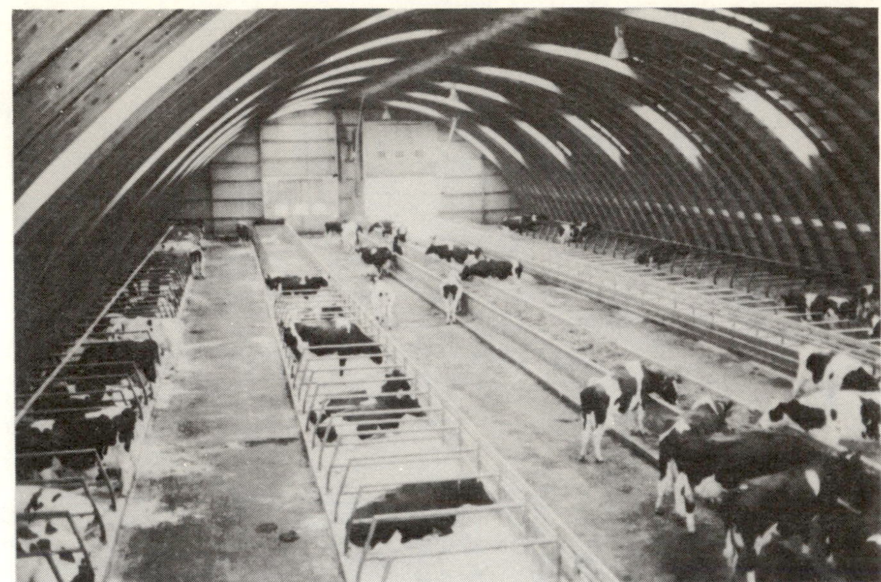

Figure 32-1. Fiberglass-reinforced plastic panels located in the roof of this gothic arched roof dairy building provide all the light that is needed during daylight hours. A total panel area of 8 to 10 percent of the floor area is adequate to provide this illumination level.

ever, by adding reinforcing to it, a material which approaches the strength of steel can be obtained. The most commonly used reinforcing is glass fiber and the product obtained is known as fiber glass reinforced plastic or (FRP). Glass fibers increase the stiffness, impact resistance, strength and overall stability of plastic. FRP panels are most often used as skylights in pole frame buildings and as interior lining materials in milking centers.

Flame retardants. One of the undesirable features of plastic is that most types burn easily and produce large quantities of toxic gas when they do burn. Chemicals which retard the spread of fire are frequently added to plastics used in building materials in order to obtain products which meet building code requirements. Most frequently added materials contain antimony, bromine, chlorine, nitrogen, phosphorus, or boron.

Kinds of Plastics

There are nearly 50 different families of plastics produced today and each of these families may have dozens of variations within it. And, more are being developed every day. Some of the plastics which are frequently found in construction are described in the following paragraphs.

Acrylonitrite-butadine-styrene (ABS). This material is a relatively low cost plastic with good strength and impact properties. It is easily worked and can be glued or solvent welded. Construction uses include waste and vent pipes for plumbing.

Acetal copolymers. Good resistance to heat, organic solvents, inorganic salts, lubricants, and hot air. Used in plumbing components.

Methyl methacrylate polymers (acrylics). These plastics have good transparency and high resistance to yellowing or discoloration. They have extremely high coefficients of thermal expansion (this means they expand and contract quite a bit with changes in temperature). They can be softened or dissolved by alcohols and strong solvents. Acrylics have been widely used in the formulation of paints. Acrylic glazing panels are now being used in solar collectors.

Urea formaldehyde and melamine formaldehyde (amino resins). These materials are frequently molded into specific products or shapes. They are thermoset plastics. Melamine is used in wall paneling and in adhesives for particle board and plywood. Urea based products are frequently used for electrical wiring components.

Epoxy. This family of plastics is widely used in the manufacture of adhesives, surface coatings, and in construction of electrical devices.

Perfluoroalkoxy (PFA). Known more generally as teflon, this material has good chemical resistance and anti-stick properties. It is also able to perform under wide temperature extremes and has good flammability resistance. It is used for electrical wire insulation, and for corrosion resistant linings in pumps and plumbing fittings.

Phenolic resins. This family of thermosets is used as adhesive and in fabrication of molded products. They frequently contain a large percentage of filler material. Common usage includes plywood and particle board glue, electrical plugs, and paneling.

Polyethylene (PE). PE is manufactured in three different densities. Chemical resistance, toughness, and strength are achieved with additives. Clear polyethylene (no additives) has poor resistance to ultra violet light. PE is used for cold water pipe, foundation drain pipe, vapor barrier material, and as a covering for greenhouses. It is the most economical of the plastics.

Polyvinyl. Thermoplastic material made from vinyl chloride (PVC), vinyl acetate, or vinylidene chloride. These low cost materials can be modified to give high strength, flame resistance, and good weatherability. It is commonly used for hot and cold water supply lines, drainage systems, and for electrical conduit.

Urethane. Depending on its particular formulation, urethane can be used to make machine parts, cushioning for the furniture industry, or lightweight rigid insulation. In agricultural construction, insulation has been its most popular application. Urethane is frequently foamed using freon or another inert gas, which increases its insulating value slightly. However, over long periods of time this gas tends to leak out, reducing the overall R-value of the insulation. Even so, urethane is one of the best insulating materials available today.

Polystyrene. Polystyrene can also be manufactured in a variety of densities for different applications. It too, has become popular in construction as a lightweight water resistant insulation.

CHAPTER **33**

Fasteners for Wood Construction

Most builders and contractors, and even some designers, spend a considerable amount of time selecting the right size and quality of lumber for a particular location, and relatively little time worrying about fasteners. A structural assembly is no stronger than its weakest link and this lack of attention usually results in the joints or connectors being the weakest link in a wooden building. In fact, looking back over our experiences during the past 20 years, well over 90% of all the building failures we have observed were the direct result of failure to use enough fasteners or the right fasteners for the job.

Fastening Strength

For any particular type of fastener, there are a number of factors which influence just how much load it can carry or transfer from one member to another. It is important to have a general understanding of these factors both from the standpoint of initial construction and in order to have a general idea of what causes failure.

Moisture content. In general, the higher the moisture content of the wood, the less an individual fastener will hold. Test results have shown that nails driven into green or wet wood develop nearly the same strength as they would in dry wood, as long as the wood remains green or wet. However, as wood dries out, it tends to shrink away from the nails, reducing the load carrying ability. Nails used in wood subjected to repeated wetting and drying may have a holding capacity that is only 25% of what they would hold in dry wood.

Moisture can also lead to corrosion of metal fasteners. A building which has withstood design loadings for many years may suddenly fail because metal fasteners used in its construction have gradually rusted away.

Direction of load. Wood is much stronger when loads are applied along the grain than it is when loaded across the grain. Since fasteners transfer load directly to the wood, direction has a major effect on how much the individual fastener can be expected to hold.

Density. The heavy dense hardwoods will grip or hold fasteners more securely and have greater internal or compressive strength than the lighter weight woods. This property is measured in terms of specific gravity and woods have been classified into four groups based on their density. The lower the group number, the better the fastener holding ability.

Table 33-1. **Grouping of Selected Woods According to Their Ability to Withstand Fastener Loadings**

Group	Typical Species
I	White Ash, Yellow Birch, Hickory, Sugar Maple, Red and White Oak
II	Douglas Fir and Larch, Southern Yellow Pine
III	Dense Redwood, Hemlock, Northern Pine, Spruce, Cypress
IV	Balsam Fir, Cedar, White Pine

Duration of load. Wood's ability to withstand high loads for short periods of time and lesser loads for long periods also holds true for fasteners. Allowable design loads for wood fasteners are based on an expected load duration of 10 years.

Defects. Splits, checks, and knots all have a negative effect on the ability of wood fasteners to transfer load. Wood used for critical structural members in a building should be selected so that fasteners can be located in areas relatively free of defects.

Nails

Nails are by far the most commonly used mechanical fastener in wood construction. They are available in a wide variety of sizes, shapes and materials designed to meet almost any type of loading or exposure conditions. Types of nails generally used in farm construction include:

Common. This is a general purpose wire nail used in framing.

Box. Similar to the common nail except that they have a smaller diameter. This is helpful when nailing wood which has a tendency to split. Box nails are generally used to fasten wall sheathing, subflooring, and roof decking.

Spikes. Similar to common nails except for a larger diameter. Spikes

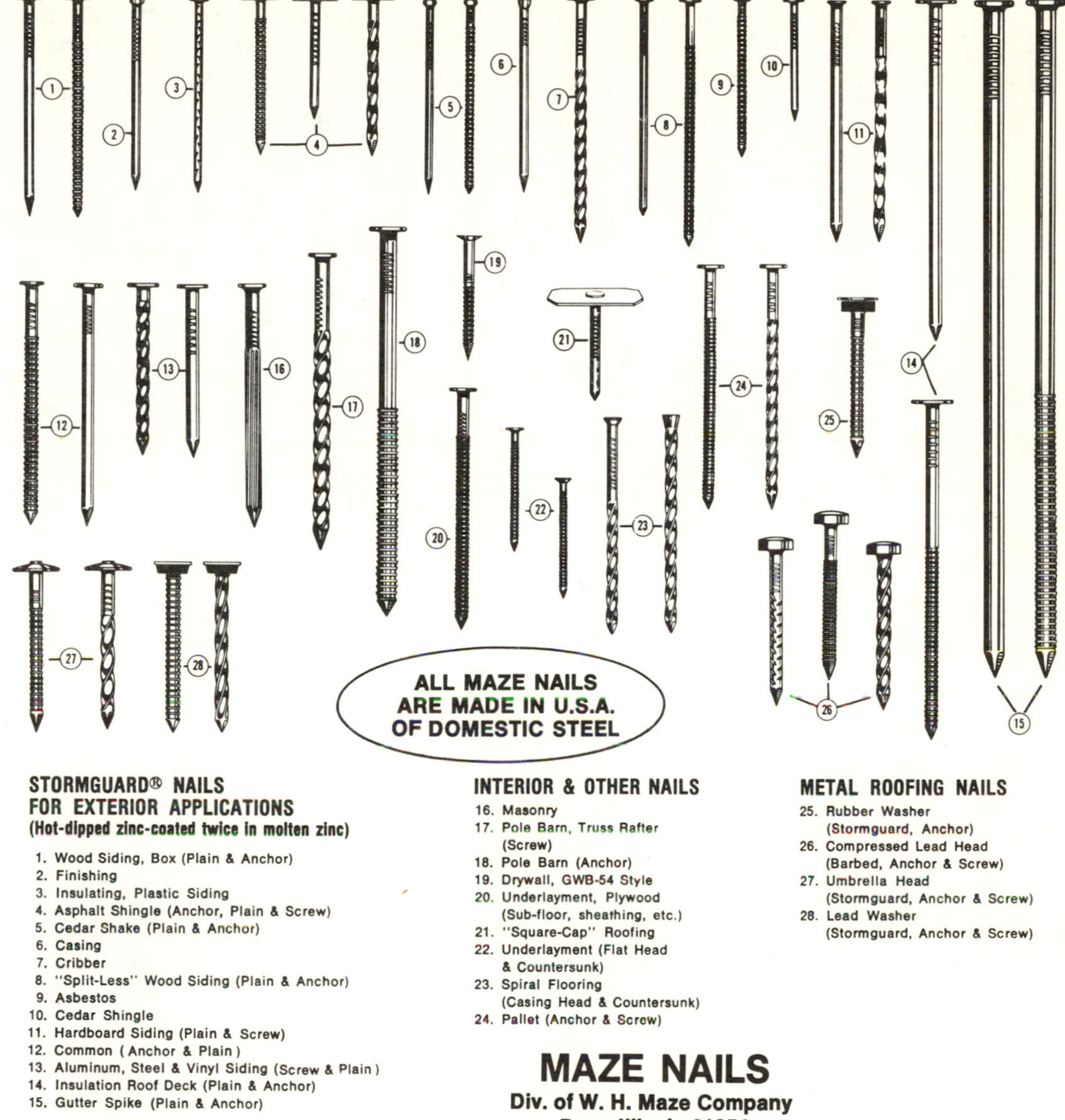

Figure 33-1. Several of the wide variety of nails available for use in the farm construction industry. (W. H. Maze Company)

are available in sizes from 10 penny up. They are used in fabrication of heavy structural members such as laminated girders and in girder to pole connections.

Deformed shank nails. Sometimes referred to as "pole barn nails," these fasteners have either ringed or threaded shank portions which improve their holding ability. They are often used to secure framing members to treated poles or posts because their increased withdrawal resistance helps offset the lubricating effect of the oil used with some preservatives.

Casing or finish nails. These fasteners have a small diameter shank and a small head which can be easily countersunk for interior finish work.

Most nails are sized by the penny (abbreviated as "d"), a term which has little relationship to either size or cost of the particular nail. Table 33-2 lists sizes for different penny sized nails. Specialty nails such as roofing nails and large spikes are usually sized in terms of their actual length.

Table 33-2. **Actual Sizes for Nails**

Penny Size	Length	Diameter in Inches				Nails
(d)	(In.)	Common	Box	Spike	Deformed Shank	per Lb
6	2	.113	.098	—	.12	150
8	2.5	.131	.113	—	.12	106
10	3	.148	.128	.192	.135	70
12	3.25	.148	.135	.192	.135	65
16	3.5	.162	.135	.207	.148	50
20	4	.192	.148	.225	.177	31
30	4.5	.207	—	.244	.177	24
40	5	.225	—	.263	.177	18
50	5.5	.244	—	.283	.177	14
60	6	.262	—	—	.177	11

The load carrying capacity of nails is specified in terms of direction (either lateral or withdrawal), nail size and type, and the species or group of the wood being fastened. In general, the larger the diameter, the greater the lateral load carrying ability. Withdrawal resistance increases both with increased diameter and increased penetration.

It should be pointed out that loads shown in Tables 33-3 and 33-4 are the design loads allowable for long time loading, not how much a particular nail will hold at the time it is initially driven. Initial load capacity is always higher than the tabulated loads.

Some nails are coated with material to improve their withdrawal

Table 33-3. **Allowable Lateral Design Loads for Nails***

Nail	Lateral Design Load Allowed in Lbs			
Size	Group I Species	Group II Species	Group III Species	Group IV Species
6d	77	63	51	41
8d	97	78	64	51
10 & 12d	116	94	77	62
16d	132	107	88	70
20d	171	139	113	91
30d	191	154	126	101
40d	218	176	144	116
60d	276	223	182	146

**Point of nail must penetrate the second piece of wood to a depth equal to 10 to 14 times the nail diameter in order to develop maximum load carrying ability.*

Table 33-4. **Withdrawal Design Loads in Lbs per Inch of Penetration in Side Grain of Seasoned Wood**

Wood Species	Common Nails				Deformed Shank Nails*		Spikes				
Group	8d	12d	16d	20d	30-60d	70-90d	12d	16d	20d	40d	60d
I	64	72	79	94	94	110	94	101	110	128	138
II	39	44	49	57	57	67	57	61	67	79	84
III	21	23	25	30	30	35	30	33	35	41	45
IV	16	18	20	24	24	28	24	25	28	32	35

**Values for smaller deformed shank nails are the same as common nail values.*

resistance. Most of these coatings lose much of their effectiveness after 1 or 2 months of service. For this reason, coated nails are generally recommended only for rough service, short-lived items such as packing crates or pallets.

There are several standard construction practices which help improve the load carrying ability of a nailed joint.

1. Drive nails at an angle rather than straight through one piece into the next.
2. Use a longer nail and drive it through and clinch across the grain rather than along or parallel to it.
3. Use toenailing to fasten ends of framing to headers or sills rather than nailing through the header into end grain.
4. Use as large a nail as possible without causing excessive splitting.

Screws

Screws have not been a popular fastener for construction of farm buildings, mainly because of the extra labor involved. Recently, however, new types

Table 33-5. **Selection and Usage of Common Nails in Farm Construction**

Connection	Number and Size of Nail
Toenailing joist to sill	3-8d
Nailing 1x6 subflooring	2-8d at each joist
Plate to joist or sill	16d every 16 in.
Toenailing studs to plate	4-8d
Double plate-fastening together	16d every 16 in.
Fabricated header	16d every 16 in. on each edge
Ceiling joist to plate toenail	3-8d
Ceiling joist lap joint	3-16d
Rafter to plate-toenail	3-8d
1 inch diagonal bracing	2-8d
Built up beams	20d-every 32 in. on each edge
Purlins to rafters (2x4 flat)	2-10d at each rafter
Purlins to rafters (2x4 on edge)	1-50d at each rafter
Sidewall grits to posts (2x4)	2-16d at each post
Sidewall grits to posts (2x6)	3-16d at each post

of self tapping screws which can be driven with electric or air powered machines have become popular for fastening metal roofing and siding to wood support members. These self tapping screws usually have a hexagonal head to facilitate power driving and a neoprene rubber washer to seal the underside of the head against the metal.

Screws have a much better withdrawal resistance than do nails. This has led directly to their superior performance in fastening roof coverings, particularly when purlin material is green or wet at the time of installation.

Bolts

Bolts are sometimes used as fasteners, particularly in joints where larger sized members are being fastened together. The strength of a bolted joint is almost always limited by the ability of the particular wood to resist crushing or failure due to direct loading by the bolt. Bolted joints should be designed by someone familiar with wood types and bolt strengths. Design information can be obtained in the ''National Design Specification for Wood Construction'' published by the National Forest Products Association.

General recommendations concerning bolted joints include the folowing.

1. Center to center distance between bolts resisting a load parallel to the grain should be at least four times bolt diameter.
2. For a joint in tension, the bolt nearest the end of the wood piece should be at least seven times the bolt diameter for softwoods or five times the bolt diameter for hardwoods, away from the end.
3. Joints in compression may have bolts located as close as four times the bolt diameter from the end of the piece.
4. For joints loaded parallel to the wood grain, bolts should be a minimum of 1.5 times the bolt diameter from the edge of the piece.

The strength of a bolted joint is affected to a large extent by the size and quality of the bolt holes drilled in the wooden members. A hole that is too large prevents the bolt from transferring load uniformly to the wooden member. Too small a hole can lead to splitting of the wood when the bolt is driven. Bolt holes should be sized so that bolts can be inserted with a slight amount of tapping with a wooden mallet. Rough holes caused by a dull bit or too rapid a feed rate also prevent uniform transfer of load.

Metal rings known as timber connectors are sometimes used to improve the load carrying capacity of a bolted joint. These connectors are designed to transfer most of the joint load between members. The bolt in a connector joint serves mainly to hold the pieces together and keep the connector in place. Connectors usually require a special tool to cut the groove in which they fit.

Figure 33-2. Formed sheet metal truss plates used to assemble prefabricated trusses. These plates are usually pressed into the wood using rollers or hydraulic presses specified by the manufacturer of the plates.

Metal Connectors

Two types of connectors fabricated from sheet metal are widely used in the farm construction industry. They are the truss plate connector and the framing anchor. Both are usually constructed of zinc plated (galvanized) steel to improve their service life under moist conditions.

Truss plates are made by several manufacturers and are fabricated with a series of teeth designed so that they can be pressed into the wood framing members the plate is connecting. Truss plates are generally available only to truss fabricators who are licensed by the plate manufacturer. The fabricator purchases the plates and uses them in conjunction with locally purchased lumber to assemble trusses. The manufacturer usually provides the fabricator with a series of standard truss designs as well as an engineering service to accommodate any unusual applications.

Framing anchors are sheet metal brackets available in several shapes which are intended to increase the strength of a joint beyond what is possible with conventional types. These, along with their applications, are illustrated in Figure 33-3.

Glue

Glue is a commonly used fastener for wood members which are fabricated

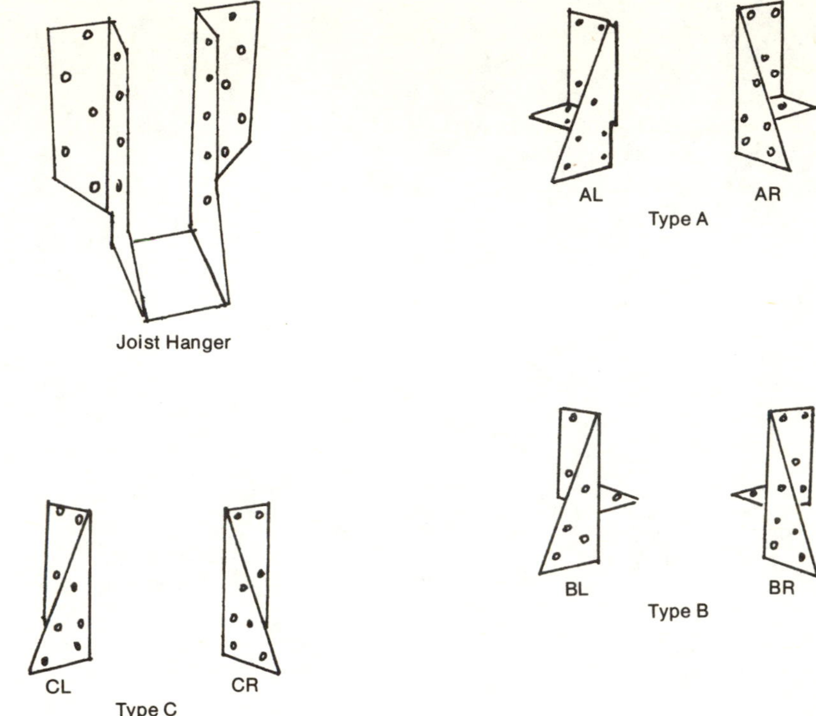

Figure 33-3. The framing anchors illustrated are constructed of galvanized sheet metal and can be used to meet a variety of hold-down or fastening needs in farm construction.

under factory conditions. Glue holds together plywood, laminated beams, and many of the prefabricated mill work components used in building. It provides a strong, lightweight, and durable fastener—provided it is properly selected, applied and cured.

A good glue joint will be stronger than the wood itself. In fact, when a glued assembly fails, it is normally the wood next to the joint which fails, and not the wood itself. In order to insure maximum performance from a glued joint, several conditions must be met.

1. Wood must be dry (less than 15% moisture), free of dirt, oil, or any other coatings.
2. Joints must be well made so that wood members to be glued fit together well.
3. Treated wood must be cleaned of all surface oil or residue before gluing.
4. Temperatures must be well above freezing, and preferably above 70° before using glue.
5. Glue must be mixed, spread and clamped in strict accordance with the manufacturer's instructions.

Farm construction generally requires a glue that is either moisture resistant or completely waterproof. Other characteristics which may be important for a particular job include cost, gap filling ability, pressure requirements for cure, working life of mixed glue, and color of the glue line. The two types of glue usually recommended for farm construction are resorcinol resin and casein.

Resorcinol resin glue comes as a powder, mixes with a special hardener and is applied at room temperature. Joints can be clamped with nails using one nail for each 8 square inches of glue area. It has a dark colored glue line and most kinds require temperature above 70° for proper curing. It will fill small gaps between joint members and is extremely moisture resistant.

Casein glue is an animal protein type glue which is mixed with water and applied at room temperature. It provides a colorless glue line with only medium resistance to moisture. It is usually less expensive than resorcinol glue.

Construction Adhesives

A large number of adhesives are now available to meet construction needs for on the job assembly of components. Adhesives are used to secure subflooring to joists, attach gypsum board, and fasten decorative wall paneling. These adhesives do not set up rapidly, retain some flexibility when cured, and are often waterproof or highly water resistant. These adhesives do not completely eliminate the use of nails, but do reduce nailing to a minimum in many applications. They usually result in increased rigidity for the overall structure and can help eliminate such annoyances as squeaking floors. Construction adhesives are usually packaged in dispenser type tubes which fit standard open frame caulking guns.

Part V

Environmental Control

CHAPTER **34**

Insulation

The most important single element in the environmental control system for a farm building is insulation. Insulation is defined as any material that reduces the rate at which heat is transferred from one area to another. Nearly all building materials have some insulating value; however, the term insulation is usually reserved for those materials which have a relatively high resistance to heat flow. Typically these materials are light in weight and contain large numbers of dead air spaces within them.

Heat is transferred from one location to another by conduction, convection and radiation, either singly or in any combination. Conducted heat passes from one place to another by warming the material that separates a warm area from a cold area. Convected heat is transmitted by a moving fluid such as circulating air. Radiation involves the passage of heat through a space without warming the space. A good example of heat transfer by radiation is the energy we get from the sun.

The driving force for all heat transfer is temperature. Heat always flows from warm places to cooler ones. The greater the temperature difference, the greater the heat flow will be.

Why Insulate?

Insulation has several functions in a farm building. First, it helps conserve heat during periods of cold weather. Conservation of animal or bird body heat is necessary to maintain desirable housing conditions. Second, insulation helps reduce the rate of heat gain during hot weather. The temperature of exterior building surfaces can be as much as 50° F above outside temperatures on a warm sunny summer day. Insulation helps prevent this heat from reaching the area where animals are housed.

Insulation helps control interior surface temperatures. Slowing the rate of heat flow through the wall and ceiling areas helps keep interior surfaces warmer during winter months. Warmer surfaces help prevent the

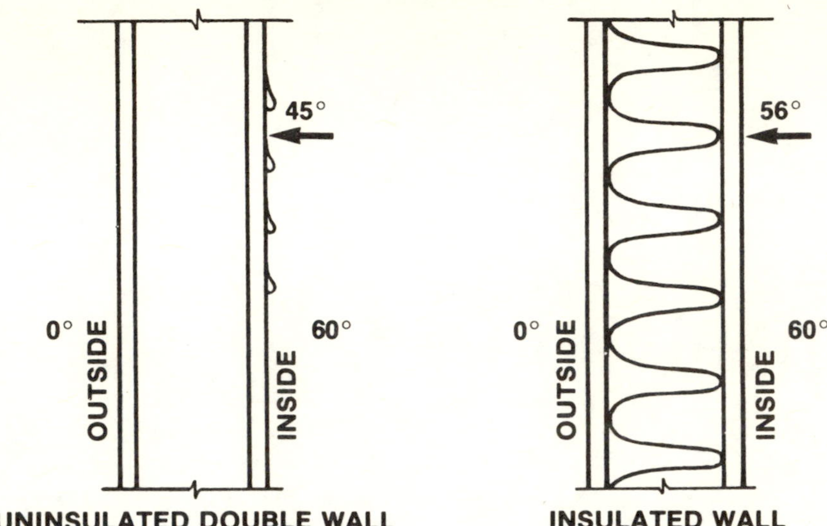

Figure 34-1. In the high-moisture environment of a livestock housing unit, cold walls mean condensation during cold winter weather. Insulation helps keep walls warm and reduces the incidence of condensation, as illustrated here. (Purdue University)

formation of condensation (either water or frost). They also improve the interior comfort level for animals housed within the building.

Finally, insulation is an investment which will pay a high rate of return for the entire life of the structure. In many types of buildings, insulation will save enough body heat to eliminate the need for purchasing supplemental heating. In others, it will reduce fuel costs enough to completely pay for itself within 2 to 3 years.

Types of Insulation and Use

The most common types of insulation are bulky, porous, lightweight materials with countless air spaces. The heavier and denser a material is, the poorer its insulating properties are. Generally, the more air spaces in a material, the better it insulates. Some building materials such as wood are good insulators; others such as concrete and metal are very poor insulators.

Manufactured insulation can be purchased in several forms. Answering the following questions will help you determine the best type for your job.

1. How is it to be used? Is it purely for insulation purposes or does it need to have some structural qualities?
2. How adaptable is it to the particular use?
3. What is its relative cost?
4. Can it be installed easily?

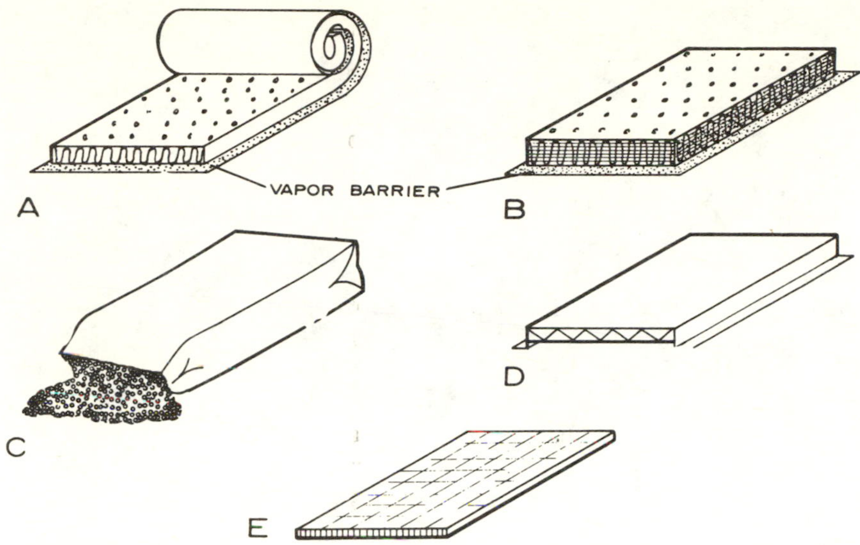

Figure 34-2. It makes no difference what kind of insulation you use provided it is installed properly. The important thing is to achieve the recommended "R" value. Illustrated are: (A) blanket, (B) batt, (C) loose fill, (D) reflective foil (not recommended for agricultural usage), and (E) rigid board type. (USDA)

Loose fill. This type of insulation is especially adaptable for use in buildings with flat ceilings and an overhead access space. It is usually installed by blowing it into place with a small blower and a vacuum cleaner sized hose. Care must be taken to avoid excessive settling if fill insulation is used in sidewalls.

Loose fill is packaged in paper bags and is made from a variety of materials. Most common types are fiber glass, rock wool, cellulose, vermiculite, and granulated cork. Loose fill is normally the least expensive insulating material in terms of cost per unit of insulating value. It must be protected from moisture with an adequate vapor barrier.

Batts or blankets. This form of insulation is the most economical for use in sidewalls of farm buildings. The most commonly found materials in batt insulation are fiber glass and rock wool. Batts do not have the tendency to settle over time as does fill insulation. Batts must be protected from moisture and physical contact by animals.

Batts and blankets are available in thicknesses from 1 to 8 inches and in widths to fit 16, 24, and 48 inch spacing of framing members. They come either as plain batts or rolls, with or without attached vapor barriers.

Insulation board. This material is typically made of wood by-products or some other cellulose type material. It has some physical strength as well as insulating ability and is frequently used as sheathing in conventional stud frame buildings. For use in livestock buildings, it must be treated to resist moisture.

Figure 34-3. Fill type insulation is easily applied when the building is nearly complete by using a blower and hose system to distribute material.

Some insulation boards are available with a vapor barrier on one side. Insulation board must be protected from physical damage if used in an area accessible to animals or birds. Follow the manufacturer's recommendations for installing on spaced supports in a ceiling, roof or wall.

Joints should be covered with a vapor proof tape to prevent moisture from penetrating to other building components when insulation board is used for interior lining. The most common use for insulating board in farm buildings is for insulation under metal roofing. The board is placed directly over roof purlins and under the metal roofing. It reduces summer heat gains and helps control condensation during the winter.

Rigid insulation. Rigid material is needed in applications where insulation must be able to withstand some load conditions. Typical applications include perimeter insulation for concrete foundations, under slab insulation for buildings with heated floors, and roof decking for flat or built up roofs. Rigid insulations are also gaining rapid acceptance for use as sheathing for sidewalls of buildings which require supplemental heat.

Materials used to make rigid insulations include expanded polystyrene and polyurethane, foam glass, and asphalt impregnated materials.

Reflective insulation. Made from metallic foil, this insulation is highly efficient in resisting downward flow of heat and radiant heat. It is effective in keeping out summer heat and allows the interior of the building to cool rapidly at night. Foil insulation is not a good choice for winter insulation in farm buildings. Reflective material loses its insulating value rapidly when covered with dust or corrosion.

Foam in place materials. These are made by foaming organic materials

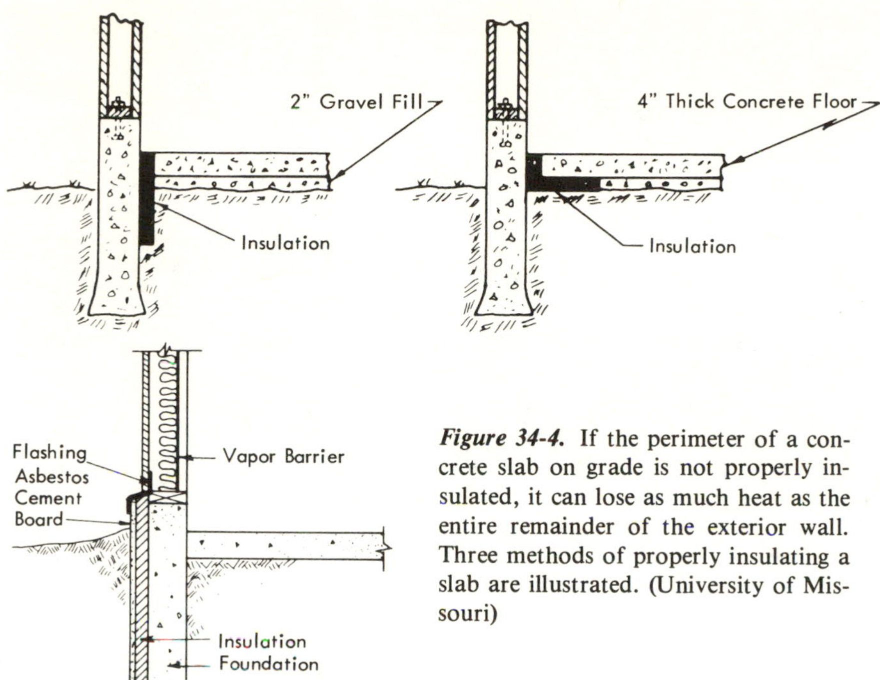

Figure 34-4. If the perimeter of a concrete slab on grade is not properly insulated, it can lose as much heat as the entire remainder of the exterior wall. Three methods of properly insulating a slab are illustrated. (University of Missouri)

with air or inert gasses. Polystyrene, polyurethane, and urea-formaldehyde compounds are usually used. Foams may or may not have good moisture resistance, depending on their cellular structure. Open celled foams such as the urea formaldehyde types should not be used without a protective vapor barrier. Closed cell foams such as polystyrene and urethane are sufficiently resistant to water vapor to eliminate the need for a vapor barrier.

Some foams can be sprayed directly on interior or exterior surfaces of buildings to form a continuous and complete insulating layer. If used on the exterior, a weatherproof coating is sprayed on over the foam to protect it from sunlight and precipitation.

Foams produce large amounts of toxic gas and heavy smoke when they burn. Some will also burn at a very rapid rate. For these reasons, many insurance companies are reluctant to provide coverage for buildings insulated with foam unless they are adequately protected with a fire resistant coating.

Foams are generally the most expensive of the common insulating materials.

Lightweight concrete. Concrete additives are sometimes used as a means of increasing the insulating value while retaining the desirable features of concrete construction. Some materials (expanded shale or mica, ground corncobs, and wood shavings) when substituted for some of the concrete aggregates will increase insulation value, but at a considerable reduction in strength. At present, no additive has been able to improve insulating value of concrete without this reduction in strength.

Insulation Ratings

Insulation, as well as other building materials, can be rated according to its ability to resist the flow of heat. This rating is commonly referred to as the R-value. The R-values for several insulations and building materials are listed in Table 34-1. The R-value may be given per inch of thickness, or for the total thickness of a material.

R-value is an additive property; 2 inches will have twice the value of one inch. Also, individual R-values for all the materials in a given section of a structure can be added together to obtain a total R-value.

Several years ago, most insulation materials were either rock wool or fiber glass. These two materials have similar insulating ability and it became common practice to specify insulation in terms of inches of thickness. Today, there are many different insulations on the market, each with its own characteristics. The R-value measure was developed as the only way to fairly compare the insulating abilities of one material with another.

Some insulation manufacturers quote R-values for their products on an installed basis. This allows them to include insulation values for other assumed components of the wall, ceiling, or floor and provides a higher total value for their product. Make sure you are comparing R-values for insulation only when you start comparing products. If the material has different R-values quoted for its use in wall, ceiling and floor, it is being quoted on an installed basis.

Other commonly used measures of insulating value are "K," "C," and "U" values. The K value gives the amount of heat (British Thermal Units—Btu) per hour which will pass through a piece of material one inch thick and 1 foot square when the temperature difference between the two sides is 1°F. The C value is similar to K, except it is given for the total thickness of material, not just for a 1 inch thickness. For example, a K value for fiber glass insulation of .27 would be equal to a U value of .09 for a 3 inch thick batt. The U value (overall coefficient of heat transfer) is the amount of heat in Btus that will pass through a complete wall, ceiling, or floor section, one foot square, in one hour with a temperature difference of 1°F. U value is equivalent to 1 ÷ R-value. K, C, and U values are primarily used in engineering design calculations and are of little use to the general public.

Recommended Levels of Insulation

The proper amount of insulation for a building is purely an economic decision. The cost of insulation is balanced against the cost of purchased energy to arrive at an optimum level. The answer will depend on building type and use, occupancy level, price of supplemental heat or cooling

Table 34-1. **R-values for Commonly Used Insulation and Building Materials**

Material	Thickness (Inches)	R-Value
Insulation		
Fiber glass batts	1	3.5
Rock wool batts	1	3.5
Extruded polystyrene (plain)	1	4.0
Extruded polystyrene (freon expanded)	1	5.0
Expanded polystyrene (bead board)	1	3.5
Milled paper or wood pulp (cellulose)	1	3.1-3.7
Sawdust or shavings	1	2.2
Rock wool—fill	1	2.5-3
Fiber glass—fill	1	2.5-3
Vermiculite	1	2.2
Expanded polyurethane	1	6.3
Urea—formaldehyde foam	1	4.2-5.5
Building components		
Wood door-solid core	1-3/4	2.2
Above door w/stormdoor		3.2
Metal door—urethane core	1-3/4	2.5
Metal door—polystyrene core	1-3/4	2.1
Windows—single glazing		.9
Windows with storm		1.8
Insulating glass—3/6 in. air space		1.5
Insulating glass—1/2 in. air space		1.7
Building materials		
Brick—common	4	1.0
Concrete block	8	1.1
Lightweight block	8	2.0
Lightweight block w/ cores filled with insulation	8	3.0
Beveled wood siding	1/2	.8
Plywood	3/8	.6
Wood-hardwoods	1	.9
Wood-softwoods	1	1.25
Gypsum board	1/2	.5
Hardboard	7/16	.7
Particle board	1	1.1
Insulating sheathing	25/32	2.1

energy, and expected temperature difference between inside and outside. Farm buildings are usually separated into three general classifications for purposes of making insulation recommendations.

Cold buildings. No attempt is made to maintain any particular temperature level within the building. Actual temperatures will fluctuate up and down with outside temperatures. A small amount of insulation is often recommended under the roof of these structures to control summer heat and winter condensation.

Cool buildings. These buildings are maintained at temperatures which are optimum for animal production during winter months. Supplemental heat is not used. Insulation is used to contain sufficient animal body heat to maintain desired temperatures. Examples include egg production buildings and swine finishing units.

Warm buildings. Structures which require supplemental heat to maintain desired interior temperatures. Examples include milking centers, brooding buildings, and farrowing houses.

Table 34-2 provides general recommendations for insulation levels in these three types of structures, based on expected winter temperature conditions.

***Table 34-2.* Suggested Minimum Insulation Levels for Farm Buildings**

	Building Type					
	Cold		Cool		Warm	
Location	Wall	Ceiling	Wall	Ceiling	Wall	Ceiling
Northern States	—	4-6	12	24	18-21	33
Central States	—	4-6	9	12-16	13	24
Southern States	—	4-6	6	10-14	10-14	22

Moisture Problems

All of the air which we deal with in farm buildings contains some moisture in the form of water vapor. In the vapor form, water molecules are free to move in any direction without limit unless they are confined by a building. When confined, some of the molecules are continually striking the walls, ceiling and floor of the building. The number of collisions depends on the amount of moisture in the air and the force of the collisions is referred to as vapor pressure. Vapor pressure is expressed in inches of mercury (just like barometric pressure).

Any time there is a difference in vapor pressure between two areas, water vapor moves from the high pressure area to the lower pressure area. This movement will continue to take place until the pressures equalize. The ability of a material to allow water vapor to move through it is called permeability and it is measured in units called perms.

1 Perm = 1 grain of water per hour per square foot per inch of mercury pressure difference (7,000 grains of water = 1 lb)

If a material has a permeability of 1 or less, we regard it as a good preventer of moisture movement and refer to it as a vapor barrier. Most building materials are highly permeable and are not good vapor barriers. Table 34-3 lists perm ratings for several materials.

Warm air has the capability of holding more water vapor than cool air. In fact, the water holding capacity of a cubic foot of air doubles with every 20°F temperature increase. The actual water vapor content of air relative to its maximum capacity is called relative humidity.

The air inside farm buildings contains more moisture than outside air. This results in vapor pressure which causes molecules of water to move through wall, ceiling and floor components. As long as temperatures are nearly equal between inside and outside, no problems will be caused. Unfortunately, during winter months colder outside temperatures result in cold surfaces located somewhere within the typical construction section. When water vapor comes in contact with a cold surface, it condenses into free water (just as it does on the outside of a glass of ice water). If the cold surface is inside a wall or ceiling section, the condensed water will saturate insulation, promote decay or rusting of structural members, and lead to paint or roofing failures on the building.

We prevent moisture problems like these by installing a vapor barrier. A vapor barrier prevents water vapor from reaching cold surfaces where it can condense. A vapor barrier should be used whenever insulation is installed. The only exception is for those cases where the material itself has such a low permeability that it provides both an insulation and a vapor barrier.

One of the best vapor barriers for farm construction is polyethylene plastic film. It is low cost, easily installed, and not affected by corrosive elements normally found in agricultural environments.

Table 34-3. **Permeability of Construction and Vapor Barrier Materials**

Material	Perm Rating
3/8 in. Gypsum board	50
1/4 in. Exterior plywood	.7
1/4 in. Interior plywood	1.9
Extruded polystyrene 1 in. thick	1.2
Urea formaldehyde foam	32
Aluminum foil	0
Polyethylene film (4 mil thick)	.08
Metal roofing	0
Aluminum paint—2 coats	.4
Oil base paint on wood—3 coats	.3-1.0

No vapor barrier is perfect. Even if it has zero permeability, normal construction practice will cause it to be punctured by nails or have openings cut in it for electrical outlets. In normal wall construction, this does not present any problems. There will be enough air circulation around and through most sidings to remove moisture much faster than it can get through small holes in the vapor barrier. Ceilings present a different problem though. Most roof coverings have permeability close to zero. This means moisture which gets through the ceiling vapor barrier will be trapped by the roofing. We prevent this from happening by installing ventilation openings between the ceiling and the underside of the roofing. Three general types are used. They are soffit or eave vents, gable end vents, and ridge or roof opening vents. Different types are sometimes used in combination to provide more positive air flow. The best combination is the

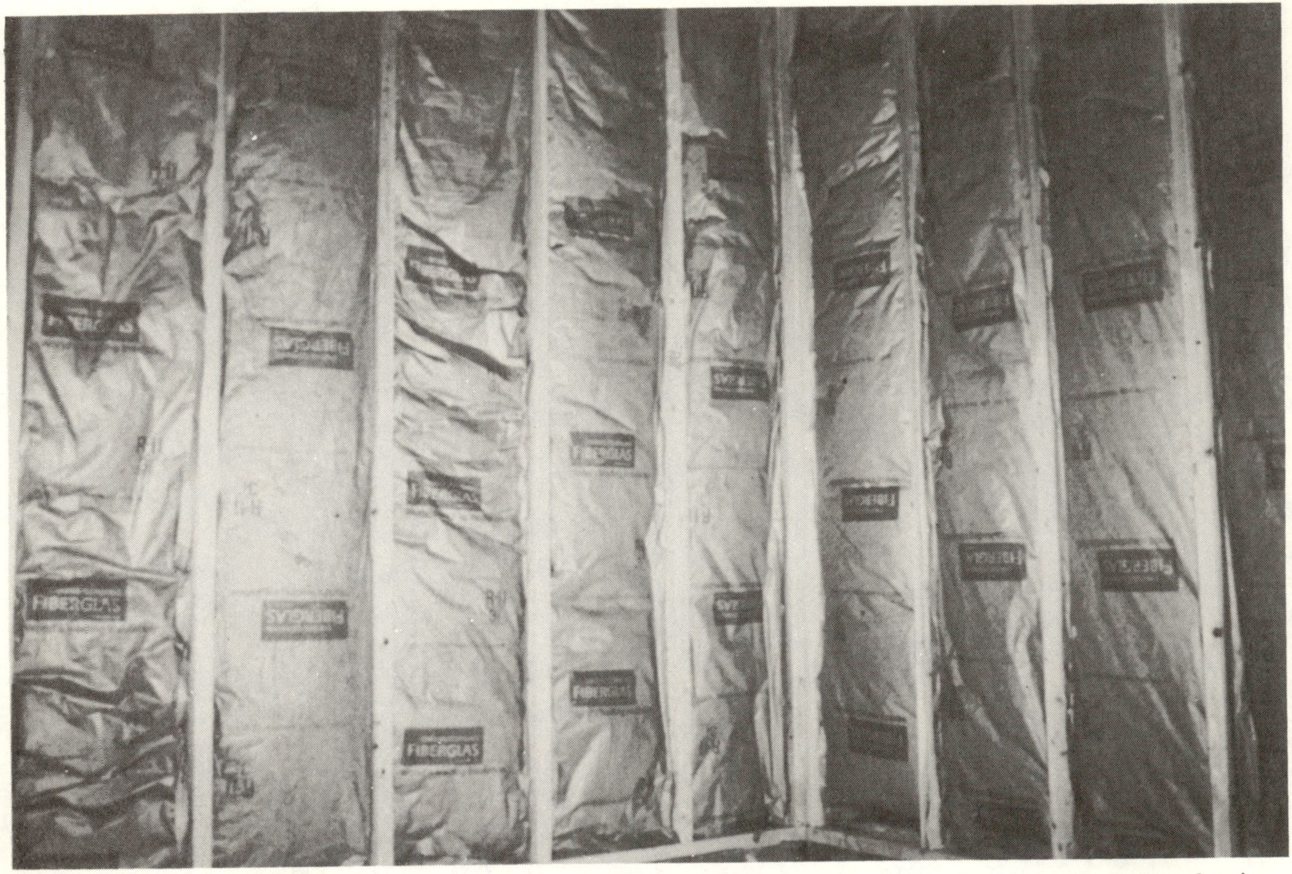

Figure 34-5. This blanket type insulation is faced with an asphalt-impregnated paper that serves as a vapor barrier. It is satisfactory for use in shops, homes, and other relatively dry areas. It should be covered with a layer of polyethylene film to provide a vapor barrier when used in a milking parlor or livestock housing building.

ridge and soffit vent system. Air enters through a screened vent under the eaves, moves up along the under side of the roof collecting any accumulated moisture, and exits at a continuous ridge vent. Ventilators are sized based on the square footage of ceiling area they are required to protect. A total ventilator area of 1 square foot per 150 square feet of ceiling area is sufficient to control moisture under almost any conditions.

CHAPTER 35

Ventilation

All successful livestock housing buildings must incorporate some type of planned ventilation system in order to provide an environment which will allow maximum animal productivity. A good ventilation system must accomplish four objectives.

1. Provide fresh air to meet the respiration needs of the animals.
2. Control moisture buildup within the structure.
3. Move enough air to dilute any airborne disease organisms produced within the building.
4. Control and/or moderate temperature extremes.

Each of the four provisions requires some optimum rate of air exchange. Experience has shown that if a reasonable degree of temperature control is provided for, the other three objectives will usually be met in a properly insulated building.

The basic process which occurs with all successful ventilation systems is as follows: cool, dry air is drawn into the building; heat and moisture are added to the air; and warm, wet air is expelled from the building. Failure to provide for any part of this process will result in failure of the ventilation system.

Insulation

Thermal insulation is an important part of all ventilation systems. It helps conserve animal heat and reduce supplemental heat required to warm ventilation air. It also maintains interior surface temperatures above the condensation point to minimize the presence of free water within the building. Chapter 34 details information on the correct levels of insulation for different types of livestock housing units.

Exhaust Systems for Warm Buildings

A warm confinement building is one which is closed, insulated, and operated in such a manner as to provide inside temperatures which are higher than, and usually independent of, outside temperature during winter months. A mechanical ventilation system is an essential part of the warm confinement building and the most often used mechanical system is the exhaust type (sometimes called negative pressure) system. This method of ventilation uses an exhaust type fan, usually located in the sidewall, to create a partial vacuum in the building by exhausting air to the outside. Fresh outside air is then drawn into the building and distributed through a planned inlet system.

Air Requirements

Air requirements vary with animal size and outside environmental conditions. The ideal system would be infinitely variable, moving just enough air to satisfy respiration needs during cold weather, up to a maximum rate which would eliminate heat stress during hot weather. Unfortunately, the equipment and control cost for such a system is prohibitive today.

The best compromise appears to be a system capable of providing three levels of air movement. The lowest or *winter minimum* provides enough air to meet respiration requirements and operates continuously. This low level provides all air necessary during periods of extremely cold weather or in buildings where a supplemental heating system is in operation. A thermostat may be used to shut off this minimum level in the event that building temperature should ever drop near the freezing point.

An intermediate or *winter normal* rate is used in addition to the winter minimum to provide a measure of interior temperature control. Fans providing this rate are regulated with reverse acting thermostats which turn them on when room temperature exceeds the set point.

The high level or *summer* rate is intended to provide some measure of temperature control during summer months. Summer rate fans are controlled by thermostats to turn them on when interior temperature reaches some set level, usually 80° to 90° F.

Table 35-1 presents recommended ventilation rates for different types of livestock housed in warm confinement buildings. Rates shown at each level are totals and not additive. This means that a total of 120 cubic feet per minute (cfm) per 250 pound pig is required for summer ventilation. This would be delivered by a winter minimum fan delivering 10 cfm, a winter normal moving 25 cfm, and a summer fan providing 85 cfm, all operating to make up the 120 cfm total.

Ventilation rates based on animal weight or per animal tend to eliminate housing density as a factor in ventilation system performance. Rates based on air changes per hour for the building neglect variation in animal heat and moisture production associated with different housing

Table 35-1. **Recommended Ventilation Rates for Livestock in Warm Confinement Buildings**

Animal	Desired Room Temp (°F)	CFM Winter Minimum	CFM Winter Normal	CFM Summer
Sow & litter	60-80	20	20	210
40 lb Pig	70	2	15	36
100 lb Pig	60	5	20	48
150 lb Pig	60	7	25	72
250 lb Pig	60	10	35	120
Dairy cow	55	35	100	200
Dairy calf	55	10	50	75
Beef per 1,000 lbs	55	15	100	200
Poultry per lb	55-60	.125	.5	1
Horse per 1,000 lbs	55	25	100	200

densities. For example, a 40 by 200 foot poultry house with 10,000 birds in cages needs a different ventilation rate than the same sized building with 4,000 birds in a floor operation.

Summer rates given in Table 35-1 provide a reasonable degree of temperature control at an economical operating level. Higher rates provide slightly lower temperatures; however, they cannot be economically justified.

The desired room temperatures indicated in table 35-1 provide a basis for adjustment of controls for fans at the winter normal level. Temperatures given are those which give optimum animal performance.

Fans

Fans used in livestock buildings are subjected to dusty and corrosive environments. They must be designed and constructed to withstand these conditions or they will not perform satisfactorily. When selecting fans, make sure they are designed for agricultural use. Look for sealed motors and bearings, heavy duty blades, and solid construction.

Ventilation fans must work against a partial vacuum and often exhaust into an oncoming wind. Because of this, they must be capable of delivering their required capacity against these load conditions. This load is referred to as static pressure and is measured in terms of inches of water. Fans selected should be able to deliver rated volume of air against 1/8 inch of static pressure. This is the amount of pressure required to raise the level of a column of water 1/8 inch. It is not much pressure, but it is not uncommon for the air delivery of a poorly designed fan to drop by 25% to 30% when subjected to this pressure as compared to air delivery against no pressure.

The Air Moving and Conditioning Association (AMCA) is an independent organization which tests and rates fans. Fans which carry the AMCA rating will deliver the rated amount of air under normally expected operating conditions.

In modern, well constructed farm buildings, fans provide the vacuum which causes fresh air to enter the building. They are not relied on to provide air distribution as they were in older, poorly constructed buildings. Because of this, fan location is not a critical item in system design. They should be located where they are convenient to install and service, and out of reach of animals within the building. The recommended maximum distance between a fan and the farthest corner of the area it serves is 125 to 150 feet. This recommendation prevents the accumulation of large volumes of warm, stale air next to the fan.

Fans which are intended to cycle on and off should be equipped with louvers. Louvers prevent the entry of cold air and birds during periods when the fans are not operating. Fans should also be provided with protective guarding or screening to prevent injuries to either animals or people who work around them.

The most commonly used fan controller is the *reverse acting thermostat* which is simply a switch which turns on when the temperature rises to its set point. It is called reverse acting because it acts in reverse of a normal heating thermostat which closes on temperature decrease.

Other controls including timers and variable speed motor controllers are outlined in Table 35-2. Controls are also subjected to dusty corrosive environment and should be selected on their ability to withstand these conditions.

Air Inlets

Air inlets are the single most important element in the exhaust type ventilation system. They are responsible for both control and distribution of the incoming ventilation air. Poorly designed or maintained inlets are the number one cause of ventilation system failure.

Every good inlet must have two characteristics: 1) it must be adjustable to accommodate variation in air flow rates between winter and summer, and 2) it must be placed so that fresh air will be delivered to all parts of the building.

The most popular type inlet for exhaust systems is the adjustable slot inlet. This consists of a continuous slot area open to a source of fresh air

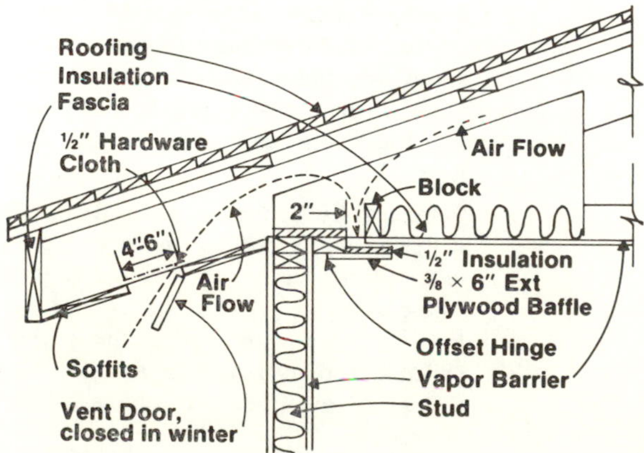

Figure 35-1. The slot inlet located at the top of one or both long exterior walls has become the most popular method of providing outside air for the exhaust type ventilation system. The ability to adjust slot width to accommodate changing needs throughout the year is an essential part of the design. (Purdue University)

with some type of adjustable baffle or control board to vary its width. Slots are usually located along the long dimension of the building at the junction of the wall and ceiling. They may also be located in the ceiling itself, usually down the center of the building.

General recommendations on slot locations are as follows:

Table 35-2. **Controls Used for Fans in Ventilation Systems**

Control	Use
Low temperature cut off	Thermostat used to shut off winter minimum fans in the event of unusually cold weather or heating system failure.
Time clock (percentage timer)	Provides variable winter minimum which can be adjusted as animal size increases. Usually found in brooding or nursery buildings.
Thermostat	Temperature activated on-off switch. In multiple fan systems, thermostats can be set a few degrees apart to provide incremental rate increases.
Time clock/thermostat	Combination controller which provides temperature activated control for warm weather and a variable guaranteed minimum rate in cold weather.
Humidistat	A desirable but, to date, unreliable method of turning fans on and off based on the amount of moisture in the air.
Throttling	Provides variable ventilation rates by restricting fan delivery. Usually accomplished by thermostat controlled power louvers.
Reversing	Provides exhaust in winter and pressure in summer by either electrical reversal or by turning fans around in their housing.
2-Stage thermostat	Provides high and low ventilation rates when used in conjunction with a two speed fan motor. The thermostat provides automatic switching between high and low speed, depending on temperature.
Solid state	Temperature activated controller used with variable speed fan motors to provide infinite variation in air delivery. These units are good in theory, but delivery rates at slow speeds are highly variable and may lead to air distribution problems when low volumes of air are needed.

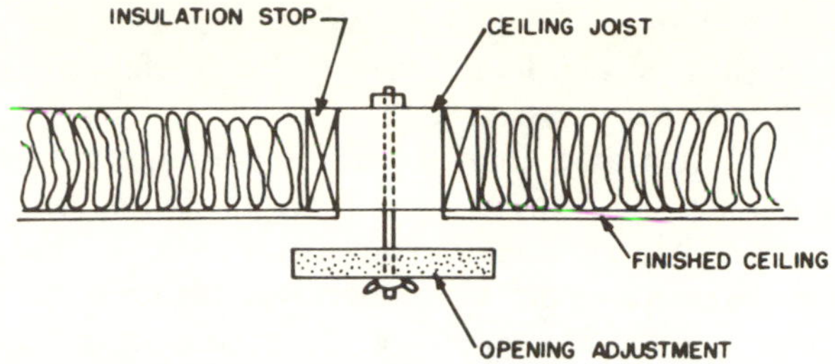

Figure 35-2. A center slot is sometimes used in addition to sidewall slots in wide buildings or in buildings that have very low ventilation requirements. Air movement through the center slot is less affected by wind than it is with sidewall slots; an important factor when dealing with very low rates. (University of Missouri)

1. Buildings up to 30 feet wide: Use either a center ceiling slot or a slot along one of the outside walls.
2. Buildings 30 to 48 feet wide: Slots along both of the long outside walls.
3. Buildings over 48 feet wide: Use slots along both of the long outside walls and one or more ceiling slots.

Slot width is based on the amount of air it is to admit to the building when the static pressure difference between inside and outside is .04 inch. At this pressure a 1 inch wide slot 1 foot long will admit 50 cfm. A 2 inch wide slot will admit 100 cfm and a 3 inch wide slot, 150 cfm.

Example problem: A 28 by 100 foot swine finishing building is used for 300 hogs. Find the width of the slot inlet required.

Solution:

(1) 300 hogs at their final weight of 220 pounds will require a summer rate of 120 cfm each or a total of 36,000 cfm (from Table 35-1).

(2) If we locate slots along both outside walls, we will have a total of 200 feet of slot.

$$\frac{36000 \text{ cfm}}{200 \text{ ft}} = 180 \text{ cfm per foot of slot.}$$

(3) $$\frac{180 \text{ cfm}}{50 \text{ cfm per inch width}} = 3.6 \text{ inches}$$

(4) A slot width of 3.6 inches will be required. It will have to be adjustable to accommodate the lower air requirements during winter months.

Manure Pit Ventilation

Buildings with slotted floors and manure storage areas often have ventilation systems modified to remove any toxic gasses which may occur in the pit area. Toxic gasses are either lighter than air or heavier than air. Gasses lighter than air will rise into the animal housing area and are rapidly removed by conventional ventilation systems. No special provision need be made for removal of these gasses.

Gasses which are heavier than air tend to build up in the pit and then move up into the housing area where their weight keeps them next to the floor. These gasses can be diluted and removed from the building by exhausting the winter minimum ventilation rate through the manure pit. This can be done by either locating the winter minimum fan(s) in the pit or by constructing a duct from the pit to the fan(s). Although heavy gasses in the pit will flow to the fans or ducts, some distribution of outlets is desirable in larger buildings. Maximum distance from the farthest point in the pit to the outlet should be restricted to 100 to 125 feet.

The amount of ventilation air moved down through the floor slots should be restricted to the winter minimum. Higher rates can cause manure to dry on the sides of the slats, plugging the slot area and can also create excessive drafts on the animals.

Pressure Systems For Warm Buildings

Several companies have developed pressurized fan ventilation systems for warm livestock housing units. These systems typically use perforated polyethylene tubes to distribute a mixture of recirculated inside air and fresh outside air through the building. The amount of fresh air introduced is controlled by a power louver which is thermostatically controlled. This

Figure 35-3. A pressure-ventilation system using a perforated plastic tube for air distribution is an effective way to solve many of the problems associated with mechanical ventilation of buildings requiring minimum amounts of outside air.

system has become popular in buildings which house very young animals and use supplemental heat. It provides three major advantages over conventional exhaust systems in these types of facilities.

1. It overcomes the problem of controlling relatively small amounts of air with conventional exhaust systems.
2. Air distribution is not adversely affected by changing outside wind patterns.
3. Fresh outside air is blended with warmer inside air before it is introduced into the animal housing area. This reduces the incidence of cold drafts.

Pressure type systems are generally used to provide only for winter ventilation needs. Conventional exhaust systems with slot inlets are used to accommodate higher summer rates. Some type of planned air outlet may be required in buildings which normally use large amounts of outside air.

Natural Ventilation for Cold Confinement Buildings

A cold confinement building is one in which little or no attempt is made to control temperatures within the structure. These buildings are designed and operated so that natural air movement provides the required ventilation. Buildings adaptable to natural ventilation include small housing units such as calf hutches or individual farrowing houses, cattle housing buildings, and swine finishing units.

Experience has shown that there are several items in building design and location which influence performance of natural ventilation systems. These are described in the following paragraphs.

Building Orientation

Since we rely on energy provided by nature to accomplish natural ventilation, it is important that we place the building in such a manner that it will intercept a maximum amount of energy (in this case, wind energy). In much of the United States, prevailing winter winds are from the North and Northwest. In summer, they usually shift to a southerly direction. Buildings with the long dimension or ridge running East-West can make maximum use of prevailing winds.

If there are some unusual wind patterns around your farmstead, this general recommendation may have to be altered to fit your situation. Things which cause unusual wind patterns are high hills, tall buldings or trees. If you suspect abnormal wind patterns in the area where your building is to be located, spend some time observing wind direction before making a final decision on building orientation.

It is desirable to place naturally ventilated buildings on the upwind side of other structures on the farmstead. This helps prevent natural air flows from being blocked off. If this is not possible, a greater than normal separation between buildings should be used. A minimum distance of 80 to 100 feet will avoid most interference problems.

Wall Openings

Wall openings admit air that makes natural ventilation work. If the building is properly oriented, there is no need to provide openings in the end walls of the building. The south wall should have a 3 to 4 foot high opening the full length of the building. This opening should start 4 to 5 feet above the floor and extend to the ceiling or eave line. In poultry or in swine buildings, this opening is frequently covered with movable curtains or panels which may be adjusted to provide some measure of temperature control. Dairy and beef buildings frequently leave the entire south wall open.

The south wall opening accomplishes two things. It provides good access to cooling summer breezes, and it admits a maximum amount of winter sunshine to help keep the interior of the building dry.

The north wall requires two openings. A continuous 4 to 6 inch wide opening at the top of the wall (often located between the rafters) provides an entrance for fresh air required to prevent moisture buildup during winter months. Additional openings which can be closed in winter are needed for summer ventilation. These summer openings are often provided by a continuous or nearly continuous 2-½ to 3 foot wide opening covered by hinged doors or removable panels.

Ridge Opening

An important part of the natural ventilation system in gable roofed buildings without ceilings is the continuous ridge opening. The ridge opening permits the release of warm moist air which tends to collect next to the roof and thus helps control condensation on the under side of the roofing material. It also provides a chimney effect which helps draw fresh air into the building even on days when there is little or no wind movement.

Several types of ridge openings and ventilators have been used to accomplish this ventilation. One of the most economical and successful solutions is to provide a continuous opening by leaving the ridge cap off the building. The opening width should be a minimum of 1-½ inches for each 10 feet of building width or 6 inches, whichever is wider. The opening may be covered with a raised roof section if desired; however, a cover may tend

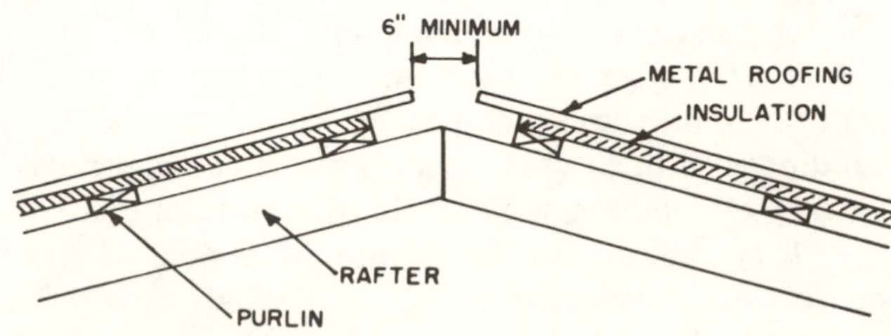

Figure 35-4. Section view of the construction of a continuous-ridge ventilation opening. (University of Missouri)

Figure 35-5. In spite of the fact that the ridge is completely open, the chimney effect caused by natural wind action and animal heat keeps both rain and snow out of this building.

to funnel wind blown rain or snow into the building. Experience has shown that very little rain or snow enters a ridge opening as long as there are animals in the building to provide heat for the chimney effect to work.

Insulation

Traditionally, insulation has not been used in naturally ventilated buildings. However, as we learn more about desirable animal environment and apply natural ventilation to different types of buildings, insulation is recommended in many cases. Insulation helps control summer heat gains from solar radiation on the roof and also conserves animal heat during winter. The conserved heat combined with close management of ventilation openings can result in a natural ventilation system which functions nearly as well as mechanical systems in some types of confinement buildings.

Draft Control

As long as the wind comes from the right direction and at the right speed, air distribution and drafts are not usually problems in naturally ventilated buildings. However, when the wind blows against the end wall of the building, undesirable air patterns or drafts can result within the building. Drafts frequently are the result of air movement within the building which is perpendicular to the ridge or lengthwise. This movement can be broken up by using solid cross partitions within the building.

Troubleshooting Ventilation Systems

When a ventilation system fails or partially fails, it produces problems which are easy to recognize, but often hard to solve. The following section lists common symptoms of system failure and probable causes.

The first step in system problem diagnosis is to verify the complaint. A properly designed and operating ventilation system produces an environment desirable for livestock, not people. Workers who have never experienced a properly operating system will often report the building is too cold or that too much air is moving through.

Symptom	*Possible Causes*
Building colder than desired, even though outside temperature is normal.	1. Fan set at too low a temperature or control calibration is off. 2. Building not properly insulated. 3. Animal density is low. If building is not at capacity, there may not be sufficient heat for the system to work. 4. Air inlets not adjusted properly. 5. Insulation is wet. Results when vapor barrier is not used or when it is installed on wrong side of the insulation.
Building too warm.	6. Fan controls set too high. 7. Not enough fan capacity installed. 8. Fans not delivering rated capacity because of dirt on blades, shrouds, and louvers. 9. Air inlets not properly adjusted or clogged with dust particles. 10. Any unusual obstruction around either the intake or exhaust side of fans.
Excessive moisture in building. Air feels damp and heavy.	11. Not enough ventilation. Tip off will be too warm a temperature. 12. Too much ventilation. Tip off will be cool temperature. Air is not being allowed to warm enough to pick up moisture. 13. Leak in waterers or plumbing system. 14. Unvented gas heaters. 15. Disease outbreak in livestock.

Symptom	*Possible Causes*
Excessive condensation on interior surfaces.	16. Extremely cold outside weather. Problem will go away when it warms up. 17. Single glazing on windows. Opening window slightly at top will usually solve this. 18. See also causes 2, 5, and 11 to 15.
Excessive drafts and/or hot spots at different locations within the building.	19. Poorly adjusted inlets. 20. Air flow is short circuited due to an open window or door. 21. See also causes 7 to 10.
Fans not working.	22. Fuse blown or circuit breaker tripped or defective. 23. Thermal protection in motor tripped. May be due to dust accumulation if system has been working satisfactorily. 24. Defective thermostat. 25. Defective fan motor.
Controls not working properly.	26. Controls defective. 27. Control settings not properly calibrated. 28. Sensing units not properly located. Sensing units should be located where they respond to true room conditions. A good location is in the center of the room just above reach of the animals.
Fuel costs excessive in supplemental heat system.	30. Controls improperly calibrated or adjusted. Heating system may be set too high or fan control too low, resulting in too much outside air being moved through the building. Only the winter minimum rate should be used when the heating system is in operation. Fans used to provide higher rates should be adjusted so that they will not come on until temperature is 5°F above the furnace shut off temperature.

CHAPTER **36**

Heating Systems

Many farm buildings require some type of supplemental heating system to provide animal comfort, to keep temperatures above freezing, or to maintain desirable working conditions. Many of the heating systems used in residential and light industrial buildings can be used equally well in farm buildings. Others cannot. This chapter reviews basic types of heating units, their application to agriculture, fuel selection, and system sizing.

Warm Air Systems

The warm air furnace or heater traditionally provides the largest heating system at the least cost. The conventional unit pulls air from the heated space either directly or through a return duct, passes it over a heat exchanger where it is warmed, and discharges it back to the space to be heated. The entire system is often controlled by a single thermostat which turns heater and fan on in response to a call for heat. The heating unit or furnace is available in a wide variety of sizes, shapes, and fuel types to accommodate almost any need.

Conventional recirculating types of warm air heating systems *cannot* be used in livestock housing facilities. The dusty conditions associated with this type of environment make it nearly impossible to keep air handling and heat exchanger equipment as clean as it needs to be in order to function effectively. Recirculating warm air heating systems can be used in greenhouses, farm shops, and milking centers.

Several manufacturers produce warm air heating units for agricultural buildings which are not of the recirculating type. These heaters take clean air directly from outside, warm it, and discharge it into the heated area. These heaters are normally used in livestock housing areas where the added air can offset a part of normal ventilation air. They are usually installed so that heated air is discharged directly into the building at a single point

Figure 36-1. This is a ventilation makeup air heater. It is a type of warm air heating unit designed to avoid the normal dust problems associated with the use of warm air heaters in farm buildings. Outside air is drawn into the heater, warmed up, and discharged into the building. This warm air offsets some of the air needed for winter ventilation—hence the name, ventilation makeup heater. A major disadvantage is that products of combustion are also discharged into the building.

adjacent to the heater. This single point discharge does not provide as uniform a temperature throughout the heated area as does a conventional ducted distribution system.

Hot Water Systems

Over the years, hot water heating systems have proven to be one of the more durable and trouble free heating methods for agricultural buildings. They eliminate the problems of dust recirculation and most components are relatively long lived.

The boiler or heating unit operates separately from the distribution system. It maintains a reservoir of hot water at the temperature set on its thermostat (140° to 215° depending on the type of distribution system). Heat is distributed through a pipe and/or radiator system by a circulating pump controlled by a thermostat located in the heated area.

In dust free areas, finned tube radiator pipes are used to improve heat transfer from the distribution system. These radiators are not satisfactory in livestock housing because they soon become clogged with dust. Black iron pipe without fins is often used as the radiator unit in dusty areas.

Hot water heat can be zoned for areas with different heat require-

Figure 36-2. This fan-forced hot water unit acts like an automobile radiator in distributing heat from water heated at a central boiler. It works well in farm shops, milking centers, and other low-dust environments. It has not been too satisfactory in livestock housing because of the dust problem.

ments. Zoning is usually accomplished by using a separate circulating pump and distribution loop for each area.

Radiant Heaters

Radiation is a method of heat transfer which is not easily understood by many persons. It involves the direct transfer of heat from a hot object to a cooler one. Radiation is the heat transfer method by which we receive all of our energy from the sun. Radiation can be used to heat people or animals and not the air around them. That is why you can feel comfortable standing in the sun on the south side of the barn on a January day when air temperature is well below freezing. Radiation is a straight line heat transfer process. If you are standing in the shade or out of direct line with a radiant heater, you won't receive any heat.

The process of radiant heat transfer makes it an ideal heat for many agricultural uses, at least in theory. For example, it can be used to:

1. Heat baby pigs without making sows uncomfortably warm.
2. Keep milkers warm in a milk parlor with doors which are constantly opening and closing.
3. Keep you warm while you are working on a machine in an open front building.
4. Brood chickens by heating them directly and not warming up the entire building.

There are two types of radiant heaters in general usage: electric and gas. Electric heaters are available in a variety of types ranging from simple heat lamps to large wall or ceiling mounted panels. Gas heaters normally use a burner to heat a ceramic element which radiates heat.

The major problem with radiant heaters has been control. Since they heat objects and not air, conventional thermostats cannot be used to turn them on and off satisfactorily. Another factor is that when they are off, nothing is heated. This causes problems during periods when outside temperatures fluctuate.

New controllers are now on the market which can sense the heat energy output of radiant heaters and can regulate output by controlling the fuel or electric energy input. These devices are fairly expensive; however, their cost can be recovered fairly quickly in reduced energy costs, particularly for systems used on a year-round basis.

Table 36-1. **Comparison of Heating Systems for Agricultural Uses**

	Warm Air	Hot Water	Radiant
Advantages	Low first cost. Wide variety of equipment. Systems available for any fuel type. Summer cooling can utilize same duct work.	Can be used to warm air on floors. Small systems can use hot water heater as a boiler. Easily zoned to provide different temperatures for various areas. Easy to locate boiler in a separate building.	Heats objects, not air. Easily used for spot heating.
Disadvantages	Recirculation of dust. Distribution ducts require space.	High initial cost. Needs freeze protection if taken out of service in winter. Radiator pipes add to room cleaning problems.	Either on or off operation unless complex controls are used. Limited number of fuel sources. Straight line heat transfer. Heater must be located in area where heat is used.

System Sizing

Supplemental heating systems for agricultural buildings are designed to maintain desired interior temperatures at the time when outside temperature is at its expected minimum. Outside minimums used for design purposes are shown in Figure 36-3.

For calculation purposes, heat loss from a building, which must be offset by the heating system, is divided into two components: conductive and infiltrative loss. Conductive loss is the heat which flows directly

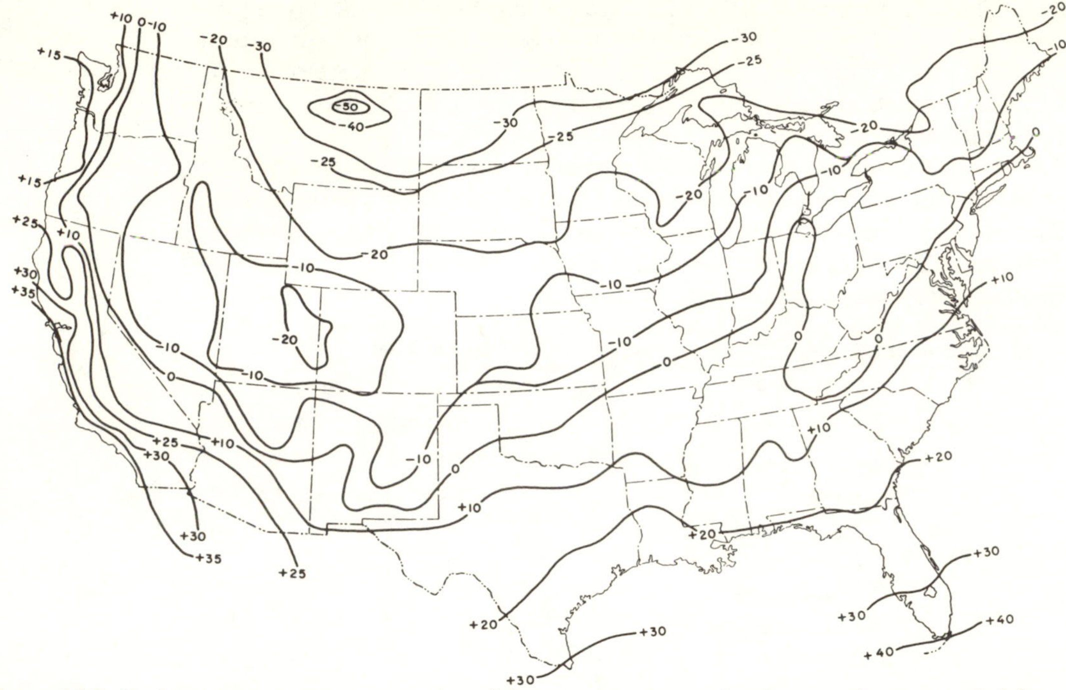

Figure 36-3. Design temperatures are not the minimum temperature that has ever been recorded for a given location. They only represent the normally expected minimum for the area. It is expected that outside temperatures will be lower than the design minimum less than 3 percent of the time during winter months. (USDA)

through the walls, ceiling and floor of a building. It is usually calculated separately for each component, as well as for door and window areas. Values are then summed for total conductive loss. The formula for calculating conductive loss is as follows.

Heat Loss $= \frac{A}{R} \times \triangle T$, *where:*

Heat loss is in Btu per hour.

A = Area of the component in square feet

R = R-Value of the component

$\triangle T$ = Temperature difference in degrees F between desired inside temperature and outside winter design value.

Infiltrative loss represents the energy required to warm up ventilating air or the air which leaks into the building. Buildings with ventilation systems use an air volume equivalent to the winter minimum rate to calculate infiltrative losses. Buildings without mechanical ventilation are usually calculated at a rate of one complete air change per hour. The formula is:

Heat Loss $= .018 \times \triangle T \times V$, *where:*

Heat Loss is in Btu per hour

.018 = a constant

$\triangle T$ = Temperature difference

V = Ventilation rate in cubic feet *per hour* or total volume of heated area in cubic feet for buildings without ventilation systems.

Total heat loss is the sum of conductive and infiltrative loss. This total can be used directly to determine the size of the supplemental heating unit in Btu's per hour. A more accurate, but less used, method would be to take this total heat figure and subtract expected animal heat production from it. This results in a smaller sized heating system. Most designers prefer not to use this technique because it can result in an undersized heating system in the event that the building is only partially full when minimum outside temperatures occur.

Example problem. Calculate the size of supplemental heater required in a 16 sow farrowing house. Dimensions of the house are 24 by 50 by 8 foot. It is insulated with R-13 in sidewalls and R-24 in the ceiling. There are no windows and two 3 by 7 foot doors. Desired inside temperature is 60° and the winter minimum design temperature is 0°.

Solution.

Conductive losses:

Component	*Area*		*R*		*ΔT*		*Heat Loss*
Wall	8 × (24 + 24 + 50 + 50)	÷	13	×	60	=	5,464
Ceiling	24 × 50	÷	24	×	60	=	3,000
Doors	2 × 7 × 3	÷	2.2*	×	60	=	1,161
							9,625 Btu

Infiltrative Loss:

16 sows × 20 cfm × 60 min/hr × .018 × 60 = 20,736 Btu

TOTAL HEAT LOSS = 30,361 Btu

*Value from Table 34-1 in Chapter 34.

A heater which would supply a minimum of 30,000 Btu per hour would be adequate for this farrowing house.

There is another interesting lesson to be learned from our example problem. Note that the heat required to warm ventilating air is more than twice the amount lost through the walls, ceiling and doors. This is a typical result for a well insulated livestock building. Many producers tend to over ventilate livestock buildings in an attempt to control odors. If we used a winter minimum rate of 30 cfm per sow instead of the recommended 20, we would increase the required size of the heating system by 25%. Actual operating costs would be increased by an even greater percentage. That's why it is important not to over ventilate, particularly in buildings where supplemental heat is being used.

Selecting a Fuel

Engineers use Btu as a measure of energy needs. A Btu is a British Thermal

Unit. It is technically defined as the amount of heat required to raise 1 pound of water 1° F. In more practical terms, it is about equal to the energy we get from burning an old fashioned wooden match.

Table 36-2. **Energy in Fuels**

Fuel	Selling Unit	Heat Content (Btu/Selling Unit)	Average System Efficiency (%)	Available Btu per Selling Unit
Natural gas	100 cu ft	100,000	80	80,000
LP-gas	Gallon	92,000	80	73,600
#2 Oil	Gallon	140,000	70	98,000
Electricity	Kwhr	3,413	100	3,413
Coal	Ton	25 million	65	16.25 million
Wood	Cord*	27.5 million	65	17.9 million

**1 cord of air dried hardwood at 20% moisture content;*
1 cord = 128 cubic feet.

Fossil fuels or electricity supply virtually all of the energy used on farms today. The selection of a particular type of fuel for your farm application should be based on the following:

1. Availability and dependability of the fuel supplier.
2. Type of heating system you plan to use.
3. Present fuel costs and your best estimate of future price trends among the various types of fuel.

Fuel is converted into heat energy by some type of burner or conversion system. With the exception of electrical resistance heaters, none of these systems are able to extract all of the heat from their fuel source. Some heat is always lost up the chimney or through the heat distribution system in the building. Table 36-2 lists common fuel types, their heat content, average system efficiencies, and how much you can expect to get out of them.

If you want to know which fuel is least expensive, you need to compare costs on the basis of cost per available Btu. A common question we receive is, "Which is less expensive, LP-gas or electricity?" Figure 36-4 will enable you to make this comparison for yourself.

Example: Suppose you are able to purchase natural gas at a cost of 43¢ per 100 cubic feet (some companies refer to this unit as a therm). What would other fuels be priced at if they were the same cost per available Btu?

Drawing a horizontal line across the chart in Figure 36-4 at the 43¢ mark for natural gas will give you the following answers.

LP-gas	40¢ per gallon
#2 Oil	53¢ per gallon
Electricity	1.9 ¢ per Kwhr
Coal	$88 per ton
Wood	$98 per cord

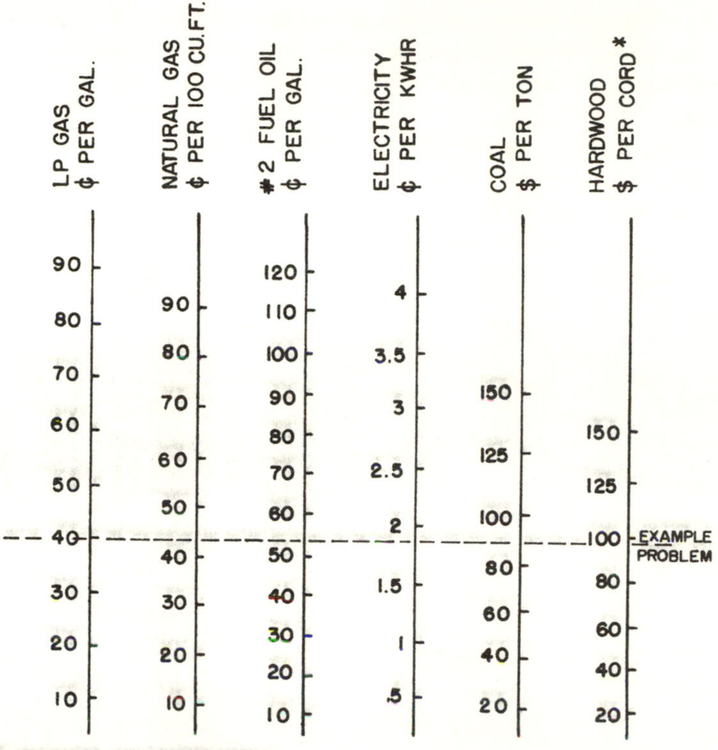

Figure 36-4. Fuel cost equivalents based on normally expected system efficiencies. (University of Missouri)

Don't forget that fuel is not the only cost in operating a heating system. Depreciation, repairs, maintenance, and the amount of labor required to operate it are all costs of heating. If you don't have time to take care of a wood burning unit or need a system with completely automatic controls, the system using the least expensive fuel source may not be the best solution for you.

Ventilation Heat Exchangers

It is possible to substantially reduce supplemental heat required to warm ventilating air by using a ventilation air heat exchanger. These usually consist of some type of duct which is divided lengthwise by a thin sheet of metal. Warm, moist exhaust air is passed through one half of the duct as it is blown from the building. The incoming cold air is brought in through the other half of the duct. Heat from the exhaust air is transferred or exchanged through the metal divider plate from the warm exhaust air to the cold inlet air. Some engineers have reported that systems of this type can recapture more than 50% of the energy normally exhausted by the ventilation system.

Ventilation air heat exchangers must be designed to accommodate two problems. First, they must be accessible for cleaning. Dust in the exhaust air will collect rapidly in the warm side of the exchanger duct. This dust will act as an insulator, reducing the efficiency of heat exchange. Second, as heat is exchanged, a large amount of condensation will occur in the exhaust duct. The duct must be constructed to contain this water and pitched to allow it to either run to the outside of the building or to a collecting drain. If it is drained to the outside, it will need to be disposed of in such a way that ice buildup will not be a problem during cold weather.

CHAPTER **37**

Alternate Energy Systems

Production agriculture in the United States uses only about 3% of the total energy consumed in the country. An even smaller percentage is used within farm buildings. In spite of this, energy cost does represent a major input for many livestock producers. During the past several years, we have seen a growing interest in the possibility of reducing energy costs or eliminating dependency on outside sources through adoption of alternate energy systems. The two sources which have received the most attention are solar and wind.

Solar Energy Systems

Solar energy is free! And, there is a never ending, unlimited supply of it. Unfortunately, systems required to collect and distribute solar energy are not free and just when you need energy the most, solar is probably going to be unavailable because of darkness or cloud cover. As a result, solar systems often end up as a more expensive energy source than some of the more traditional heating systems.

On a clear day at 40° North latitude (the 40° latitude line runs right through the heart of America's agricultural production area) the amount of solar energy that strikes a flat horizontal surface is equivalent to 1,780 Btu's per square foot. This ranges from a high of 2,650 Btu's in June to a low of 780 Btu's in December. Using these values, we find that a flat surface slightly larger than 5x5 feet would receive energy equivalent to 1 gallon of LP-gas on a clear June day.

Unfortunately, several factors prevent us from either receiving or using this theoretical ideal. First, the sun does not shine every day. Depending on where you are located, it may shine less than half the possible time or as much as 80% + of the time. For any location, this percentage of possible sunshine will vary throughout the year, with the lowest percentage usually occurring during the normal winter heating season. We still receive solar radiation on cloudy days, but generally at too low a level to be used effectively in any presently available collection system.

Atmospheric contamination also affects the amount of solar energy we receive. Dust, haze, smog and moisture all decrease the amount of energy we receive from the sun.

No mechanical system is 100% efficient. Just as we are not able to extract all the energy from a gallon of oil, we cannot capture all of the sun's energy. Current research shows that we can capture 40% to 60% of the solar energy that strikes a particular collector, with most being in the 40% range.

Finally, collector orientation affects the energy capture. Ideally, a collector would be oriented with its surface perpendicular or exactly at right angles to the sun's rays from morning until night. This requires a fairly expensive tracking device and some means of re-aiming the collector. A more practical solution is to fix the collector at some compromise angle and accept a reduction in efficiency.

Collector Types

Active or planned solar collectors fall into two general types: flat plate and concentrating collectors.

Concentrating collectors gather the sun's rays from a relatively large area and focus them on a single point. If you ever used a magnifying glass to start a fire by focusing the sun's rays, you were using a concentrating collector. In the field of solar collection, parabolic shaped mirrors are used instead of a magnifying glass. The effect is the same.

Concentrating collectors can create extremely high temperatures (over 2,000°F). They can be used to generate steam which can be used directly or to power generators. Concentrating collectors require precisely constructed surfaces and a tracking device to follow the sun during the day. Because of this, they are relatively expensive and require continuous maintenance. We generally don't consider them for agricultural uses because we rarely need the high temperatures they provide.

The flat plate collector requires no tracking device to capture the sun's energy. It absorbs energy directly from the sun, as well as indirect or diffuse radiation reflected off nearby buildings, ground or clouds. Flat plate collectors are capable of providing temperatures up to 150° to 200°F and are relatively simple to build. These factors make the flat plate collector the logical choice for agricultural space heating.

There are many different designs for flat plate collectors, but all have two basic characteristics: 1) a flat plate to absorb solar radiation, and 2) a circulating fluid to pick up heat from the plate and transport it to the point of use. The two fluids most commonly used are air and water.

Air collectors. An air collector can be as simple as a bare sheet of metal, like a metal roof, painted a flat black to absorb as much energy as possible, with air blown underneath in a duct of some type. This type of collector is known as a bare plate collector.

A second type, known as a covered plate collector uses a transparent cover of glass or plastic with the heat collecting air moving between the cover plate and the dark colored absorber. The transparent cover reduces heat loss from the absorber plate and improves the overall efficiency of collection.

A third type, called a suspended plate collector, has air circulated both above and below the absorber plate to pick up absorbed heat. This type provides still greater collection efficiency.

Water collectors. A water collector has the same basic components as an air collector: an absorber plate and a transfer medium. The difference is in how the medium is passed over the absorber.

The basic water collector consists of an absorber plate, generally with water tubes attached, a cover, and insulation behind the absorber plate. Heat from the absorber plate is removed by the water circulating in the tubes. Another type of water collector has no water tubes. The water simply flows down over the absorber in a sheet or in an open channel if the absorber is corrugated. The type with tubes is generally more efficient, but the open channel type generally costs less.

Freezing in the winter can be a problem with water collectors. You can get around that problem by draining the collector when it's not in use or by

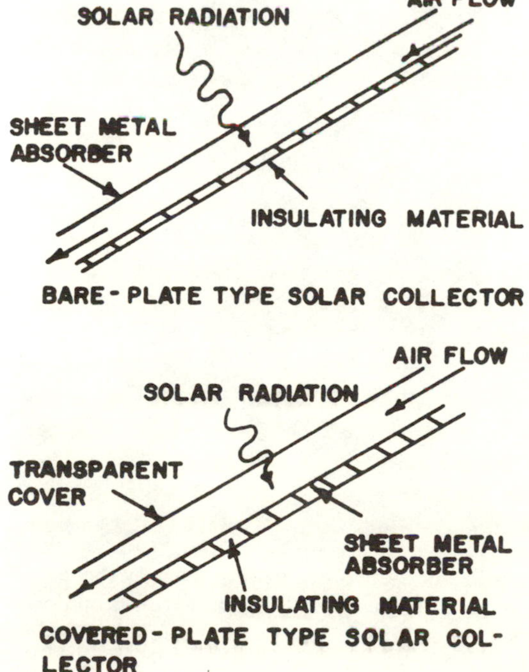

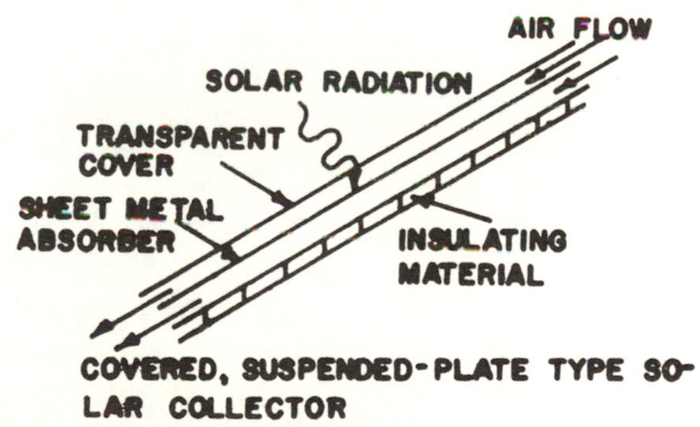

Figure 37-1. Cross-sectional diagrams of the three types of flat-plate collectors used in farm applications.

adding antifreeze to the water. Other problems with water solar collectors include leaks in the plumbing and metal corrosion.

Solar air heaters are the most common choice for livestock housing because of the water collector's disadvantages and because air collectors don't require a heat exchanger for space heating.

Collector Efficiency

The efficiency of a solar collector is defined as the ratio of the amount of useful heat collected to the total amount of solar radiation striking the collector surface during any time period.

One of the problems with flat plate systems designed to date has been the relatively low efficiency compared to other heating systems. Efficiencies are low because of the high losses in collection and transport of solar energy. Heat is lost through the front, sides, and back of the collector, by reflection from the cover, and by direct radiation from the heated flat plate. Typical day long efficiencies for different types of flat plate collectors are

Figure 37-2. Solar heat gain for a collector system can be improved by the use of reflectors. This farrowing house has a south facing-wall collector with drop-down reflector panels made of plywood painted white. The reflectors fold up during summer months to shade the collector.

presented in Table 37-1.

Instantaneous efficiencies (collector efficiency at an instant during the day when everything is right) can be considerably higher than the average day long efficiency. Remember this when evaluating manufacturer's or designer's claims for a particular type of collector.

Several modifications of the basic collectors will improve efficiency. If the collector will operate at more than 50°F difference between the outside air temperature and the circulating medium's temperature, you can increase efficiency by adding an additional cover. Each additional cover reduces convection and radiation loss. But by adding a cover, you increase cost and reflection losses from the glass or other material. An optimum number of covers must be found. Two covers are best for home collectors, while one cover is sufficient for livestock housing.

Table 37-1. **Day Long Collection Efficiencies of Different Types of Flat Plate Collectors Used in Agricultural Applications**

Type	Efficiency (%)
Plastic tube type	25
Bare plate	30
Covered plate	35
Suspended plate	40
Suspended plate with 2 covers	45

Another way to improve efficiency is by selecting the best absorbing surfaces. An absorber can be treated chemically so that it will absorb most of the radiation striking it without reradiating much of the absorbed heat out to the surroundings. This treatment is fairly expensive, but it increases efficiency when you need higher temperatures.

Figure 37-3. This commercially produced hot water heating system preheats hot water and supplies some of the space heat for this milking center.

Figure 37-4. Solar systems can be simple. This combination farrowing and nursery building has the south slope of the roof covered with transparent fiberglass-reinforced plastic instead of the usual metal. During winter, the ventilation air is drawn from the solar-heated attic space instead of directly from outside. Sidewalls of this building are concrete sandwich panels constructed on site by the owner and his son.

Figure 37-5. This partially below-ground swine nursery unit is using a south wall solar collector and storage unit developed by Kansas State University to provide preheating for the ventilation air.

Reflectors can also increase the amount of radiation striking the collector face. You may want to make other modifications, including various absorber plate designs that are more efficient—overlapping glass or corrugated, finned, or bonded tube-in-sheet design.

Weigh improvements in efficiency against the increase in cost and maintenance requirements of the system. Usually, the more efficient a collector is, the more costly it is. A less efficient but also less costly collector may prove to be more cost-effective in delivering a given amount of heat. As new design, manufacturing and installation developments occur, the relative cost effectiveness of alternate collectors will undoubtedly change.

Collector Construction

Solar collectors are being made of many different materials and in a wide variety of designs. The materials used should be able to resist weather, as a roof or wall must, and the adverse effects of the sun's radiation. Water collectors should resist freezing and corrosion or clogging due to acidity, alkalinity, hardness of water, or the water-antifreeze mixture. Air collectors should be able to resist dust, moisture, and breakage of the glazing (transparent cover) due to hail, thermal expansion, or other causes. Your goal is a design that will economically produce useful heat with a minimum of repair, maintenance, and replacement of parts.

Cover materials. Glass is most often the cover for solar collectors used for space heating of homes or industrial or public buildings.

Figure 37-6. This lean-to type collector system with rock storage supplied nearly one-third of the energy in this poultry brooding building in southwest Missouri during the 1979-80 heating season. Savings averaged nearly 20 gallons of LP gas per day.

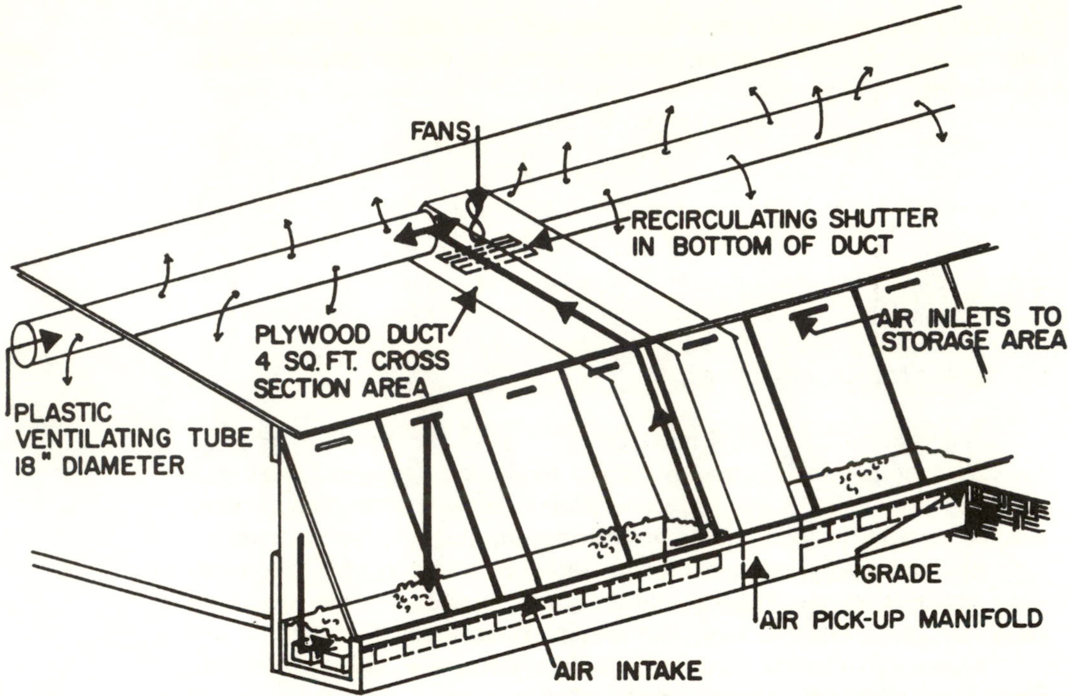

Figure 37-7. Pictorial view of the retrofitted solar collection and storage system shown in Figure 37-6.

Glass reduces convection losses. It is also a good transmitter of the incoming solar radiation but radiates almost no heat from the absorber surface to the surroundings. This is the so-called "greenhouse" or "heat-trap" effect. This effect explains why the inside of your car gets hot on a warm summer day. The window glass traps the heat in the car.

However, all of the heat is not trapped by glass covers. The glass absorbs some of the heat radiated from the absorber, which causes the glass temperature to rise; and some heat is lost due to the temperature difference between the glass and surroundings.

Both single strength and double strength window glass are commonly used. Eighty-seven percent of the incoming solar radiation can pass through the glass; the rest is either reflected or absorbed in the glass.

Where there is high danger of hail or vandals breaking the glass, a one-half inch wire mesh can protect the glass from damage. The screen shades the glass and decreases the effective collector area by about 15%, so the total collector area must be increased accordingly.

Plastic films or sheets are also used as cover materials. Only a few types now available can withstand the sun's rays for more than one or two years. With plastics, solar radiation is 92% transmittable, but the pastics do not perform as well as a heat trap. They permit up to 30% of the long wave radiation to be radiated to the surroundings from the absorber. For livestock buildings or for temporary installations, the plastics do have certain advantages. They are flexible, which helps them withstand wind, hail and other elements, and are easier to install and cheaper than glass. They provide a convection barrier in the same way glass does. In some designs with two covers, one layer of glass is used along with a layer of plastic underneath.

Greenhouse grade fiberglass is most often used as a cover in livestock buildings. It performs about the same way as glass except somewhat less solar radiation is transmittable—80% versus 87% for glass. Also, it is less likely to break with expansion or contraction of the collector housing.

Absorber plates. Absorber plates should:

- Absorb as much of the sun's radiant energy as possible.
- Lose as little heat as possible to the surroundings.
- Transfer the heat retained to a circulating medium.

An absorber plate painted black will absorb more radiant energy than any other plate color. A black surface can absorb about 95% of solar radiation. A flat black paint should be used to reduce possible reflection.

Special coatings may reduce the amount of heat radiated from the plate to surroundings. These coatings absorb the same amount of radiant energy as regular black surfaces, but emit or radiate much less.

Materials generally used for collector plates are copper, plywood, aluminum, and steel. Copper is the most expensive, but also has the highest thermal conductivity. Steel is the least expensive but also has the lowest conductivity of the three. For water heating collectors especially, the conductivity is important. For copper, the water tubes, which are bonded to the absorber plate, may be spaced farther apart than for a material with less conductivity. If the entire area of the absorber is swept by the transfer fluid, the conductivity of the plate is much less important.

Another important consideration is the bond of the water tubes to the plate. The soldering connection must be good or efficiency will suffer. Such bonding is more of a problem with aluminum. Some plates are bonded tube-in-sheet design, like many refrigerator shelves used to be. This provides good thermal contact.

For air collectors, wood and plastics have been used as absorber plates. They generally do not perform quite as efficiently as the metals, but are sometimes acceptable since the cost per square foot of collector might be reduced. Surface area of the plate also affects heat transfer in air collectors. Many designs include fins or corrugations to increase this area, thereby increasing heat transfer.

The housing may be a wooden, sheet-metal or fiber-reinforced plastic frame. A wood frame needs moisture-resistant backing. Paint sheet metal frames to prevent rusting.

Secure the cover sheet firmly with weather-resistant gaskets that allow expansion and contraction of the cover, yet keep moisture out. This expansion/contraction joint is especially important with glass covers, since glass expands one and one-half times more than steel and two times more than wood. This joint is not nearly as important for plastic or fiberglass covers.

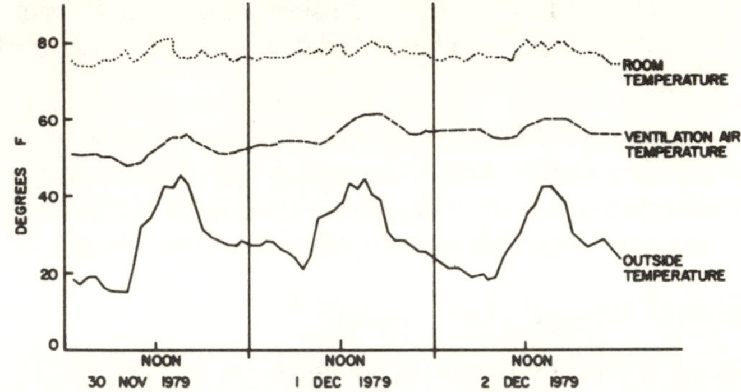

Figure 37-8. This graph illustrates typical performance of a collector with storage system used to preheat ventilation air used within the animal housing unit. The area between outside air temperature and the temperature of the ventilation air represents the energy supplied by the solar system. (University of Missouri)

Add insulation to the back and exposed sides of the collector to reduce heat loss in those directions.

Stagnation temperatures, which occur during periods when the solar system does not operate, can approach 300°F in flat plate collectors. For this reason, select insulating materials that can withstand high temperature without deteriorating. Mineral wool materials (fiberglass and rock wool) are most often used for collector insulation.

Wind

Wind has been used as a source of energy for agriculture for nearly 2,500 years. The first windmills used for grinding grain appeared in the Middle East around 200 to 400 B.C. In the United States, wind machines were used extensively for pumping water from the early 1800's up until the mid-1950's. For the last 30 years of this period, wind powered generators provided small amounts of electrical energy for areas which were not yet served by rural electric lines. The virtual disappearance of wind powered energy systems was the result of many factors. Among the more important of these were the following.

1. Agriculture's needs for energy were growing far beyond the ability of wind machines to produce it.
2. Commercially produced electricity became available in almost unlimited quantities at a reasonable cost. The water pumped by a $2,500 windmill could now be pumped by a $40 electric motor at an annual cost of less than $50.
3. Wind is not a reliable energy source. When you need energy the most, the wind is likely to be unavailable. Today's farm operations rely heavily on timeliness and cannot survive without a dependable and reliable power source.

The two things for which wind powered devices appear to have the most potential today are the pumping of water and the heating of water (either directly or with an electrical heating unit). Both of these energy consuming operations have storage capabilities which can even out or moderate the wide variations in wind power availability.

There are two factors which determine how much power can be obtained from a particular wind machine: the speed of the wind, and the amount of wind or area which is swept by the rotor or propeller.

Power = .00502 × Area × (wind speed)^3, *where:*

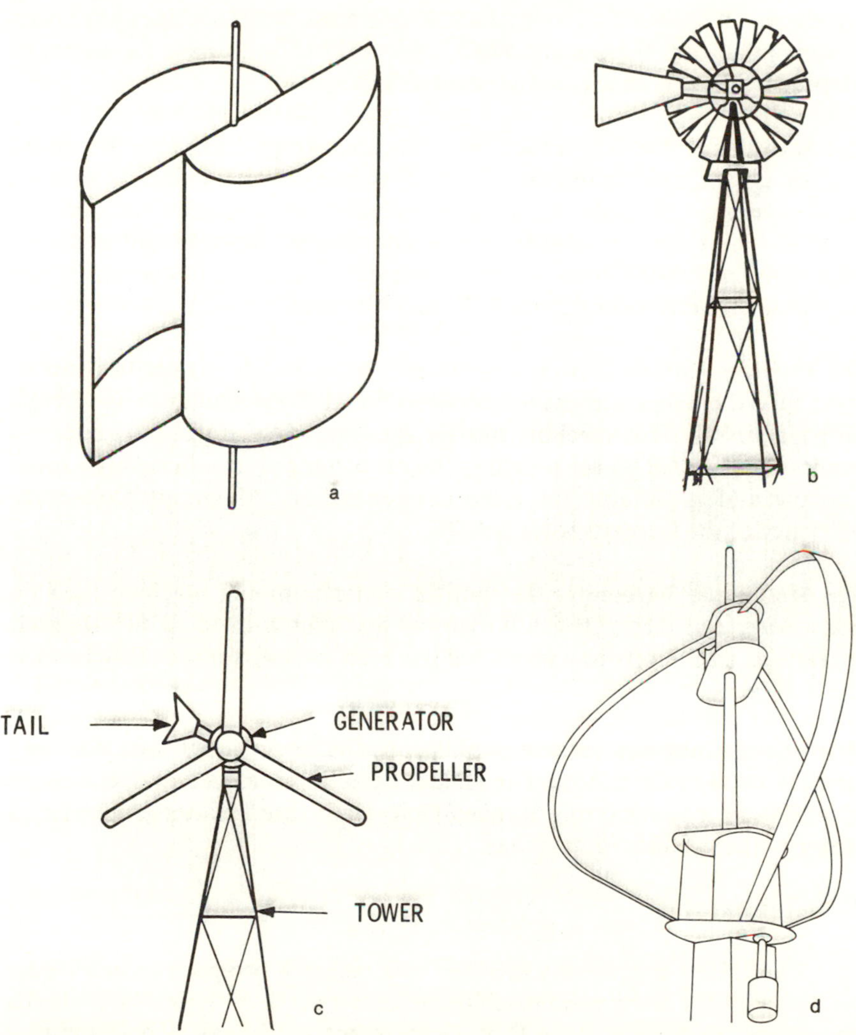

Figure 37-9. Four different types of wind machines: (a) a Savonius rotor, (b) the multiblade turbine familiar to farmers throughout the country, (c) the three-bladed high-speed propeller used to generate electricity on many farms before the days of REA, and (d) the Darrieus rotor (this illustration shows a small Savonius rotor installed as a starter on the Darrieus machine). (Michigan State University)

Power is expressed in watts

.00502 = a constant

Area = Area swept by the rotor or propeller in square feet

Wind speed = Average speed in mph

It is not possible for any wind machine to extract all of the energy from the wind. The theoretical maximum efficiency is about 59%. Most actual machines operate at less than half of this theoretical maximum.

There are several types of wind machines available today. These can be classed as either horizontal or vertical axis machines, depending on the orientation of their main power shaft. Horizontal shaft machines have been more popular over the years; however, vertical axis units have the ability to adapt more quickly to varying wind directions.

The Savonius Rotor is a vertical axis machine which turns at a low speed and has a high starting torque. The high starting torque makes it an ideal water pumping unit and the slow speed means that balance is not a critical item. Savonius rotor machines can be constructed from 55 gallon drums with only a limited amount of fabrication required. Savonius rotor machines have efficiencies in the 15% to 18% range.

The Darrieus Rotor is also a vertical axis machine. It usually has two or three curved blades which have a cross sectional shape similar to an aircraft wing or airfoil. This machine has an extremely low starting torque and requires an external power source to start it turning. It is a fairly high speed machine and is suitable for electrical generation. Maximum theoretical efficiency of the Darrieus rotor is 38%.

The Multiblade Turbine is the familiar water pumping machine used on many American farms. It is a horizontal axis unit with 15 to 40 blades. It operates at a relatively low speed and has high starting torque. Efficiency is about 30%.

High speed propellers became popular on small generators used on many farms from the 1920's through the mid-1950's. It has a maximum efficiency of 47% and a low starting torque. Units with three blades are easier to balance than two bladed machines.

Research

The USDA is presently involved in a research program to investigate the potential for using wind machines to offset some of agriculture's needs for energy. In addition, the U.S. Department of Energy is developing a testing program to evaluate the performance of commercially available units. As time goes on, we will be in a much better position to evaluate these units. Some of the factors listed below represent problems which must be solved by research and development or they will limit the potential for wind machine use.

Figure 37-10. This is a high-speed wind turbine being used to generate electricity in an experiment being conducted at Iowa State University.

1. Present machines require at least a 7 mph wind and most reach their maximum output when wind speed reaches 25 mph. At speeds above 25 mph, many machines are designed to automatically shut down.
2. Many areas of the country do not have enough wind to operate wind machines. An average annual wind velocity of 8 mph is required in order to generate any practical amount of electrical energy.
3. Icing of blades can be a severe operational problem during winter months in northern areas of the country.
4. Most electrical devices are designed to operate on alternating current at a frequency of 60 cycles per second. Wind powered generators which generate alternating current (AC) produce a frequency which varies with wind speed. Many systems generate direct current which must be converted into AC before it can be used to operate motors and other appliances.
5. Presently available wind machines are usually rated at a specific wind speed (normally 20 to 25 mph). The actual in service output of these machines is likely to be less than 25% of the rated capacity. In other words, a machine rated at 6 Kwhr can be expected to produce less than 1.5 Kwhr on a continuous year-round basis.

Appendix A

University Agricultural Engineers

Working drawings for hundreds of farm buildings are distributed through agricultural engineering departments at land grant universities. These are generally available through county extension offices, or you can write to the Extension Agricultural Engineer at your state university about your specific needs. Their addresses are listed below.

Alabama
Auburn University
Auburn, AL 36830

Alaska
University of Alaska
Fairbanks, AK 97701

Arizona
University of Arizona
Room 430, Agricultural Sciences Building
Tucson, AZ 85721

Arkansas
P.O. Box 391
Little Rock, AR 72203

California
University of California
Davis, CA 95616

Colorado
Colorado State University
Fort Collins, CO 80523

Connecticut
University of Connecticut
Storrs, CT 06268

Delaware
University of Delaware
Newark, DE 19711

Florida
University of Florida
Frazier Rogers Hall
Gainesville, FL 32601

Georgia
University of Georgia
Athens, GA 30602

Hawaii
University of Hawaii
3050 Maile Way
Honolulu, HI 96822

Idaho
University of Idaho
Moscow, ID 83843

Illinois
University of Illinois
Urbana, IL 61801

Indiana
Purdue University
Lafayette, IN 47907

Iowa
Iowa State University
Davidson Hall
Ames, IA 50011

Kansas
Kansas State University
Seaton Hall
Manhattan, KS 66506

Kentucky
University of Kentucky
Lexington, KY 40546

Louisiana
Louisiana State University
Baton Rouge, LA 70803

Maine
University of Maine
Orono, ME 04469

Maryland
University of Maryland
College Park, MD 20742

Michigan
Michigan State University
East Lansing, MI 48824

Minnesota
University of Minnesota
Agricultural Engineering Building
St. Paul, MN 55108

Mississippi
Mississippi State University
Mississippi State, MS 39762

Missouri
University of Missouri
Columbia, MO 65211

Montana
Montana State University
Bozeman, MT 59717

Nebraska
University of Nebraska
Lincoln, NE 68503

Nevada
University of Nevada
Reno, NV 89507

New Hampshire
University of New Hampshire
Pettee Hall
Durham, NH 03824

New Jersey
Cook College—Rutgers University
Biological & Agricultural Engineering Department
New Brunswick, NJ 08903

New Mexico
New Mexico State University
Las Cruces, NM 88003

New York
Cornell University
Riley-Robb Hall
Ithaca, NY 14853

North Carolina
North Carolina State University
P.O. Box 5906
Raleigh, NC 27650

North Dakota
North Dakota State University
Fargo, ND 58105

Ohio
Ohio State University
2073 Neil Hall
Columbus, OH 43210

Oklahoma
Oklahoma State University
Stillwater, OK 74074

Oregon
Oregon State University
Corvallis, OR 97331

Pennsylvania
Pennsylvania State University
Agricultural Engineering Building
University Park, PA 16802

Rhode Island
University of Rhode Island
Kingston, RI 02881

South Carolina
Clemson University
Clemson, SC 29631

South Dakota
South Dakota State University
Brookings, SD 57006

Tennessee
University of Tennessee
P.O. Box 1071
Knoxville, TN 37901

Texas
Texas A & M University
303 Agricultural Engineering Building
College Station, TX 77843

Utah
Utah State University
Logan, UT 84322

Vermont
University of Vermont
Burlington, VT 05401

Virginia
VPI & SU
Blacksburg, VA 24061

Washington
Washington State University
Pullman, WA 99164

West Virginia
West Virginia University
Morgantown, WV 26506

Wisconsin
University of Wisconsin
460 Henry Hall
Madison, WI 53706

Wyoming
University of Wyoming
P.O. Box 3354
Laramie, WY 82071

Two areas of the country have formed regional organizations which also develop plans and informational materials relating to the farm structures area. Their addresses are as follows:

Midwest Plan Service (MWPS)
Iowa State University
Davidson Hall
Ames, IA 50011

Northeast Regional Agricultural Engineering Service (NRAES)
Cornell University
Riley-Robb Hall
Ithaca, NY 14853

Appendix B

System International (SI) Units Of Measurement

With the exception of the United States, all countries of the world have adopted the SI or "metric" system of measurement. Even Great Britain, where the system of measurement we now use was developed, has now converted to SI. We already use the so-called metric system for many of our routine measurements around the farm. The most common of these are found in the area of medication where we specify and use milligrams and cubic centimeters. Many of the products we buy are now labeled in both English and SI units, and some are even packaged in the SI module. As time goes on, the U.S. will be completely converted to SI and you will be as familiar with kilograms, tonnes, hectares, and Pascals as you now are with bushels, feet, rods, and horsepower.

The International System has only six basic units of measurement. They are:

meter (m) - unit of length or distance

second (s) - unit of time

kilogram (kg) - unit of mass, or as it is more commonly used, weight

kelvin (K) - unit of temperature

ampere (A) - electrical current

calendula (cd) - light intensity

The basic units are given prefixes to indicate larger or smaller quantities. For example, a kilometer is 1,000 meters and a centimeter is equivalent to 1/100 of a meter. A few of the more commonly used prefixes are listed in Table B-1.

Basic units are combined to describe physical properties with more than one dimension. For example, crop yields are expressed in kilograms per hectare. Some of these combinations are given special names which frequently honor persons who were associated with the scientific world. Examples are the Pascal, used to measure pressure and the Joule in heat measurement.

Table B-1. **Partial Listing of Approved Prefixes for SI Units**

Prefix	Symbol	Multiplier
mega	M	100,000
kilo	k	1,000
hecto	h	100
deka	da	10
deci	d	.1
centi	c	.01
milli	m	.001

Table B-2. **SI Units Used in Common Agricultural Measurements**

Quantity	Use	SI Unit	Symbol
Area	land measurement	hectare	ha
	building size	square meters	m^2
Torque	engine torque	Newton meter	N.m
Energy	heat quantity	joule	J
	machine use	kilowatt-hour	kW.h
	solar radiation	watts per sq. m.	$W.m^2$
Force per unit			
Length	beam load	newtons/meter	N/m
Length	machinery size	millimeters	mm
	building materials	millimeters	mm
	field dimensions	meter	m
	longer distances	kilometer	km
Mass	crop yield	kilograms/hectare	kg/ha
	machinery	kilograms	kg
	truck load capacity	kilograms	kg
		metric tonnes	t
	surface coatings	$grams/meter^2$	g/m^2
	flow rates-air and water	kilogram/second	kg/s
Power	engine output	kilowatt	kW
Pressure	hydraulic or air	kilopascal	kPa
Thermal Cond.	heat flow through material	watts per meter per degree Kelvin	W/m.K
Velocity	vehicle speed	kilometer/hour	km/h
	air velocity	meters/second	m/s
Volume	engine displacement	cubic centimeters	cm^3
	earth fill, buildings	cubic meter	m^3
	liquid, grain tanks	liter	L
	liquid application rate	liter/hectare	L/ha
	air flow rates	$meter^3/second$	m^3/s
	fuel consumption	liter/hour	L/h

Table B-3. **Conversion Factors for English to SI Units**

Multiply	By	To Get
acres	.4047	hectares or $hectometers^2$
acres	4047	square meters
Btu	1055	joules
Btu	.0002928	kilowatt-hours
Btu/hour	.2931	watts
bushels	.03524	cubic meters
bushels	35.24	liters
cubic feet	.02832	cubic meters
cubic feet	28.32	liters
cubic inches	16.39	cubic centimeters
cubic inches	.00001639	cubic meters
cubic inches	.01639	liters

Multiply	By	To Get
cubic yards	.7646	cubic meters
cubic yards	764.6	liters
feet	30.48	centimeters
feet	.3048	meters
feet per minute	.508	centimeters per second
feet per second	30.48	centimeters per second
foot pounds	1.356	joules
foot pounds/minute	.00002260	kilowatts
gallons	3785	cubic centimeters
gallons	.003785	cubic meters
gallons	3.785	liters
gallons per minute	.06308	liters per second
horsepower	.7457	kilowatts
inches	2.54	centimeters
inches	.254	meters
statute miles	1.609	kilometers
miles per hour	26.82	meters per minute
ounces	28.349	grams
fluid ounces	.02947	liters
pecks (U.S.)	8.8096	liters
liquid pints	.4732	liters
pounds	453.59	grams
pounds per cubic foot	16.02	kilograms per cubic meter
pounds per sq foot	4.882	kilograms per sq meter
quarts	.9463	liters
square feet	.0929	square meters
square yards	.8361	square meters
tons (2,000 lbs)	.9078	tonnes
yards	.0009144	kilometers
yards	.9144	meters

Appendix C

Beam And Floor Joist Load Capacities

Table C-1. **Total load capacity for uniformly distributed loads on wooden beams made of No. 2 Douglas Fir. For loads which are concentrated at the center of the beam, reduce total load capacity by one-half.**

	Beam size (Inches)					
Span (Feet)	**4 x 6**	**4 x 8**	**4 x 10**	**4 x 12**	**4 x 14**	**4 x 16**
10	1,470	2,555	4,159	4,988	5,874	6,761
12	1,225	2,129	3,465	4,988	5,874	6,761
14	1,050	1,825	2,970	4,394	5,874	6,761
16	919	1,596	2,599	3,845	5,333	6,761
18	817	1,419	2,310	3,418	4,741	6,280
20	735	1,277	2,079	3,076	4,267	5,652
22	688	1,161	1,890	2,796	3,879	5,138
24	612	1,064	1,732	2,563	3,555	4,710

	Beam Size (Inches)					
Span (Feet)	**6 x 6**	**6 x 8**	**6 x 10**	**6 x 12**	**6 x 14**	**6 x 16**
10	2,310	4,296	6,618	8,011	9,405	10,798
12	1,925	3,580	5,745	8,011	9,405	10,798
14	1,650	3,069	4,924	7,216	9,405	10,798
16	1,444	2,685	4,308	6,314	8,701	10,798
18	1,283	2,387	3,830	5,612	7,734	10,195
20	1,155	2,148	3,447	5,051	6,960	9,176
22	1,050	1,953	3,133	4,592	6,328	8,342
24	962	1,790	2,782	4,209	5,800	7,646

	Beam Size (Inches)				
Span (Feet)	**8 x 8**	**8 x 10**	**8 x 12**	**8 x 14**	**8 x 16**
10	5,859	9,025	10,925	12,825	14,725
12	4,882	7,834	10,925	12,825	14,725
14	4,185	6,714	9,839	12,825	14,725
16	3,661	5,875	8,609	11,865	14,725
18	3,255	5,222	7,653	10,546	13,903
20	2,929	4,700	6,887	9,492	12,512
22	2,663	4,273	6,261	8,629	11,375
24	2,441	3,917	5,739	7,910	10,427

Span (Feet)	Beam Size (Inches) 10 x 10	10 x 12	10 x 14	10 x 16
10	11,431	13,838	16,245	18,652
12	9,923	13,838	16,245	18,652
14	8,505	12,464	16,245	18,652
16	7,442	10,906	15,029	18,652
18	6,615	9,694	13,359	17,611
20	5,954	8,725	12,023	15,850
22	5,412	7,931	10,930	14,409
24	4,961	7,270	10,019	13,208

Table C-2. **Allowable floor loads in pounds per square foot for various joist sizes and spacings. Values are based on use of No. 2 Douglas Fir having an allowable bending stress of 1450 psi.**

Nominal Size and Spacing		Joist Span in Feet 4	6	8	10	12	14	16	18	20	22	24
2 x 4	12 in. O.C.	94	41	23	15							
	16 in. O.C.	70	30	17	11							
	24 in. O.C.	47	20	11	7							
2 x 6	12 in. O.C.	261	174	114	73	50	37	28				
	16 in. O.C.	196	130	85	54	37	27	21				
	24 in. O.C.	130	87	57	36	25	18	14				
2 x 8	12 in. O.C.		229	172	127	88	64	49	39	31		
	16 in. O.C.		172	129	95	66	48	36	29	23		
	24 in. O.C.		114	86	63	44	32	24	19	15		
2 x 10	12 in. O.C.			219	175	143	105	80	63	51	42	35
	16 in. O.C.			164	131	107	78	60	47	38	31	26
	24 in. O.C.			109	87	71	52	40	31	25	21	17
2 x 12	12 in. O.C.				213	178	152	119	94	76	63	53
	16 in. O.C.				160	133	114	89	70	57	47	39
	24 in. O.C.				106	89	76	59	47	38	31	26

Note: Loads calculated in this table are based on strength of the wood, not on how much it will bend or deflect under load. This table should not be used in residential construction or any other building where it is important not to have "springy" floors.

INDEX

D

E

F

G

H

I

J

L

M

T

U

V

W

Z